Water and Power in Past Societies

THE INSTITUTE FOR EUROPEAN AND MEDITERRANEAN ARCHAEOLOGY
DISTINGUISHED MONOGRAPH SERIES

Peter F. Biehl, editor-in-chief
Sarunas Milisauskas and Stephen L. Dyson, editors

The Magdalenian Household: Unraveling Domesticity
Ezra Zubrow, Françoise Audouze, and James G. Enloe, editors

Eventful Archaeologies: New Approaches to Social Transformation in the Archaeological Record
Douglas J. Bolender, editor

The Archaeology of Violence: Interdisciplinary Approaches
Sarah Ralph, editor

Approaching Monumentality in Archaeology
James. F. Osborne, editor

The Archaeology of Childhood: Interdisciplinary Perspectives on an Archaeological Enigma
Güner Coşkunsu, editor

Diversity of Sacrifice: Form and Function of Sacrificial Practices in the Ancient World and Beyond
Carrie Ann Murray, editor

Climate and Cultural Change in Prehistoric Europe and the Near East
Peter F. Biehl and Olivier P. Nieuwenhuyse, editors

Water and Power in Past Societies
Emily Holt, editor

WATER AND POWER
IN PAST SOCIETIES

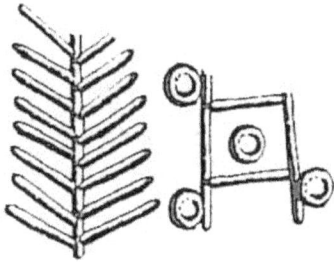

IEMA Proceedings,
Volume 7

EDITED BY
Emily Holt

STATE UNIVERSITY OF
NEW YORK PRESS

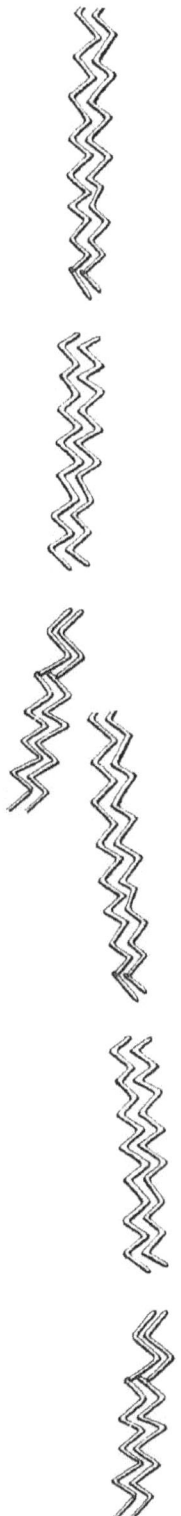

Logo and cover/interior art: A vessel with wagon motifs from Bronocice,
Poland, 3400 B.C. Courtesy of Sarunas Milisauskas and Janusz Kruk,
1982, Die Wagendarstellung auf einem Trichterbecher au Bronocice,
Polen, *Archäologisches Korrespondenzblatt* 12: 141–144

Published by
State University of New York Press, Albany

© 2018 State University of New York

All rights reserved

For information, contact
State University of New York Press, Albany, NY
www.sunypress.edu

Library of Congress Cataloging-in-Publication Data

Names: Holt, Emily, 1980- editor.
Title: Water and power in past societies / edited by Emily Holt.
Description: Albany : State University of New York Press, [2018] | Series: SUNY
    series, The Institute for European and Mediterranean Archaeology distinguished
    monograph series | Includes bibliographical references and index.
Identifiers: LCCN 2017017027 (print) | LCCN 2018024455 (ebook) | ISBN
    9781438468778 (e-book) | ISBN 9781438468754 (hardcover   ) | ISBN
    9781438468761 (paperback   )
Subjects: LCSH: Water and civilization.
Classification: LCC CB482 (ebook) | LCC CB482 .W387 2018 (print) | DDC 930.1—
    dc23
LC record available at https://lccn.loc.gov/2017017027

10 9 8 7 6 5 4 3 2 1

Contents

Illustrations

Figures

TABLES

CHAPTER ONE

Water and Power in Past Societies

An Introduction

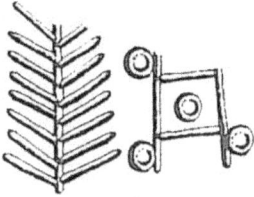

Emily Holt

Water is occupying an increasingly large part of our contemporary environmental consciousness. Over the past decade, a slow trickle of popular scholarship, such as the epilogue to Tom Standage's *A History of the World in Six Glasses* (2006), has become a flood of volumes analyzing water's role in the past, present, and future. Brian Fagan's *Elixir* (2011), Charles Fishman's *The Big Thirst* (2012), James Salzman's *Drinking Water: A History* (2013), and David Sedlak's *Water 4.0* (2014) are just a few examples of this trend. The global public is becoming more aware of water as a contested resource, recognizing that access to water and its distribution and control are sources of empowerment or disenfranchisement, wealth or poverty, health or illness throughout the world. As users of interconnected water systems, we are also confronting the reality that water is likely to become increasingly contested in the future, as global climate change is "fundamentally water access change" (Scarborough and Lucero 2011).

Growing popular interest contributes to bringing water research to the foreground in archaeology as well as in other fields. However, the archaeology of water has a long history that predates the popular discussion by several decades. Beginning with the so-called hydraulic hypothesis put forward by Karl Wittfogel in the 1950s (Wittfogel 1957), archaeologists have long been interested in the social and political consequences of controlling water. While the original hydraulic hypothesis has been criticized, rejected, reconsidered, and reformulated many times over, the essential role water plays in all societies has kept water a constant in archaeological studies of human power structures.

Discussions of the archaeology of water often open with the truism that water is a human necessity, which is one way of tackling the immensity of water as a subject of inquiry and putting it into a universal framework. Focusing on the biological imperative for humans, animals, and plants to take in water encourages archaeologists to think about the power implications of water in places where it is scarce, spatially discontinuous, or seasonally absent. Many early studies of the archaeology of water focused on areas that fit these geographical descriptions, making irrigation networks a persistent subject of interest for archaeologists.

However, focusing solely on the consumption of water can eclipse the fact that water is an equally powerful resource in areas that do not experience water insecurity as it is generally formulated. Water can have potent political and symbolic meanings without being scarce. Water that is not directly consumed—such as ocean and seawater, coastal marshes, and brackish lagoons—can facilitate travel and transportation, provide additional resources, and form a component of cosmologies. While these types of water have figured prominently in archaeological studies, they have generally been considered under different theoretical frameworks than studies of fresh water. It is only more recently that these types of water have also been considered under "the archaeology of water," perhaps due to our growing awareness of climate change and the interconnectedness of all earth's water.

The goal of this volume is to provide a broad sample of case studies addressing different types of water and different ways that water is incorporated into human power structures. The goal of this introduction is therefore to orient the reader with respect to the diverse theoretical perspectives that have been taken to discuss water in past societies as well as to introduce the following chapters. Because useful water theory has been developed not only in archaeology but also in related fields such as cultural anthropology, human geography, and history, I draw on case studies from a variety of disciplines to illustrate recurring themes in our understandings of water.

WATER: A TOTAL SOCIAL FACT

Water's very fundamentality can make it overwhelming as a category of inquiry. The fact that water is omnipresent in human society, yet present in different amounts and varying forms, seems to both invite and defy attempts to theorize it. For the past century, scholars throughout the social sciences as well as governmental and nongovernmental organizations have looked for ways to conceptualize the pervasiveness of water in human experience, often with the long-term goal of improving water management and mitigating water-related crises. Because the theory applied in archaeological studies has developed in connection with these influential trends, often specifically referencing them and contributing to them, I will begin this introduction with a general overview of the development of water theory before focusing specifically on water in archaeological thought.

Cultural anthropologists Ben Orlove and Steven Caton have recently applied Mauss's concept of a "total social fact" to the study of water (2010). By "total social fact," Mauss meant "social phenomena that cut across virtually all domains of society" (2010:402). Orlove and Caton observe that "Water connects domains of life such that the water used in one will affect the water used in others." Similarly, Veronica Strang paraphrases Lévi-Strauss in observing that water is good "for thinking with," citing the fact that water "permeates all organic things and kinds, including humankind, flowing through and connecting the various micro and macro scales at which they interact" (2015:133).

While these observations may seem intuitively obvious, they emerge from a line of critical analysis of human relationships with water that has been developing primarily since the late twentieth century. For most of the preceding century, the dominant paradigm in the study and management of water has been the hydrologic cycle. The original concept of the hydrologic cycle (Horton 1931) served to define hydrology as a field of study with a particular body of experts. The hydrologic cycle was presented as apolitical and specifically natural, occurring independently of human behavior.

Beginning around the early 1970s, the broad theoretical framework of political ecology began to challenge the assumption that ecological models such as the hydrologic cycle were either apolitical or independent of human behavior. I will not try to summarize the development of political ecology here since there are already many useful summaries (e.g., Robbins 2004). It is important to note, however, that many approaches to water in human society began to apply a political ecology perspective, and this approach has continued to be influential in water studies. Managerial approaches to water used by governmental and nongovernmental organizations promote and respond to particular perceptions of water that often privilege industry, well-funded lobbies, and specific social groups (Fernandez 2014).

The questioning of the natural world as apolitical and independent of human behavior that began with political ecology continued during the late twentieth century. As the inherent separation of nature and society was increasingly questioned by cultural theorists such as Lefebvre (1991) and Latour (1993), scholars of water history began deconstructing the sociopolitical relationships that created specific water uses. Swyngedouw's (1999) influential study of water management in late-nineteenth and early-twentieth-century Spain was explicitly critical of the hydrologic cycle as a sufficient framework for understanding water history. Drawing on Latour and the political ecology framework, Swyngedouw showed that Spain's status as a water-poor nation was part of socioeconomic and political discourses promoted by influential thinkers in the arts and government.

Roughly around the same time, the term *hydrosocial cycle* began appearing in works of human geography as an alternative to the hydrologic cycle (Bakker 2002). Critical geographers Linton and Budds (2014) have recently sought to advance the hydrosocial cycle as a useful conceptual framework, defining the term as "a socio-natural process by which water and society make and remake each other over space and time." Conceptualizing water as part of the hydrosocial cycle encourages researchers to follow water as it moves in society, rather than focusing on a single point of access. The importance of this approach has been demonstrated by numerous studies in cultural anthropology, which have found that different types of water may not be interchangeable within particular cultural frameworks because the specific trajectories of water affect its physical and social properties. For example, the treated water supplied by a mining company may not be an acceptable substitute for the flowing water the company diverts for its productive processes (Li 2013). Similarly, the recycling of wastewater for irrigation can have long-term consequences different from the consequences that using fresh water would have (Barnes 2014).

The interconnectedness of all water through the hydrosocial cycle is perhaps exemplified by the connection between current climate change and a variety of water-related challenges to the resilience of human systems. In the field of human geography, Kirsten Hastrup (2009) has proposed the term *waterworlds* to describe the pervasive interconnections of water in human life. Posing this term in the context of responding to climate change–related disasters, Hastrup divides contemporary waterworlds into the melting ice, the rising seas, and the drying lands. Her conceptualization is particularly useful because it highlights the connectedness among different kinds of water and water-related disasters rather than treating the world's different kinds of water as separate.

A final important influence in water scholarship that is highlighted by Hastrup's waterworlds is the human security perspective. The United Nations established the Human Security Unit in 2004 with the goal of protecting essential human freedoms by protecting people from critical and pervasive threats (UNHSU 2009:5). The human security approach emphasizes the interconnectedness of seven different types of security: economic, food, health, environmental, personal, community, and political. Some social scientists have begun adopting a human security perspective in their work, and the value of this perspective in the integrated world of water is clear. While access to sufficient water may appear most related to environmental security, it also has effects in food production, health, and economic enterprises. Problems in any of these securities may lead to threats to personal and community security, and perhaps even political security. Cultural anthropologists Wutich and Brewis (2014) apply a human security perspective to a cross-cultural study of water use, finding that necessary amounts of water vary, but having enough water as it is culturally defined is essential for well-being.

ORGANIZING WATER, ORGANIZING PEOPLE

As a total social fact, water relates constantly to human power struggles and has been a consideration in archaeological studies of sociopolitical structures from the beginning of the discipline. I will not attempt to provide a complete history of the study of water in archaeology here, since such syntheses have been undertaken before (e.g., Billman 2002) and the list of scholars who have contributed important insights to the archaeological scholarship on water is too long to cite in its entirety. Instead, I present several broad theoretical categories into which archaeological understandings of water often fall, including ethnographic and historical studies where they have been influential. Also, it is important to acknowledge at the outset that all approaches to water are inherently linked. We cannot separate biology from culture or the human systems we create from our daily lived experiences and the environments in which they occur.

WATER MANAGEMENT AND PRODUCTION

The idea that irrigation leads to social and political complexity can be traced in Western thought to Karl Marx (Avinieri 1969:7). It is then found in the work of V. Gordon Childe (1950) and Julian Steward (1949, 1955). This "hydraulic hypothesis" was most fully developed by Karl Wittfogel in his work *Oriental Despotism: A Comparative Study of total Power* (1957). One of the earliest explicit considerations of the role of water in creating inequalities in the past, the hydraulic hypothesis presents water as an essential resource requiring top-down management to successfully meet the needs of populations. In this model, everyone needs access to water, but the nature of information gathering and actualization means that only a few people can be controlling the water, which results in the formation of power hierarchies.

The hydraulic hypothesis has been heavily critiqued on both ethnographic and archaeological grounds (Adams 1960; Billman 2002; Butzer 1976; Lanning 1967; Leach 1959; Mitchell 1973). Many subsequent studies have shown that the need for equitable water management often promotes and maintains social equality, or at least diffused corporate heterarchies, in areas where states are unable to assert their dominance (Coward 1979; Hunt and Hunt 1976; Ostrom 1992; Trawick 2001). The work of Braemer et al. (2009) in Syria, Thomas Glick (1970) in medieval Valencia, and Helena Kirchner (2009) in the Balearics provide a sample of specifically archaeological examples. However, the hydraulic hypothesis has also been found to continue to have explanatory power, especially when considered broadly in conjunction with other social processes that may be taking place in societies reliant on irrigation (Davies 2009; Sidky 1997).

The managerial requirement of irrigation networks may not be sufficient to cause the development of social hierarchies; however, the economic and political advantages of controlling water—and products that rely on water—may promote hierarchy formation (Haas 1982; Moseley 1974, 1975; Stanish 1994). In semiarid areas, access to water, the land improved by irrigation, or the fruits of newly irrigated lands can be bestowed as gifts on loyal or particularly meritorious followers (Sidky 1997:1008–1009).

The hydraulic hypothesis focused on water as a resource in agricultural production, but water is also essential for some kinds of industrial production. Differential water access can result in differential levels of economic success, as has been observed for mining communities in ancient Greece (Van Liefferinge et al. 2014).

WATER, IDEOLOGY, AND DISPLAY

The tendency to view water primarily from an economic, engineering, and managerial perspective does not do justice to the many ways humans interact with water (Swyngedouw 2004). Ideological and symbolic interactions with water can also be important sources of sociopolitical power. One influential line of research in the ideological control of water was initiated by Clifford Geertz (1972, 1980), who proposed that irrigation in modern Bali is organized at the local level, defined by the *subak,* through the rituals of the rice cult. This hypothesis was critiqued by Hobart (1982), whose study of one *subak* showed a serious mismatch between the activities of agriculture and the rituals of the rice cult. Further studies by J. Stephen Lansing (Lansing 1987, 1991; Lansing and Kremer 1993) indicated that *subak*s participate in a supra-local organization system controlled not by the state government, but by the religious organizations of the Balinese water temples. Alternative explanations of Balinese water management have been offered (Hauser-Schäublin 2003, 2011; Lansing et al. 2005), but the ideological relationships between water and power structures remain central to the system.

The strategy of maintaining sociopolitical power by controlling water-related ritual has been noted ethnographically in other cultures as well (e.g., Håkansson 1998), and numerous archaeological examples have been discussed, with the symbolic aspects of Maya water management being a particular focus (Isendahl 2011; Luzzadder-Beach et al. 2016; Scarborough 1998). Water is also used symbolically to display political dominance through monumental constructions (Harrower 2009), curry public favor with gifts of water (Longfellow 2011), and build elite identity through conspicuous consumption (Novák 2002; Jones and Robinson 2005).

WATER AND CONNECTIVITY

One of water's powers that was particularly important in the preindustrial world is the way in which it facilitates transportation and the exchange of goods, ideas, and people. The connectivity offered by water of varying types and the differential effects of this connectivity on the people who harnessed it is a major current in archaeological, historical, and ethnographic studies.

The effects of water connectivity have long been a focus of study in Mediterranean archaeology and history. It is often observed that the connectivity offered by the Mediterranean Sea was a dominant force in the development of the ancient Greek world (Pomeroy et al. 1999). Detailed analyses of sea-based connectivity as creating a distinctly Mediterranean way of life have been developed by Braudel (1972), Horden and Purcell (2000), and Broodbank (2013). More localized studies have examined the Cyclades (Broodbank 2002) and the Nile Delta (Wilson 2012), and the differential benefits of sea travel as opposed to land travel in the Roman Mediterranean can be explored in Stanford's ORBIS Project (Scheidel and Meeks, http://orbis.stanford.edu/).

The social and economic outcomes of water connectivity have also been a pronounced focus in archaeological and ethnographic scholarship on the island cultures of Polynesia and Melanesia. Malinowski's seminal study of the Kula ring (1932) and the many subsequent studies that have challenged and elaborated his original work (Dalton 1977; Damon 2002; Weiner 1976) may be the most obvious examples. Other studies highlighting this connectivity include those of the trade relationships of the Vitiaz Strait (Harding 1967, Lilley 1988), the Port Moresby area of Papua New Guinea (Allen 1984), the Arawe Islands (Gosden and Pavlides 1994), and the chiefdoms of the Philippines (Junker 1999).

EXPERIENCING WATER

Another broad approach to water is a relational materiality or phenomenological approach, found in the work of anthropologists such as Veronica Strang (2008, 2015) and Matt Edgeworth (2011) as well as some human geographers (Walker et al. 2011). This approach advocates a departure from an anthropocentric understanding of human-environmental relationships to one in which other material agents—such as water—take active roles in mutually constituting landscapes and humans' lived experiences of them. Substances such as water are considered to have agency, or if not agency, a stubborn materiality that pushes back against humans' attempts to completely control them. The materiality of water can be pleasant or onerous, biddable or ungovernable, helpful or harmful. The practices of living with the substance of water result in emergent phenomena that defy the nature/culture divide.

One trend in phenomenological approaches to water focuses on water as an element of the human creation of landscapes and places (Harmanşah 2014). In this approach, the symbolic power of water as it appears in springs, caves, rivers, and other natural features is accessed and harnessed, as in the evocative example of the sacred Maya landscape of freshwater pools in Cara Blanca, Belize, analyzed by Lisa Lucero and Andrew Kinkella (2014). Naturally occurring waterscapes are sometimes echoed or recreated by human efforts, as they were in the case of the Maya through the building of temples, and as has been argued by Colin Richards (1996) for water-filled ditches surrounding the henges of Neolithic Britain. Such sacred or symbolic landscapes are often interpreted and reinterpreted over time, creating layers of self-referential meaning.

CLIMATE AND HUMAN ECOLOGY

Water is undeniably a critical factor in climate change, and many archaeologists have approached human interactions with water in the past through the interpretive lens of changing climate. Scholars have identified the lack of water resulting from adverse climate change as being linked to the collapse of complex societies in cultures as diverse in time and place as the southern Levant in the Late Bronze Age (Langgut et al. 2013) and the Maya in the Terminal Classic Period (Haug et al. 2003). While narratives that are too deterministic and fail to account for human adaptability have been criticized in rebuttals such as *Questioning Collapse* (McAnany and Yoffee 2010), our contemporary experiences leave little doubt that climate change can be a major factor affecting human behavior.

One current approach that highlights an ecological perspective is human niche construction. Human niche construction looks at how humans modify their environments to make them more favorable, resulting in new ecological niches. Water management of all kinds, particularly irrigation systems, can usefully be considered using the model of human niche construction because water management systems not only create long-term change in the resources available to humans (Wilkinson et al. 2015; Zhu et al. 2015), they also result in different ecosystems that present new health conditions and challenges for the humans who create them (Kloos and David 2002).

WATER AND POWER IN PAST SOCIETIES

The diverse collection of papers presented here results from the conference Water and Power in Past Societies, the 8th Visiting Scholar Conference of the Institute for European and Mediterranean Archaeology, held at the University at Buffalo on April 11–12, 2015. These papers were chosen to present a wide range of theoretical and methodological approaches, as well as to provide geographical and chronological breadth. In addition to providing specific case studies that will be of interest to scholars in each geographical region, these papers demonstrate detailed applications of the theoretical perspectives discussed above.

The first part of this volume—Productive Power and the Ecological History of Waterscapes—includes case studies that highlight the relationships between water and different kinds of production, with particular focus on how production is situated in trajectories of political economy. Examples of agricultural, pastoral, and industrial production are located within specific waterscapes that simultaneously offer possibilities and create limitations for producers. Within each waterscape, repeated human actions interact with local geography to build histories of production with important consequences for understanding productive relationships at any given point along the trajectory. Such histories of water-based production are present in most current waterscapes, and archaeological inquiry can provide the background for understanding how these waterscapes should be viewed.

Christopher T. Morehart opens Part I with a chapter contrasting two raised-field or *chinampa* farming systems in the southern and northern regions of the Basin of Mexico. He traces their histories of integration with local and state-level institutions, providing a critique of exclusively bottom-up models of water management with important implications for assessing the sustainability of traditional agricultural systems.

Eva Kaptijn traces social organization in the longue durée as it relates to irrigation in the Zerqa Triangle, Jordan. Her chapter highlights the effects of geography and sunk costs on the long-term persistence of the Zerqa Triangle irrigation system while tracing the changing social organizations that have managed the system in response to different political realities.

In a chapter that complements the two agricultural studies, Emily Hammer argues that mobile pastoralism is the "other half of the story" of sustainable adaptation to dry environments. While irrigation in dry environments may bring water to the crops that need them, mobility takes an alternative approach by bringing animals to water. Additionally, small-scale water management projects such as check dams and cisterns serve to permanently improve the landscape for mobile pastoralists while requiring only minimal upkeep.

Finally, Kim Van Liefferinge provides an important counterpoint to the studies focusing on food production by examining the role of water in industrial production in the mining industry of classical period Laurion, Greece. Van Liefferinge finds that the differential potential to gather water offered by specific locations for ore-processing workshops had long-term effects on the workshops' success.

The second part of this volume—Waterscapes, Power Plays, and Display—includes case studies of water used to legitimize power symbolically. These studies draw on theories of elite identity, viewership, and phenomenology to understand how people experience water displays and their role in maintaining power structures. While two of the studies address water and display in dry areas, Part II opens with a study of water symbolism in a geographical region that is not semiarid and that does not experience water scarcity by current definitions, emphasizing that water can be a powerful symbolic resource in any environment.

Brenda Longfellow provides a detailed assessment of how elite male identity in the early Roman Republic was tied to the control of nature. Control of nature was often expressed through controlling water in the pools and fountains that were essential parts of elite homes. As water control became established as a familiar, private expression of elite male power, some individuals began using the same symbolic elements to transfer expressions of power into public spaces, contesting and legitimizing their positions in Roman Republican society and government.

Leigh-Ann Bedal provides a contrasting study of the breakdown of an elite-supported water system. During the Hellenistic and Roman periods, the Nabateans of the desert city of Petra engineered a complex hydraulic system to supply both practical needs and impressive water displays. As Petra's economy declined in Late Antiquity, the extensive hydraulic system fell into disuse, replaced by localized systems supporting much smaller populations.

Michael J. Harrower compares the role of water in ancient Southwest and Southeast Arabia (Yemen and Oman), showing how the timing and intensity of water availability can lead to different ways of monumentalizing water management. Water in Oman was primarily available through continuously flowing springs, leading to social organizations of water sharing that were expressed in communal tombs. Conversely, water in Yemen was available in the form of destructive flash floods that encouraged more hierarchical forms of labor organization, expressed in water diversion architecture.

The third part of this volume—Coastal Water—presents case studies that analyze water as a transportation resource. Drawing on observations about the utility of water for encouraging long-distance travel and decreasing transportation costs, these studies present ways in which knowledge of and access to sea routes differentially shaped the success of ancient communities.

Christopher Prescott, Anette Sand-Eriksen, and Knut Ivar Austvoll examine the control of coastal waterways as a source of power in Late Neolithic and Early Bronze Age Norway. They find that the ability to control navigational bottlenecks through the threat of force probably contributed to the formation of small-scale chiefdoms in these specific, strategic locales.

Similarly, Jennifer L. Gaynor's chapter shows how the frequently overlooked fortresses of the nonurban maritime hub of Tiworo, in central Indonesia, were key strategic points in attempts by Western colonial powers to control the trade in nutmeg and cloves. Power relationships in the archipelago were spatially discontinuous and essentially personal, defying attempts to understand them through land-based models.

Justin Leidwanger provides a complementary perspective by examining small-scale maritime trade in Roman-period Cyprus. Leidwanger uses a GIS approach to analyze the significance of low-level connectivity offered by small ships and minimally developed ports, finding that even these modest opportunities had a significant effect on the development of rural economies.

The final part of this volume—Water Archaeology: Pasts, Presents, Futures—presents four case studies that exemplify how archaeology can inform our understanding of water management in the longue durée, including insights for present and future water management. Archaeology's time-depth as a social science offers unique perspectives and information that no other field can provide (e.g., Ljungqvist et al. 2015).

Matt Edgeworth begins Part IV with an analysis of rivers in England and Wales showing how a millennium of human-river entanglement has resulted in a contemporary waterscape providing thousands of opportunities for small-scale hydropower development. Through their mutual agency, rivers and the communities that live near them interact to create hybrid entities shaped by—and offering possibilities for—both human and natural systems.

Ömür Harmanşah provides an analysis of the political ecology of water in Central Anatolia, focusing on how running field projects entangles archaeologists in contemporary water politics. Salvage projects in particular, conducted before major planned construction projects, often involve contested water rights between local communities and supralocal governmental interests. Archaeologists may choose to engage with these water politics or not, but they cannot escape being part of the "geology of belonging" of these particular water systems.

Sturt Manning's contribution addresses the fact that assessments of potential water-related crisis inevitably involve reconstructing local and regional hydrologies, which can vary over long spans of time. Manning combines detailed evidence for precipitation drawn from tree ring–based reconstructions to address the frequency of crisis-inducing drought in Anatolia and the Levant in the past millennium. Manning finds that, while local and short-term food shortage was probably common, longer-term and widespread famine were very rare, though potentially historically pivotal.

Vernon L. Scarborough's chapter closes the volume with a comparative study that addresses one of the biggest theoretical questions currently facing water archaeologists: Does our research have something to say about water management in the present and future? Examining the southern lowland Maya on the Yucatan Peninsula and the ancestral Puebloan populations occupying Chaco Canyon of the U.S. Southwest, Scarborough identifies important similarities in water and environmental management and their relationship to social instability.

CONCLUSIONS

Water as a subject of study resembles water as a physical substance: it simultaneously creates, crosses, and defies boundaries. Water's many manifestations and the ways people interact with them refuse to be easily generalized. Finding a single common denominator for understanding water is a challenge, and one that many scholars would argue against. While I would agree that there is no "right approach" to water, some common themes have emerged during the production of this volume that deserve to be highlighted.

The first is the necessity of a longue durée perspective in the study of water. Whether the theoretical focus of a study emphasizes the ecological or the social, water cannot be separated from its local socionatural histories.

A second important theme is the labor demands of water. All water is managed in some way, and the demands of this management call for organizational solutions. This leaves open the possibility of choosing either more egalitarian or more hierarchical social structures. At the same time, the demands of water are juxtaposed with the potentials of water. Water can make life easier, for example, by providing a means of faster, cheaper transportation. Like water's demands, water's potentials also present opportunities to create hierarchies, and they reward those who can master the technologies that unlock them.

A final important theme is water's inherent symbolic power. Regardless of the nature of their environments, humans cannot distance themselves from water. Whether in wet surroundings or dry, water is a daily experience in some form or another, creating inescapable, lived meanings that can be harnessed to justify and express hierarchy—or to resist it.

Because of its daily essentiality, water offers constantly repeated opportunities for interpretation, management, and control. In the context of these quotidian experiences of water, different ways of gathering and applying knowledge, different definitions of what is desirable and valuable, different goals for agro-pastoral and industrial production, and different understandings of how to value natural resources come into conflict. In the past as in the present, these conflicts are often resolved in favor of those who possess greater social, political, and economic capital.

ACKNOWLEDGMENTS

I would like to thank the Institute for European and Mediterranean Archaeology and the University at Buffalo, State University of New York, for hosting Water and Power in Past Societies, the 8th IEMA Visiting Scholar Conference. I would also like to thank Peter Biehl and Stephen L. Dyson for their mentorship during my year as the IEMA Postdoctoral Fellow.

REFERENCES CITED

Adams, R. McC. 1960 Early Civilizations, Subsistence, and Environment. In *City Invincible: A Symposium on Urbanization and Cultural Development in the Ancient Near East*, edited by C. H. Kraeling and R. McC. Adams, 269–295. University of Chicago Press: Chicago.

Allen, J. 1984 Pots and Poor Princes: A Multidimensional Approach to the Role of Pottery Trading in Coastal Papua. In *The Many Dimensions of Pottery: Ceramics in Archaeology and Anthropology*, edited by S. van der Leeuw and A. C. Pritchard, 409–473. University of Amsterdam: Amsterdam.

Avinieri, S. (editor) 1969 *Karl Marx on Colonialism and Modernization*. Anchor Books: New York.

Bakker, K. 2002 From State to Market?: Water Mercantilización in Spain. *Environment and Planning A* 34:767–790.

Barnes, J. 2014 Mixing Waters: The Reuse of Agricultural Drainage Water in Egypt. *Geoforum* 57:181–191.

Billman, B. R. 2002 Irrigation and the Origins of the Southern Moche State on the North Coast of Peru. *Latin American Antiquity* 13:371–400.

Braudel, F. 1972 *The Mediterranean and the Mediterranean World in the Age of Philip II*. Translated by S. Reynolds. Harper Colophon Books, New York. Original edition, 1949, Colin, Paris.

Braemer, F., D. Genequand, C. Dumond Maridat, P.-M. Blanc, J.-M. Dentzer, D. Gazagne, and P. Wech 2009 Long-Term Management of Water in the Central Levant: The Hawran Case (Syria). *World Archaeology* 41:36–57.

Broodbank, C. 2002 *An Island Archaeology of the Early Cyclades.* Cambridge University Press: Cambridge.

Broodbank, C. 2013 *The Making of the Middle Sea: A History of the Mediterranean from the Beginning to the Threshold of the Classical World.* Oxford University Press, Oxford.

Butzer, K. W. 1976 *Early Hydraulic Civilization in Egypt.* University of Chicago Press: Chicago.

Childe, V. G. 1950 The Urban Revolution. *The Town Planning Review* 21:3–17.

Coward, E. W. 1979 Principles of Social Organization in an Indigenous Irrigation System. *Human Organization* 38:28–36.

Dalton, G. 1977 Aboriginal Economies in Stateless Societies. In *Exchange Systems in Prehistory,* edited by T. K. Earle and J. E. Ericson, 191–212. Academic Press: New York.

Damon, F. H. 2002 Kula Valuables: The Problem of Value and the Production of Names. *L'Homme* 162:107–136.

Edgeworth, M. 2011 *Fluid Pasts: Archaeology of Flow.* Bristol Classical Press (Bloomsbury Academic): Bristol.

Davies, M. I. J. 2009 Wittfogel's Dilemma: Heterarchy and Ethnographic Approaches to Irrigation Management in Eastern Africa and Mesopotamia. *World Archaeology* 41:16–35.

Fernandez, S. 2014 Much Ado about Minimum Flows . . . Unpacking Indicators to Reveal Water Politics. *Geoforum* 57:258–271.

Geertz, C. 1972 The Wet and the Dry: Traditional Irrigation in Bali and Morocco. *Human Ecology* 1:23–39.

Geertz, C. 1980 *Negara: The Balinese Theater State in the Nineteenth Century.* Princeton University Press: Princeton.

Glick, T. 1970. *Irrigation and Society in Medieval Valencia.* Harvard University Press: Cambridge.

Gosden, C., and C. Pavlides 1994 Are Islands Insular? Landscape vs. Seascape in the Case of the Arawe Islands, Papua New Guinea. *Oceania* 29:162–171.

Haas, J. 1982 *The Evolution of the Prehistoric State.* Columbia University Press: New York.

Håkansson, T. N. 1998 Rulers and Rainmakers in Precolonial South Pare, Tanzania: Exchange and Ritual Experts in Political Centralization. *Ethnology* 37:263–283.

Harding, T. G. 1967 *Voyagers of the Vitiaz Strait.* University of Washington Press: Seattle.

Harmanşah, Ö. 2014 Event, Place, Performance: Rock Reliefs and Spring Monuments in Anatolia. In *Of Rocks and Water: Towards an Archaeology of Place,* edited by Ö. Harmanşah, 140–168. Oxbow Books: Oxford and Philadelphia.

Harrower, M. 2009 Is the Hydraulic Hypothesis Dead Yet? Irrigation and Social Change in Ancient Yemen. *World Archaeology* 41:58–72.

Hastrup, K. 2009 Waterworlds: Framing the Question of Social Resilience. In *The Question of Resilience. Social Responses to Climate Change,* edited by K. Hastrup, 11–30. The Royal Danish Academy of Sciences and Letters: Copenhagen.

Haug, G. H, D. Günther, L. C. Peterson, D. M. Sigman, K. A. Hughen, and B. Aeschlimann 2003 Climate and the Collapse of Maya Civilization. *Science* 299:1731–1735.

Hauser-Schäublin, B. 2003 The Precolonial Balinese State Reconsidered: A Critical Evaluation of Theory Construction on the Relationship between Irrigation, the State, and Ritual. *Current Anthropology* 44:153–181.

Hauser-Schäublin, B. 2011 Land Donations and the Gift of Water. On Temple Landlordism and Irrigation Agriculture in Pre-Colonial Bali. *Human Ecology* 39:43–53.

Hobart, M. 1982 Padi, Puns, and the Attribution of Responsibility. In *Natural Symbols in Southeast Asia*, edited by G. B. Milner, 55–88. School of Oriental and African Studies: London.

Horden, P., and N. Purcell 2000 *The Corrupting Sea: a Study of Mediterranean History*. Blackwell: Oxford.

Horton, R. E. 1931 The Field, Scope, and Status of the Science of Hydrology. *Transactions, American Geophysical Union* 12:189–202.

Hunt, R. C., and E. Hunt 1976 Canal Irrigation and Local Social Organization. *Current Anthropology* 17:389–411.

Isendahl, C. 2011 The Weight of Water: A New Look at Pre-Hispanic Puuc Maya Water Reservoirs. *Ancient Mesoamerica* 22:185–197.

Junker, L. J. 1999 *Raiding, Trading, and Feasting: The Political Economy of Philippine Chiefdoms*. University of Hawai'i Press: Honolulu.

Kirchner, H. 2009 Original Design, Tribal Management and Modifications in Medieval Hydraulic Systems in the Balearic Islands (Spain). *World Archaeology* 41:151–168.

Kloos, H., and R. David 2002 The Paleoepidemiology of Schistosomiasis in Ancient Egypt. *Human Ecology Review* 9:14–25.

Langgut, D., I. Finkelstein, and T. Litt 2013 Climate and the Late Bronze Collapse: New Evidence from the Southern Levant. *Tel Aviv: Journal of the Institute of Archaeology of Tel Aviv University* 40:149–175.

Lanning, E. 1967 *Peru before the Incas*. Prentice-Hall: Englewood Cliffs, NJ.

Lansing, J. S. 1987 Balinese "Water Temples" and the Management of Irrigation. *American Anthropologist* 89:326–341.

Lansing, J. S. 1991 *Priests and Programmers: Technologies of Power in the Engineered Landscape of Bali*. Princeton University Press: Princeton.

Lansing, J. S., and J. N. Kremer 1993 Emergent Properties of Balinese Water Temple Networks: Coadaptation on a Rugged Fitness Landscape. *American Anthropologist* 95:97–114.

Lansing, J. S., L. Pedersen, and B. Hauser-Schäublin 2005. Discussion: On Irrigation and the Balinese State. *Current Anthropology* 46:305–308.

Latour, B. 1993 *We Have Never Been Modern*. Harvard University Press: Cambridge.

Latour, B. 2004 *The Politics of Nature: How to Bring the Sciences into Democracy*. Harvard University Press: Cambridge, MA, and London.

Leach, E. R. 1959 Hydraulic Society in Ceylon. *Past & Present* 15:2–26.

Lefebvre, H. 1991 *The Production of Space*. Blackwell: Oxford.

Li, F. 2013 Contesting Equivalences: Controversies over Water and Mining in Chile and Peru. In *The Social Life of Water*, edited by J. R. Wagner, 18–35. Berghahn Books: New York and Oxford.

Lilley, I. 1988 Prehistoric Exchange across the Vitiaz Strait, Papua New Guinea. *Current Anthropology* 29:513–516.

Linton, J., and J. Budds 2014 The Hydrosocial Cycle: Defining and Mobilizing a Relational-Dialectical Approach to Water. *Geoforum* 57:170–180.

Ljungqvist, F. C., P. J. Krusic, H. S. Sundqvist, E. Zorita, G. Brattström, and D. Frank 2015 Northern Hemisphere Hydroclimate Variability over the Past Twelve Centuries. *Nature* 532:94–98.

Longfellow, B. 2011 *Roman Imperialism and Civic Patronage: Form, Meaning, and Ideology in Monumental Fountain Complexes*. Cambridge University Press: Cambridge and New York.

Lucero, L. J., and A. Kinkella 2014 A Place for Pilgrimage: The Ancient Maya Sacred Landscape of Cara Blanca, Belize. In *Of Rocks and Water: Towards an Archaeology of Place*, edited by Ö. Harmanşah, 13–39. Oxbow Books: Oxford and Philadelphia.

Luzzadder-Beach, S., T. Beach, S. Hutson, and S. Krause 2016 Sky-Earth, Lake-Sea: Climate and Water in Maya History and Landscape. *Antiquity* 90:426–442.

Malinowski, B. 1932 *Argonauts of the Western Pacific. An Account of Native Enterprise and Adventure in the Archipelagoes of Melanesian New Guinea*. Dutton: New York.

McAnany, P., and N. Yoffee (editors) 2010 *Questioning Collapse: Human Resilience, Ecological Vulnerability, and the Aftermath of Empire*. Cambridge University Press: Cambridge.

Mitchell, W. P. 1973 The Hydraulic Hypothesis: A Reappraisal. *Current Anthropology* 14:532–534.

Moseley, M. E. 1974 Organizational Preadaptation to Irrigation: The Evolution of Early Water-Management Systems in Coastal Peru. In *Irrigation's Impact on Society*, edited by T. E. Downing and M. Gibson, 77–82. University of Arizona Press: Tucson.

Moseley, M. E. 1975 *The Maritime Foundations of Andean Civilization*. Cummings: Menlo Park, CA.

Novák, M. 2002 The Artificial Paradise: Programme and Ideology of Royal Gardens. In *Sex and Gender in the Ancient Near East*, edited by S. Parpola and R. M. Whiting, 443–460. The Neo-Assyrian Text Corpus Project, Part II: Helsinki.

Orlove, B., and S. C. Caton 2010 Water Sustainability: Anthropological Approaches and Prospects. *Annual Review of Anthropology* 39:401–415.

Ostrom, E. 1992 *Crafting Institutions for Self-Governing Irrigation Systems*. Institute for Contemporary Studies Press: San Francisco.

Pomeroy, S. B., S. M. Burstein, W. Donlan, and J. T. Roberts 1999 *Ancient Greece: A Political, Social, and Cultural History*. Oxford University Press: Oxford.

Richards, C. 1996 Henges and Water: Towards an Elemental Understanding of Monumentality and Landscape in Late Neolithic Britain. *Journal of Material Culture* 1:313–336.

Robbins, P. 2004 *Political Ecology: A Critical Introduction*. Blackwell: Malden, MA.

Jones, R. and D. Robinson 2005 Water, Wealth, and Social Status at Pompeii: The House of the Vestals in the First Century A.D. *American Journal of Archaeology* 109:695–710.

Scarborough, V. L. 1998 Ecology and Ritual: Water Management and the Maya. *Latin American Antiquity* 9:135–159.

Scarborough, V. L., and L. Lucero 2011 The Non-Hierarchical Development of Complexity in the Semitropics: Water and Cooperation. *Water History* 2:185–205.

Sidky, H. 1997 Irrigation and the Rise of the State in Hunza: A Case for the Hydraulic Hypothesis. *Modern Asian Studies* 31:995–1017.

Stanish, C. 1994 The Hydraulic Hypothesis Revisited: Lake Titicaca Basin Raised Fields in Theoretical Perspective. *Latin American Antiquity* 5:312–332.

Steward, J. H. 1949 Cultural Causality and Law: A Trial Formulation of the Development of Early Civilizations. *American Anthropologist* 51:1–27.

Steward, J. H. 1955 *Irrigation Civilizations: A Comparative Study*. Pan American Union: Washington, DC.

Strang, V. 2008 The Social Construction of Water. In *Handbook of Landscape Archaeology*, edited by B. David and J. Thomas, 123–130. Left Coast Press: Walnut Creek CA.

Strang, V. 2015 Fluid Consistencies. Material Relationality in Human Engagements with Water. *Archaeological Dialogues* 21:133–150.

Swyngedouw, E. 1999 Modernity and Hybridity: Nature, Regeneracionismo, and the Production of the Spanish Waterscape, 1890–1930. *Annals of the Association of American Geographers* 89:443–465.

Swyngedouw, E. 2004 *Social Power and the Urbanisation of Water: Flows of Power.* Oxford University Press: Oxford.

Trawick, P. B. 2001 Successfully Governing the Commons: Principles of Social Organization in an Andean Irrigation System. *Human Ecology* 29:1–25.

United Nations Human Security Unit. 2009. Human Security in Theory and Practice: An Overview of the Human Security Concept and the United Nations Trust Fund for Human Security.

Van Liefferinge, K., M. van den Berg, C. Stal, R. Docter, A. De Wulf, and N. E. C. Verhoest 2014 Reconsidering the Role of Thorikos within the Laurion Silver Mining Area (Attica, Greece) through Hydrological Analyses. *Journal of Archaeological Science* 41:272–284.

Walker, G., R. Whittle, W. Medd, and M. Walker 2011 Assembling the Flood: Producing Spaces of Bad Water in the City of Hull. *Environment and Planning A* 43:2304–2320.

Weiner, A. B. 1976 *Women of Value, Men of Renown: New Perspectives in Trobriand Exchange.* University of Texas Press: Austin.

Wilkinson, T. J., L. Rayne, and J. Jotheri 2015 Hydraulic Landscapes in Mesopotamia: The Role of Human Niche Construction. *Water History* 7:397–418.

Wilson, P. 2012 Waterways, Settlements, and Shifting Power in the North-Western Nile Delta. *Water History* 4:95–117.

Wittfogel, K. A. 1957 *Oriental Despotism: A Comparative Study of Total Power.* Yale University Press: New Haven.

Wutich, A., and A. Brewis 2014 Food, Water, and Scarcity: Toward a Broader Anthropology of Resource Insecurity. *Current Anthropology* 44:444–468.

Zhu, T., M. W. Ertsen, and N. C. van der Giesen 2015 Long Term Effects of Climate on Human Adaptation in the Middle Gila River Valley, Arizona, America. *Water History* 7:511–531.

PART I

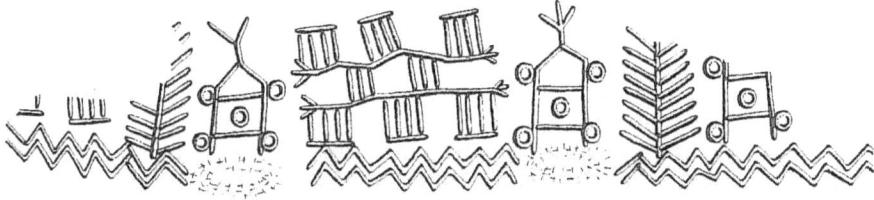

Productive Power and the
Ecological History of Waterscapes

CHAPTER TWO

The Political Ecology of Chinampa Landscapes in the Basin of Mexico

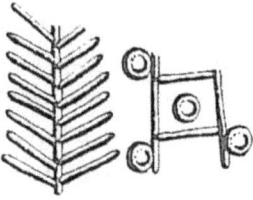

Christopher T. Morehart

Abstract   *Research in political ecology pushes scholars to trace how human inter-action with the landscape is shaped by broader conditions in the political economy. Archaeology has a powerful role to play in this endeavor. Archaeological research provides scales in time and space that few other fields can access. The scope of our gaze enables us to examine how peoples' relationship to land and water is connected not only to a wider political economy but, moreover, to a historical political economy. This project requires we move beyond highly localized perspectives focused on the bottom-up in order to understand how local relationships, institutions, and landscapes are conditioned by a changing and dynamic political economic history. This chapter pursues this goal by comparing two case studies of raised field, chinampa agriculture in the Basin of Mexico: the chinampas of the southern Basin of Mexico and the chinampas of Xaltocan in the northern Basin. Both these systems have dynamic relationships to the development and expansion of state polities. However, their trajectories diverge greatly, and the sustainability of these systems, both physically and in the social imaginary, cannot be understood without articulating local landscapes with long-term histories in the ecological, social, political, and economic fabric of Mexico.*

Archaeological research on land and water always has been in dialogue with politics in some form. Even today, the ghost of Karl Wittfogel lurks in the background of many studies on human-water relationships. For Wittfogel, a centralized political organization emerges from the need to administer large-scale hydraulic projects. Small-scale irrigation systems do not necessitate such evolutionary developments, he argued. But as systems become larger and more integrated, a threshold is reached—an "administrative creation point" (Wittfogel 1957:109)—that fosters increased political complexity and the centralization of despotic regimes. Wittfogel's ideas stimulated substantial discussion in social evolutionary theory (i.e., Armillas 1971; Pálerm 1973; Sanders and Price 1968; Steward 1955). But they have long been criticized on both empirical and conceptual grounds (i.e., Adams 1974; Coward 1980; Earle 1978; Erickson 1993; Feinman 2006; Hunt 1988; Hunt et al. 2005; Kelly 1983; Lansing 1991; Leach 1959; Mabry 1996, 2000; Marcus and Stanish 2006; Netting 1993; Price 1994; Scarborough 2003; Woodbury 1961). We now know that not only do states not necessarily emerge from irrigation projects but, more significantly, farming households and their local relationships are more commonly responsible for irrigation projects' creation, administration, and often their sustainability (Erickson 2006; Ostrom 1990).

Many reasons exist to be critical of Wittfogel (informing on his colleagues and his support of the House Un-American Activities committee should remain high on the list [Price 2004]). However, his recognition that irrigation systems require particular institutions and that the form and structure of irrigation systems relate in some translatable way to the nature of these institutions was important for a basic reason: water integrates in a way that prevents the independence of farming households. Institutions specify the kinds of rules, rights, entitlements, expectations, and duties necessary to manage irrigation systems of varying size, integration, and complexity, including those without centralized administrative control (Ostrom 1990; Schlager and Ostrom 1992).

Articulating local institutions to macro-regional political and economic processes is a challenging goal. It requires efforts to understand how progressively global and historical dynamics play out in physical and social landscapes and condition people's practices and relationships (Roseberry 1989; Wolf 1982). Such work is of fundamental importance to the comparative study of sustainability. Archaeologists and scholars of socioecological systems have studied how local institutions and landscapes mesh with a broader political economy. Focusing on the bottom-up is a significant means, methodologically and interpretively, to understand how socioecological relationships are structured and operate (Erickson 2006; Thurston and Fisher 2006). For scholars of people (anthropologists, archaeologists, historians, geographers, sociologists, etc.), the bottom-up represents a basic unit of analysis. Archaeologists particularly excel at understanding how processes develop from the bottom up given the physically material and localized nature of our work. The household, community, and even the broader landscape have served as units of bottom-up study, offering textured insight into social relationships as they exist through recurrent, everyday practices (Erickson 1993, 2006; Netting 1993; Robin 2006).

Yet this perspective in archaeology should not overemphasize the autonomy of the local (Janusek and Kolata 2004; Morehart and Eisenberg 2010). Paradoxically, positioning farmers, their households, or their communities as autonomous can minimize the ingenuity, flexibility, and adaptability of their strategies in relation to broader constraints (Morehart 2010:82). Archaeologists empirically study the past from the bottom up and must first consider local organizational processes in terms of the day-to-day process of making a living. But local organizational patterns in daily life may be highly structured by nonlocal forces that, nonetheless, operate locally. Extreme bottom-up views would inhibit considerations of how households and communities situate within broader, and often highly variable, political economic landscapes. Netting's research, for example, pushed social scientists toward detailed analyses of household autonomy in land management. But he also observed that smallholders often are, in fact, peasants subordinate to elites (Netting 1993:187). Erickson is one of the leading archaeological advocates for bottom-up positions in the archaeological study of agrarian landscapes. But he also stressed that "what raised fields and other landscape capital systems did was to tie farmers to the land, making them relatively immobile and subject to labor taxes and tribute" (Erickson 1993:411). Situating the local into the extralocal is a fundamental methodological and inferential strength in archaeology (Brumfiel 1992), though the effect of such frequently unequal relationships on the sustainability of landscapes and socioecosystems has received less attention than broader climatological and demographic processes.

In research on contemporary social and ecological interactions, an emphasis on local, bottom-up processes also exists. Responding to Hardin's (1968) erroneous and reactionary oversimplification of how people manage and benefit from common property, these researchers have shown that property relationships are dynamic and that local people have created durable institutions to sustainably manage ecosystems. This work is focused on eliciting and modeling the institutional relations, rules, and norms that comprise a socioecological system (e.g., Janssen et al. 2012; Miller and Page 2007; Ostrom 1990; Poteete et al. 2010; Schlager and Ostrom 1992). The focus on the local system is a strength and a limitation. It enables researchers to understand the dynamics of norms and how such norms translate into the operation and sustainability of local socioecosystems. As a systems approach, however, scholars offer models of "nested systems" to pursue broader relationships, which are highly abstract, interpretively cumbersome, and often include variables, processes, and systems that are comparatively incompatible and devoid of human actors, intentions, etc. (Brumfiel 1992:559; Cowgill 1975:506). In eliciting the rules and norms of institutions, points of stress that jeopardize sustainability often appear through the actions of local individuals and users, typically classed as free riders, holdouts, defectors, stationary bandits, etc. Norms are followed, enforced, or disregarded depending on the structure of local relationships. On the one hand, this approach allows researchers to see inequality in a broader social landscape as it affects local systems and their sustainability (Janssen et al. 2012). On the other hand, ironically similar to Hardin's views, much of this work places the major responsibility for sustainability on the shoulders of local decision makers rather than a broader and historical political economy.

Local resource users represent a group of human actors we can observe directly. We can also study nonhuman actors—things, places, and landscapes—as they interdigitate with local relationships (Robbins 2012). But many human actors in regional political ecologies are less obvious and operate through increasingly global consortiums whose effects are often more tangible than their agency (Paulson and Gezon 2005). If we are able to place the responsibility for sustainability or unsustainability on the shoulders of local people, we should also attempt a similarly "democratic" distribution of "blame" on the shoulders of multiple historical factors that directly impact local people but which they may have limited ability to navigate.

These bottom-up approaches in archaeology and socioecology emphasize local dynamics and how they change in relation to broader historical factors. This approach is central to the growing field of political ecology. At its most basic level, political ecology is the study of cultural ecology, or how humans interact with the environment, with an eye on the political economy, or the differential distribution of wealth and power in society (Blaikie and Brookfield 1987; Paulson et al. 2005:17; Peet and Watts 1996; Robbins 2012). Political ecologists examine how people interact with the physical environment while physically and discursively navigating institutional relations that exist at multiple scales, particularly those that affect but transcend local systems (Escobar 1999; Paulson and Gezon 2005; Peet and Watts 1996; Rocheleau 1999). Examining the nature of the local institutional milieu is the primary means to understand the political ecology of environmental interaction. But research on political ecology stresses that local processes are shaped by broad historical forces as well as "agents" that have the ability to affect and to transcend local systems, such as NGOS, transnational corporations, regional, national, and global elites, leaders, and political regimes, etc. (Pauslon et al. 2006). The actions of these entities and the processes that they either create or perpetuate are both local and extralocal and must be incorporated into our understandings of landscapes.

CHINAMPA CASE STUDIES

In this spirit, I now turn to two case studies on *chinampa* farming in the Basin of Mexico to examine differing configurations of landscape and social and political institutions. The Basin of Mexico is a closed hydraulic plateau between 2500 and 2700 m asl (Figure 2.1). Large-scale settlement surveys during the 1960s and 1970s documented the regional demographic profile of the region (Sanders et al. 1979). Settlements of pottery-using farmers are first observable in the archaeological record by the Early Formative period (ca. 1500 BCE). The macro-regional settlement system went through several periods of growth and decline up to the present, often in direct response to the influence of political systems and their policies, including small and expansionary states (i.e., empires). People practiced agriculture of varying levels of intensity, depending on the local environment, demography, and political economy. Their practices took advantage of the mosaic distribution of resources across the landscape, which included the high sierra, the foothills of the surrounding piedmont, rivers and streams, alluvial deposits, and lakes and lagoons.

The lakes in particular offered important resources for local populations and for the financing of entire political economies. Prior to the arrival of the Spanish in the sixteenth century and the elaborate lake drainage projects that continue to today, the Basin of Mexico was characterized by an interconnected system of lakes and lagoons, which varied in elevation, size, and salinity (Ezcurra et al. 1999; Mathes 1970; Sanders et al. 1979). Texcoco was the largest, central lake. It was also the lowest in elevation and was saline. The waters of Lake Texcoco were a powerful threat to the stability of settlements. In the fifteenth century, for example, the Aztec empire constructed a long dike to separate the waters of Texcoco from their urban capital at Tenochtitlan, creating an anthropogenic lake referred to as Lake Mexico. The dike, attributed to the Texcoco king Nezahuacoyotl, protected Tenochtitlan and its lands from flooding and also protected the freshwaters of Lakes Xochimilco and Chalco, located to the south, which

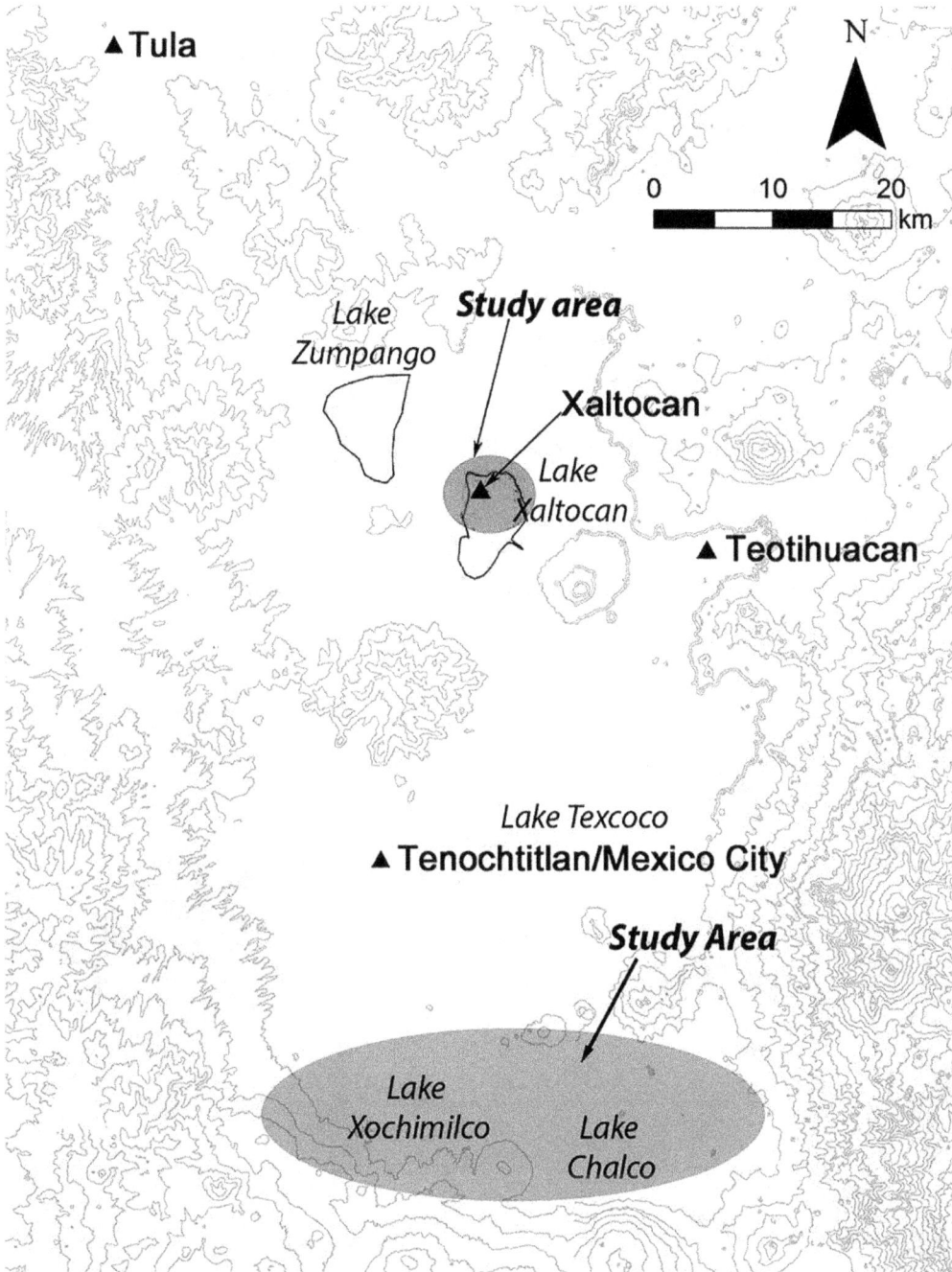

FIGURE 2.1 Map of the Basin of Mexico showing areas and sites discussed in text.

was an important agricultural zone for the empire (see below). Lakes Zumpango and Xaltocan were the northernmost lakes. They were largely brackish systems, though their salinity varied over time (Frederick et al. 2005) and also offered important agricultural resources (see below). These lakes periodically overflowed into Texcoco, increasing the larger lake's salinity and flooding problems. Indeed, the role of the northern lakes in urban flooding was recognized by both the Aztecs and the Colonial Spanish. The Aztecs constructed another dike to separate these waters from Texcoco, creating a lake called Lake San Cristóbal or Ecatepec (Candiani 2014). Moreover, the earliest Spanish efforts to drain the lakes focused first on diverting springs that fed Lakes Zumpango and Xaltocan (Morehart 2010).

The word *chinampa* derives from the Nahuatl term *chinamitl,* which means an area enclosed by hedges or canes (Molina 1944:21). Chinampas represent elevated agricultural plots, usually long and narrow, separated by canals in a wetland environment (Ávila Lopez 1991, 2006; Frederick 2007; Palerm 1973; Rojas Rabiela 1991; Sanders 1957; Santamaría 1912; West and Armillas 1950) (Figure 2.2). They are comparable to other raised field systems in the New World (Morehart 2012a). Raised field farming in particular has been highlighted as an agricultural technology that is very productive and highly sustainable when managed from the bottom up (e.g. Erickson 1993, 2006; Iriarte et al. 2012; Renard et al. 2011).

Chinampa farming in particular is often stressed as an innovative form of Traditional Ecological Knowledge and has appeared in efforts to employ traditional practices to improve

FIGURE 2.2 Modern chinampa in Xochimilco, Mexico.

local agrarian economies and ecosystems. Chinampas have existed in the Basin of Mexico for more than 1,000 years. Their longevity has led ecologists not only to study the highly local nature of chinampa farming but to introduce chinampas into similar ecosystems elsewhere as part of efforts to improve ecological and economic stability (Gomez-Pompa and Jimenez-Osornia 1989; Gómez-Pompa et al. 1982; Jiménez-Osornio 1995, 1999). These efforts have not been successful (Gómez-Pompa and Jiménez-Osornio 1989:245–246). The failure of these projects was not entirely environmental but, rather, organizational and structural. The experimental plots, even if they were ecologically well planned, did not mesh with how local institutions and communities were tied into a national economic system that shaped land allocation, agrarian production, debt, investment, etc.

Although unsuccessful, this work offers a useful lesson. It points to a need to transcend bottom-up research and to examine the connections between a local milieu and the broader forces operating in a political economy that shapes the sustainability of socioecosystems and peoples' livelihoods. The stress on "tradition" can open our eyes to alternative means of interacting with landscapes and resources (Berkes 2012). But it is necessary to unpack and question our ideas and often our valorization—if not romanticization—of tradition. Traditional ecological practices have histories that shape their sustainability across time and space. Research on chinampa farming offers an excellent opportunity to situate agrarian practices and water management in history—to study how local practices and relationships were shaped by changing political, economic, and environmental processes. In the Basin of Mexico, two primary areas were sites of intensive chinampa agriculture: Lakes Xochimilco and Chalco in the southern Basin and Lake Xaltocan in the northern Basin. The comparisons I discuss below demonstrate very different histories. But they share one similarity: their histories are the product of how broader, political ecological processes have shaped local relationships and landscapes.

SOUTHERN LAKES

The most well-known chinampas in the Basin of Mexico are those associated with the Aztec empire, located in the southern freshwater lakes of Xochimilco and Chalco (Figure 2.1). The developmental relationship between the Aztec state and chinampa agriculture is not entirely clear. It is based on an incomplete mosaic of archaeological data and historical sources. Prior to the formation of the Aztec empire, chinampas seem to have existed on a limited scale from the Classic to Middle Postclassic periods (ca. 300–1350 CE), especially along the lake edges adjacent to communities (Coe 1964; Parsons 1976, 1991; Parsons et al. 1985). Once the Aztec Triple Alliance formed, however, the empire conquered this region in the early mid-fifteenth century CE, led by the king Itzcoatl (Armillas 1971; Parsons 1976, 1991; Rojas Rabiela 1991; West and Armillas 1950). The Codex Mendoza, for example, lists Xochimilco as one of Itzcoatl's conquests; the toponym is depicted with a chinampa-like motif adjacent to a burning house, indicating conquest (Berdan and Anawalt 1992:17, folio 6r) (Figure 2.3). The Aztec state did not emerge from these intensive hydrological projects but, instead, imposed itself upon the previous strategies of conquered peoples (Morehart 2010:129). Chinampa creation was

FIGURE 2.3 Representation of Xochimilco in the Codex Mendoza, emphasizing its conquest (adapted from Berdan and Anawalt 1992).

intertwined with the need for foodstuffs and to maintain imperial control both over formerly independent communities and over allied nobles through gifts or grants of land (Hicks 1991; Luna 2014; Nichols 2004:274; Parsons 1976).

Research on the southern lakes' chinampas exhibits very different attempts to understand the relationships between sociopolitical institutions and the landscape. Scarborough (1991:127) observed that the chinampas required corporate investments for their creation and upkeep. Sanders and Price (1968:177), however, argued that with the abundance of fresh water in these lakes, the chinampas lacked the integration requiring a high level of cooperation and coordination. Yet others still observed the presence of the state, not only given the large-scale engineering projects the state financed, such as Nezahuacoyotl's dike, that prevented flooding salt waters from the central lakes into the chinampas, but also through the study of the landscape itself. Using remote sensing data and survey, for example, Pedro Armillas (1971:660) argued that the chinampa system was comprised by a highly standardized grid of fields and canals that covered between 9,000 and 12,000 ha (see also Luna 2014). Armillas argued that this standardized landscape, created in a short period of time, was the product of the Aztec empire. Such expansionist, systematic development (Doolittle 1984; Scarborough 2003) may reflect the state's disregard for or appropriation of local social and physical entitlements in order to increase tax revenue while increasing workers' dependence on the state. Chinampa produce would come to support as much as one-half of the urban population of Tenochtitlan, the Aztec capital (Armillas 1971; Parsons 1976). Parsons (1976) went beyond a state-centric view to model the institutional complexity that affected chinampa production. He argues chinampa produce flowed through multiple, overlapping institutions via rent from tenant farmers on noble estates, tribute from local landholding communities or barrios (known as *calpolli*), and market trade. Most chinampa fields during this time, as Luna's (2014) recent research demonstrates, were not articulated to preexisting communities and were likely fields of tenants dependent upon absentee landowners.

Although these farmers were associated with differing institutions, lands were nonetheless worked by commoners (Gibson 1964). Both tenant farmers on noble estates and farmers in calpolli communities appear to have maintained similar standards of living and undertaken a similar range of activities, pointing up the importance of local, bottom-up perspectives. For example, Elizabeth Brumfiel found similarities in practices and access to resources in an analysis of artifacts from Xico, a chinampa community (Brumfiel 1991). Paleoethnobotanical research by Popper (1995), moreover, demonstrated that local chinampa farmers developed complex forms of traditional ecological knowledge on farming techniques, soils, water, and plants. In fact, many agriculturalists in rural and urban areas maintained house lots adjacent to chinampa fields (Avila López 1991:141; Calnek 1972; Parsons et al. 1985). The household, thus, represented the basic unit of production and management (Netting 1993).

Differing views on the institutional structure of chinampa production are not necessarily in conflict with one another but reflect the ways in which landscapes form and farmers strategize in relation to political, social, and economic institutions. Clearly, state finance was necessary for key projects that maintained the hydraulic qualities of the southern lakes. As Scarborough (1991:130) notes, "chinamperos were at the service of the state bureaucracy, since only the state could control and regulate water levels." The correctness of Armillas's conclusion that the standardized system was the product of state hydraulic engineering requires further study. But such systematic changes would not necessarily create greater hydraulic integration at the local level. Despite the large size of the chinampa zone, a diminished need for extra-household systems of coordination, which Sanders and Price (1968) argued, may have characterized the system's operation and management, supporting the evidence of farming household autonomy that Elizabeth Brumfiel (1991) and Popper (1994) documented.

Many questions on the role of chinampas in the historical and political ecology of the Aztec empire remain to be studied (see Luna 2014). The temporal relationships between chinampa agriculture and major political economic changes are not well understood, but the data we have suggest future areas of work. For example, did tenant farms exhibit less longevity compared to chinampas associated with landholding communities? Was the livelihood of tenant farmers more precarious given their dependence on the stability of the Aztec state, which was conquered in the sixteenth century? Were chinampas connected to landholding communities not only older but also more resilient? That is, did the institutional structure of local communities buffer chinamperos from changes in the political economy compared to tenant farmers? Or was the reverse the case? Did Spanish efforts to transform land into an alienable good offer opportunities for tenants to own land, simultaneously eroding the institutional structure of landholding communities? These questions can be addressed through further fieldwork and can be easily operationalized into testable research.

The focus on the association between the Aztecs and chinampa farming often overshadows the role of chinampas throughout history. Avila López's (1991, 2006) pioneering research on chinampas in Iztapalalapa and Mexicaltzingo, also in the southern basin, documented fundamental shifts in the structure and form of chinampas from prehispanic to colonial times. While retaining lengths similar to earlier, fossil chinampas, colonial chinampas were much wider (approximately 12 m wide versus 3 m wide for earlier chinampas) (Avila López 1991:139). Illuminating some of the questions posed above, these shifts reflect changing systems of land tenure after Spanish conquest. Despite the increase in the size of individual fields, however, the overall area chinampas occupied decreased greatly due to transforming property regimes, ecological changes affecting hydrology, and restructuration of regional and subregional economies. The number of chinampas bequeathed to heirs also decreased throughout the colonial period. By the sixteenth to seventeenth century, chinampa parcels were increasingly treated as inheritable private property often with their previous connections to corporate entities obscured or deemphasized (Cline 1984, 1986; Cline and León Portilla 1984; Kellogg 1995). Transformations in tenure also were tied to changing gender relations. In sixteenth-century legal cases, for example, women increasingly sought to assert their control over the ownership of chinampas and strongly disputed contrary claims, while litigation involving men centered more on rural lands (Kellogg 1995:33, 44). These shifts were due to the erosion of indigenous rules governing corporate tenure, changing patterns of wealth and impoverishment, indigenous demographic decline, the draining of the lakes, and the ways the Spanish developed and expanded urban centers (Bojórquez Castro and Villa Rodríguez 1995; Kellogg 1995:149).

Today the chinampas of Xochimilco still exist, but they occupy a fraction of their former area. Bojórquez Castro and Villa Rodríguez (1995:90) estimate a 99 percent reduction in the number of chinampas from 1500 to 1995. During much of the twentieth century, Lake Xochimilco was almost completely dry as waters that formerly drained into the area were diverted for industry or to support urban services (Narchi 2013:180; Torres et al. 1994). The government responded by pumping in wastewater from Cerro de la Estrella and other treatment plants. Salinization is an increasing problem, and the southern lakes are contaminated with heavy metals, pathogenic microorganisms, and detergents (Bojórquez Castro and Villa Rodríguez 1995:90; Quiñónez 2005). The declining and increasingly dangerous quality of the water has led to an almost 50 percent reduction of consumable cultigens in the past 50 years (Canabal 1997:141; Crossley 1999:118; Narchi 2013:190). Large-scale floriculture, for which Xochimilco is "traditionally" known, was a direct response to water contamination. The center of Xochimilco and its chinampas are now a World Heritage site (since 1987). Main canal systems are open to tourists, who can take guided boat tours while drinking beer, eating food, and listening to mariachi music, blissfully unaware of the historical and political ecology (Figure 2.4).

FIGURE 2.4 The tourist landscape of Xochimilco, showing decorated boats used for canal tours.

NORTHERN LAKES

Other raised field systems in the Basin of Mexico, however, exhibit remarkably differing political ecological histories. In the northern basin, a chinampa system was constructed around the pre-Aztec city center of Xaltocan in a lake of the same name (Morehart 2010, 2012a; Morehart and Frederick 2014; Nichols and Frederick 1993) (Figure 2.1). Xaltocan was an independent kingdom during the Early and Middle Postclassic periods (ca. 1000–1350 CE). At its height between the thirteenth and fourteenth centuries, the kingdom had more than 5,000 local inhabitants with connections ranging from the southern Basin of Mexico to present-day northern Hidalgo. Xaltocan financed its complex political economy from tribute, market exchange, and intensive, raised field agriculture (Brumfiel 2005).

Using satellite imagery, air photos, geomorphological trenches, and excavation units, we documented the chinampa system's size to be more than 1,500 ha (Morehart 2010, 2012a; Morehart and Frederick 2014) (Figure 2.5). This system was highly integrated hydraulically. Unlike the fresh waters of the southern Basin of Mexico, Lake Xaltocan fluctuated between saline to brackish conditions through much of its history (Frederick et al. 2005). However, key freshwater systems flowed into the lake basin, such as the

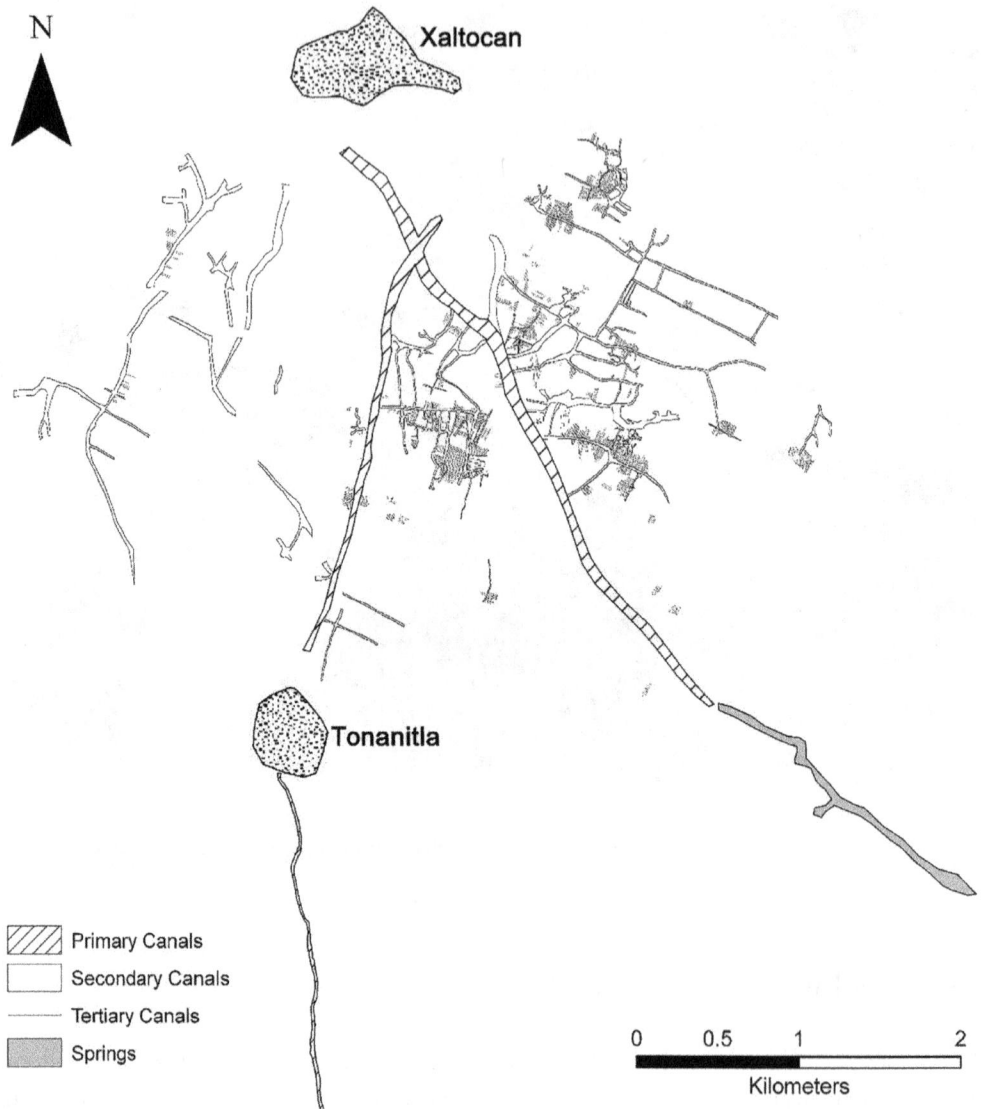

FIGURE 2.5 Plan map of Xaltocan's chinampa system, based on excavations, satellite imagery, and aerial photos.

Cuauhtitlan River to the southwest and, significantly, a series of springs that emerged at the base of a local hill, known today as Cerro Chiconautla. The layout of the raised field system incorporated these springs. A large, primary canal was constructed to channel its waters into secondary canals that distributed water throughout the system and narrow tertiary canals that surrounded individual fields.

I estimate that at its height, the chinampa system could have supported approximately 15,000 people, three times the estimated population of the community, and would have required approximately 1,300 full-time farmers (Morehart 2010, 2014). As in the southern Basin, farming households seem to have maintained a degree of autonomy over productive decisions. Farmers cultivated a range of crops, including maize, beans, squash, and chenopodium (Morehart 2010). We also recovered substantial quantities of pine charcoal within the field system. Pine is not locally available and inhabits higher elevations surrounding the central basin. It was likely a trade good used extensively as household fuel. Its presence in the chinampas suggests that chinamperos employed household waste, such as hearth ash, to enhance soil productivity. Moreover, we recovered many large jar, or olla, sherds from canal deposits. The vast majority of these either had handles at the rim or extremely flared necks. Despite the immediate presence of lake water, this may suggest that farmers employed pot irrigation to water individual plants, an extremely labor-intensive form of manual irrigation (Scarborough 1991; Wilken 1987).

Farmers produced crops to maintain the institution of the family and household, to participate in the market, and to pay tribute or taxes to institutions connected to the state (Morehart 2014; Morehart and Eisenberg 2010). However, maintaining key hydraulic features and administering the distribution of water required institutions that linked the community of water users. The system was far smaller than the later chinampa zone in the south but well above scalar stress thresholds in terms of size and number of potential users (Hunt 1988; Mabry 1996; Uphoff 1986). Interestingly, the number of users is higher than most figures of landed corporate groups documented in sixteenth-century central Mexico, such as the calpolli (see Carrasco 1964). Hence, farmers would have required the organization of multiple corporate groups to minimize dilemmas stemming from their fragmentation as the polity grew in size and complexity. This appears to have been exactly what occurred. The chinampa system grew dramatically in size and use intensity from the eleventh to the fourteenth century. It appears to have been an ecologically well-managed system with no clear evidence of degradation. Chemical analysis of soil samples suggested high amounts of freshwater influx and low salt levels, and diatom analysis indicated an alkaline environment similar to the southern basin lakes (Frederick et al. 2005:107; Morehart 2010:199–202).

The ecological system appears to have been more sustainable than the political one. Xaltocan was conquered toward the end of the fourteenth century CE, almost 50 years prior to the formation of the Aztec empire (Brumfiel 2005). The impact of war and conquest affected the community of chinamperos; the institutions they formed to manage water did not survive the collapse of the political system, and the chinampa system was abandoned. Many of the rulers and residents fled to Hidalgo, Tlaxcala, Puebla, and even Xochimilco, where towns or barrios named Xaltocan exist today (Morehart and Frederick 2014). Significantly, the chinampa system was not reinitiated when the Aztec state expanded into the region about 50 years later, despite their investment in chinampas to the south. I suggest this occurred due to both organizational and ecological reasons. Organizationally, the Aztecs made no effort to reinstall indigenous rulers. Local residents subject to the Aztecs were pulled in many tributary directions, producing cotton cloth as well as serving as warriors and laborers on noble estates. Interestingly, the Codex Mendoza, which lists the tribute requirements for all towns and provinces in the Aztec empire makes little mention of Xaltocan (Berdan and Anawalt 1992). The town is listed in the codex's section on dynastic history and military conquest and again in another section listing towns that provided warriors for garrisons. In other words, both top-down and bottom-up conditions prevented the formation of sustainable hydraulic institutions necessary to engage in chinampa farming at previous levels. Ecologically, the conquest of Xaltocan created environmental conditions detrimental to intensive, wetland farming. The Aztecs diverted the Cuauhtitlan River away from the Xaltocan lake basin to open up arable land elsewhere. Although the springs remained, insufficient freshwater influx existed for raised field farming in the now seasonal lagoon, which drastically increased the salinization of local soils. The springs emerged from Cerro Chiconautla, and Late Postclassic period terracing on the hill and surrounding land use for other communities likely further reduced the amount of water.

From the sixteenth to the nineteenth century, Spanish and Mexican land surveyors described Xaltocan's lands as barren, arid, and nitrous (Morehart 2010:147). Residents in the area supported themselves through salt production and fishing. The first Spanish efforts to drain the lakes centered on diverting the Chiconautla springs and the Cuauhtitlan River, though local residents opposed this project (Morehart 2010:154). Nevertheless, the first effort to drain the lakes, the Gran Desagüe, was completed by 1604 and expanded in the late nineteenth century and early twentieth century. By the mid-twentieth century, many of the former chinampa lands were converted into highly standardized agricultural plots, known as *ejido*. The springs that once fed the area were finally tapped via deep wells to provide water for Mexico City's urban population in the 1950s, permanently draining the seasonal lagoon. To irrigate their fields, farmers today obtain water from Mexico City. As in the southern basin, this water is contaminated with heavy metals and bacteria (Ezcurra et al. 1999:91; Vega-López et al. 2009; Vega-López et al. 2012). With changes to the Mexican constitution in 1992, it is now possible to sell ejido land (Hamilton 2002). With farmers unable to compete with foreign grain commodities from the United States (made possible via NAFTA), corporate developers are buying land and building shopping malls and massive condominium complexes in former agricultural areas, fundamentally altering local institutions and entire ecosystems. Local organizations in Xaltocan have responded by asserting their autonomy over community lands and fostering events that celebrate the town's history (Morehart 2012b).

Unlike the southern lakes, Xaltocan's chinampas do not occupy a central place in the popular imagination of tourists or the national consciousness of Mexico. Many residents, young and old, however, recall a local legend about the loss of the waters. According to the myth, a powerful lord named Awítsotl (who shares the name of a fifteenth-century Aztec king known for his ill-fated hydraulic policies) owned the wealth of Xaltocan: the freshwater springs that fed the lake. Residents became dissatisfied with his rule and captured him to take him to jail via canoe. Awítsotl, however, transformed into an aquatic animal, drowned his captors, and escaped, taking with him the town's wealth. One local resident observed that "the waters dried up, all went with Awítsotl. Only some swallows have returned, but only to say 'you have done bad by chasing away our love, as he was the owner of the water; today you will stay miserable'" (Barlow 1999:184). Although this myth places the blame on residents for violating a sacred covenant, the disappearance of water did not result from unsustainable local institutions. Instead, it is the result of policies implemented by transforming political economic institutions from the fifteenth to the twenty-first century that operate on an increasingly global scale.

Conclusion

The two case studies discussed here offer basic points of similarity and contrast. In both cases, individual farming households were the main unit of production and management. But also, both cases exhibit the importance of understanding the institutional milieu. Chinampa farming in the southern Basin of Mexico was connected directly to the political economy of the state. This does not mean that the state was involved in the management or the administration of raised field farming, despite the state's role in financing and organizing major hydraulic projects. The relationship between land and the state was built around multiple, often overlapping institutions, which included households, communities, tenant farmers, and noble estates. In Xaltocan, we have more data on the structure of the raised field system across time and space but less information on the structure of the institutional landscape given the paucity of historic texts describing the system. Yet the integrated nature of the irrigation system required the formation of institutions capable of transcending the household and possibly multiple corporate groups. At Xaltocan, we have an excellent example of how political instability can negatively impact the sustainability of a socioecosystem dependent on stable institutions that linked farmers together. Organizational and ecological factors influenced both the abandonment of the chinampa landscape and the fact that chinampa farming was not reinitiated later. In the southern lakes, chinampa farming has persisted much longer. But even here, this persistence is not simply the continuation of tradition. Rather, the changing political economies of the Aztecs and, especially, the Spanish empires shaped land tenure and hydrology. Chinampa farming did not persist, it changed as ecosystems were modified, population declined, and land was converted to an alienable good.

Both areas, moreover, have been modified continually throughout Mexico's history, especially with the expansion of urban services for a growing Mexico City and land and water reforms. These processes have caused unprecedented levels of degradation and pollution. The tradition of chinampas continues to exist in the minds of people. Where Xochimilco's chinampas have become a national and international treasure, visited and consumed by tourists, the history of Xaltocan's chinampas is embedded within local myths of the loss of an entire ecosystem.

Recognizing the political ecology of landscapes has important implications for the archaeological study of ancient landscapes and water management. First, it allows us to go beyond hyper-simplified characterizations of social relations and governance, such as household autonomy versus state control or bottom-up versus top down. Second, it allows archaeologists to consider how the sustainability of social and ecological systems depends not only on local relationships but also on the local impact of more expansive institutions across the political economy. In so doing, archaeologists can better capture the reality of past socioecological systems and produce narratives of the past that are more in dialogue with processes occurring within the contemporary world. Doing so also fosters a historically engaged archaeology with a gaze not locked into the distant past but with eyes on the past, present, and future.

ACKNOWLEDGMENTS

I would like to thank Emily Holt for inviting me to the 8th annual IEMA conference on water and power in past societies. My thinking on how to study this issue benefited greatly from the contributions and, especially, the wonderful conversations. The work I've been doing the past ten years in the Basin of Mexico has been supported by many institutions, including the National Science Foundation, Wenner Gren, the National Geographic Society, Fulbright Hays, Digital Globe, Inc., Northwestern University, Georgia State University, Arizona State University, the Instituto Nacional de Antropología e Historia de Mexico, and the Universidad Nacional Autónoma de México. I also acknowledge the following individuals: Elizabeth Brumfiel, Jeffrey Parsons, Charles Frederick, Enrique Rodriguez, Kristin De Lucia, John Millhauser, Lisa Overholtzer, and Daniel Vallejo. Finally, my work in Xaltocan is not possible without the support of the municipality of Nextlalpan, the delegation of Xaltocan, the Casa de la Cultura of Xaltocan, the Museum of Xaltocan, the organization of the common lands and ejido of Xaltocan, and the Civil Association of the Great Kingdom of Xaltocan.

REFERENCES

Adams, R. M. 1974 Historic Patterns of Mesopotamian Irrigation Agriculture. In *Irrigation's Impact on Society*, edited by T. Downing and M. Gibson, pp. 1–6. University of Arizona Press, Tucson.

Armillas, P. 1971 Gardens on Swamps. *Science* 175(4010):653–661.

Avila López, R. 1991 *Chinampas de Iztapalapa*, D. F. Instituto Nacional de Antropología e Historia, Mexico, D.F.

Avila López, R. 2006 *Mexicaltzingo: Arqueologia de un Reino Culhua-Mexica*. 2 vols. Conaculta, Mexico, D.F.

Barlow, Robert H. 1999 Textos de Xaltocan. Estado de México. In *Escritos Diversos*, edited by J. Monjarás Ruiz and E. Límon, pp. 169–195. vol. VII. Instituto Nacional de Antropología e Historia, Mexico, D.F.

Berdan, F. F., and P. R. Anawalt. 1992 *The Codex Mendoza, Vol IV: Pictorial Parallel Image Replicas of Codex Mendoza with Transcriptions and Translations of the Spanish Commentaries and Translations of the Spanish Glosses*. University of California Press, Berkeley.

Berkes, F. 2012 *Sacred Ecology*. Routledge, New York.

Bojórquez Castro, L., and F. Villa Rodríguez. 1995 El Ecosistema Lacustre. Xochimilco y el Deterioro de las Chinampas. In *Presente, Pasado y Futuro de las Chinampas*, edited by T. Rojas Rabiela, pp. 85–137. Centro de Investigaciones y Estudios. Superiores en Antropologia Social, Hidalgo y Matamoros, Tlalpan.

Brumfiel, E. 1991 Agricultural Development and Class Stratification in the Southern Valley of Mexico. In *Land and Politics in the Valley of Mexico*, edited by H. R. Harvey, pp. 43–62. University of Mexico Press, Albuquerque.

Brumfiel, E. 1992 Breaking and Entering the Ecosystem: Gender, Class, and Faction Steal the Show. *American Anthropologist* 94:551–567.

Brumfiel, E. 2005 Conclusions: Production and Power at Xaltocan. In *Production and Power at Postclassic Xaltocan,* edited by E. M. Brumfiel, pp. 349–360. Instituto Nacional de Antropología e Historia, Mexico, D.F.

Calnek, E. E. 1972 Settlement Pattern and Chinampa Agriculture at Tenochtitlan. *American Antiquity* 37:104–115.

Canabal, B. 1997 *Xochimilco una Identidad Recreada*. Universidad Autónoma Metropolitana, Unidad Xochimilco, Coyoacán, D.F.

Carrasco, P. 1964 Tres Libros de Tributo del Museo Nacional de México y su Importancia para los Estudios Demográficos. In 35th International Congress of Americanists, 1962, vol. 3, pp. 373–378. Mexico City.

Cline, S. 1984 Land Tenure in Late Sixteenth-Century Culhuacan. In *Explorations in Ethnohistory: Indians of Central Mexico in the Sixteenth Century*, edited by H. R. Harvey and H. J. Prem, pp. 277–311. University of New Mexico Press, Albuquerque.

Cline, S. 1986 *Colonial Culhuacan, 1580–1600: A Social History of an Aztec Town*. University of New Mexico Press, Albuquerque.

Cline, S., and M. León-Portilla. 1984 *The Testaments of Culhuacan*. UCLA Latin American Center Nahuatl Studies Series, UCLA Latin American Center Publications, Los Angeles.

Coe, M. D. 1964 The Chinampas of Mexico. *Scientific American* 210–211:90–98.

Coward, E. W. 1980 Irrigation Development: Institutional and Organizational Issues. In *Irrigation and Agricultural Development in Asia: Perspectives from the Social Sciences*, edited by E. W. Coward, pp. 15–28. Cornell University Press, Ithaca.

Cowgill, G. 1975 On Causes and Consequences of Ancient and Modern Population Changes. *American Anthropologist* 77:505–525.

Crossley, P. 1999 Sub-Irrigation and Temperature Amelioration in Chinampa Agriculture. PhD Dissertation, University of Texas.

Doolittle, W. E. 1984 Agricultural Change as an Incremental Process. *Annals of the Association of American Geographers* 74:124–137.

Earle, T. 1978 *Economic and Social Organization of a Complex Chiefdom, the Halelea District, Kaua'i, Hawaii*. Anthropological Papers 63. Museum of Anthropology, University of Michigan, Ann Arbor.

Erickson, C. 1993 The Social Organization of Prehispanic Raised Field Agriculture in the Lake Titicaca Basin. In *Economic Aspects of Water Management in the Prehispanic New World*, edited by V. L. Scarborough and B. L. Isaac, pp. 369–426. Greenwich, CT: JAI Press.

Erickson, C. 2006 Intensification, Political Economy, and the Farming Community: In Defense of a Bottom-up Perspective of the Past. In *Agricultural Strategies*, edited by J. Marcus and C. Stanish, pp. 233–265. Cotsen Institute of Archaeology, Los Angeles.

Escobar, A. 1999 After Nature: Steps to an Antiessentialist Political Ecology. *Current Anthropology* 40(1): 1–30.

Ezcurra, E., M. Mazari-Hiriart, I. Pisanty, and A. Guillermo Aguilar. 1999 *The Basin of Mexico: Critical Environmental Issues and Sustainability*. New York: United Nations University Press.

Feinman, G. M. 2006 The Economic Underpinnings of Prehispanic Zapotec Civilization: Small-Scale Production, Economic Interdependence. In *Agricultural Strategies*, edited by J. Marcus and C. Stanish, pp. 255–280. Cotsen Institute of Archaeology, Los Angeles.

Frederick, C. D. 2007 Chinampa Cultivation in the Basin of Mexico: Observations on the Evolution of Form and Function. In *Seeking a Richer Harvest: The Archaeology of Subsistence Intensification, Innovation and Change*, edited by T. L. Thurston and C. T. Fisher, pp. 107–124. Springer Scientific Publishing, New York.

Frederick, C. D., B. Winsborough, and V. Popper. 2005 Geoarchaeological Investigations in the Northern Basin of Mexico. In *Production and Power at Postclassic Xaltocan*, edited by E. M. Brumfiel, pp. 71–116. Instituto Nacional de Antropología e Historia, Mexico, D.F.

Gibson, C. 1964 *The Aztecs under Spanish Rule: A History of the Valley of Mexico, 1519–1810*. Stanford University Press, Stanford.

Gomez Pompa, A., and J. J. Jiménez Osornio. 1989 Some Reflections on Intensive Tradition Agriculture. In *Food and Farm: Current Debates and Policies,* edited by K. Truman and C. Gladwin, pp. 231–253. University Press of America, New York.

Gómez-Pompa, A., H. L. Morales, E. Jiménez Ávila, and J. Jiménez Ávila. 1982 Experiences in Traditional Hydraulic Agriculture. In *Maya Subsistence: Studies in Memory of Dennis E. Puleston*, edited by K. V. Flannery, pp. 327–340. Academic Press, New York.

Hamilton, S. 2002 Neoliberalism, Gender, and Property Rights in Rural Mexico. *Latin American Research Review* 37(1):119–143.

Hardin, G. 1968 The Tragedy of the Commons. *Science* 162:1243–1248.

Hicks, F. 1991 Gift and Tribute: Relations of Dependency in Aztec Mexico. In *Early State Economies. Political and Legal Anthropology*, edited by H. J. M. Claessen and P. van de Velde, pp. 199–213. vol. 8. Transaction Publishers, New Brunswick.

Hunt, R. C. 1988 Size and the Structure of Authority in Canal Irrigation Systems. *Journal of Anthropological Research* 44:335–355.

Hunt, R. C., D. Guillet, D. R. Abbott, J. Bayman, P. Fish, S. Fish, K. Kintigh, and J. A. Neely. 2005 Plausible Ethnographic Analogies for the Social Organization of Hohokam Canal Irrigation. *American Antiquity* 70:433–456.

Iriarte, J., M. Power, S. Rostain, F. Mayle, H. Jones, J. Watling, B. Whitney, and D. McKey. 2012 Fire-Free Land Use in Pre-1492 Amazonian Savannas. *Proceedings of the National Academy of Sciences of the USA* 109:6473–6478.

Janssen, M. A., F. Bousquet, J. Cardenas, D. Castillo, and K. Worrapimphong. 2012 Field Experiments on Irrigation Dilemmas. *Agricultural Systems* 109:65–75.

Janusek, J. W., and A. L. Kolata, 2004 Top-Down or Bottom-Up: Rural Settlement in the Lake Titicaca Basin, Bolivia. *Journal of Anthropological Archaeology* 23:404–430.

Jiménez Osornio, J. J. 1995 Componentes Esenciales de la Tecnologia Chinampera. In *Presente, Pasado y Futuro de las Chinampas*, edited by T. Rojas Rabiela, pp. 77–83. Centro de Investigaciones y Estudios. Superiores en Antropologia Social, Hidalgo y Matamoros, Tlalpan.

Jiménez Osornio, J. J. 1999 Componentes Ecologicos Esenciales de la Tecnologia Chinampera. In *Los Camellones y Chinampas Tropicales: Memorias del Simposio-Taller Internacional sobre Camellones y Chinampas Tropicales*, edited by J. J. Jiménez Osornio and V. M. Rorive, pp. 120–130. Ediciones de la Universidad Autonoma de Yucatan, Merida.

Kellogg, S. 1995 *Law and the Transformation of Aztec Culture, 1500–1700*. University of Oklahoma Press, Norman.

Kelly, W. W. 1983 Concepts in the Anthropological Study of Irrigation. *American Anthropologist* 85:880–886.

Lansing, S. 1991 *Priests and Programmers: Technologies of Power in the Engineered Landscape of Bali*. Princeton University Press, Princeton.

Leach, E. 1959 Hydraulic Society in Ceylon. *Past and Present* 15:2–26.

Luna Golya, G. 2014 Modeling the Aztec Agricultural Waterscape of Lake Xochimilco: A GIS Analysis of Lakebed Chinampas and Settlement. PhD Dissertation, Anthropology Department, University Park, The Pennsylvania State University.

Mabry, J. B. 1996 The Ethnology of Local Irrigation. In *Canals and Communities: Small-Scale Irrigation Systems,* edited by J. B. Mabry. University of Arizona Press, Tucson.

Mabry, J. B. 2000 Wittfogel Was Half Right: The Ethnology of Consensual and Nonconsensual Hierarchies in Irrigation Management. In *Hierarchies in Action: Cui Bono?,* edited by M. W. Diehl, pp. 3–30. Center for Archaeological Investigation, Southern Illinois University, Carbondale.

Mathes, W. M. 1970 "To Save a City" The Desague of Mexico–Huehuetocal, 1607. *The Americas* 26:419–438.

Marcus, J., and C. Stanish. 2006 Introduction. In *Agricultural Strategies*, edited by J. Marcus and C. Stanish. Cotsen Institute of Archaeology, Los Angeles.

Miller, J. H., and S. E. Page. 2007 *Complex Adaptive Systems: An Introduction to Computational Models of Social Life*. Princeton University Press, Princeton.

Molina, A. 1944 *Vocabularo en Lengua Castellan y Mexicana*. Ediciones Cultura Hispanica IV. Colección de Incunables Americanos, Madrid.

Morehart, C. 2010 The Archaeology of Farmscapes: Production, Place, and the Materiality of Landscape at Xaltocan, Mexico. PhD Dissertation, Department of Anthropology, Northwestern University, Evanston.

Morehart, C. 2012a Mapping Ancient Chinampa Landscapes in the Basin of Mexico: A Remote Sensing and GIS Approach. *Journal of Archaeological Science* 39:2541–2551.

Morehart, C. 2012b What If the Aztec Empire Never Existed? The Prerequisites of Empire and the Politics of Plausible Alternative Histories. *American Anthropologist* 114:267–281.

Morehart, C. 2014 The Potentiality and the Consequences of Surplus: Agricultural Production and Institutional Transformation in the Northern Basin of Mexico. *Economic Anthropology* 1:154–166.

Morehart, C. T., and D. T. A. Eisenberg. 2010 Prosperity, Power, and Change: Modeling Maize at Postclassic Xaltocan, Mexico. *Journal of Anthropological Archaeology* 29:94–112.

Morehart, C., and C. Frederick. 2014 The Chronology and Collapse of Pre-Aztec (Chinampa) Agriculture in the Northern Basin of Mexico. *Antiquity* 88:531–548.

Narchi, N. E. 2013 Deterioro ambiental en Xochimilco: Lecciones para el cambio climático Global. *Veredas* 27:177–219.

Netting, R. 1993 *Smallholders, Householders: Farm Families and the Ecology of Intensive, Sustainable Agriculture*. Stanford University Press, Stanford.

Nichols, D. 2004 The Rural and Urban Landscapes of the Aztec State. In *Mesoamerican Archaeology: Theory and Practice*, edited by J. Hendon and R. A. Joyce, pp. 265–284. Blackwell, Oxford.

Nichols, D., and C. D. Frederick. 1993 Irrigation Canals and Chinampas: Recent Research in the Northern Basin of Mexico. In *Economic Aspects of Water Management in the Prehispanic New World*, edited by V. L. Scarborough and B. L. Isaac, pp. 123–150. JAI Press, Greenwich, CT.

Ostrom, E. 1990 *Governing the Commons: The Evolution of Institutions for Collective Action.* Cambridge University Press, Cambridge.

Palerm, Á. 1973 *Obras Hidráulicas Prehispánicas en el Sistema Lacustre del Valle de México.* Instituto Nacional de Antropología e Historia, Mexico, D.F.

Parsons, J. 1991 Political Implications of Prehispanic Chinampa Agriculture in the Valley of Mexico. In *Land and Politics in the Valley of Mexico*, edited by H. R. Harvey, pp. 17–42. University of New Mexico Press, Albuquerque.

Parsons, J. 1976 The Role of Chinampa Agriculture in the Food Supply of Aztec Tenochtitlan. In *Cultural Change and Continuity: Essays in Honor of James B. Griffin*, edited by C. Cleland, pp. 233–257. Academic Press, New York.

Parsons, J. R., M. Parsons, V. Popper, and M. Taft. 1985 Chinampa Agriculture and Aztec Urbanization in the Valley of Mexico. In *Prehistoric Intensive Agriculture in the Tropics*, edited by I. Farrington. vol. 232. BAR International Series, Oxford.

Paulson, S., and L. L. Gezon (editors). 2005 *Political Ecology across Spaces, Scales, and Social Groups.* Rutgers University Press, New Brunswick, NJ.

Paulson, S., L. Gezon, and M. Watts. 2005 Politics, Ecologies, Genealogies. In *Political ecology across Spaces, Scales, and Social Groups*, edited by S. Paulson and L. Gezon, pp. 17–37. Rutgers University Press. New Brunswick, NJ.

Peet, R., and M. Watts (editors). 1996 *Liberation Ecologies: Environment, Development and Social Movement.* Routledge, London.

Popper, V. 1995 Nahua Plant Knowledge and Chinampa Farming in the Basin of Mexico: A Middle Postclassic Case Study. PhD Dissertation, Department of Anthropology, University of Michigan.

Poteete, A. R., M. A. Janssen, and E. Ostrom. 2010 *Working Together: Collective Action, the Commons, and Multiple Methods in Practice.* Princeton University Press, Princeton.

Price, D. H. 1994 Wittfogel's Neglected Hydraulic/Hydroagricultural Distinction. *Journal of Anthropological Research* 50:187–204.

Price, D. H. 2004 *Threatening Anthropology: McCarthyism and the FBI's Surveillance of Activist Anthropologists.* Duke University Press, Durham.

Quiñónez, C. 2005 *Chinampas y Chinamperos: Los horticultores de San Juan Tezompa.* Universidad Iberoamericana.

Renard, D., J. Iriarte, J. Birk, S. Rostain, B. Glaser, and D. McKey. 2011 Ecological Engineers ahead of Their Time: The Functioning of Pre-Columbian Raised-Field Agriculture and Its Potential Contributions to Sustainability Today. *Ecological Engineering* 45:30–44.

Robbins, P. 2012 *Political Ecology.* Wiley-Blackwell, Malden, MA.

Robin, C. 2006 Gender, Farming, and Long-Term Change. *Current Anthropology* 47:409–433.

Rocheleau, D. 1999 Sustaining What for Whom? Differences of Interest within and between Households. In *Managed Ecosystems: The Mesoamerican Experi*ence, edited by U. Hatch and M. E. Swisher, pp. 31–47. Oxford University Press, Oxford.

Rojas Rabiela, T. 1991 Ecological and Agricultural Changes in the Chinampas of Xochimilco-Chalco. In *Land and Politics in the Valley of Mexico*, edited by H. R. Harvey, pp. 275–290. University of New Mexico Press, Albuquerque.

Roseberry, W. 1989 *Anthropologies and Histories: Essays in Culture, History, and Political Economy.* Rutgers University Press, New Brunswick, NJ.

Sanders, W. 1957 Tierra y Agua (Soil and Water): A Study of the Ecological Factors in the Development of Meso-American Civilizations. PhD Dissertation, Harvard University.

Sanders, W. T., J. R. Parsons, and R. S. Santley. 1979 *Basin of Mexico: Ecological Processes in the Evolution of a Civilization.* Academic Press, New York.

Sanders, W. T. and B. J. Price. 1968 *Mesoamerica: The Evolution of a Civilization.* Random House, New York.

Santamaría, M. 1912 *Las Chinampas del Districto Federal.* La Secretaria de Fomento, Mexico.

Scarborough, V. L. 1991 Water Management Adaptations in Nonindustrial Complex Societies: An Archaeological Perspective. In *Archaeological Method and Theory*, edited by M. B. Schiffer. vol. 3. The University of Arizona Press, Tucson.

Scarborough, V. L. 2003 *The Flow of Power: Ancient Water Systems and Landscapes.* School American Research Press, Santa Fe.

Schlager, E., and E. Ostrom. 1992 Property-Rights Regimes and Natural Resources; A Conceptual Analysis. *Land Economics* 68(3):249–262.

Steward, J. (editor) 1955 *Irrigation Civilizations: A Comparative Study.* Pan American Union, Washington, DC.

Torres, P., B. Canabal, and G. Burela. 1994 Urban Sustainable Agriculture: The Paradox of the Chinampa System in Mexico City. *Agriculture and human values* 11(1):37–46.

Thurston, T. L., and C. T. Fisher (editors). 2007 *Seeking a Richer Harvest: The Archaeology of Subsistence Intensification, Innovation and Change.* Springer, New York.

Uphoff, N. 1986 *Improving International Irrigation Management with Farmer Participation: Getting the Process Right.* Westview Press, Boulder, CO.

Vega-López, A., F. A. Jiménez-Orozco, L. A. Jiménez-Zamudio, E. García-Latorre, and M. L. Domínguez-López. 2009 Phase I Enzyme Induction in Girardinichthys viviparus, an Endangered Goodeid Fish, Exposed to Water from Native Localities Enriched with Polychlorinated Biphenyls. *Archives of Environmental Contamination and Toxicology* 57(3):561–570.

Vega-López A., C. I. Carrillo-Morales, H. F. Olivares-Rubio, M. Lilia Domínguez-López, and E. A. García-Latorre. 2012 Evidence of Bioactivation of Halomethanes and Its Relation to Oxidative Stress Response in Chirostoma riojai, an Endangered Fish from a Polluted Lake in Mexico. *Archives of Environmental Contamination and Toxicology* 62(3):479–493.

West, R., and P. Armillas. 1950 Las Chinampas De México, Poesía y Realidad de los Jardines Flotantes. *Cuadernos Americanos* 50:165–182.

Wilken, G. 1987 *Good Farmers: Traditional Agricultural Resource Management in Mexico and Central America.* University of California Press, Berkeley.

Wittfogel, K. A. 1957 *Oriental Despotism: A Comparative Study of Total Power.* Yale University Press, New Haven.

Wolf, E. R. 1982 *Europe and the People without History.* University of California Press, Berkeley.

Woodbury, R. B. 1961 A Reappraisal of Hohokam Irrigation. *American Anthropologist* 63:550–560.

CHAPTER THREE

Irrigation and Social Organization

A Longue Durée Perspective from the Jordan Valley

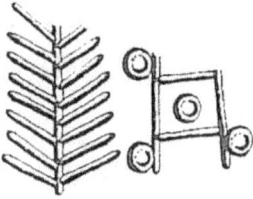

Eva Kaptijn

Abstract   *Irrigation structures society and society, in its turn, determines the functioning of an irrigation system. This dialectic relationship allows archaeologists to gain insights into the social organization of irrigation. Anthropologists studying irrigation have compared a large number of irrigating societies and formulated generalities that occur in most case studies. In this article these generalities are evaluated with regard to the Zerqa Triangle, Jordan Valley, where an irrigation system of more or less the same layout was used in three different periods and societies. In the first example, the early modern period, ca. 1940s and 1950s, the social organization is known and fits the formulated generalities about irrigation system size and social structure very well. In the Mamluk system, 1250–1516 CE, the association between the size of irrigation system and social structure does not seem to work, but in this case the prerequisite of ethnoarchaeological comparability is not met, as during the Mamluk period the region was the focus of cash crop production tightly controlled by external powers instead of internally regulated. Archaeological evidence suggests that ethnographic comparisons are sound regarding the Iron Age IIa/b society (1000–725 BCE). While little is known about the social organization of Iron Age irrigation based on archaeology, the cross-cultural comparison allows us to suggest that irrigation was possibly managed via council organization.*

IRRIGATION AND SOCIAL ORGANIZATION

While it is clear that social organization and the organization of irrigation systems mutually influenced each other in the past, it is often very difficult archaeologically to get an understanding of social organization. To overcome this problem, archaeologists and other social scientists have searched for cross-cultural generalities: instances in which societies, around the globe, resolved similar problems in similar ways (Marcus and Stanish 2005:8). Cross-cultural analogies provide by no means universal truths; for every generality, several exceptions can be found (Uphoff 1986:51). Nevertheless, these cross-cultural generalities can be helpful to guide our thinking regarding the potential ways irrigation might have been organized in past societies.

Many scholars agree that there seems to be a relationship between number of irrigators (or size of the irrigation system) and complexity of organization (a modified version of a portion of Wittfogel's hydraulic hypothesis) (see, e.g., Marcus and Stanish 2005:4). Large irrigation systems incorporating many people are more often organized via complex bureaucratic institutions than small-scale systems with only a few people. However, what exactly is denoted by small-scale or large-scale remains undefined (Marcus and Stanish 2005:6).

This article will investigate whether these general characteristics also apply to the Zerqa Triangle and whether they can improve our understanding of the way the irrigation system functioned in societies for which we have only archaeological data. Some studies have attempted to quantify these generalities on scale of the irrigation system and its social organization (Hunt 1988; Kappel 1974; Mabry 2000; Uphoff 1986). These will be evaluated and tested on three different irrigation societies in the Zerqa Triangle using essentially the same irrigation system. It should be stressed that both size or scale and complexity should be regarded as continua and that fixed thresholds are not likely to exist.

Although there exists no strict link between size of the irrigable area and the structure of organization, several studies into modern irrigation communities have suggested that systems larger than ca. 100 ha (1 km²) are unlikely to be organized acephalously (e.g., Hunt 1988:347; see for more examples Mabry 1996:10; Uphoff 1986:53). Alternatively, people have argued that the focus should not lie on the size of the area, but on the number of irrigators (e.g., Mabry 2000). Based on comparative research among modern and historic irrigation systems, Kappel has, for example, argued that systems that exceed ca. 5,000 people are mostly not organized by local assemblies or councils (Kappel 1974:163). If an irrigation community consists of a higher number of people, irrigation is most often arranged by some central authority.

Alternatively, Uphoff, trying to assess the possibilities for greater farmer participation, examined 50 case studies together describing more than 100 irrigation systems all over the globe (Uphoff 1986). Based on these cases he argued in favor of grouping systems according to levels of irrigation complexity. The simplest single-level irrigation systems consist of a single canal that both taps the water source and feeds the fields (Uphoff 1986:46). In a two-level system the canal that brings water to the field branches off from the canal that taps the river or spring. The greater the number of canals that exist between the destination fields and the source, the higher the level of the irrigation system. While irrigation systems are usually (technically) analyzed starting from the main canal that taps the source and then followed downstream identifying secondary, tertiary, etc. canals branching off, Uphoff advocates that (social) investigations should start with the canal that feeds the fields because the primary canal in a four-level system has a different status than the primary canal in a one-level system (Uphoff 1986:50). From case studies, Uphoff identified several regularities that seemed to be linked to the different levels. The one-level systems encompass a small group of people. Land and water are usually equitably distributed and organization of irrigation is a communal affair shared by all those involved. These systems are relatively independent (Uphoff 1986:46). In two-level systems, two or more basic units are dependent on the same water source, which usually necessitates a second level of organization to allocate water or arbitrate in disputes. This is often horizontally instead of vertically organized, that is to say, through cooperation between similar systems that have no central supervision (Uphoff 1986:47). When more levels are present in the irrigation system, the organization becomes increasingly formalized and may involve an external/independent institution that organizes and controls the functioning of the irrigation system. In larger, higher-level irrigation systems more people are involved, but there is also less personal interaction. In these cases explicit rules and regulations as well as clear sanctions are usually needed for the system to function satisfactorily (Uphoff 1986:52). Uphoff has tentatively quantified the link between levels in the irrigation system and size of the command area. Single-level systems are usually smaller than 40 ha (100 acres), two-level systems range between ca. 40–400 ha, three-level systems (or level 3 in higher-level systems) are ca. 400–4000 ha, and four levels encompass a terrain of 4000–40,000 ha (Uphoff 1986:53).

The danger in looking at ethnographic examples to explain archaeological situations is, of course, that one is comparing apples with oranges (Wendrich 2002:8). Trustworthy information can only be attained when similar phenomena are compared. More precisely, it should be certain that one is not comparing similar outcomes of distinct processes, but that the factors leading to certain results are comparable (Wendrich 2002:8–9, fig.1-1). With this problem in mind, considerable attention will be paid to what is known about the sociopolitical and socioeconomic situations of the societies that created the irrigation systems, independent of the systems themselves.

REGIONAL SETTING

The Zerqa Triangle is located on the eastern side of the Jordan Valley, about halfway between Lake Tiberias and the Dead Sea. The area of research constitutes the triangle formed by the River Jordan in the east, the Wadi Rajib in the north, the hills leading up to the Jordanian plateau in the east and the Zerqa river in the southeast (see Figure 3.1). This area is located between ca. 200 and 280 m below sea level. Temperatures in the valley are high. Today, average day temperatures reach up to 39° C during summer and are 19° C during the coldest winter month (Nedeco and Dar al-Handasah 1969; Jordan Meteorological Department), meaning that the potential evaporation is also high. The average modern yearly rainfall amounts to 270 mm. This lies above the 250 mm threshold normally considered to be the minimum amount needed for dry farming (Wirth 1971:92). However, the interannual variability is high and varied between 118 and 501 mm within the scope of four years. Decades of measurements, namely, since 1933, show that yearly amounts below 250 mm occurred 12 times over the past 30 years, with six years of less than 200 mm and three years of less than 150 mm (Nedeco and Dar al-Handasah 1969; Jordan Meteorological Department). For a stable permanent society, dry-farming is therefore not an option in the Zerqa Triangle. Furthermore, excavations have revealed the remains of crops that cannot be cultivated with the bare minimum amount of precipitation for dry-farming, for instance, flax and sugar cane, especially considering the potential evapotranspiration rates prevalent in the Jordan Valley. The 250 mm isohyet is an easy threshold that works well as a rough guideline. However, to critically evaluate the potential for dry-farming, other critical factors such as interannual variability, timing of precipitation, humidity, and potential evapotranspiration as well as the cropping system must be taken into account.

The modern climate is, of course, not representative of the past. With regard to the periods discussed in this paper, namely, the Iron Age IIa/b (ca. 1000–750 BCE) and the Mamluk period (1250–1516 CE), several proxies give information. Analysis of land snail shells from the Negev suggest a gradual drying and warming trend between 2000 BCE and 1500 CE (Rosen 2007:89). More or less comparable results are provided by the Soreq cave speleothems showing that between ca. 2000 and 1000 BCE the climate was comparable to that of today followed by gradually drier and warmer conditions reaching a peak around 400 BCE (Bar-Matthews et al. 2003:fig.13). Dead Sea levels show small-scale fluctuations between ca. 1000 and 550 BCE, again followed by drier conditions, evidenced by a drop in lake levels, until 370–350 BCE (Frumkin and Elitzur 2002:337; Rosen 2007:94). With regard to the Mamluk period, several climatic proxies suggest that around 1200 CE, the climate was relatively moist (Luterbacher et al. 2012:158). In all, during the Iron Age the climate seems to have been similar to today or slightly drier and warmer, while the start of the Mamluk period witnessed a peak in moisture availability, but during this period conditions became drier again. The Zerqa Triangle will therefore probably always have been located on the edge of the dry-farming zone. To ensure resilience against dry spells and fluctuations in timing of rainfall, irrigation will have been vital in this region if a stable sedentary society was to be maintained.

The Irrigation System

Until the reorganization of land and water resources in the 1960s, a system of irrigation was used that tapped the water of the Zerqa River at three locations and distributed it over the entire valley plain by means of a network of canals (see Figure 3.1). This gravity flow system utilized the gentle slope of the area to carry the water across the valley plain in small open canals made from stone, mud, branches, and occasionally plaster. Physical remains, old photographs, and oral accounts suggest that also the three main canals were relatively small (ca. 1–1.5 m wide and 1 m deep). To irrigate specific fields water was led into certain canals while others were closed off by simple dams also made of stones, branches, and mud (Kaptijn 2009:306; Kooij 2007; Tarawneh 2014:39).

Calculations have demonstrated that in a year with average rainfall the water of the Zerqa, Jordan's second largest perennial stream, was sufficient to fully irrigate the entire plain when cultivated with the crops common in the Mediterranean region, for instance, wheat, barley, pulses, vegetables, and some fruits. Only in exceptionally dry years and/or

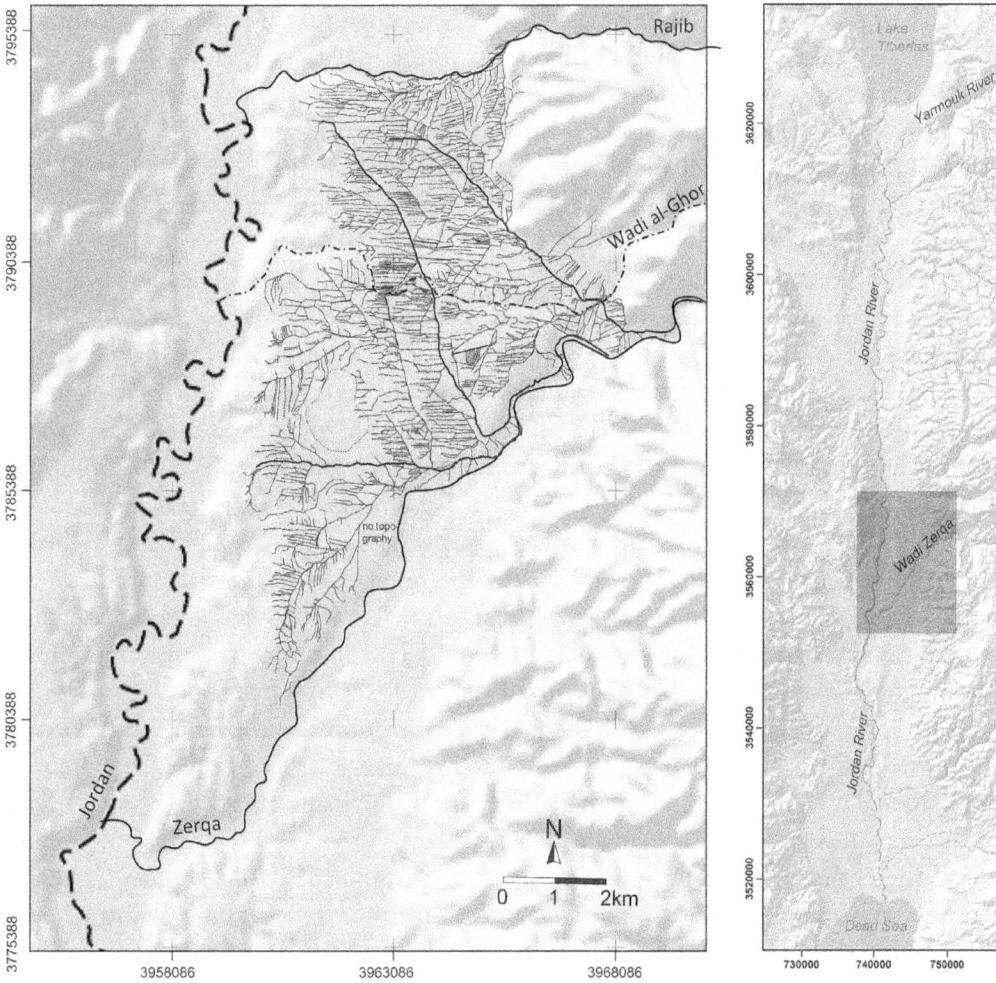

FIGURE 3.1 The Zerqa Triangle with the premodern irrigation system (irrigation canals outside the Zerqa Triangle have not been depicted).

when cultivating very water-demanding crops might water stress have occurred (Kaptijn 2009:339–376).

The earliest historical records mentioning this system, albeit a smaller version, date back to the second half of the nineteenth century (D'Albert de Luynes 1874:133–135; Merrill 1881:382). At that time the Jordan Valley was in the process of becoming resettled after a period in which only temporary occupation in winter by Bedouins was the norm (Kaptijn 2009:313–317). The settled farmers that were described by nineteenth-century scholars traveling through the region stated that the canals had always been there; "neither they, nor their fathers had anything to do with their construction" (Merrill 1881:283). All that farmers had to do to bring a new piece of land under cultivation was to clean out and repair the old canals (Merrill 1881:282). Because there was as good as no permanent occupation and no (large-scale) agriculture in the Jordan Valley between ca. 1600 and

1800 CE, the canals must have originated in the next period that saw intensive agriculture, that is, the Mamluk period. This assumption is corroborated by archaeological evidence. During the "Settling the Steppe" survey two water mills from the Mamluk period were discovered that were fed by early modern main canals (Kaptijn 2009:282–283). This leads to the conclusion that the location of at least two of the three main canals was the same in both periods, thereby giving this part of the irrigation system an age depth of at least 500 years.

The Mamluk period, 1250–1516 CE, was not the period during which the irrigation system was first installed. Although there is no physical evidence of canals, it is likely that the system was created during the Late Bronze Age (1550–1200 BCE). During this period the number of settlements increased rapidly (Kaptijn 2014). Additionally, this period is the first time sites were located in the middle of the plain away from the natural water sources that had been the foci of settlement in previous periods (Kaptijn 2014:323, 325). The only way to bring water to the agricultural fields, assuming that fields were located near the villages, would have been by means of irrigation canals crossing the valley plain. Given the topography of the Zerqa Triangle, the number of possible locations for the main canals is limited. In order to cover an area as large as possible, one canal had to tap the Zerqa far upstream and run along the hill flanks to the northwest. Other canals had to circumnavigate a higher badland area located north of the Zerqa just after its entrance into the plain (Figure 3.1) and allow for the downstream incision of the Zerqa that was already in place before the Iron Age started, that is, before 1200 BCE (Hourani et al. 2008:432). This means that the best locations for main canals are roughly those of the early modern (pre-1960) main canals. The early modern main canals ran along most of Late Bronze and Iron Age settlements, and a similar location of main canals in those periods may therefore be considered. The irrigation system and its history have been described in detail elsewhere (Kaptijn 2009:301ff; 2010).

Early Modern Society

The way the irrigation system functioned, as well as the organization of society, is well known for the early modern period (pre-1960). This period is incorporated here because many parallels can be drawn between early modern and Iron Age irrigation societies. Furthermore, it is a way to test the general trends attested in cross-cultural analogies.

Early modern society in the Jordan Valley was a society in transition; pastoral nomadic Bedouins gradually became settled agriculturalists. This process started around 1850 and was largely finished just over a century later, although even today a few Bedouin families camp in this region during the winter months. During the period discussed here, ca. the 1940s and 1950s, irrigation was organized by the local inhabitants without state interference and several tribes, each with its own territory, occupied the region.

Concerning the link between complexity of social organization and size of the irrigable area, it is clear that the Zerqa Triangle exceeded the limit of acephalous organization by far. The area irrigated by the three main canals encompassed 9.3 km² (canal 1), 5.3 km²

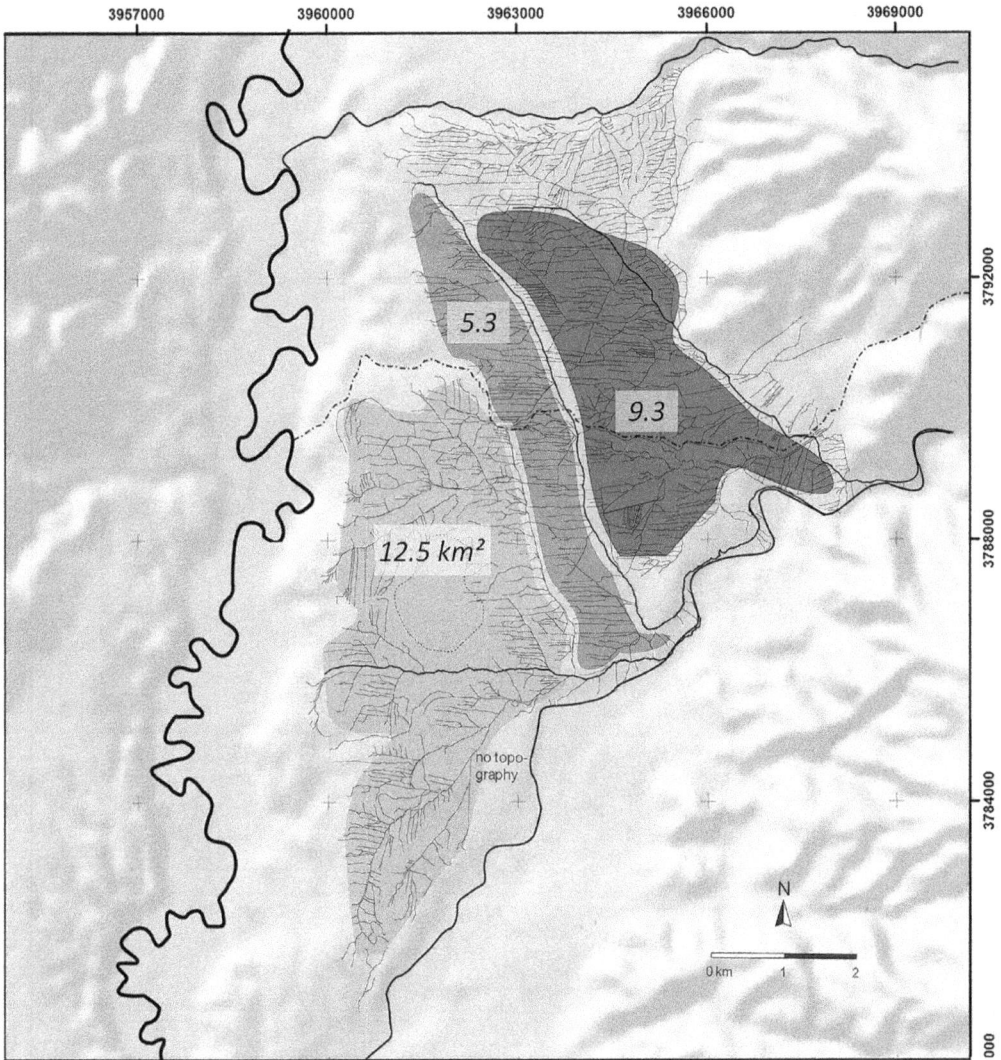

FIGURE 3.2 Area irrigated per main irrigation canal.

(canal 2), and 12.5 km² (canal 3) respectively (Figure 3.2). These numbers fall within the range of Uphoff's three-level systems. A look at the irrigation system shows that in most cases three levels of canals were present, although in some parts of the system several canals interconnected, making a strict flow sequence difficult to reconstruct (see Figure 3.3). It is clear that several basic level one units can exist together within a tribe's territory. At the same time, the territories of several tribes, whose borders coincided with the distribution areas of canals, made up the area irrigated by a single main canal. The three main canals together formed the irrigation system of the Zerqa Triangle. Based on Uphoff's level model, the Zerqa Triangle was thus most likely organized by a council of representatives.

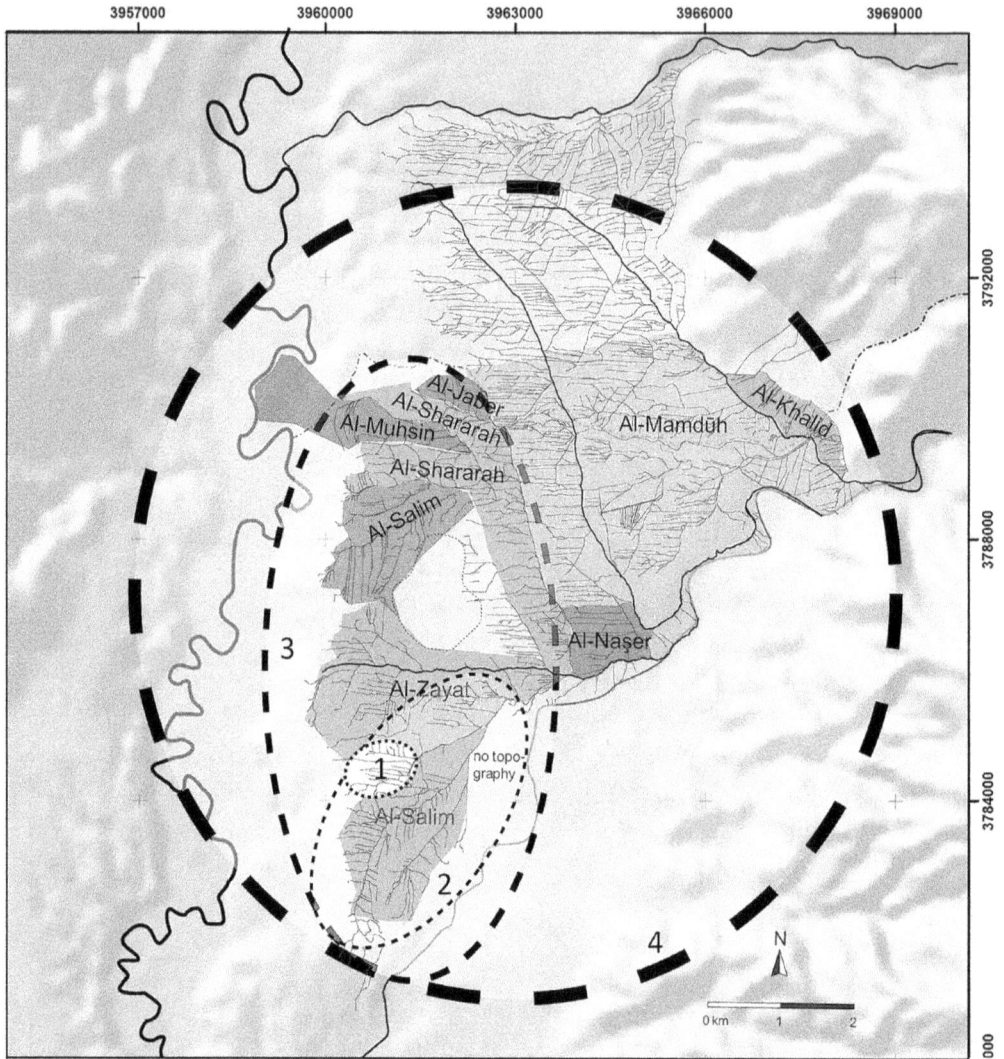

FIGURE 3.3 Levels of canals in the Zerqa Triangle irrigation system with tribal territories.

Kappel's generalization of 5,000 people being the limit for organization via a council can also be evaluated for the early modern period. Official census data are available for 1952 when the first housing census was conducted. In this census it was recorded that before 1950, 118 houses existed in the Zerqa Triangle (i.e., the Deir 'Alla district) and another 188 were built between 1951 and 1955 (Layne 1994:44). Assuming an average household size of five to seven persons (based on slightly later census data from the region), this gives a population density of 590–826 people before 1950. This number is roughly corroborated by aerial photographs taken in 1953 (Royal Jordanian Geographic Centre). In these photographs the exact number of structures present in the irrigation area of each main canal can be counted (Figure 3.4). Of course, from above it cannot be

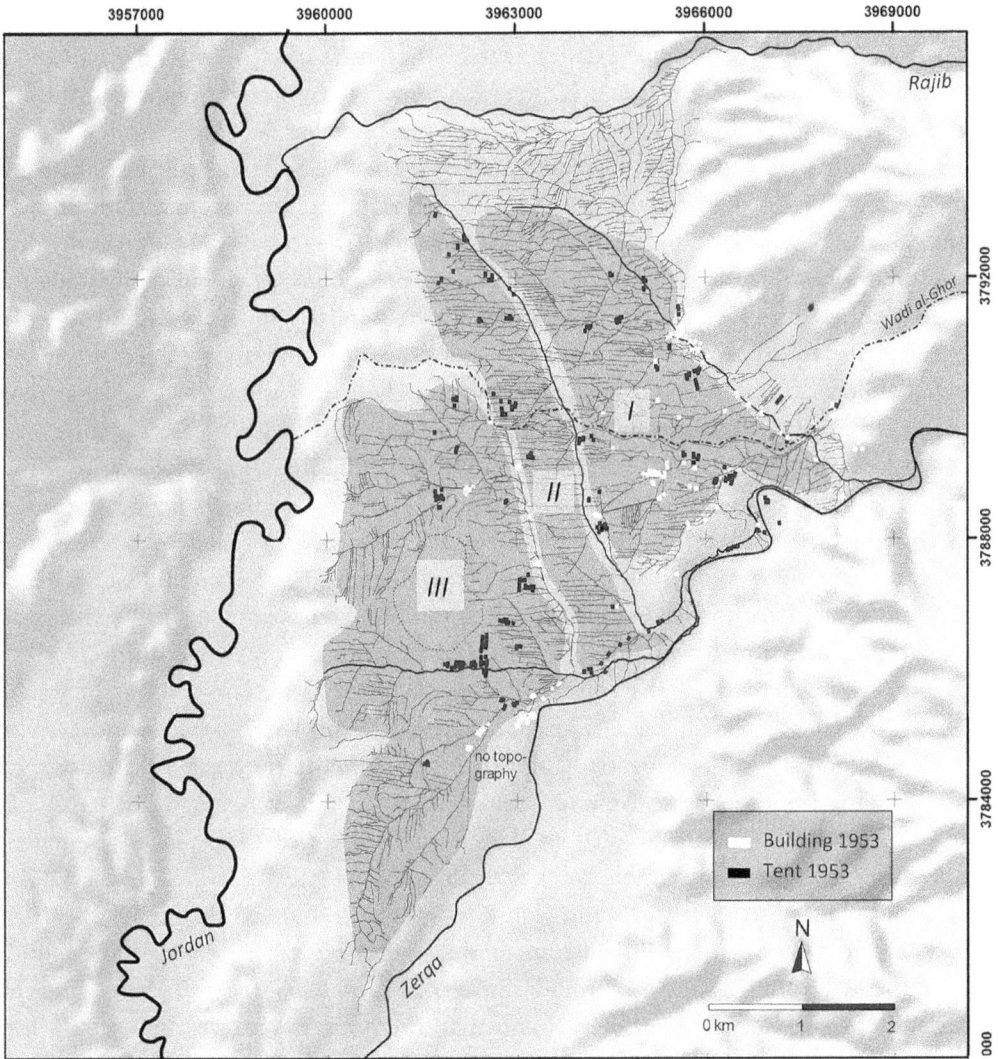

FIGURE 3.4 Black goat hair Bedouin tents and buildings, based on aerial photographs Winter 1953 (aerial photograph courtesy of Royal Jordanian Geographic Institute).

determined whether a structure was used for habitation or had some other purpose. The actual number of buildings used for housing will therefore be lower than the counted amount. However, 192 structures can be counted, which is of the same order of magnitude as the number of houses of the census.[1] More importantly, the photographs show the presence of a group of inhabitants that was not registered in the censuses, namely, mobile tent dwellers.

During the 1950s a large portion of society was still mobile and only remained in the valley during the winter months. When the tents are counted on the aerial photographs it is clear that there were more tents than houses, that is, 239 tents versus 192 houses or ca. 1,195–1,673 tent dwellers and ca. 960–1,344 people living in permanent structures. This combined number is well below the 5,000 persons limit suggested by Kappel. It is uncertain to what extent the tent dwellers participated in the irrigation system. Tents were often located in areas that had not yet been brought under cultivation.

Reference to cross-cultural analogies thus suggests that irrigation in the Zerqa Triangle during the early modern period could well have been organized by councils or representatives of the different segments in the wider community. Ethnographic studies confirmed this organization for the early modern period. The irrigated region was divided over several tribes (Figure 3.3). While the tribes were autonomous within the boundaries of their own territory and agriculture was organized completely independently inside the tribal area, the irrigation system was shared and its daily organization joined the tribes together. Informants who could remember the pre-1960s irrigation system related that every day the tribal leaders would come together and decide which areas were to be irrigated (Tarawneh 2014:38). Decisions with regard to the irrigation system were made jointly by representatives from all tribes, usually the sheikhs. Maintenance of the main canals was also conducted jointly by all tribes that shared their water. There was one person in charge of water distribution, and he would measure the amount of water to be let into a canal via notches on a stick. One unit of water measured on the stick was regarded as sufficient to irrigate ten hectares of land. As many canals fed different tribal territories, representatives of the concerned tribes would oversee the division of water. This would occur on a daily basis (Kaptijn 2009:306; Tarawneh 2014:38–39).

The ethnohistorical investigations provide information on the social organization of the irrigation system that is unlikely to be attained based on archaeology and cross-cultural parallels alone. During the early modern period there were clear power differences between the tribes that are visible in the organization of the irrigation system. There existed two types of tribes, the so-called Hurr tribes who considered themselves the original occupants of the region and superior to the second type of tribes, the Ghawarneh tribes. There were two Hurr tribes and the territory of one of these, the Mamduh, was clearly bigger and had more fertile land than the other tribes (see Figure 3.4). The territory of the second Hurr tribe, the Shararah, did not differ in size or location from the Ghawarneh territories. However, if the irrigation system is taken into account, the difference clear. The largest Hurr tribe had the use of two of the three main canals. All other tribes shared the third canal. The second Hurr tribe was first to divert water from that canal to its territory and all Ghawarneh territories were located downstream and stood therefore in a dependent relationship towards the Hurr tribe (Kaptijn 2009:382). A more detailed description of the organization of the early modern irrigation system is given elsewhere (Kaptijn 2009, 2010, 2015; Tarawneh 2014:38–39).

IRON AGE VILLAGE COMMUNITIES

During the Iron Age (IA) IIa/b period, 1000–725 BCE, the Zerqa Triangle was located on the border between Ammon to the southeast and Israel to the west. While in the previous IA I period the focus of the Jordan Valley sites, including the Zerqa Triangle, had been toward the west (Herr 2014:657), the outlook during the IA II period was to Ammon. The borders of Ammon are not precisely known. The center was clearly its capital Rabbath-Ammon, modern Amman, and the area surrounding it. However, where its boundaries lay exactly is not clear. In the Bible, "the lands along the course of the Yabboq," which is firmly identified as the Zerqa, were considered to belong to the Ammonites (Deut. 2:37). While the region undoubtedly did not belong to the Ammonite heartland, the region was incorporated in the Ammonite network of interaction based on the presence of Ammonite-style pottery, artifacts, and inscriptions (Kooij and Ibrahim 1989; Yassine and Teixidor 1986). Petrographic and chemical provenance analysis of IA IIc and III (734–332 BCE) pottery from Tell Deir 'Alla and Tell Mazar (see Figure 3.5) have revealed a continuous and intensive ceramological exchange network with central Transjordan and only limited exchange with southern Palestine, while the majority was produced locally (Groot 2011:262; 2012). Unfortunately, no such information is available for the IA IIa/b, but the persistence of this division throughout the IA IIc-III irrespective of sociopolitical changes suggests the stability of this network.

While there is sufficient evidence that Israel and Judah may be called early states during this period, Ammon cannot be considered as such. Apart from the capital Rabbath-Ammon, large cities were absent, as were urban planning, strong central authority, etc. (LaBianca and Younker 1998:409). Instead, Ammon can perhaps best be regarded as a tribal kingdom. The different political entities in the southern Levant all had tribal origins and literary sources suggest Ammonite society still contained strong tribal links (LaBianca and Younker 1998:405; Younker 2014:762). A very strong increase in number of sites is visible during the IA II (from 15 in IA I to 97 in IA II) (Younker 2014:761). This was accompanied by intensification of agriculture, but not at the complete expense of mobile pastoralism (LaBianca and Younker 1998:407). The settlement pattern can be regarded as a so-called three-tiered settlement hierarchy with one large site (Rabbath-Ammon), a few medium-sized sites (5–10 ha) and many small sites (<2.5 ha) (Younker 2014:761). This system is often taken as indicative of a more complex sociopolitical organization. However, Younker rightfully argues that the scale of the settlements and the settlement hierarchy in Ammon were very small, especially when compared to, for example, Mesopotamia, which makes it unwarranted to regard Ammon as a complex, integrated, and centrally controlled political unity (Younker 2014:762).

In the Zerqa Triangle, the IA IIa/b period is the most densely settled period until today. A large number of tell sites existed (see Figure 3.5), but these were all small (<1.5 ha and most <0.5 ha). Excavations revealed quite tightly settled villages focusing on subsistence farming (Petit 2009; Kooij and Ibrahim 1989; Yassine and Steen 2012). The intensive "Settling the Steppe" survey as well as pottery studies suggest that society included a component of mobile pastoralists, possibly with people shifting between these subsistence modes relatively easy (Groot 2011:144; Kaptijn 2009:409–410; in press).

In all, the Iron Age Zerqa Triangle seems to have been a rural farming area dominated by a considerable number of small villages, hamlets, and farmsteads. While borders were fluid and shifted over the course of the Iron Age as a whole, the Zerqa Triangle was always located on the periphery of these entities. Although the material culture clearly shows influences from and contacts with neighboring regions, especially with Ammon, a

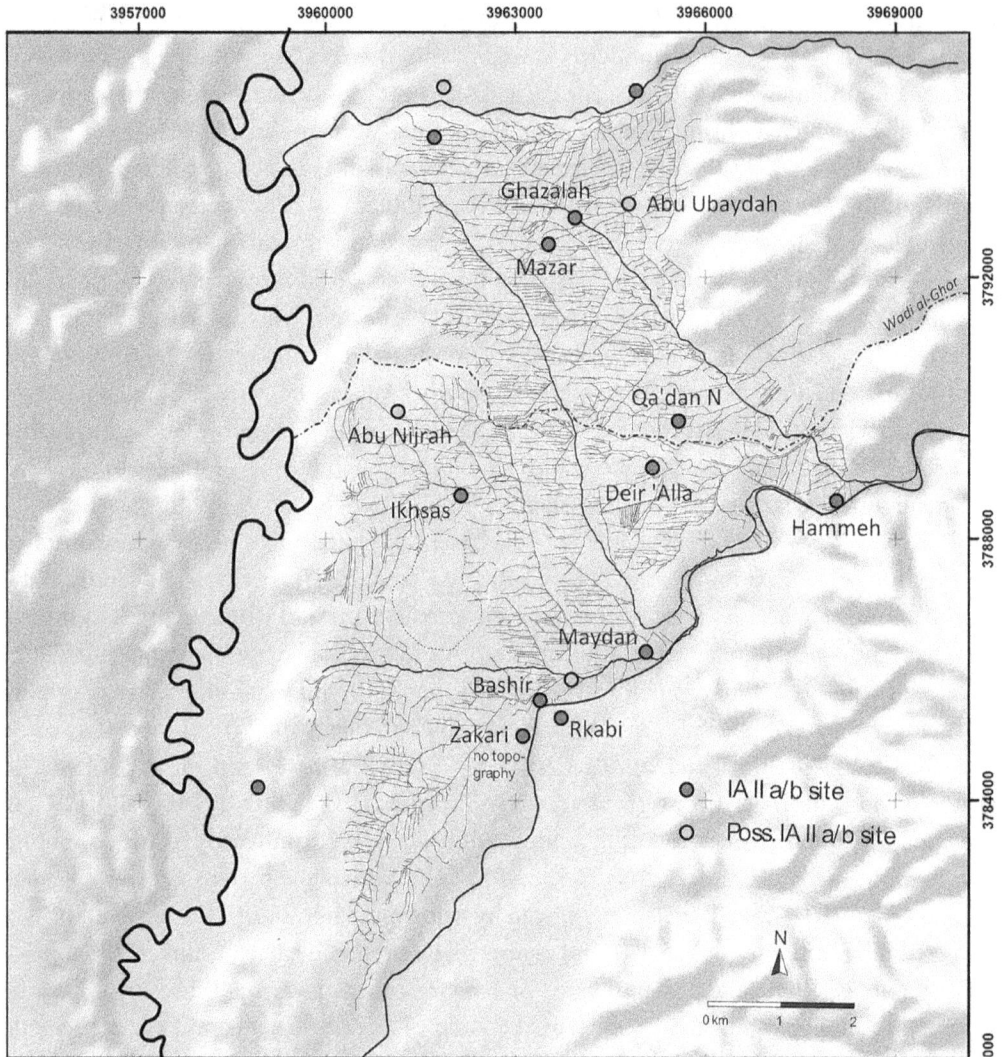

FIGURE 3.5 Iron Age IIa/b sites (plotted on the early modern irrigation system).

strict central control by an external authority or state is not likely. The Zerqa Triangle was, therefore, most likely autonomous with regard to its organization of land and water division.

Quite a large number of IA IIa/b settlements have been identified in the Zerqa Triangle, in all, 19 tell settlements (Figure 3.5). Reconstructing population density in archaeology is notoriously difficult. Several different methods and calculations have been proposed mostly based on ethnographic parallels or excavated floor plans, (e.g., Broshi 1993; Lehmann 2004; Naroll 1962; Shiloh 1980; Sumner 1979). Most ethnographic examples stem from flat surface sites, while in the Zerqa Triangle all sites are tells. Because of the space restrictions tells often have much denser occupation. One of the IA IIa/b tells, Tell Deir 'Alla, has seen extensive excavation. A fire has preserved the IA IIa/b layer very well while all artifacts were left in place. The excavator, Gerrit van der Kooij, has performed a "use of space" analysis on these remains and attempted to identify the housing units of a nuclear family (Kooij 2002). In the excavated part of the site, 11.4 percent of the total area occupied in the IA IIa/b, seven such units can be identified. Using a nuclear family size of five to seven people based on ethnographic parallels (Kramer 1982:159–160; Lehmann 2004:152; Qutaifan 1990:70; Sumner 1979:169–170), a total population of 300–330 people for Tell Deir 'Alla and an average of 440–600 p/ha can be assumed. Excavations in the Zerqa Triangle at smaller sites suggest that these sites may have had slightly lower densities. For the unexcavated sites an average population density of ca. 350–550 p/ha is therefore assumed for the IA IIa/b period. All sites have been surveyed by Lucas Petit, who also established estimates of occupied area per period (Petit 2009:161–189). With these data a tentative population estimate can be given for the IA IIa/b in the area irrigated by the Wadi Zerqa (see Table 3.1). There is evidence that also the Iron Age IIa/b society contained a mobile pastoral component (Kaptijn 2009:196–197, 407–409). If we assume a mobile population that was of equal proportion to that in the early modern period, then the number of people remains under Kappel's threshold, namely, 2,880–4,840 inhabitants.

The absence of actual irrigation canals dating to the Iron Age makes an evaluation of the number of canal levels difficult. The position of several sites in the middle of the plain at considerable distances away from the Zerqa suggests that more than one level existed. However, without the layout of the actual irrigation canals no further information can be deduced.

The Iron Age settlement pattern is characterized by a large number of small villages dispersed throughout the valley. This is markedly different from a settlement pattern in which the population is concentrated in a small number of large settlements. There are no archaeological indications that suggest a settlement hierarchy among these sites. Tell Deir 'Alla and Tell Mazar

TABLE 3.1
IRON AGE VILLAGES WITH ESTIMATED AREA OF OCCUPATION AND NUMBER OF INHABITANTS (ARRANGED PER IRRIGATION CANAL)

Canal I Site	Area occupied in IA (ha)	Inhabitants	
		5p	7p
Deir Alla	0.7	245	385
Qa'dan N	0.1	35	55
Hammeh	0.5	175	275
Mazar	1.5	525	825
Ghazalah	0.2	70	110
Abu 'Ubaydah	?	?	?
	3	**1050**	**1650**

Canal III Site	Area occupied in IA (ha)	Inhabitants	
		5p	7p
Bashir	0.4	140	220
Ikhsas	0.5	175	275
Zakari	0.4	40	220
Maydan	0.1	35	55
Abu Nijrah	?	?	?
Rkabi	?	?	?
	1.4	**390**	**770**

are slightly larger, but there is no evidence to suggest they had a different socioeconomic or sociopolitical status in this period. These distinct villages, therefore, suggest that there were several different groups of irrigators participating in the irrigation system.

Based on cross-cultural analogies, the Iron Age community in the Zerqa Triangle might have organized the irrigation system via a group of representatives of the different units partaking in the system. The available archaeological information, that is, the dispersed settlement pattern and the absence of a developed settlement hierarchy, suggests that an organization by representatives is a likely option; the different participants in the system needed to cooperate to be able to irrigate a large portion of the plain and the number of irrigators or units (villages) is too large for this to have taken place by acephalous, face-to-face contact.

Mamluk Imperial Control

During the Mamluk period, 1250–1516 CE, the Zerqa Triangle cannot be considered a peripheral area located on the edge of control of a central authority as it had been during the other two periods. At this time, the Jordan Valley formed the agricultural center from which a considerable portion of the empire's wealth derived. Politically and culturally, however, the region was as much a marginal area as ever.

An important component of Mamluk economy, social life, and export was formed by sugar (Sato 2015). Sugarcane is a tropical crop that needs high temperatures and ample water to produce a good crop. Within the Mamluk Empire the locations where sugarcane could be successfully cultivated were therefore limited. The Jordan Valley and the Zerqa Triangle in particular was one of those areas (the Nile Valley was the other large sugar-producing area in the region).

While Mamluk government mostly left the existing agricultural organization and, where present, the system of water division in place, they actively took control of the management of sugarcane production (Walker 2006:80). Sugarcane was cultivated on special estates. These estates were owned by wealthy entrepreneurs who did not reside locally. In the later years of the Mamluk Empire the sultan amassed an ever-greater number of estates (Ashtor 1981:99, 101).

No physical evidence in the form of boundary markers, maps, etc. remains to determine the location and extent of these estates. There are, however, some indications what the plantations may have looked like in the Zerqa Triangle. In sugarcane the level of sucrose rapidly degrades after harvest of the plant (Galloway 1989:16). In order to maximize the sugar yield, the cane had to be crushed and the resulting juice boiled down to the point where it crystallized as soon as possible. Processing facilities were therefore located in close proximity to the fields. In this area the crushing was done in watermills. In the Zerqa Triangle, four Mamluk sugar-production sites including a watermill were found, as well as one without traces of a mill (Franken and Kalsbeek 1975; Kaptijn 2009:262–291; Steiner 2008). It is assumed that the cane crushed in a mill derived from the fields surrounding it and did not travel a great distance or pass other mills.

The irrigation system supports this view and provides more detailed insight into the potential layout of these plantations. To turn the heavy millstones of these mills, a considerable stream flow would have been needed. Furthermore, during harvest time the mills would have been in operation day and night, a practice alluded to in historical sources (LaGro 2002:34) and possibly attested by the large numbers of lamps discovered at excavated mills (Stern 2001; Taha 2009:188). This implies a considerable and permanent supply of water. In the Zerqa Triangle this is only available in the main canals. As discussed above, two of the Mamluk watermills were connected to main canals of the early modern period.

Because the mills were connected to the main canals and the fields were in all likelihood surrounding the mills, it is very likely that the water of the main canal that fed the mill was used to irrigate the fields that supplied the cane processed in the mill. Although canals were interconnected in the Zerqa Triangle system, which makes boundaries less clear, a reconstruction of potential sugar estates has been made based on the early modern irrigation system (see Figure 3.6).

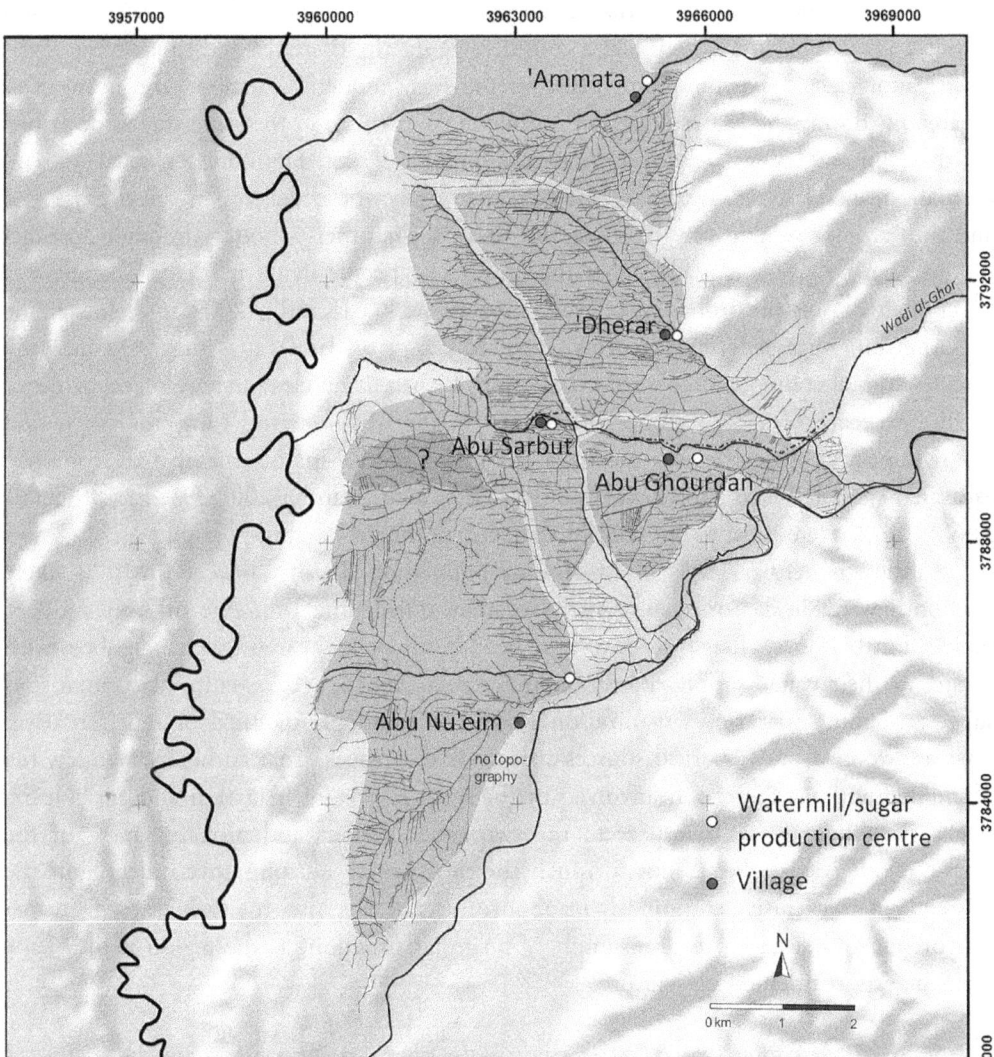

FIGURE 3.6 Mamluk villages, sugar-production centers, and reconstructed plantations (plotted on the early modern irrigation system).

The location of villages in close proximity to the sugar production centers also suggests a more unified land division than in the other periods. In the early modern period and Iron Age, a larger number of smaller settlements existed throughout the area, suggesting a relatively fragmented system of land use/ownership. The location of Mamluk villages seems to be linked to main irrigation canals and sugar production centers. Some corroboration for the reconstructed estates is provided by a historical record that relates that in 1398 CE the governor of Syria, while traveling through the Jordan Valley, arrested emir Ǧulbān. This emir was at that time on the lands (estates?) allotted to him by the sultan located at 'Ammata and 'Addliyeh. The northernmost reconstructed estates both contain a tell and modern village that still carry those names (LaGro 2002:18).

While the locations of the main Mamluk irrigation canals have been identified, lower-order canals remain elusive. The size of the irrigated area is not exactly known, but the location of the sugar production centers throughout the plain, for instance, Tell Abu Sarbut, suggests that the system had a considerable distribution area and thus several levels of irrigation canals, possibly comparable to the early modern situation. The number of inhabitants during the Mamluk period is difficult to calculate in the same way as described for the Iron Age period (see above). Excavations have been far more restricted and no (partial) village plans are available. However, the number of settlements is drastically lower and sites are not significantly larger in size than in the other periods. Although no exact number can be given, it is clear that the number of people living in Zerqa Triangle was lower than during the Iron Age or early modern period (Kaptijn 2009:364). Given the importance of sugarcane (and hence year-round claims on land), it is suggested that any mobile pastoral component of society was limited. There is no clear archaeological evidence for the existence of such a group. In contrast to the Iron Age and early modern period not ovicaprines, but cattle was the most dominant species in the assemblages from two excavated sites, Tell Abu Sarbut and Tell Abu Ghourdan (Kaptijn 2009:394; Es 1995:table 1, 65). Cattle were most likely used in the sugar industry for transport purposes.

Although neither levels of canals nor population density are certain, it is likely that both were similar or even a bit lower than during the Iron Age or early modern period. Furthermore, villages seem to have been less dependent upon their neighbors with regard to their water supply. Based on these characteristics, cross-cultural comparisons suggest Mamluk irrigation organization would fit within the council or representatives type. However, from historical sources it is clear that an external authority, namely, the Mamluk Empire, was actively involved in the organization of irrigation and agriculture. The main difference with respect to the two other periods and probably most of the cross-cultural case studies is not so much the presence of a strong government, but the existence of an exclusive commodity or opportunity: in this case, the cash crop sugarcane. The present-day situation is an example of a similar situation, as the region is today the focus of export-oriented agriculture.

MODERN IRRIGATION IN THE EASTERN JORDAN VALLEY

With the construction of the King Abdullah Canal, or East Ghor Canal, in 1966 the irrigation system that had been in place for several millennia came to an end. Where previously the Zerqa Triangle had been in a privileged position as it was the only user of the Zerqa water, after 1966 water from the Zerqa and Yarmouk rivers had to be shared with the more arid areas of the Jordan Valley. Irrigation was completely reorganized and both land and water came under jurisdiction of the Jordan Valley Authority (Tarawneh 2014:59). In this new form, irrigation in the Zerqa Triangle stopped being a regional-scale undertaking organized by a council of representatives. Instead, the area became part of a supraregional system that was governed by an external state-led authority and had a strong focus on export-oriented agriculture.

CONCLUSIONS

Generalities based on cross-cultural parallels can never be used to determine the social organization of an archaeological irrigation system. It can, however, be used as a model through which the social aspects of irrigation systems can be investigated. Archaeological results, however, should always form the basis of any hypotheses. The early modern and Iron Age case studies have shown that size of the irrigation system (in area or people) indeed influences the mode of social organization of that system to a large extent. The Mamluk example, on the other hand, demonstrated an exception. The opportunity to cultivate a cash crop and manufacture a very profitable commodity led to the involvement of external actors in a system that, when only judging by size, could well have been organized by a council. Although very little information on the actual irrigation system was available for the Iron Age, the use of cross-cultural generalities in combination with archaeological information on the settlement pattern and settlement hierarchy has provided a better understanding of the social organization of the irrigation system, thereby demonstrating the worth of cross-cultural generalities in archaeological studies.

ACKNOWLEDGMENTS

This article was written within the framework of the project "Belgian Archaeological Expeditions to the Orient. Heritage in Federal Collections," funded by the Belgian Science Policy (Belspo) and carried out at the Royal Belgian Institute of Natural Sciences. It builds on research undertaken within the project "Settling the Steppe. The Archaeology of Changing Societies in Syro-Palestinian Drylands during the Bronze and Iron Ages," funded by the Netherlands Organization for Scientific Research and carried out at the Faculty of Archaeology of Leiden University, the Netherlands.

NOTE

1.   Because information on the yearly increase of houses between 1951 and 1955 is missing, I assume an even growth, i.e., ca. 37 per year. This results in 193 houses at the end of 1952.

REFERENCES CITED

Ashtor, E. 1981 Levantine Sugar Industry in the Late Middle Ages: A Case of Technological Decline. In *The Islamic Middle East 700–1900: Studies in Economic and Social History*, edited by A. L. Udovitch, pp. 91–132. Princeton Studies on the Near East. The Darwin Press, Princeton.

Bar-Matthews, M., A. Ayalon, M. Gilmour, A. Matthews, and C. J. Hawkesworth. 2003 Sea-Land Oxygen Isotopic Relationships from Planktonic Foraminifera and Speleothems in the Eastern Mediterranean Region and Their Implication for Paleorainfall during Interglacial Intervals. *Geochimica et Cosmochimica Acta* 67(17):3181–3199.

Broshi, M. 1993 Methodology of Population Estimates: The Roman-Byzantine Period as a Case Study. In *Biblical Archaeology today, 1990. Proceedings of the Second International Congress on Biblical Archaeology.* Jerusalem, June–July 1990, pp. 420–425. Israel Exploration Fund Israel Academy of Sciences and Humanities, Jerusalem.

D'Albert de Luynes, H. T. 1874 *Voyage d'exploration a la mer Morte, a Petra, et sur la rive gauche du Jourdain* (published posthumously by Melchior Vogüé). Arthus Bertrand, Paris.

Es, L. van. 1995 Faunal Remains Form Tell Abu Sarbut, A Preliminary Report. In *Archaeozoology of the Near East II: Proceedings of the Second International Symposium on the Archaeozoology of Southwestern Asia and Adjacent Areas*, edited by H. Buitenhuis and H.-P. Uerpmann, pp. 88–96. Backhuys, Leiden.

Franken, H. J., and J. Kalsbeek. 1975 *Potters of a Medieval Village in the Jordan Valley. Excavations at Tell Deir 'Alla: A Medieval Tell, Tell Abu Gourdan, Jordan.* North-Holland ceramic studies in archaeology 3. North-Holland publishing company, American Elsevier, Amsterdam, Oxford, New York.

Frumkin, A., and Y. Elitzur. 2002 Historic Dead Sea Level Fluctuations Calibrated with Geological and Archaeological Evidence. *Quaternary Research* 57:334–342.

Galloway, J. H. 1989 *The Sugar Cane Industry. An Historical Geography from Its Origins to 1914.* Cambridge Studies in Historical Geography. Cambridge University Press, Cambridge.

Groot, N. F. C. 2011 All the Work of Artisans. Reconstructing Society at Tell Deir 'Allā through the Study of Ceramic Traditions: Studies of Late Bronze Age Faience Vessels and Iron IIc-III Ceramics from Tell Deir 'Allā, Jordan. Unpublished PhD thesis, Delft University of Technology.

Groot, N. F. C. 2012 Production and Exchange of Ceramics in the Central Jordan Valley during Iron Age IIc. In *Tell el-Mazar II: Excavations on the Mound 1977–1981*, edited by K. Yassine and E. J. v. d. Steen, pp. 41–45. BAR international series 2430. Archaeopress, Oxford.

Herr, L. G. 2014 The Southern Levant (Transjordan) During the Iron Age I Period. In *The Oxford Handbook of the Archaeology of the Levant: c. 8000–332 BCE*, edited by M. Steiner and A. E. Killebrew, pp. 649–659. Oxford University Press, Oxford.

Hourani, F., E. Kaptijn, L. P. Petit, G. van der Kooij, and O. al-Ghul. 2008 Dayr 'Alla Regional Project: Settling the Steppe. Third campaign 2006. *Annual of the Department of Antiquities of Jordan* 52:427–443.

Hunt, R. C. 1988 Size and the Structure of Authority in Canal Irrigation Systems. *Journal of Anthropological Research* 44(4):335–355.

Jordan Meteorological Department: from website: http://www.jometeo.gov.jo/.

Kappel, W. 1974 Irrigation Development and Population Pressure. In *Irrigation's Impact on Society*, edited by T. E. Downing and M. Gibson, pp. 159–167. Anthropological Papers 25. University of Arizona Press, Tucson.

Kaptijn, E. 2009 *Life on the Watershed. Reconstructing Subsistence in a Steppe Region Using Archaeological Survey: A Diachronic Perspective on Habitation in the Jordan Valley.* Sidestone Press, Leiden.

Kaptijn, E. 2010 Communality and Power Irrigation in the Zerqa Triangle, Jordan. *Water History* 2(2):145–163.

Kaptijn, E. 2014 The Late Bronze and Iron Age Cultural Landscape of the Eastern Jordan Valley: The Start of a Long Tradition. In *Exploring the Narrative: Jerusalem and Jordan in the Bronze and Iron Ages*, edited by N. Mulder, J. H. Boertien, and E. van der Steen, pp. 23–35. Bloomsbury, Edinburgh.

Kaptijn, E. 2015 Irrigation and Human Niche Construction. An Example of Socio-Spatial Organisation in the Zerqa Triangle, Jordan. *Water History* 7(4):441–454.

Kaptijn, E. In press Subsistence Stability in Irrigating Societies. A Diachronic Perspective from the Jordan Valley. In *New Agendas in Remote Sensing and Landscape Archaeology in the Near East*, edited by M. Altaweel, G. Philip, and D. Lawrence. Studies in Ancient Oriental Civilization. Chicago Oriental Institute, Chicago.

Kooij, G. van der. 2002 Use of Space in Settlements—An Exercise upon Deir Alla-IX. In *Moving Matters. Ethnoarchaeology in the Near East. Proceedings of the International Seminar Held at Cairo 7–10 December 1998*, edited by W. Wendrich and G. v. d. Kooij, pp. 63–73. CNWS publications 111. Research school of Asian, African and Amerindian studies, University Leiden, Leiden.

Kooij, G. van der. 2007 Irrigation Systems at Dayr 'Alla. In *Studies in the History and Archaeology of Jordan IX*, edited by F. al-Khraysheh, pp. 133–144. Department of Antiquities of Jordan, Amman.

Kooij, G. van der, and M. M. Ibrahim. 1989 *Picking up the Threads . . . : A Continuing Review of Excavations at Deir 'Alla, Jordan*. Rijksmuseum van Oudheden, Leiden.

Kramer, C. 1982 *Village Ethnoarchaeology. Rural Iran in Archaeological Perspective*. Studies in Archaeology. Academic Press, New York.

LaBianca, Ø. S., and R. W. Younker. 1998 The Kingdoms of Ammon, Moab, and Edom: The Archaeology of Society in Late Bronze/Iron Age Transjordan (ca. 1400–500 BCE). In *The Archaeology of Society in the Holy Land*, edited by T. E. Levy, pp. 401–415. Leicester University Press, Leicester.

LaGro, H. E. 2002 *An Insight into Ayyubid-Mamluk Pottery: Description and Analysis of a Corpus of Mediaeval Pottery from the Cane Sugar Production and Village Occupation at Tell Abu Sarbut in Jordan*. Unpublished dissertation, Faculty of Archaeology, University of Leiden, Leiden.

Layne, L. L. 1994 *Home and Homeland: The Dialogics of Tribal and National Identities in Jordan*. Princeton University Press, Princeton.

Lehmann, G. 2004 Reconstruction the Social Landscape of Early Israel: Rural Marriage Alliances in the Central Hill Country. *Tel Aviv* 31:141–193.

Luterbacher, J., R. García-Herrera, S. Akcer-On, R. Allan, M.-C. Alvarez-Castro, G. Benito, J. Booth, U. Büntgen, N. Cagatay, D. Colombaroli, B. Davis, J. Esper, T. Felis, D. Fleitmann, D. Frank, D. Gallego, E. Garcia-Bustamante, R. Glaser, F. J. Gonzalez-Rouco, H. Goosse, T. Kiefer, M. G. Macklin, S. W. Manning, P. Montagna, L. Newman, M. J. Power, V. Rath, P. Ribera, D. Riemann, N. Roberts, M.-A. Sicre, S. Silenzi, W. Tinner, P. C. Tzedakis, B. Valero-Garcés, G. van der Schrier, B. Vannière, S. Vogt, H. Wanner, J. P. Werner, G. Willett, M. H. Williams, E. Xoplaki, C. S. Zerefos, and E. Zorita. 2012 A Review of 2000 Years of Paleoclimatic Evidence in the Mediterranean. In *The Climate of the Mediterranean Region*, edited by P. Lionello, pp. 87–185. Elsevier, Oxford.

Mabry, J. B. 1996 The Ethnology of Local Irrigation. In *Canals and Communities. Small-Scale Irrigation Systems*, edited by J. B. Mabry, pp. 3–30. Arizona studies in human ecology. Arizona University Press, Tucson.

Mabry, J. B. 2000 Wittfogel Was Half Right: The Ethnology of Consensual and Non-Consensual Hierarchies in Irrigation Management. In *Hierarchies in Action: Cui Bono?*, edited by M. W. Diehl, pp. 284–294. Center for Archaeological Investigations Occasional Papers 27. Southern Illinois University, Carbondale.

Marcus, J., and C. Stanish. 2005 Introduction. In *Agricultural Strategies*, edited by J. Marcus and C. Stanish, pp. 1–13. Cotsen Advanced Seminar. Cotsen Institute of Archaeology Press, Los Angeles.

Merrill, S. 1881 *East of the Jordan: A Record of Travel and Observation in the Countries of Moab, Gilead, and Bashan*. C. Scribner's sons, London.

Naroll, R. 1962 Floor Area and Settlement Population. *American Antiquity* 27(4):587–589.

Nedeco and Dar al-Handasah. 1969 Annex B Climate and hydrology. In *Jordan Valley Project. Agro- and Socio-Economic Study. Final Report*. The Hashemite Kingdom of Jordan. Jordan river and tributaries regional corporation. Dar al-Handasah consulting engineers and Netherlands Engineering Consultants (NEDECO), Beirut and The Hague.

Petit, L. P. 2009 *Settlement Dynamics in the Middle Jordan Valley during Iron II-III*. BAR International Series 2033. Archaeopress, Oxford.

Qutaifan, W. 1990 Al-'Aluk. In *Part-Time Farming: Agricultural Development in the Zarqa River Basin, Jordan*, edited by M. Mundy and R. Saumarez Smith, pp. 60–111. Institute of Archaeology and Anthropology, Yarmouk University, Irbid.

Rosen, A. M. 2007 *Civilizing Climate. Social Responses to Climate Change in the Ancient Near East*. Altamira Press, Lanham.

Sato, T. 2015 *Sugar in the Social Life of Medieval Islam*. Islamic Area Studies. Brill, Leiden.

Shiloh, Y. 1980 The Population of Iron Age Palestine in the Light of a Sample Analysis of Urban Plans, Areas, and Population Density. *Bulletin of the American Schools of Oriental Research* 239:25–35.

Steiner, M. L. 2008 Tell Abu Sarbut: The Occupation of a Rural Site in the Ayyubid-Mamluk Periods. In *Sacred and Sweet. Studies on the Material Culture of Tell Deir 'Alla and Tell Abu Sarbut*, edited by M. L. Steiner and E. J. van der Steen, pp. 157–195. Ancient Near Eastern Studies Supplement Series 24. Peeters Publishers, Leuven.

Stern, E. J. 2001 The Excavations at Lower Horvat Manot: A Medieval Sugar-Production Site. *'Atiqot* 42:277–308.

Sumner, W. M. 1979 Estimating Population by Analogy: An Example. In *Ethnoarchaeology. Implications of Ethnography for Archaeology*, edited by C. Kramer, pp. 164–174. Columbia University Press, New York.

Taha, H. 2009 Some Aspects of Sugar Production in Jericho, Jordan Valley. *In A Timeless Vale. Archaeological and Related Essays on the Jordan Valley in Honour of Gerrit van der Kooij on the Occasion of his Sixty-Fifth Birthday*, edited by E. Kaptijn and L. P. Petit, pp. 181–191. Leiden University Press, Leiden.

Tarawneh, M. F. 2014 *Rural Capitalist Development in the Jordan Valley. The Case of Deir 'Alla—The Rise and Demise of Social Groups*. Sidestone Press, Leiden.

Uphoff, N. 1986 *Improving International Irrigation Management with Farmer Participation. Getting the Process Right*. Westview Studies in Water Policy and Management. Westview Press, Boulder, CO.

Walker, B. J. 2006 The Role of Agriculture in Mamluk-Jordanian Power Relations. *Bulletin d'études orientales* 57:79–99.

Wendrich, W. 2002 Moving Matters, an Introduction. In *Moving Matters. Ethnoarchaeology in the Near East. Proceedings of the International Seminar Held at Cairo 7–10 December 1998*, edited by W. Wendrich and G. van der Kooij, pp. 7–12. Research school of Asian, African and Amerindian studies, University Leiden, Leiden.

Wirth, E. 1971 *Syrien. Eine geographische Landeskunde.* Wissenschaftliche Länderkunden Band 4/5. Wissenschaftliche Buchgesellschaft, Darmstadt.

Yassine, K., and E. J. van der Steen. 2012 *Tell el-Mazar II: Excavations on the Mound 1977–1981.* BAR international series 2430. Archaeopress, Oxford.

Yassine, K., and J. Teixidor. 1986 Ammonite and Aramaic Inscriptions from Tell el-Mazar in Jordan. *Bulletin of the American Schools of Oriental Research* 264:45–50.

Younker, R. W. 2014 Ammon during the Iron Age II period. In *The Oxford Handbook of the Archaeology of the Levant: c. 8000–332 BCE*, edited by M. L. Steiner and A. E. Killebrew, pp. 757–769. Oxford University Press, Oxford.

CHAPTER FOUR

Water Management by
Mobile Pastoralists in the Middle East

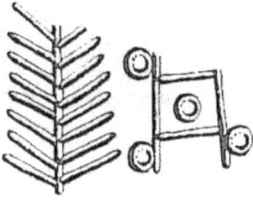

Emily Hammer

Abstract *Archaeologists typically study ancient water management through the surviving material manifestations of irrigation schemes and runoff systems constructed by sedentary agricultural communities. Another important component to water sustainability in the past was population mobility, in particular by transhumant pastoral groups. On the large scale, mobile pastoralism is about bringing animals to the best available or most accessible water and pastures rather than bringing water and fodder to animals. Pastoralism is a water management strategy that involves a different conception of landscape, space, and resources than dry farming or irrigation agriculture. In addition to following precipitation and snowmelt patterns, transhumant pastoralists also sometimes construct water-harvesting features in their pasture and camping areas to increase the amount of water available. Archaeological survey work in southeastern Turkey provides an example of sustainable local water manipulation schemes by mobile pastoralists of the last 600–700 years. Water collection and soil enhancement structures constructed by these pastoralists can be best understood as landscape anchors: geographic foci that structured the spatial organization of local landscapes. Although small-scale and locally managed, the water and pasture improvement features examined by the archaeological survey in Turkey have had enduring impacts on local land use that are demonstrable through archaeological and environmental analysis.*

INTRODUCTION

Pastoralism is a water management strategy that involves a different conception of landscape, space, and resources than dry farming or agriculture. Ancient water management is typically studied through the surviving material manifestations of water engineering features such as irrigation canals and runoff systems. However, these and other ways of artificially transporting and collecting water, usually constructed by sedentary farming societies, are only half the story of long-term sustainable water management in the Middle East. The other component to water sustainability in the past was mobility, in particular by transhumant pastoral groups. On the large scale, mobile pastoralism is about bringing animals to the best available and most accessible water and pastures rather than bringing water and fodder to animals.

Archaeologists have often perceived mobile pastoralism in the Middle East as a kind of alternative "fallback" subsistence strategy pursued by communities under unfavorable, external circumstances: drought, soil salinization, political collapse, and a lack of available agriculturally productive land (e.g., Adams 1978:334; Hole 2007:197). An alternate perspective more aligned with some sociological and anthropological literature on the relative stability and vulnerability of pastoral groups instead focuses on the internal factors sustaining pastoral production systems and sees mobile pastoralism as a set of active, effective strategies for managing resources such as water in order to increase the reliability of production (e.g., Beck and Huang 2011; Roe et al. 1998). Mobility itself is an effective technology for water management, as are animals themselves, which serve as easily moveable stores of liquid, calories, and capital. Small-scale water capture systems are a third important water management strategy used by mobile pastoralists. Such systems are designed to keep rainfall, runoff, and snowmelt distributed across the landscape, thereby increasing the amount of water available and expanding the range of usable pasture.

In the first part of this paper, ethnographic studies from across the Middle East are synthesized as a source of ideas both about natural water use by mobile pastoralists, activities that are typically invisible archaeologically, as well as water engineering strategies of these groups that may be visible archaeologically. In the second part of the paper, an archaeological case study in southeastern Turkey provides an example of sustainable local water manipulation schemes by mobile pastoralists of the last 600–700 years. To illustrate water engineering strategies, an archaeological case study in southeastern Turkey provides an example of sustainable local water manipulation schemes by mobile pastoralists of the last 600–700 years. Mobile groups altered marginal areas to improve water availability and pasture quality for themselves and their animals. Water collection and soil enhancement structures can be best understood as geographic foci that structured the spatial organization of local landscapes, what I have elsewhere termed "landscape anchors" (Hammer 2014). Although small-scale and locally managed, water and pasture improvement features have had enduring impacts on local land use that are demonstrable through archaeological and environmental analysis.

WATER AND SUBSISTENCE RISK IN THE MIDDLE EAST

In the Middle East, rain falls in episodic, erratic seasonal patterns often with a high degree of inter-annual variation (Beaumont et al. 1976:65–72). Low mean annual rainfall and inter-annual variation can cause both agricultural and pastoral subsistence systems to experience fluctuation in their productivity level. Communities in the premodern

Middle East had to develop risk management strategies in an attempt to reduce variance in annual production and reduce the vulnerability of food systems to failure or collapse.

Agricultural, agropastoral, and pastoral societies use two distinct approaches to managing risk of subsistence failure: diversification and intensification (Marston 2011). *Diversification* strategies attempt to reduce variance in subsistence returns by varying the kinds of foods produced and their location and time of production. Specific diversification strategies include crop species diversification, spatial diversification (scattering of fields, population mobility, and sharing of food or food production efforts), and temporal diversification (food storage and crop scheduling) (Marston 2011:191–194). *Intensification* strategies attempt to reduce the chance that food production will fall below the starvation threshold in any given year by increasing production well beyond this threshold. Specific intensification strategies include deliberate overproduction and irrigation (Marston 2011:194–195). Mobile pastoralists engage in species diversification by varying herd composition (often shifting the balance between sheep and goats in a herd in the Middle East [Cribb 1991:28]) and spatial diversification through population mobility and sharing of food or food production efforts. Temporal diversification is an internal element of all pastoral systems, as animals are mobile food and capital stores that can be slaughtered, bartered, or sold throughout the production cycle (e.g., Cribb 1991:34; Roe et al. 1998:41). Mobile pastoralists also can engage in intensification strategies by increasing their herd size beyond that needed for subsistence (Cribb 1991:29–34) and by increasing the quality and quantity of water and graze in their seasonal pastures through water capture systems like those described below.

Many attempts to reduce variance in food production in the past involved direct or indirect manipulation of water availability. Sedentary farmers in arid or semiarid river plains and certain hilly environments reduced risk by directly increasing the amount of water available for crops through the construction of surface or subsurface irrigation canals (Wilkinson 2003:71–99, 155–172) and runoff collection systems (Bruins 1986; Evenari et al. 1982). These water engineering systems intensify agricultural production and diversify the sources of water available for human consumption and crop watering. Irrigation not only boosts agricultural yield and increases the variety of crops that may be grown, but also helps spatially and temporally diversify crop production by extending agricultural fields and extending the growing season. Sedentary farmers in semiarid steppes and plains that could in some years support dry farming intensified agricultural production by more indirectly manipulating soil moisture through manuring practices and fallow regimes (Wilkinson 1982, 1994).

Another indirect but highly successful means of manipulating water availability is through population mobility. Irrigation canals, qanat/flaj/karez channels, runoff farms, and other systems that were created and maintained by sedentary farming societies usually form the center of discussions of ancient water management in the Middle East. Less studied are the alternative strategies through which ancient societies thrived in these same environments without developing engineered water systems. Water can be effectively "managed" by accessing it where it is seasonally available at or near the ground surface and where it is naturally stored in depressions, moisture-retentive soils, and wild vegetation. Mobile pastoralism is an often-overlooked component of water management in the historical and ancient Middle East.

MOBILE PASTORALISM AND WATER

Mobile pastoralism is a set of subsistence systems involving the herding of domesticated herbivores in multiple areas with seasonally available pasture and water (Figures 4.1 and 4.2). In the ancient and premodern Middle East, mobile pastoralists herded combinations of cattle, sheep and goats, camels, and water buffalo (Barfield 1993:93–130; Cribb 1991; Hammer and Arbuckle 2017). Pastoral mobility with these herd animals can vary in scale in terms of distance, time, and community size/composition. Herders may move their animals short distances of only a few kilometers, or regional distances of up to several hundred kilometers in a given year according to customary practice, the territory they control, or the availability of water and graze (Barfield 1993:96–97; Johnson 1969).[1] Socially, politically, and/or environmentally influenced patterns of transhumance or migration may cause pastoralists to change the location of their campsite and/or pastures only a few dozen times per year (Bates 1973; Black-Michaud 1986:2), several dozen (Skogseid 1993:223), or more than one hundred times (Barth 1964:15). Pastoralists may be organized into social and political units of any size, from a few households to large tribal confederations (Barfield 1993:107–115). Mobile herders may

FIGURE 4.1 Photograph of shepherd taking herds to the Tigris River to drink, Diyarbakır province, southeastern Turkey.

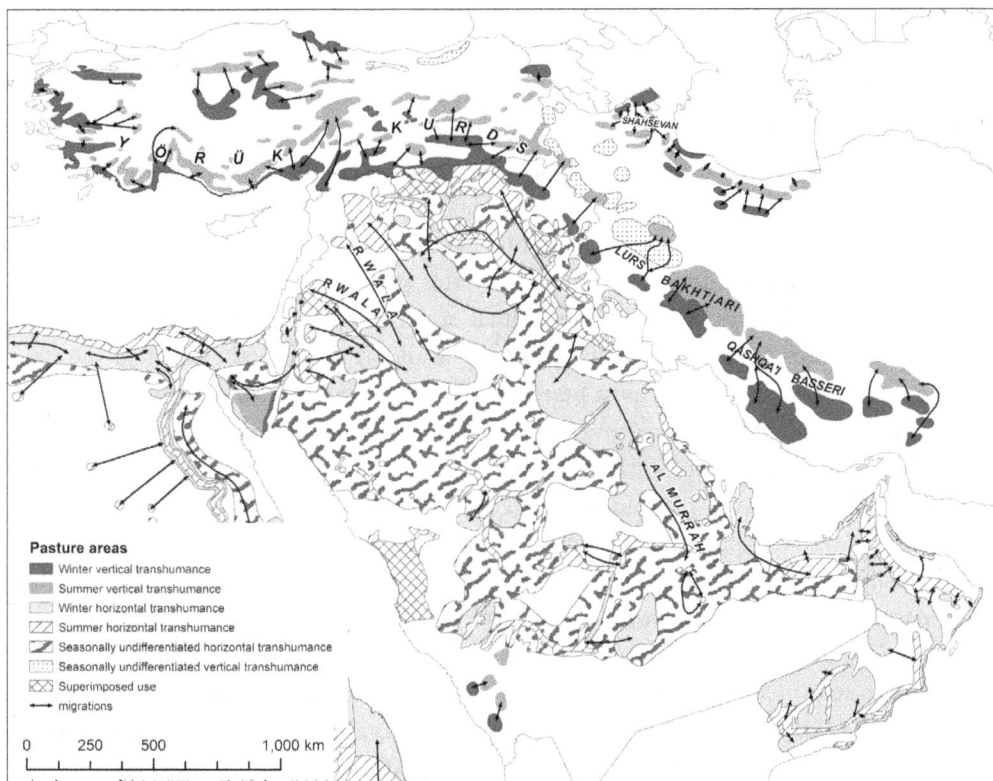

Pasture areas
■ Winter vertical transhumance
▨ Summer vertical transhumance
▦ Winter horizontal transhumance
▧ Summer horizontal transhumance
▨ Seasonally undifferentiated horizontal transhumance
▨ Seasonally undifferentiated vertical transhumance
▨ Superimposed use
↔ migrations

0   250   500   1,000 km

FIGURE 4.2 Map of the Middle East showing some documented examples of vertical and horizontal pastoral migration between winter and summer pastures as they existed in the early twentieth century. After *Tübinger Atlas des Vorderen Orients* (Wehling 1992). The migration routes of groups mentioned in the text are labeled.

form a specialized subgroup of society, where herding takes them away from their kin, or they may be accompanied on seasonal migrations by their entire household or even their entire community (Cribb 1991:25–27).

The location of water sources and the nature, volume, and quality of these sources affect mobile pastoral social structure and land-use systems. Most obviously, the availability of enough water fit for domestic and animal consumption affects the locations, sizes, and relative clustering or dispersion of seasonal campsites and pasture areas (Cribb 1991:135–138, 143; Hole 2004: 77). Water may be more or less important as a locational factor depending on rainfall patterns, the species of herd animal, and whether or not animals are lactating (Horne 1980:14; 1994:42–43, 62–65; Lancaster and Lancaster 1999:214–215). The location, size, and quality of pasture, as with any vegetation cover, is additionally affected by soil moisture, rainfall, temperature, and snowfall patterns. The spatial distribution of reliable water and pasture sources can affect local and regional patterns of conflict and cooperation among different mobile and sedentary groups. For example, the Qashqā'i of southwest Iran had a contentious relationship with sedentary

communities they encountered during their migrations because these sedentary communities in the 1980s and 1990s increasingly enclosed small water sources such as qanat
outlets, wells, and springs that the Qashqā'i had previously been able to access (Beck
2003:297). Prior to the construction of government wells in the 1960s, the Al Murrah
Bedouin of southeast Arabia had to depend on good relations with surrounding tribes
in their winter pastures for access to well water (Cole 1975:46).

As a water management strategy, mobile pastoralism allows herders to intensify the
production of animal products and to diversify this production spatially and temporally
in four intertwined ways. First, on an annual scale, mobility allows people and their
animals to be where water and graze are locally available at a certain point of the year.
Variation exists in pastoral mobility patterns, but all in one way or another respond to
the seasonal abundance of water and graze.[2] In the deserts of Arabia, pastoralists often
move their animals between seasonal groundwater sources separated by long distances
(Cole 1975:33–36; Lancaster and Lancaster 1999:207–237) and use camels or don-
keys to carry water to any sheep and goats that are herded (Lancaster and Lancaster
1999:132–133, 214). In the steppes of Iraq, Syria, and Turkey, horizontally transhumant pastoralists move their animals between different pastures at around the same
topographical elevation, sometimes making use of low hill ranges that receive seasonal
precipitation (e.g., Danti 2000; Rowton 1974:6). In mountainous environments of the
Taurus and Zagros in Turkey, Iraq, and Iran, pastoralists engage in vertical transhumance
for the purposes of taking advantage of altitudinal differences in the seasonal availability of pasture and water (e.g., Cribb 1991:134). These pastoralists follow rainfall and
snowmelt patterns, typically using highland areas in the summer and lowland areas or
river plains in the winter.

Second, on both short- and long-term scales, a mobile lifestyle, a flexible conception of the landscape, and extensive landscape knowledge allow pastoralists to manage
risk through relocation and shifts in transhumance and residence patterns (Beck and
Huang 2011:106–107, 113–114). Mobility allows pastoralists to search for and relocate
to areas with the best resources available (Roe et al. 1998:43–44). Mobility also allows
pastoralists to respond to annual trends in water and graze distribution and to abnormal
environmental conditions that may arise (Cole 1975:35; Cribb 1991:143–144). Mobile
pastoral households and camping groups can disperse or congregate at different times
in response to local and regional changes in precipitation, water availability or access,
and pasture quality (Barth 1964; Beck 1991; Tapper 1979). The lower limit of how
many tents camped together often depended on labor needs and security issues, while
the upper limit depended on the carrying capacity of the land (Hole 2004:73–74) and
water sources (Skogseid 1993:227).

Third, mobility encourages dispersed patterns of inhabitation across the landscape.
Mobile subsistence systems can mitigate unpredictability and variation in various resources'
supply, including water, by using a larger area with a larger number of sources (Beck
and Huang 2011:124; Marx 1977:347). Especially compared to nucleated settlements
with higher population densities, dispersed seasonal inhabitation patterns are less likely
to overtax local water resources, a fact that has become evident in recent decades as

mobility restrictions have resulted in pastoralists putting increasing pressure on desert water sources (Lancaster and Lancaster 1999:226–227).

Fourth, animals serve as moveable stores of liquid and food; the herding of them in and of itself constitutes a type of water management technology. In the absence of water for human consumption, animals turn a resource that is not digestible by humans (moist grass) into a consumable liquid (milk). The Rwala Bedouin of northern Arabia and the Al Murrah Bedouin of southeastern Arabia migrated to access different groundwater resources, but largely drank milk as their main liquid intake when they could (Cole 1975:42; Lancaster and Lancaster 1999:138). Camels themselves were part of an active water management strategy for many sheep and goat pastoralists in eastern Jordan, as the larger beasts of burden were used to haul water to pastures for the smaller animals (Lancaster and Lancaster 1999:133). Animals can become a form of walking storage for seasonally available plant foods or for surplus agricultural produce, turning perishable plant products into long-lasting, easily moveable stores of dairy, meat, and capital.

MOBILE PASTORALISTS AND WATER ENGINEERING

Transhumant pastoralists also modify the landscape and invest in infrastructure to improve or increase water supplies in their seasonal territories. Water-harvesting features intensify and diversify production by increasing the amount of water available and by enhancing the quality of soil and available pasture grasses. The use of wells, natural seepages, and runoff features by mobile pastoralists has been documented ethnographically (Musil 1928:339, 346; Salamé 1955:91–92) and archaeologically (Danti 2000:25–27; Vetter et al. 2013; Ludwig 1970; Miller 1980:332–337; Rosen 1987) as means to secure supplies of water for animals, to enable flocks to remain in winter territories after surface water has evaporated, to extend the spatial range of pastures that can be accessed by herders, and to provide for animals during times of conflict.

While water management was not a focus of the major ethnographies of Middle Eastern mobile pastoral groups, all published between the 1950s and 1980s, the background descriptions of geography, daily life, and migrations contain some relevant details about these groups' water practices, their water engineering efforts, and the relationship between water and territoriality in their herding areas.

Ethnographically studied groups approached territoriality and access to water sources in two ways. Some, such as the horizontally transhumant Al-Murrah Bedouin of Arabia, recognized private rights to artificial water sources such as wells and cisterns (Cole 1975:33). Others, such as the Yomut Türkmen of northeastern Iran (Irons 1975), the Lurs of western Iran (Black-Michaud 1986), and the Saçıkara Yörük of southeastern Turkey (Bates 1973), practiced a "first come, first served" rule in the use of artificial water sources (Tapper 1979:4). Generally, everyone was entitled access to natural, free-flowing water sources such as rivers and springs. Sometimes these public water sources (rivers, canals) were located within pastures held by certain groups or individuals. In these cases, Shahsevan households in northwestern Iran established paths to these water sources. Groups whose estates had direct access to water sources allowed their animals to drink from the source, but where other pasture estates intervened, the groups with indirect access carried water to their herds via camel train (Tapper 1979:87). Over several decades, securing reliable water access became a problem for tribes in Iran because of agricultural expansion and the lowering of water tables due to irrigation. In the 1960s and 1970s the Qashqā'i of southwestern Iran relied on seasonal natural water sources, lived near their pastures, and traveled to collect water. By the 1990s, they had to assert their right to water sources by living near the sources on a permanent basis. This caused them to need to travel farther and farther away for adequate grazing (Beck 1998:62–63, 71–73).

In areas where there were no wells or rivers, runoff collection features were the primary sources of water for vertically transhumant pastoralists in winter lowland territories. The Qashqā'i excavated earthen water basins delimited by rocks and dried mud in their winter territories that collected rainwater and runoff for animal consumption. They also made use of natural pools remaining in gorges after heavy precipitation (Beck 1991). Households used runoff that collected in rock crevasses for their own consumption (Amir-Moez 2002:199). The Shahsevan dug wells in their winter pastures, which were subsequently held as private property, but they also used the runoff that collected in natural hollows and artificial reservoirs. They piled snow in these hollows and reservoirs so that animals could drink the melt (Tapper 1979).

In highland summer territories, springs and snowmelt were the primary sources of water for vertically transhumant pastoralists. The Qashqā'i lined the mouths of springs with stones to create small pools and sometimes constructed channels with stones. These channels allowed animals to drink away from the spring head, and helped avoid contamination of the water for human consumption (Beck 1991:295). The Shahsevan endeavored to ensure that snowmelt did not escape their summer pastures. They dammed flowing snowmelt in reservoirs in order to water animals and also channeled snowmelt onto hillsides in order to create irrigated meadows. Camps took water for domestic purposes from springs and not from stagnant pools of snowmelt (Tapper 1979:90).

In both winter and summer territories, vertically and horizontally transhumant pastoral groups continually maintain artificial water sources. The Qashqā'i repaired their winter runoff basins every year, eventually with concrete, and also annually repaired the channels that they constructed to divert spring water for animal consumption in summer pastures. They built no permanent structures in their summer pastures, and the only land improvements they engaged in were related to water sources (Beck 1991:295). In Arabia, mobile herders relied throughout the year on rock basins that collected runoff and rock seepage water for animals. These rock basins occurred naturally, but people improved them by regularly removing debris, silt, and stones, excavating their bases, and constructing dams to keep or divert water into the basins (Lancaster and Lancaster 1999:132–133).

Due to their repetitive seasonal use of land, mobile pastoralists had a complicated relationship with the investments they and their neighbors made in the landscape, especially those created for the purposes of collecting or conserving water supplies. Mobile pastoralists' seasonal absences in a particular territory placed limits on the effort they were willing to invest in infrastructure, which could be removed or destroyed while they were away. Nearby villagers destroyed the trees and spring channels that the Qashqā'i planted and constructed in their summer pastures because they "abhorred any physical sign that the Qermezi [Qashqā'i] claimed the land" (Beck 1991:311). On the other hand, mobile pastoral groups frequently benefited from the water engineering structures of other groups, including wells and water channels that were not held as private property. Irrigation systems in Iran provided water access and more lush wild vegetation at field edges for animal herds (Beck 1998:70; 2003:298). The 1960s state irrigation system in the Mughan Steppe of northwestern Iran had built-in places—low areas with steps—where animals could drink from the primary channel (Tapper 1997:300–301).

SMALL-SCALE WATER ENGINEERING BY
PREMODERN MOBILE PASTORALISTS IN SOUTHEASTERN TURKEY

Archaeological survey work in Diyarbakır Province, southeastern Turkey, provides an example of small-scale water engineering by pastoral nomads. In the Upper Tigris River Valley, the Hirbemerdon Tepe Survey (2007–2011, Figure 4.3 on page 50) investigated the spatial patterning of premodern mobile pastoral campsites in relationship to surrounding water features in a 47 square kilometer area (Hammer 2012, 2014; Ur and Hammer 2009). These features are both natural and constructed and include the Tigris River, seasonal drainage (wadi) systems, rock-cut cisterns, small dams, and cairns. The characteristics and arrangement of such features demonstrate how transhumant pastoralists used small-scale runoff systems to collect water and improve local pasture conditions. These sustainable systems, likely in use for the last 600–700 years, have continually shaped local patterns of inhabitation, territory, and movement (Hammer 2014).

Ethnographic and historic accounts show that long-distance transhumant pastoralism has at least a 1,000-year history in this region. Mountain-to-plain transhumance by sheep and goat pastoralists of the last millennium has been well documented in histories of the medieval Islamic dynasties based at Diyarbakır, records of the fifteenth-century Akkoyunlu nomadic confederacy, and the sixteenth- to nineteenth-century censuses of the Ottoman Empire as well as ethnographies from the early and mid-twentieth century (Bates 1973; Beşikçi 1969; Erhan 1997; Frödin 1943; Hammer and Arbuckle 2017; Hütteroth 1959; Kasaba 2009; Peacock 2010; van Bruinessen 1988; Woods 1999). The Tigris and its tributaries were often the lowland winter pasture for people who had highland summer pastures in the Taurus Mountains. Upland pastures in the Taurus are lush in the spring/summer, but under snow for five or more months in the winter; lowland valley pastures near the Tigris are plentiful in the winter but dried out in the summer due to extreme heat and drought. Before the delineation of the southern Turkish border in the 1920s, the Upper Tigris River Valley was also used as a transient camping area in spring and fall for groups moving between summer pastures in the Taurus Mountains and winter pastures in the Mesopotamian plain as far south as Mosul, Iraq, and Raqqa, Syria (van Bruinessen 1992:95–96, 189–190; Woods 1999:29–30). These general migration patterns were not the products of the control of territorial polities in southeastern Anatolia. State policies, particularly under the Ottomans, frequently resulted in changes in the specific location of certain groups' pasture areas (Gündüz 1997; Kasaba 2009; Şahin 2006:110; Sümer [Demirtaş] 1949). However, various pastoral groups used the same general areas for their summer and winter pastures in southeastern Anatolia for the last millennium,

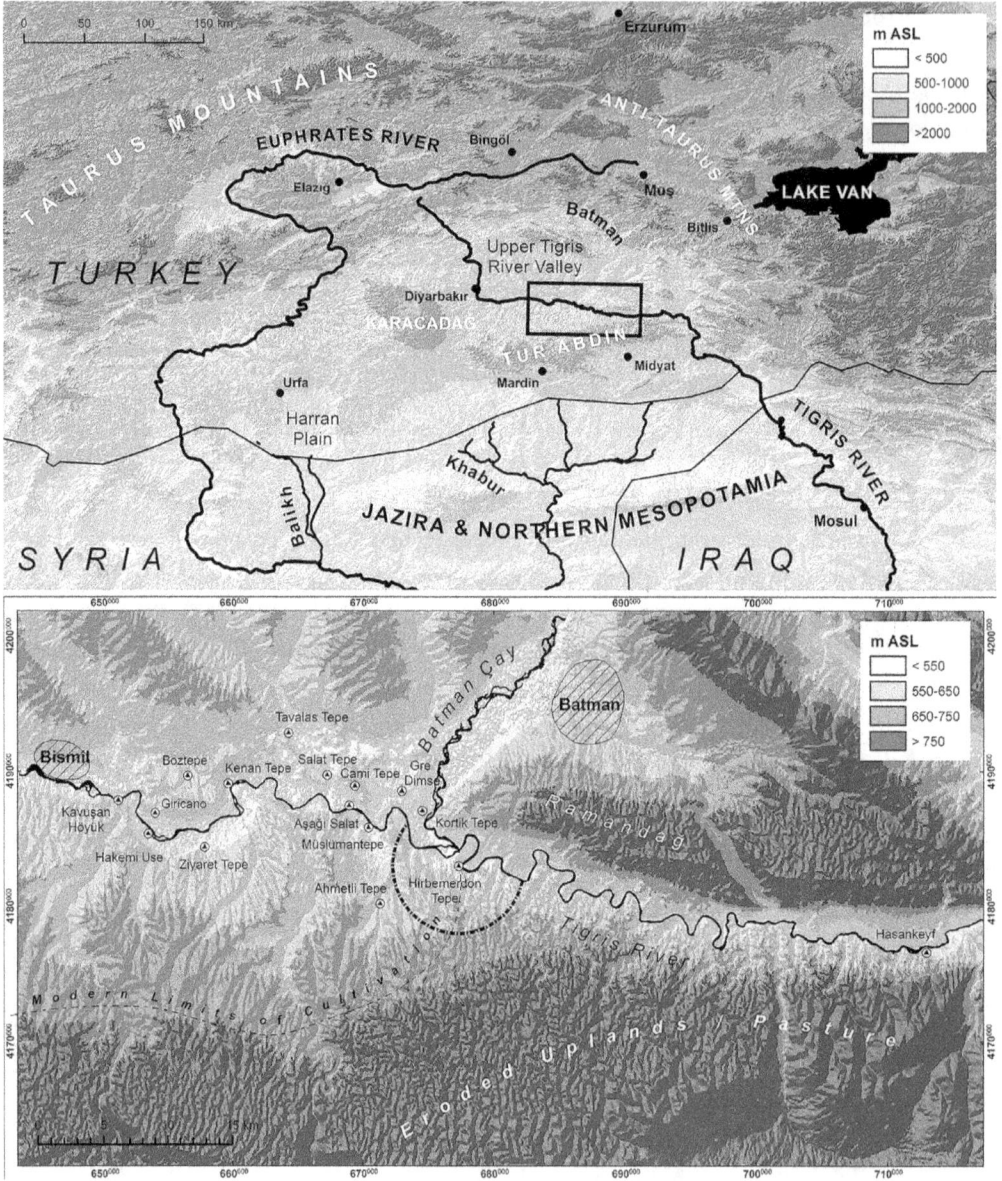

FIGURE 4.3 Location of the Hirbemerdon Tepe Survey at the interface between the Upper Tigris River Valley and eroded uplands to the east.

from the time of the influx of mobile pastoral populations from Central Asia in the eleventh century CE until the mid-twentieth century, following seasonal pasture availability, rainfall patterns, and climate.[3]

Descriptions of mobile pastoral encampments and rural land use appear peripherally in various accounts written by travelers in the Diyarbakır region over the last 200 years. While the information to be gleaned from these sources is anecdotal, they suggest that some of the general ethnographic observations about pastoralists and water discussed above were valid for earlier periods in and near the study area. Particularly relevant here, the travelers' accounts indicate that pastoralists repeatedly camped in the vicinity of constructed water features such as wells and cisterns. In the 1870s, the Yörük near Tarsus were only able to obtain water from deep rock-cut cisterns (Davis 1879:437). Türkmen encampments west of Urfa drew water from large circular cisterns up to 20 feet deep with steps (Buckingham 1827:45–46), and an encampment between Urfa and Mardin drew upon "very deep" cisterns hewn out of hard rock with carved surface channels for directing runoff water into their tanks (Buckingham 1827:143).

The Hirbemerdon Tepe Survey team employed pedestrian survey methodologies to examine an area of eroded hills beyond the boundaries of modern-day agriculture at the east edge of the upper Tigris River Valley (Hammer 2012:165–211; 2014:272–273; Ur and Hammer 2009:39). The only archaeologically detected settlements in this eastern area of 17 square kilometers are mobile pastoral campsites. The 18 campsites surveyed are mostly located in the lowest parts of the landscape, on low terraces beside deeply incised dry seasonal drainages (wadis; Figure 4.4). They are marked by low stone foundations

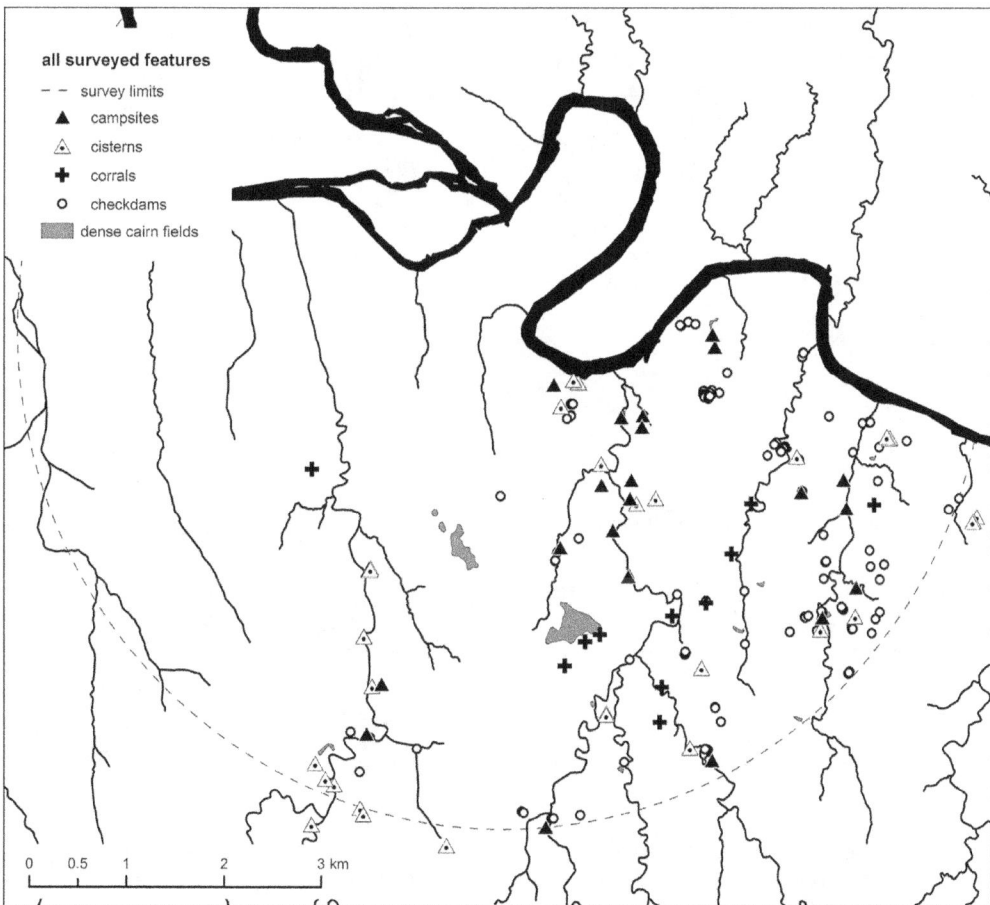

FIGURE 4.4 Location of surveyed campsites, features, and water sources in the study area.

that served as tent footings, pounded earthen tent floors, stone walled corrals, and trash middens (Figure 4.5). Some of the campsites had been inhabited in the mid to late twentieth century. Pottery found on the surface of and nearby other campsites dates to the Medieval Islamic and Ottoman periods, from the thirteenth to the early twentieth centuries CE (Hammer 2012:229–246; 2014:274–275).

A suite of landscape features designed to enhance the water and pasture resources of the immediate region surrounded each campsite examined by the archaeological survey: cisterns, small dams, and cairns (Hammer 2012:252–272; 2014:276–278). Cisterns near the campsites have been carved out of limestone bedrock in areas where large surfaces of bedrock are exposed (Figure 4.6 on page 54). The impermeable surface formed by the exposed bedrock around the cistern results in an increased amount of runoff, which is directed into the tank of the cistern by shallow rock-carved surface channels. The 29 surveyed cisterns had three different morphologies. Twenty-three pit cisterns consisted of reservoirs carved into horizontal bedrock surfaces on ridgetops or beside seasonal streambeds.

FIGURE 4.5 Photographs of campsites in the study area. (A) Twentieth-century campsite with stone corrals and tent footings. (B) Premodern campsite with collapsed and flattened stone architecture. (C) Premodern campsite with compressed earthen tent platform. The upright sticks in the photo mark postholes.

Figure 4.6 Photograph of cisterns in the study area. (A) Stepped cistern with surface water channel stretching toward the upper left corner of the photo and a spoil heap in front of the cistern entrance. (B) Pit-style bell-shaped cistern with surface channel.

The interiors of these cisterns were frequently bell-shaped, where the base of the reservoir is wider than the top. Five stepped cisterns had rectangular tanks with doorways carved into limestone slopes. Sets of three to seven stairs led from the exterior to the bottom of the tank. Stepped cisterns had the most extensive sets of shallow surface channels directing runoff toward the tank, and these channels frequently surrounded the entrance to direct water around the doorway. The entrances to stepped cisterns were often marked by large spoil heaps resulting from episodes of cistern cleaning. There is only one example of the third type of cistern, which also has a large rectangular subterranean reservoir. However, this reservoir was not accessed by stairs and has a much smaller external opening than the stepped cisterns. The carving date of six of the cisterns has been investigated using geological exposure dating methods. While the method produced only large age ranges, the results suggest that the cisterns could have been carved either recently or within the last several hundred years (Hammer and Ackert n.d., in prep).

Ancient and premodern cisterns with similar structural characteristics, including reservoirs carved from relatively soft bedrock on hillsides, stepped tank access points, and surface channels to direct runoff, have been extensively surveyed by archaeologists in the Negev and the Libyan deserts (Avni 1996; Evenari et al. 1982; Vetter et al. 2013). In the flat Libyan desert in northwestern Egypt, mounded discolored spoil heaps resulting from cistern cleaning often led surveyors to the location of cistern openings, which were more hidden from view (Vetter et al. 2013:463–465).

In the narrow valleys created by the seasonal drainage systems, series of small check dams are aligned perpendicular to the slope of hillsides (Figure 4.7). Check dams are

FIGURE 4.7 Photograph of a check dam in the study area.

found in many types of arid and semiarid environments all over the world (Beckers et al. 2013:151–152; Dennell 1982). The check dams in the survey area usually measure only a few meters across and are constructed of earth and/or stone. The accumulation of soils behind these small dams and the enhanced level of moisture in the soil surrounding the dams improve the quality of vegetation in their vicinity. During particularly wet times, small amounts of water may be impounded behind these dams and used for animal consumption.

On the plateaus between seasonal drainage systems, there are large fields of rock piles or cairns (Figure 4.8). At least some of these cairns do not appear to have marked graves, and dense concentrations of cairns are found in areas that are not currently farmed, even with the wide availability of irrigation water. Analyses using the Normalized Differential Vegetation Index (NDVI) have suggested that areas with cairns have a slightly higher natural vegetation density and soil moisture than nearby areas without cairns that have the same topographical and environmental characteristics (Hammer 2014:282). For these reasons, cairns could have been a type of pasture/soil improvement system, as the clearing of stones into piles improves the growth of wild grasses (Chang and Koster 1986:112–113). Both check dams and cairns are impossible to date without excavation, and the exact date of these features' construction remains unknown.

FIGURE 4.8 Photograph of a cairn field in the study area. One cairn is in the foreground and several others are visible in the background.

All of the surface water and pasture features described above are only effective during the winter rainy season, the time during which transhumant groups have historically been present in the region. A crucial feature of these runoff collection features is that they are designed to harness highly local, seasonal water resources. Climatic patterns in southeastern Anatolia appear to have been relatively stable for the last millennium (Bryson and Bryson 1999:13; Hütteroth 2006:22). During the summer, there is little to no precipitation, and the extreme heat causes desiccation of the soil and natural grasses. Cisterns, dams, and cairn fields catch water and retain moisture before it drains into the major streams and rivers. This is an effective and low-energy way to keep rainfall distributed across the landscape in the locations where humans and animals need it, using features that can easily be constructed and maintained by single households or camping groups. Cisterns and water-holding dams spatially and temporally extend the available water sources for human consumption, while dams and cairn fields help intensify the growth of natural pasture grasses.

Once constructed, these runoff collection features are relatively permanent improvements to the landscape that continue to function without the need for elaborate maintenance. Further, their continued use appears to have shaped camping and herding patterns over an extended period of time. In these ways, the runoff collection features constructed by pastoralists resemble the road and irrigation systems that historical ecologists term "landesque capital" (Blaikie and Brookfield 1987:9; Brookfield 2001:54–55, 216; Erickson and Walker 2009:251).

The cisterns, dams, and cairn fields are no longer in annual use, yet remained functional and effective as of 2011. Mobile pastoralism has steadily declined in southeastern Anatolia since the mid-nineteenth century (Kasaba 2009), and most remaining transhumant groups in Diyarbakır were forced to settle during the conflict between the Kurdish Worker's Party and the Turkish state, beginning in the 1980s (Jongerden 2007). Only one group of transhumant pastoralists camped in the study region during the period 2004–2010. Examination of this group's campsite and interviews with inhabitants of nearby villages indicate that they trucked in tanks of water. However, this group must have benefited from the continual pasture-improving effects of the dams and cairn fields surrounding their campsite. The openings of many cisterns are marked by large sediment heaps resulting from repeated cleaning of deposits that accumulate in the cisterns. With only a small amount of cleaning of accumulated sediment from catchment channels, the cisterns fill during the winter rains. The continued effects of the dams and cairn features is apparent in the winter and spring from the significantly denser and lusher quality of the grasses surrounding them, measured through multispectral satellite imagery (Hammer 2014:281–282).

The cisterns, dams, and cairns do more than supply necessary water and improve pasture: they also might structure local movement paths and seasonal territories. Though small-scale investments, they expanded the distribution of resources surrounding campsites. Cisterns likely affected both the inhabitation and daily herding patterns of mobile pastoralists. The seasonal drainages only contain flowing water during flash floods. The only reliable source of water in the study area is the Tigris River, which is up to five kilometers over rough terrain from some of the surveyed campsites. While herds could be taken to the river to drink, obtaining water for household consumption remains a problem. Cisterns and earthen impound dams could provide sources of water for household and animal consumption closer to the campsite and also enable the use of a wider range of pasture areas further away from the river. The modest size of the cisterns probably made them better suited for household water consumption. Without cisterns, nomadic pastoral groups might choose to camp closer to the river and shepherds might follow a much more circumscribed daily herding pattern.

Surveys of cisterns in the Negev and the Libyan deserts have connected cistern use and spatial distribution not only to runoff agricultural systems and trade routes, but also to pastoral grazing patterns. Archaeological surveys and ethnographic documentation of water sources in the Negev found that sedentary and mobile Bedouin herders in the twentieth century used scattered cisterns on hillsides located away from settlements for watering their animals. Some of these cisterns were associated with ancient pottery but no visible ancient settlements, leading archaeologists to hypothesize that they could have been used for the same purpose in the past (Avni 1996; Evenari et al. 1982:159, 400). A survey of cisterns in Marmarica (northwestern Egypt) concluded that scattered networks of cisterns closer to the Mediterranean coast in an area with higher rainfall and good pasture areas were likely constructed to benefit mobile pastoralists herding sheep, goats, and camels, while linear distributions of cisterns farther away from the coast in the desert interior were indicative of ancient transportation routes followed by donkey and camel caravans. The spacing of cisterns in the two northernmost zones of the survey area was on average 2.8 and 5.8 kilometers, respectively, distances that would have allowed animals to be herded between different cisterns on a daily basis (Vetter et al. 2013:467, 477). In these zones, cisterns were not associated with any traces of substantial architecture. One of the cisterns in the northern part of the study area was associated with a campsite with pottery from the Ptolemaic through Byzantine periods (Vetter et al. 2013:468–470).

The central role of cisterns in the Hirbemerdon area is evidenced by their distribution in relationship to campsites. Spatial analyses of topographic proximity and accessibility show that the majority of campsites are located in close proximity to cisterns (Hammer 2014:282–284) (Figure 4.9). The density of campsites and cisterns is greatest in three distinct clusters oriented north-south along major seasonal drainages. These clusters are separated from their nearest neighboring cluster by 1.5 and 2.2 kilometers. Premodern campsites in the survey area cluster around larger cisterns. In the middle cluster of the eastern survey area, the densest concentration of campsites in the survey region (six campsites) is set in the middle of a cluster of three cisterns. These campsites have different morphological and taphonomic characteristics, probably indicating that they were inhabited at different times. This archaeological pattern probably results from the repeated reoccupation of this location in part because of the advantages provided by the nearby cisterns. As previously mentioned, the openings of many cisterns are marked by large sediment heaps resulting from repeated cleaning of deposits that accumulate in the cisterns. These heaps provide further evidence for the extended use and significance of the cisterns.

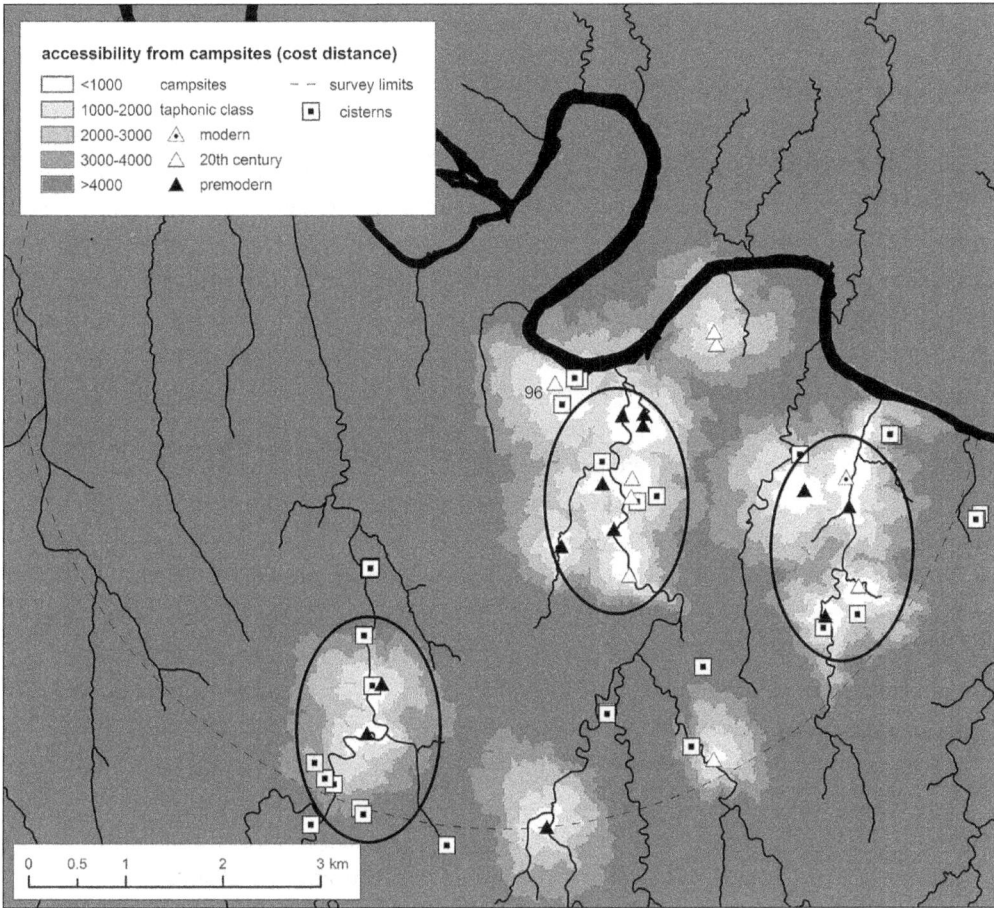

FIGURE 4.9 Map showing clusters of campsites and cisterns in the study area.

Cisterns, and possibly also check dams and cairns, were investments in the land-scape that may have not only encouraged subsequent reinhabitation by mobile pastoral groups but also have marked territory. Ethnographically, the security of pasture tenure was a major factor influencing the degree of effort invested in campsite architecture (Cribb 1991:110–112) and should also be a major factor influencing the elaboration of constructed water collection and pasture improvement system features such as cisterns, dams, and cairn fields. Islamic and customary law across the Middle East dictates that free-flowing water cannot be owned but that modified or improved water sources are private property (Lancaster and Lancaster 1999:129–131). The Ottoman Majalla (civil code) from the mid-nineteenth century formalizes and builds upon Islamic water law, recognizing three different categories of water (common, private, and public domain) and specifying that water may only be owned through collection in a reservoir, cistern, well, or constructed channel (Mallat 1995; Métral 1981:128–129, 132–133).[4] Although no specific study on historic notions of water rights in southeastern Anatolia exists, such ideas could have been a force in southeast Anatolian land-use patterns over the last millennium. The investment that pastoral groups made in creating and maintaining water collection and pasture improvement systems could either lead to or result from seasonal territorial control over specific herding and camping areas. The investment seen in the Hirbemerdon Tepe landscape—the large number of cisterns and extensive campsite infrastructure—suggests that this land was at some point in the past claimed, seasonally controlled, and annually revisited.

Over time, water collection and soil enhancement structures can be best understood as *landscape anchors*: features that are in continuous and modified use that become geographical foci orienting groups' camping, herding, and mobility patterns over long periods of time (Hammer 2014). Like road networks and irrigation systems that cause "historical path dependency" in settlement location (McGlade 1999:476–478), landscape anchors become deeply etched into the physical environment and into mobile communities' perceptions of the landscape. Migration and camping patterns are shaped by knowledge of landscape anchors, including the natural landscape of available pasture and water resources as well as notions of territory shaped by the cultural landscape of water and pasture improvement systems. For mobile pastoral groups, sustainable, locally managed water and pasture sources enhanced by the creation of cisterns, dams, and cairns become spatially fixed nodes in flexible networks of regional (interseasonal) and local (intraseasonal) movement.

Winter water availability was the most common problem among vertically transhumant Turkish and Iranian pastoral tribes in the twentieth century (Beck 1991:75; Skogseid 1993:227). For many groups, the water and pasture resources available in winter territories formed one of the primary constraints on the entire regional transhumance system. In this sense, seasonal water features constitute evidence for long-term planning in the context of the overall land-use system.

However, the suite of water and pasture improvement features should not be seen as a unified and planned system. Together they can function to improve the pasture and water resources of the local environment, and thus pastoral productivity. They are not, however, the end result of a coordinated effort or a planned scheme. Rather, the set of water and pasture features in the landscape likely grew organically and piecemeal, like irrigation and road networks that are constructed accretionally (Doolittle 1984). Each surveyed water and pasture feature likely has an individual use history. These features should be seen as nodes in a local resource network whose constituent elements change temporally. Landscape anchors may be occluded or reintroduced into the group of used features at different timescales: weekly, yearly, or generationally. This organic growth and flexible pattern of use, in combination with regional pastoral mobility, contributes to the sustainability of water, pasture, and food production.

CONCLUSION

In semiarid and arid environments of the Middle East, both sedentary agropastoral societies and mobile pastoral societies developed their own intensification and spatial-temporal diversification strategies for coping with unpredictability in water availability. Mobile pastoral societies' water strategies included *population mobility*, which allowed use of a broader range of water and pasture resources and allowed pastoralists to follow annual precipitation patterns; *flexible land-use patterns*, which allowed herders to adjust their location and herding patterns in response to spatial and temporal patterns in the available water and graze; *geographic dispersal*, which placed less stress on individual water and pasture sources; *animal technology* itself, which provided herders with mobile stores of liquid (milk), meat, and capital; and *water capture systems*, which collect runoff for human and animal consumption and sometimes improve the growth of natural pasture grasses.

Mobile pastoralism was an important component of regional and local water management systems in the premodern Middle East. As a water management strategy, mobile pastoralism is geared toward the exploitation of seasonally available surface and groundwater resources through either entirely natural means or through small-scale water engineering. Mobile pastoral households "managed" water by accessing it where it was seasonally available at or near the ground surface. For mobile pastoralists, the relationship between water and flow is opposite to that for societies practicing irrigation agriculture. Instead of channeling water to fields and households, transhumant pastoralists brought animals and households to water. Rather than annually supplying water to fixed amounts of territory, pastoral groups altered their residence patterns according to the environmental, social, and economic situation of a given year within changing territories. We might conceive of pastoral land use as a flow toward seasonal resources and seasonal water supplies.

Ethnographic studies provide the most direct evidence for patterns of entirely natural water use, as the use of relatively unmodified locations in the landscape is difficult to document from archaeological evidence. However, the archaeological study of pastoral landscapes can offer important information about small-scale water engineering projects undertaken by mobile pastoral populations in the past.

In southeastern Turkey, archaeological survey work has mapped suites of water harvesting and pasture improvement systems used by transhumant pastoralists of the last 600–700 years (Medieval Islamic and Ottoman periods), providing a case study concerning water manipulation schemes of mobile pastoralists as well as the effects of this water engineering on natural and cultural landscapes. These water harvesting and pasture improvement systems included cisterns, check dams, and cairns. All were small-scale, designed to collect seasonal surface water and keep rainfall distributed across the landscape at points where it would be most useful. The water and pasture improvement features were likely constructed and used by single households or small groups of households and required very little maintenance in order to continue functioning. The network of cisterns across the pastoral landscape may have grown in a piecemeal fashion. Despite (or perhaps because of) their small scale and low maintenance requirements, these features had an enduring impact on the landscape. The evidence for the impact of cisterns is particularly strong: their location in relationship to campsites and the characteristics of the cisterns themselves suggest that these features remained functional and effective over long periods of time, orienting and "anchoring" the camping and herding patterns of successive generations of transhumant pastoralists.

In addition to their long-term usefulness, the water and pasture improvement features constructed by pastoralists may have shaped cultural and natural landscapes because they served as markers of territory or land tenure. As full coverage survey revealed no evidence for sedentary inhabitation of the study area, the mobile pastoral groups who used the area probably only controlled the area seasonally. Ethnographically studied pastoralists in Iran struggled with gaining access to perennial water sources such as wells that they had previously used only seasonally, as these water sources were eventually enclosed by sedentary agricultural communities. However, the water and pasture improvement features studied in southeastern Turkey were not perennial water sources, but instead were only useful for collecting runoff and increasing soil moisture during the winter rainy season. Cisterns, check dams, and cairns were therefore not useful to other groups at other times during the year. Small-scale seasonally active water and pasture features such as these could have served as markers of permanence and seasonal return, both functionally and conceptually anchoring returning pastoral communities within their mobile landscape.

ACKNOWLEDGMENTS

The collection of data on mobile pastoral campsites and surrounding water features in southeastern Turkey was carried out under the Hirbemerdon Tepe Survey with the support of the General Directorate of Monuments and Museums of the Republic of Turkey and the Diyarbakır Museum. I would like to thank the survey director, Jason Ur, as well as Joshua Wright, both for the fieldwork that we carried out together and for productive conversations on a number of topics related to pastoralism and water. Funding for fieldwork and data analysis was generously provided by the U.S. National Science Foundation (BCS-1203140), the Wenner-Gren Foundation for Anthropological Research (Grant # 8411), the National Geographic Society (Grant # 8731-09), the American Research Institute in Turkey (U.S. Department of State, Education, and Cultural Affairs Fellowship), the American Schools of Oriental Research (Platt Fellowship), the Harvard University Graduate Society, and the Harvard University Department of Anthropology.

NOTES

1.   The length of ethnographically documented long-distance migration routes with sheep and goats varied in the Turkish Taurus and Iranian Zagros Mountains: Kurdish tribes in southeastern Turkey and western Iran such as the Beritanlı and Alikanlı, the Yörük, Lurs, and the Bakhtiari all followed migration routes of less than 200 kilometers in each direction, while the Basseri and Qashqā'i of southwestern Iran had migration routes longer than 250 kilometers (Digard 1981:13; Johnson 1969:160–161; Skogseid 1993). Some Qashqā'i subtribes migrated up to 600 kilometers each way (Beck 2003:294).

2.   As Cribb has noted (1991:137–138), ethnographers of mobile pastoral groups who claimed that water was not a major factor in camping patterns relied on their observations of pastoral groups during periods of the year where water was relatively abundant, and did not look at the whole annual picture.

3. Climatic models suggest that precipitation in the Diyarbakır region was within 2–4 percent of observed modern values over the last 700 years (Bryson and Bryson 1999), similar to conclusions reported long ago on the basis of Anatolian tree ring data (Hütteroth 2006).

4. The notion that water sources can be owned through occupation and intentional work seems tied to ideas in Ottoman and earlier Islamic and pre-Islamic law codes in the Middle East that dictate that people may gain ownership over "dead" lands by developing or restoring previous hydraulic installations such as irrigation canals (Lancaster and Lancaster 1999:131). Although improved water sources and collected water could be owned, Islamic law and Ottoman codes retain a "right of thirst," where people and animals may freely access running water, wells, and cisterns when survival is at stake, as long as they do not damage property (Lancaster and Lancaster 1999:130; Mallat 1995:129; Métral 1981:134).

REFERENCES CITED

Adams, R. M. 1978 Strategies of Maximization, Stability, and Resilience in Mesopotamian Society, Settlement, and Agriculture. *Proceedings of the American Philosophical Society* 122(5):329–335.

Amir-Moez, Y. 2002 The Qashqa'i. In *The Nomadic Peoples of Iran*, edited by R. Tapper and J. Thompson, pp. 190–251. Azimuth Editions, London.

Avni, G. 1996 Nomads, Farmers, and Town-Dwellers: Pastoral-Sedentarist Interaction in the Negev Highlands, Sixth-Eighth Centuries C.E. Israel Antiquities Authority, Jerusalem.

Barfield, T. J. 1993 *The Nomadic Alternative*. Prentice-Hall, Upper Saddle River, NJ.

Barth, F. 1964 *Nomads of South Persia; The Basseri Tribe of the Khamseh Confederacy*. Humanities Press, New York.

Bates, D. G. 1973 *Nomads and Farmers: A Study of the Yörük of Southeastern Turkey*. University of Michigan Press, Ann Arbor.

Beaumont, P., G. H. Blake, and J. M. Wagstaff. 1976 *The Middle East: A Geographical Study*. John Wiley, London.

Beck, L. 1991 *Nomad: A Year in the Life of a Qashqa'i Tribesman in Iran*. University of California Press, Berkeley.

Beck, L. 1998 Use of Land by Nomadic Pastoralists in Iran: 1970–1998. In *Transformations of Middle Eastern Natural Environments*, edited by J. Albert, M. Bernhardsson, and R. Kenna, pp. 58–80. Yale School of Forestry and Environmental Studies, J. Coppock and J. A. Miller, general editor. Yale University Press, New Haven, CT.

Beck, L. 2003 Qashqa'i Nomadic Pastoralists and Their Use of Land. In *Yeki Bud, Yeki Nabud: Essays on the Archaeology of Iran in Honor of William M. Sumner*, edited by N. F. Miller and K. Abdi, pp. 289–304. The Cotsen Institute of Archaeology; The American Institute of Iranian Studies; The University of Pennsylvania Museum of Archaeology and Anthropology, Los Angeles.

Beck, L., and J. Huang. 2011 Risk and Resilience among Contemporary Pastoralists in Southwestern Iran. In *Sustainable Lifeways: Cultural Persistence in an Ever-changing Environment*, edited by N. F. Miller, K. M. Moore, and K. Ryan, pp. 106–127. University of Pennsylvania Museum of Archaeology and Anthropology, Philadelphia.

Beckers, B., J. Berking, and B. Schütt. 2013 Ancient Water Harvesting Methods in the Drylands of the Mediterranean and Western Asia. *eTopoi* 2:145–164.

Beşikçi, İ. 1969 *Doğu'da Değişim ve Yapısal Sorunlar (Göçebe Alikan Aşireti)*. Sevinç Matbaası, Ankara.

Black-Michaud, J. 1986 *Sheep and Land: the Economics of Power in a Tribal Society*. Cambridge University Press, Cambridge.

Blaikie, P., and H. Brookfield. 1987 *Land Degradation and Society*. Methuen, New York.

Brookfield, H. 2001 *Exploring Agrodiversity*. Columbia University Press, New York.

Bruins, H. J. 1986 *Desert Environment and Agriculture in the Central Negev and Kadesh-Barnea during Historical Times*. MIDBAR Foundation, Nijkerk, The Netherlands.

Bryson, R. A., and R. U. Bryson. 1999 Holocene Climates of Anatolia: As Simulated with Archaeoclimatic Models. *Türikye Bilimler Akademisi Arkeoloji Dergisi* 2:1–14.

Chang, C., and H. A. Koster. 1986 Beyond Bones: Toward an Archaeology of Pastoralism. *Advances in Archaeological Method and Theory* 9:97–148.

Cole, D. P. 1975 *Nomads of the Nomads: the Al Murrah Bedouin of the Empty Quarter*. Aldine, Chicago.

Cribb, R. 1991 *Nomads in Archaeology*. Cambridge University Press, Cambridge.

Danti, M. 2000 Early Bronze Age Settlement and Land Use in the Tell es-Sweyhat Region, Syria. PhD dissertation, Department of Anthropology, University of Pennsylvania, Philadelphia.

Dennell, R. W. 1982 Dryland Agriculture and Soil Conservation: An Archaeological Study of Check-dam Farming and Wadi Siltation. In *Desertification and Development: Dryland Ecology in Social Perspective*, edited by B. Spooner and H. S. Mann, pp. 171–200. Academic Press, London.

Doolittle, W. E. 1984 Agricultural Change as an Incremental Process. *Annals of the Association of American Geographers* 74(1):124–137.

Erhan, S. 1997 An Historical Account of Identity Formation in Turkey: The Impact of Nomadism. In *Contrasts and Solutions in the Middle East*. Aarhus Universitet, Denmark.

Erickson, C., and J. Walker. 2009 Pre-Columbian Causeways and Canals as Landesque Capital. In *Landscapes of Movement: Trails, Paths, and Roads in Anthropological Perspective*, edited by J. Snead, C. Erickson, and A. Darling, pp. 232–252. University of Pennsylvania Press, Philadelphia.

Evenari, M., L. Shanan, and N. Tadmor. 1982 *The Negev: The Challenge of a Desert*. Harvard University Press, Cambridge.

Frödin, J. 1943 Les formes de la vie pastorale en Turquie. *Geografiska Annaler* XXV–XXVI:219–272.

Gündüz, T. 1997 *Anadolu'da Türkmen aşiretleri : Bozulus Türkmenleri, 1540–1640*. Bilge Yayınları, Kızılay, Ankara.

Hammer, E. 2012 Local Landscapes of Pastoral Nomads in Southeastern Turkey. PhD dissertation, Department of Anthropology, Harvard University, Cambridge.

Hammer, E. 2014 Local Landscape Organization of Mobile Pastoralists in Southeastern Turkey. *Journal of Anthropological Archaeology* 35:269–288.

Hammer, E., and R. Ackert. n.d., in prep Cosmogenic 36Cl Dating of Limestone Cisterns in Southeastern Turkey.

Hammer, E., and B. S. Arbuckle. 2017 10,000 Years of Pastoralism in Anatolia: A Review of Evidence for Variability in Pastoral Lifeways. *Nomadic Peoples* 21(2):214–267.

Hole, F. 2004 Campsites of the Seasonally Mobile in Western Iran. In *From Handaxe to Khan: Essays presented to Peder Mortensen on the Occasion of His 70th birthday*, edited by K. v. Folsach, H. Thrane, and I. Thuesen. Aarhus University Press, Oakville, CT.

Hole, F. 2007 Agricultural Sustainability in the Semi-Arid Near East. *Climate of the Past* 3:193–203.

Horne, L. 1980 Dryland Settlement Location: Social and Natural Factors in the Distribution of Settlements in Turan. *Expedition* 22(4):11–17.

Horne, L. 1994 *Village Spaces: Settlement and Society in Northeastern Iran*. Smithsonian Series in Archaeological Inquiry. Smithsonian Institution Press, Washington, DC.

Hütteroth, W.-D. 1959 *Bergnomaden und Yaylabauern im mittleren kurdischen Taurus*. Selbstverlag des Geographischen Institutes der Universität Marburg, Marburg.

Hütteroth, W.-D. 2006 Ecology of the Ottoman Lands. In *The Cambridge History of Turkey: Volume 3: The Later Ottoman Empire, 1603–1839*, edited by S. Faroqhi, pp. 18–43. Cambridge University Press, Cambridge.

Irons, W. 1975 *The Yomut Turkmen: A Study of Social Organization among a Central Asian Turkic-Speaking Population*. Anthropological papers; no. 58. University of Michigan, Ann Arbor.

Johnson, D. L. 1969 The Nature of Nomadism: A Comparative Study of Pastoral Migrations in Southwestern Asia and Northern Africa. MA Thesis, Department of Geography, University of Chicago, Chicago.

Jongerden, J. 2007 *The Settlement Issue in Turkey and the Kurds: An Analysis of Spatial Policies, Modernity, and War*. Brill, Leiden.

Kasaba, R. 2009 *A Moveable Empire: Ottoman Nomads, Migrants, and Refugees*. Studies in Modernity and National Identity. University of Washington Press, Seattle.

Lancaster, W., and F. Lancaster. 1999 *People, Land, and Water in the Arab Middle East. Environments and Landscapes in the Bilad ash-Sham*. Harwood Academic Publishers, Amsterdam.

Ludwig, W. 1970 Die Grabung auf dem Tell Habuba Kabira: die Bauwerk. *Mitteilungen Deutsches-Orient Gesellschaft* 102:37–41.

Mallat, C. 1995 The Quest for Water Use Principles: Reflections on Shari'a and Custom in the Middle East. In *Water in the Middle East: Legal, Political, and Commerical Implications*, edited by J. A. Allan and C. Mallat, pp. 127–137. I. B. Tauris Publishers, London.

Marston, J. M. 2011 Archaeological Markers of Agricultural Risk Management. *Journal of Anthropological Archaeology* 30:190–205.

Marx, E. 1977 The Tribe as a Unit of Subsistence: Nomadic Pastoralism in the Middle East. *American Anthropologist* 79:343–363.

McGlade, J. 1999 Archaeology and Evolution of Cultural Landscapes: Towards an Interdisciplinary Research Agenda. In *The Archaeology and Anthropology of Landscape*, edited by P. J. Ucko and R. J. Layton, pp. 458–482. Routledge, London.

Métral, F. 1981 Le droit de l'eau dans le code civil ottoman de 1869 et la notion de domaine public. In *L'homme et l'eau en Mediterranée et au Proche Orient II, Aménagements hydrauliques*, pp. 125–142. Travaux de la Maison de L'Orient. Maison de l'Orient : Presses universitaires de Lyon, Lyon.

Miller, R. 1980 Water Use in Syria and Palestine from the Neolithic to the Bronze Age. *World Archaeology* 11(3):331–341.

Musil, A. 1928 *The Manners and Customs of the Rwala Bedouins*. The American Geographical Society, New York.

Peacock, A. C. S. 2010 *Early Seljuq History: A New Interpretation*. Routledge Studies in the History of Iran and Turkey. Routledge, London.

Roe, E., L. Huntsinger, and K. Labnow. 1998 High Reliability Pastoralism. *Journal of Arid Environments* 39:39–55.

Rosen, S. A. 1987 Byzantine Nomadism in the Negev: Results from the Emergency Survey. *Journal of Field Archaeology* 14(1):29–42.

Rowton, M. 1974 Enclosed Nomadism. *Journal of Economic and Social History of the Orient* 17:1–30.

Şahin, İ. 2006 *Osmanlı döneminde konar-göçerler: incelemeler, araştırmalar*. Eren, İstanbul.

Salamé, M. 1955 L'elevage au Liban. *Revue de Géographie de Lyon* 30:81–101.

Skogseid, H. 1993 Nomadic Pastoralism and Land Use Patterns in Eastern Turkey: The Case of the Kurdish Beritan Tribe. In *The Middle East—Unity and Diversity: Papers from the Second Nordic Conference on Middle Eastern Studies, Copenhagen 22–25 October 1992*, edited by H. Palva and K. S. Vikør, pp. 216–231. Nordic proceedings in Asian studies, no. 5. NIAS Books, Copenhagen.

Sümer (Demirtaş), F. 1949 Bozulus Hakkında. *Ankara Üniversitesi Dil ve Tarih-Coğrafya Fakültesi Dergisi* 7(1):29–60.

Tapper, R. 1979 *Pasture and Politics: Economics, Conflict, and Ritual among Shahsevan Nomads of Northwestern Iran*. Academic Press, London.

Tapper, R. 1997 *Frontier Nomads of Iran: A Political and Social History of the Shahsevan*. Cambridge University Press, Cambridge.

Ur, J. A., and E. L. Hammer. 2009 Pastoral Nomads of the Second and Third Millennia A.D. on the Upper Tigris River, SE Turkey: Archaeological Evidence from the Hirbemerdon Tepe Survey. *Journal of Field Archaeology* 34(1):37–56.

van Bruinessen, M. 1988 The Population of Diyarbekir: Ethnic Composition and other Demographic Data. In *Evliyā Çelebi in Diyarbekir. Evliya Çelebi's Book of Travels: Land and People of the Ottoman Empire in the Seventeenth Century Volume I*, edited by M. van Bruinessen and H. Boeschoten, pp. 29–35. E. J. Brill, Leiden.

van Bruinessen, M. 1992 *Agha, Shaikh, and State: The Social and Political Structures of Kurdistan*. Zed Books, London.

Vetter, T., A-K. Rieger, and H. Möller. 2013 Water, Routes, and Rangelands: Ancient Traffic and Grazing Infrastructure in the Eastern Marmarica (Northwestern Egypt). In *Desert Road Archaeology in Ancient Egypt and Beyond*, edited by F. Förster and H. Riemer, pp. 455–484, Africa Praehistorica 27. Heinrich-Barth-Institut, Köln.

Wehling, K. 1992 Vorder Orient: Nomadismus und andere Formen der Wanderviehwirtschaft (Middle East: Nomadism and other Forms of Pastoral Migration). In *Beihefte zum Tübinger Atlas des Vorderen Orients. Reihe B, Geisteswissenschaften*. L. Reichert, Wiesbaden.

Wilkinson, T. J. 1982 The Definition of Ancient Manured Zones by Means of Extensive Sherd-Sampling Techniques. *Journal of Field Archaeology* 9:323–333.

Wilkinson, T. J. 1994 The Structure and Dynamics of Dry-Farming States in Upper Mesopotamia. *Current Anthropology* 35(5):483–520.

Wilkinson, T. J. 2003 *Archaeological Landscapes of the Near East*. University of Arizona, Tucson.

Woods, J. E. 1999 *The Aqquyunlu: Clan, Confederation, Empire*. 2nd ed. University of Utah Press, Salt Lake City.

CHAPTER FIVE

Water and Workshops

Inequality among Mining Sites in Ancient Laurion (Greece)

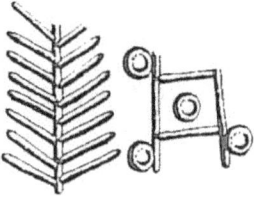

Kim Van Liefferinge

Abstract *The archaeological remains of the Athenian silver industry in the Laurion (Attica, Greece) offer a unique opportunity to study power relations among mining sites. The silver mines were exploited from the late Neolithic (4200–3100 BCE) until modern times, with a peak in the Classical period (480–323 BCE). This last phase in particular left dramatic traces in the landscape: industrial features, such as mine shafts, spoil heaps, and ore-washing workshops, were scattered throughout the Laurion. Among these remains, ore-washing workshops are the most noteworthy features. Their function became increasingly important as exploitation continued and rich ore deposits became depleted. Washeries facilitated the use of low-grade ores in silver production. However, they also confronted the miners with an environmental constraint: washeries were water-consuming installations in an area that was virtually waterless. This issue triggered the development of well-organized water management, dependent on rainwater harvesting in cisterns. The distribution of workshops in the Laurion valleys suggests that the competition for appropriate water catchments was fierce, causing both regional and local inequalities between sites. This paper explores how differential access to water sources in the Laurion contributed to such inequalities by performing hydrological analyses on water availability and the water use of workshops.*

INTRODUCTION

The Laurion, located in the southeast of Attica in Greece, was an area of great interest throughout Antiquity (Figure 5.1). Attractive for its silver resources, the region was exploited from at least the late Neolithic (4200–3100 BCE) until late Roman times

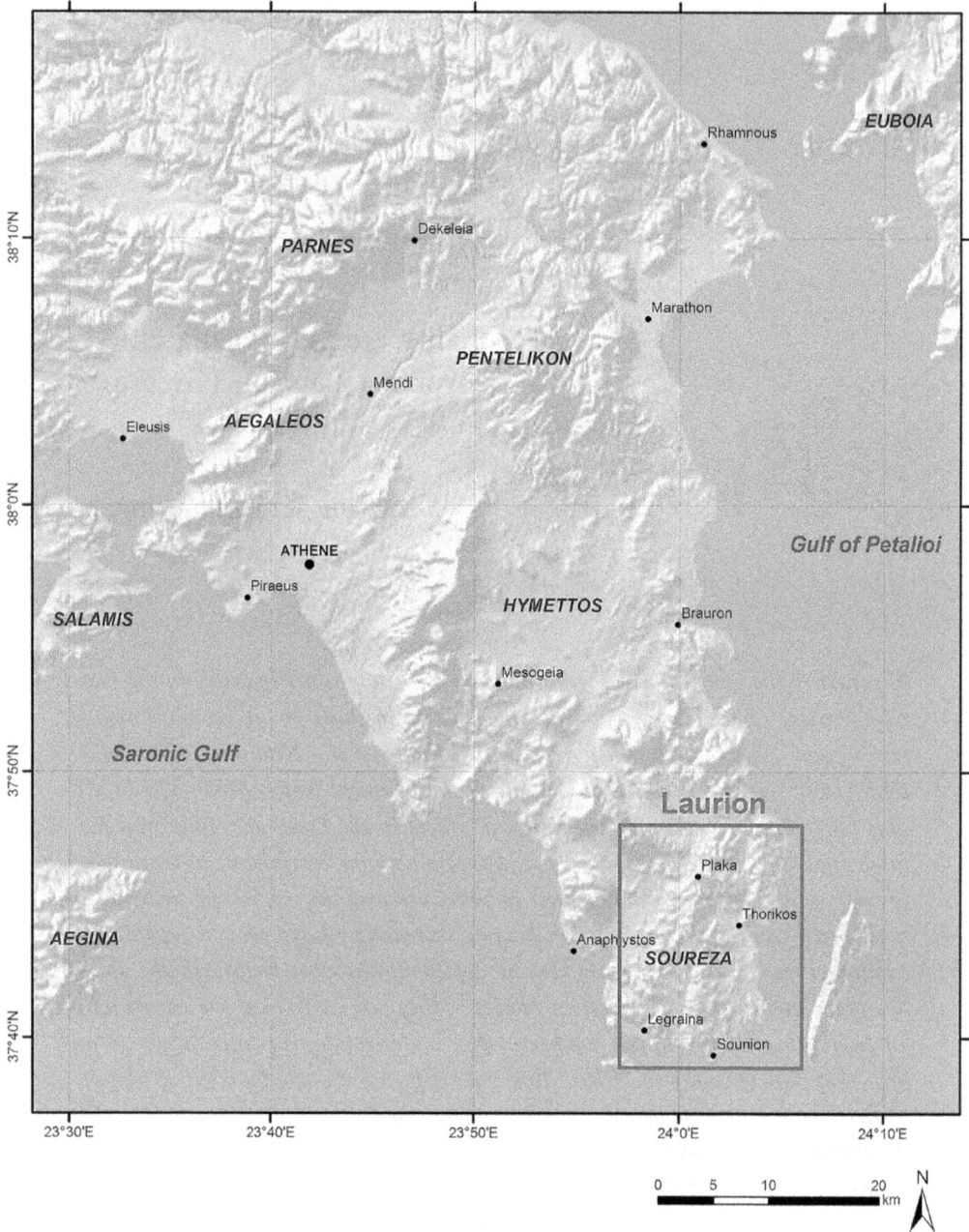

Figure 5.1 Map of Attica and the Laurion (Map by C. Stal; Van Liefferinge et al. 2014, fig. 1).

(fifth century), with a clear peak in the Classical period (480–323 BCE). This boost in mining was affected by political and economic events such as the introduction of coinage in Athens (mid-sixth century BCE),[1] the Persian wars (early fifth century BCE) and direct interference by the city-state of Athens.[2] As a result the Laurion was scattered with metallurgical features including spoil heaps, mine shafts and ore-processing workshops.

The-last mentioned features attract especial attention in the landscape. Ore-processing workshops were elaborate facilities that contained workspaces—with a washery, cisterns, storage areas, and rooms to crush and grind ores—as well as living quarters for the workers and workshop owners. Their purpose was to process and purify low-grade silver ores in the specially designed washeries.

The ore-processing procedure relied on the relative masses of different particles within the ore: because the silver was heavier than any impurities, the two could be separated by means of water. First, water was fed into the washery (Figure 5.2) from the main reservoir (Δ) through a fixed number of nozzles. Subsequently, the water flowed into a series of channels (A_1, A_2, A_3, A_4) and settling tanks (B_1, B_2, B_3). By the time it arrived in the last settling tank the water was virtually clean and ready to be reused. There is a hot debate about the specific execution of this process,[3] but scholars generally agree that the purification of silver ore took place on area E by means of either wooden scrapers (Negris 1881) or washing boards (Conophagos 1980), whereas the channels and settling tank were principally meant for the purification of water.

The layout and structure of ore washeries indicate an important environmental constraint with which metallurgists struggled: water scarcity. The climate of Classical Greece is thought to resemble the current one, with a similar annual variability in rainfall and temperature.[4] This would imply a semiarid climate, with hot and dry summers, short and

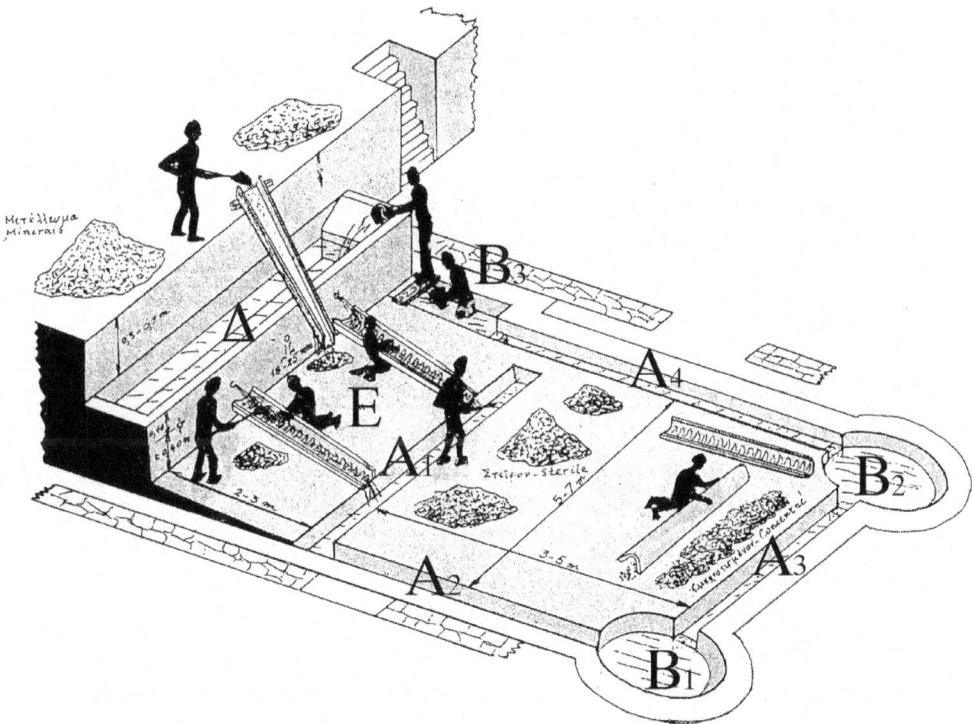

FIGURE 5.2 The purification of ore in a washery according to Conophagos (1980) (Trikkalinos 1978, fig. 8).

wet winters, and low annual rainfall rates for Attica of less than 400 m³ (Foxhall 2007). These conditions were a problem for the mining industry. Conophagos (1980:246–250) calculated that a typical four-nozzle washery used no less than 19.5 m³ water per month. Within this context, it is not surprising to see ore-processing workshops accompanied by large cisterns, and located at strategic positions facilitating the harvest of surface runoff.

It is fair to say that water availability was one of the most crucial determinants of the operation of workshops. The less water metallurgists had, the less ore they could process and, eventually, the less silver they could produce. It can be hypothesized that local and regional differences in water availability influenced the relative success of competing workshops, leading to inequality between them. These issues will be investigated through hydrological analyses of the water availability and water use of workshops located in two different areas of the Laurion, more specifically (1) the coastal area of Adami and Potami and (2) the central Laurion valleys.

Methods

Because this paper is an elaboration of a study published in *Journal of Archaeological Science* (2014), only a brief summary of the actual analyses will be provided here. This paper focuses primarily on the application of these analyses, described in the following section.

The main water source for ore-dressing workshops was rainwater, collected in cisterns from surface runoff (i.e., water that did not permeate the soil, but rather ran off the hillslopes). This allows the exploration of water management strategies through an analysis of runoff water accumulation and routing using the ArcGis software suite. In order to perform such an analysis, a digital elevation model (DEM) and a rainfall time series are required. The DEM used here was derived from topographical maps with a scale of 1:5000,[5] allowing a grid resolution of 11.6 m. The results of this analysis for the coastal and central Laurion regions can be seen in Figures 5.3a and 5.3b. The volume of water running off the hill to a certain point is called the "contributing area," defined by the number of pixels flowing to a specific point on the map. Darker colors indicate a higher number of pixels and therefore a higher concentration of water passing through a given point. The rainfall time series is a recent one taken from the rain gauge in Athens and showing a typical climatological pattern.[6]

The contribution area and rainfall time series can then be combined to compute a water balance model. This basic hydrological model allows one to calculate the change in volume of a reservoir for a given amount of time, taking into account the inflow rate and the water removed from the cistern. The inflow rate is determined by the surface runoff passing through the local inlet of the cistern. Its value can be derived from the pixel value of the contribution area. For the most part, a cistern's local inlet was an artificial channel tapping an ephemeral gully. Water can be removed from the cistern either through evaporation or for operational purposes. Since cisterns were roofed, it can be assumed that the amount of water lost through evaporation was virtually zero, meaning any water removed would have been for operational purposes. As mentioned above, Conophagos (1980:249) calculated operational water removal rate to be no less than 20 m³/month, based on a 12-hour workday. Another parameter that must be taken

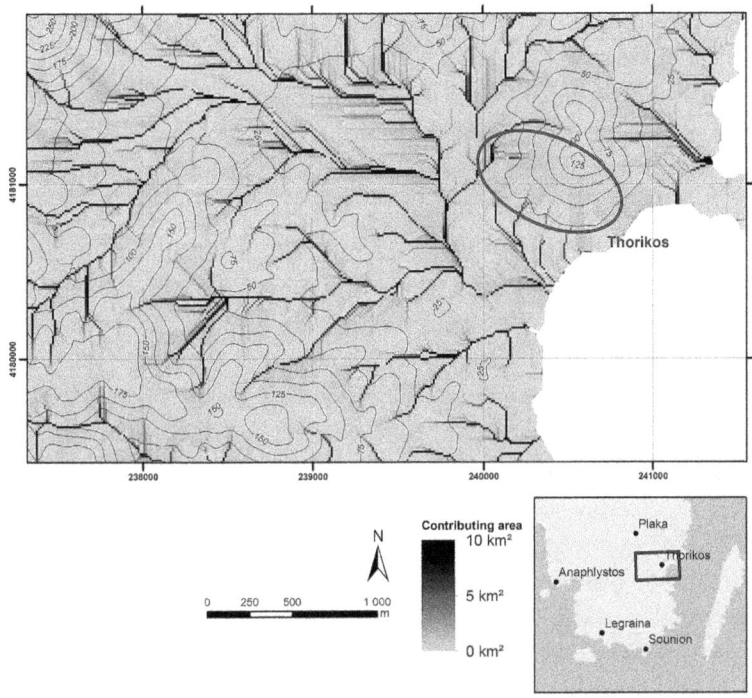

FIGURE 5.3A Contributing area map of the Thorikos region (Map by C. Stal, M. van den Berg, M. and K. Van Liefferinge; Van Lieffeiringe et al. 2014, fig. 3).

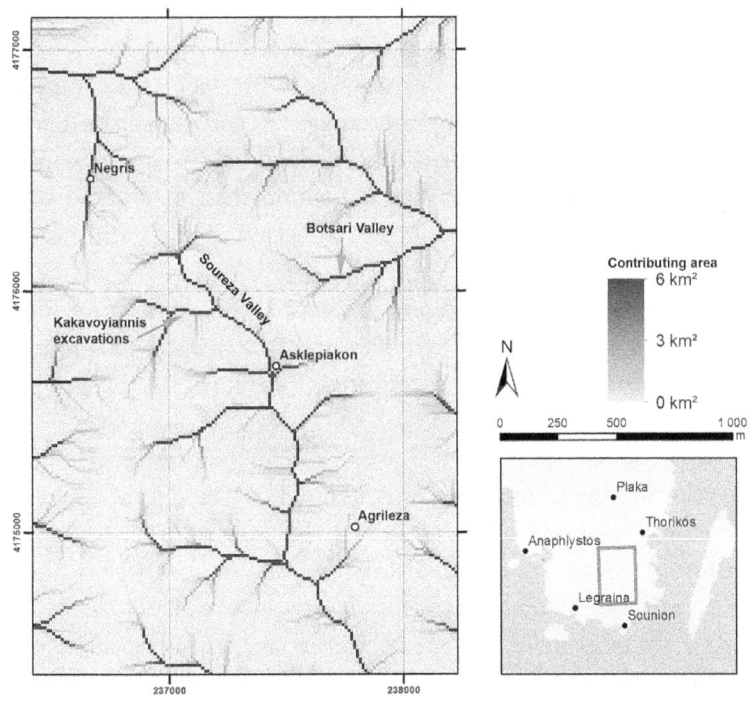

FIGURE 5.3B Contributing area map of the Laurion heartland (Map by C. Stal, M. van den Berg and K. Van Liefferinge).

into account is the capacity of the cistern. These reservoirs are generally round in shape and have average volumes of 100 to 1,000 m^3 (Conophagos 1980:253). Determining a cistern's volume is often difficult because cisterns found in the Laurion are not always entirely cleared during their excavation. Those that are, however, have an average depth between 4.5 and 5.5 m,[7] making it is reasonable to apply a 5 m depth to unexcavated cisterns in these analyses.

This analytical framework enables the estimation of not only how much water was available for ore washing, but also the percentage of time a washery would have failed to operate due to drought. This information becomes especially interesting when stepping out of a single workshop and taking the wider industrial area into account. When used carefully, it allows one to determine regional differences in the operability of workshops, and therefore to determine which areas were more or less successful for ore processing.

CASE STUDIES

The analyses compare two distinct areas in the Laurion, for which there are good excavational or survey data. First, I discuss the coastal area of the Adami and Potami plain, with the site of Thorikos as the main case study. Second, I explore the Laurion heartland, focusing specifically on the Agrileza, Asklepiakon, and Negris workshops.

ADAMI AND POTAMI PLAIN: THORIKOS (FIGURE 5.4)

Thorikos is undoubtedly the most eye-catching site in the Adami and Potami area. The site is strategically located on the two-peaked Velatouri Hill, next to the natural harbors of Porto Mandri and Franko Limani. On the lower south slope of the hill intensive excavations have been undertaken, revealing the remains of an Archaic to Early Hellenistic settlement. Nowadays the site is divided into the so-called Theatre Zone and Industrial Quarter. Multiple workshops have been located within these zones, and cluster in three complexes (Mussche 1998:56): the first area A is located in the Industrial Quarter with Mine no. 2 as its focal point. The second area B is situated west of the theatre with workshops processing ores from Mine no. 3. The data on Area C are limited because it was badly disrupted by the mining activities of *La Compagnie Française des Mines du Laurion* in the nineteenth and twentieth centuries. Therefore, this paper will focus solely on Area A and B.

In Area A, five washeries (W1, 2, 3, 12, 13) and four cisterns (C1, 2, 3, 4) have been recorded. Two of the cisterns are underground, bottle-shaped reservoirs (C2 and 3), used for domestic purposes and situated on the courtyard of Insula 2. This house incorporates a former spring, starting as a deeply eroded fault surface in the marble outcropping in the rear end of room DR. This space was probably a small shrine making use of the spring water, as indicated by the *gourna* and the niche in its northern wall. From here a large and deeply eroded fracture passes through the full length of the insula, connecting the two cisterns on the courtyard. The cisterns were partly cleared during the excavation of the insula but their volumes remain unknown.

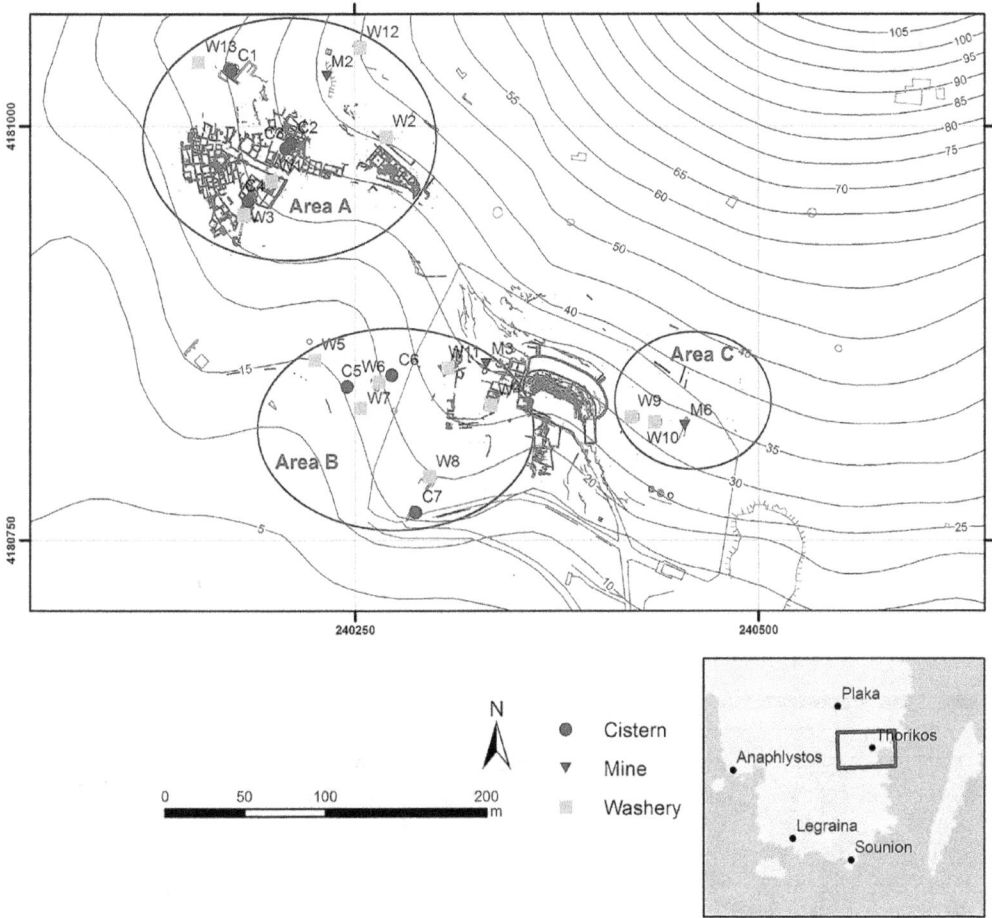

FIGURE 5.4 The metallurgy complexes (A-B-C) in Thorikos (Map by C. Stal and K. Van Liefferinge; Van Liefferinge et al. 2014, fig. 6).

The remaining cisterns in Area A are industrial reservoirs belonging to metallurgical workshops. The Cistern no. 1 workshop contains Thorikos's largest water reservoir (Van Liefferinge et al. 2011; Figure 5.5 on page 96, left). The 209 m³ cistern is situated immediately northwest of the Industrial Quarter. The cistern is partly hewn into the surrounding rock and partly built up with massive walls, giving it the strength to retain the enormous water pressure. The cistern's basin has a quadrilateral shape (with sides 9 m, 4.5 m, 7.5 m, and 5.5 m long, respectively) adjoining a small, higher zone of which the rocky underground was left unadjusted (B). This smaller area likely fulfilled several purposes: from it water could be raised more easily out of the cistern when it was not entirely full, and it could also add to the cistern's capacity in case of a higher water level. West of the cistern are a flattened working platform (C), a crushing area (D), and Washery no. 13 (E). Since this washery is not cleared, the number of nozzles cannot be determined. On the east side of the cistern are several notably organized curved walls

THORIKOS
Cistern no.1 Workshop

Crushing table
D

Washery no.13
E

Working
platform
C

A

B

F

Cistern no.1

0 3 6 12 meter

Waterproof area

THORIKOS
Washery no.1 Workshop

AX

AQ

AS

A

AU

AP

BG

AT

AD

Washery no.1

BF

BE

BD

BA

BC

AG

BL

BN

BEs

AL

AF

AE

AC

AA

BM

BO

AN

AM

AI

AH

AB

CA

BP

AJ

KB

KC

Cistern no.4

AO

KF

KE

KD

KN

Washery no.3

KO

KG

KK

0 3 6 12 meter

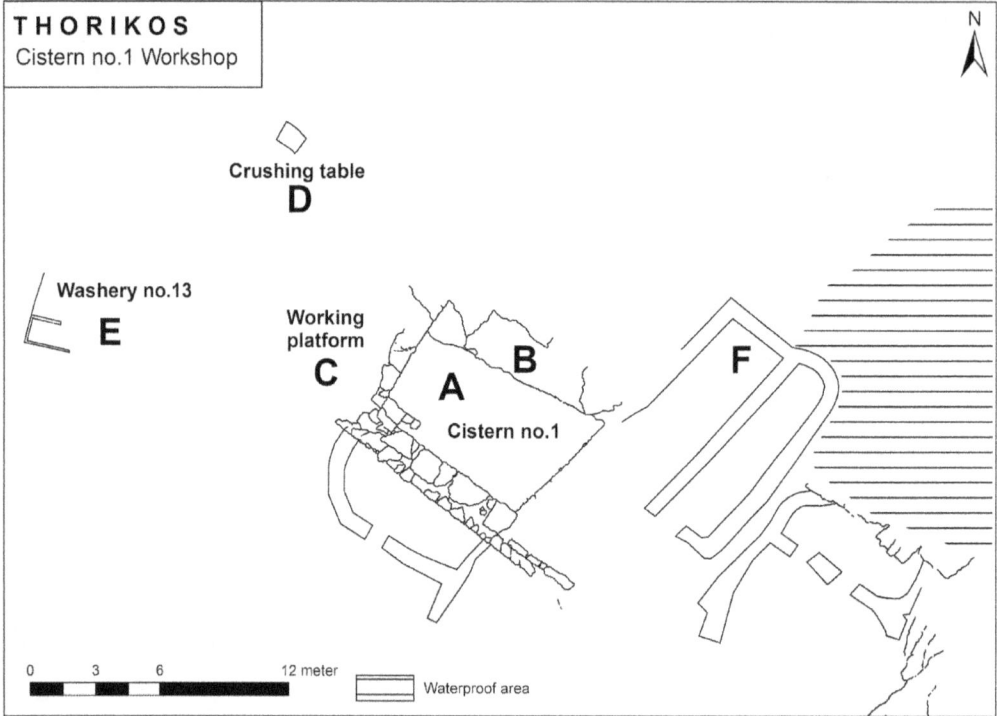

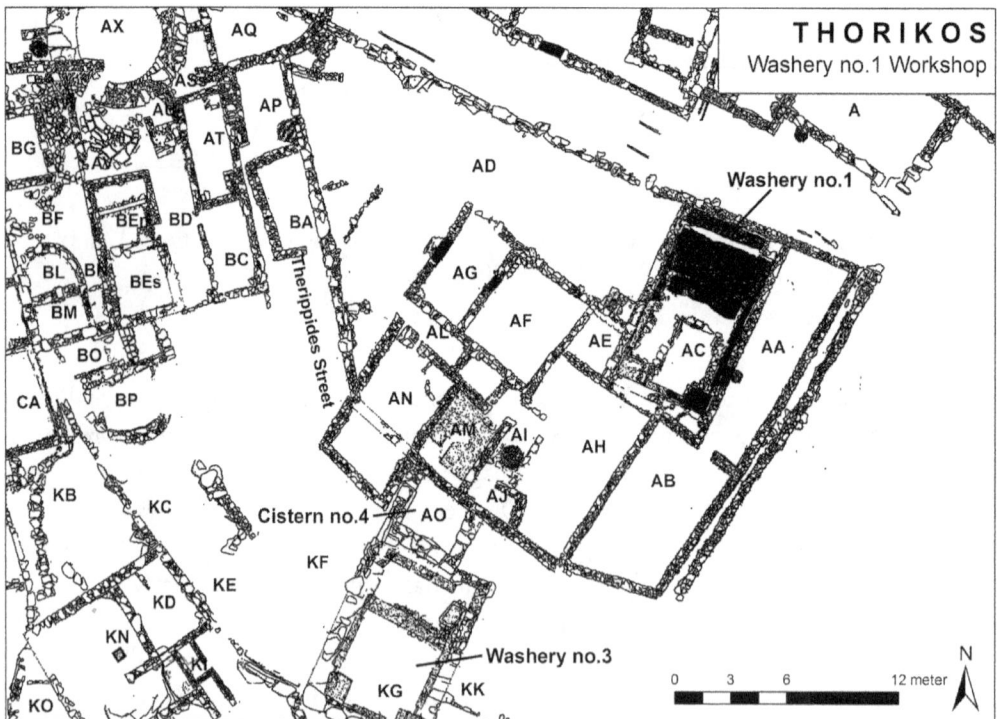

FIGURE 5.5 The Cistern no. 1 and Washery no. 1 Workshop in the Industrial Quarter, Thorikos. (After Van Liefferinge et al. 2014, fig. 7).

(F) that probably played a role in water harvesting. Linked to these walls is a large waterproof area, free of structures and fractures in the rocky underground.

The second workshop, which contains Washery no. 1 (Figure 5.5, right), is situated in the center of the Industrial Quarter (Mussche 1967:47–62, 1968, 1998:50–1). It was installed into an older residential building during the last quarter of the fifth century BCE. Besides a large courtyard, this workshop's insula contained living quarters such as a bathroom, dormitories, and a kitchen, as well as working areas. Washery no. 1 has modest dimensions (5.3 × 10.3 m) and a reservoir allowing space for four nozzles (Conophagos 1980:247). The workshop has a remarkably small cistern (no. 4) of 18 m³ at its disposal, built immediately south of the workshop, in the corner of AM and AN. The basin has a semirectangular shape (2.50 – 2.75 m × 3.00 m; depth 2.24 m) and would have collected water from the roof of the workshop. When Washery no. 1 fell out of use, Cistern no. 4 remained in use by another washery (no. 3) built against its south wall. This construction, together with the construction of rooms AQ, AP, and BA, shut off the Therippides Street, thus drastically changing traffic patterns in the Industrial Quarter (Mussche 1998:53–54).

Area B is virtually unexcavated, but several clear features can be recognized (see also Figure 5.4). The current state of research recognizes five washeries (W4, 5, 6, 7, 8, and 11) and three cisterns (C5, 6, 7). Several of these washeries and cisterns were grouped in the southwestern end of this complex: Cistern no. 6 is of the same type as the cistern found in Insula 2. Cisterns no. 5 and 7 are industrial water reservoirs, rectangular in shape and measuring 4 × 6 m. If their depth is assumed to have been 5 m, which is the average depth of Laurion cisterns, then their volume would have been approximately 120 m³. Given their locations, it could be that Cistern no. 5 was providing water to Washery no. 6 and 7, and Cistern no. 7 to Washery no. 8. Due to later disturbances and the current overgrowth, it remains unclear how the remaining washeries (no. 4, 5, and 11) organized their water supply.

Although the contributing area map of the lower slopes of the Velatouri gives somewhat different results for Areas A and B (Figure 5.6 on page 98), they have three things in common. First, rainwater harvesting depended on nonconcentrated surface runoff (i.e., runoff that flows overland as sheet flow and not through little streams). As a corollary, workshops took care of their water supply individually, relying mainly on microcatchments. Second, water availability through rainwater harvesting was low, the only exception being the southwest part of complex B. Third and most importantly, most cisterns were not erected near the most favorable water catchments of the Velatouri. This is shown by the particularly low pixel values on the contribution area map.

The water balance model seems to further confirm these trends. On the following diagram (Figure 5.7 on page 99), washery performance with respect to drought and over-use is shown as a function of the number of nozzles. The graphs also compare yearlong use (solid lines) with seasonal use from September until March (dotted lines), which are the wettest months of the year.

Starting with Area A, Cistern no. 1 has a catchment of 6 px or 864 m² on the contributing area map. The water balance model shows that Cistern no. 1 was able to serve

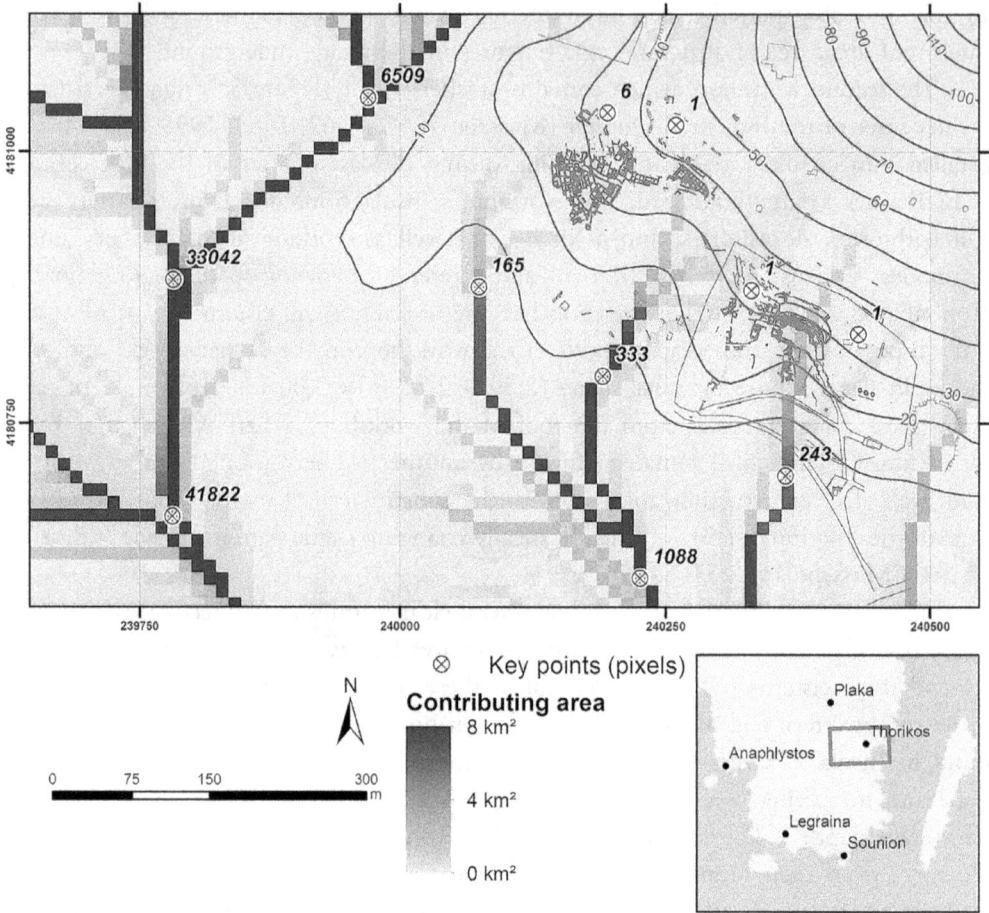

Figure 5.6 Detail of the contributing area map, showing the site of Thorikos (Map by Stal. C., van den Berg, M. and Van Liefferinge K.; Van Liefferinge et al. 2014, fig. 8).

a single four-nozzle washery throughout the year without issues, but that it would not have had any surplus water for other activities or serve as a buffer against drought. The dotted line, however, shows that a surplus would have been present during seasonable use.

For Cistern no. 4, which was significantly smaller (18 m³) and had only the roof as its catchment, the results are much less promising. Even when serving the bare minimum number of washery nozzles, this cistern's workshop would not have been able to operate continuously throughout the year. Its performance would have improved slightly during the rainy season, but even that would not have made up for the cistern's tiny capacity and water supply.

Continuing to Area B, we are confronted with a more ambiguous situation. The area southwest is one of the most favorable catchments of this zone. Cistern no. 5 collected water accumulating in a small stream and, with a catchment area of 116 px, would have been able to serve a six-nozzle washery the entire year through. During seasonal use,

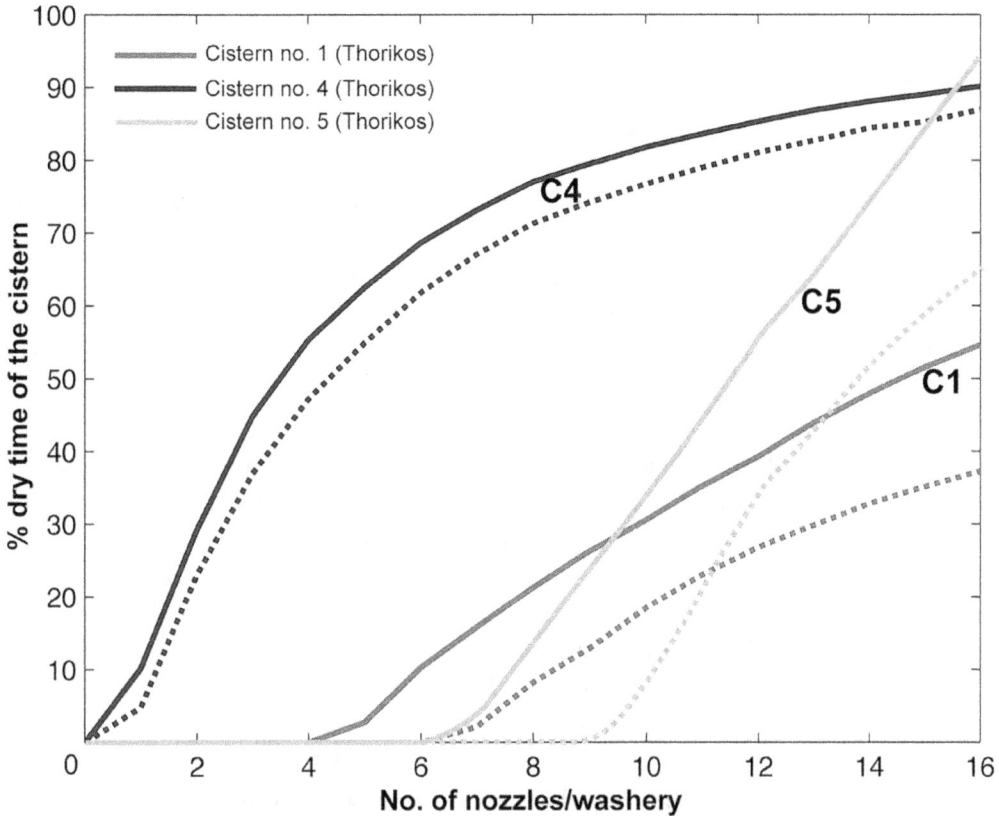

FIGURE 5.7 Water balance model of the Thorikos cisterns. The graph represents the percentage of the cistern's dry time in relation to the number of nozzles/washery. The full gray curve shows the washery's use during the full time series and the dotted lines the seasonal washery use from September until March (Graph by M. van den Berg and K. Van Liefferinge).

it would have been able to provide two average-sized four-nozzle washeries. Therefore, it becomes plausible that Cistern no. 5 was responsible for the two washeries located directly next to it, more specifically Washeries 6 and 7.

For Cistern no. 7 there are not enough data available to draw definitive conclusions, but some suggestions can be made. The cistern is located on a hillcrest, which would have hampered the collection of surface runoff at this specific location. This is shown by the low pixel values in the water balance model, which range from 1 to 2. A similar observation can be made about the workshops of Washeries no. 4 and 11.

These results are surprising for an industry so heavily dependent on water. In order to better understand these issues, it is helpful to examine other factors such as Thorikos's settlement history. A crucial evolution at the site was its transition from a markedly residential area in the fifth century BCE to an industrial one in the following century (Mussche 1998:64). The present archaeological evidence reveals two trends: workshops

were either incorporated in older houses (e.g., Washeries no. 1, 3, 4, and 11) or constructed along the borders of the former residential nucleus (e.g., Washeries no. 5, 6,
7, 13). The availability of existing infrastructure could therefore be the most vital factor
determining workshop location. Using old structures in the erection of a new workshop
would have been a double-edged sword: on the one hand, it would have required less
effort and resources; on the other hand, it would have introduced significant interference
with the workshop's water supply.

This becomes especially clear when looking more closely at the entirely excavated
Washery no. 1 workshop. Hydrological analyses reveal issues with water availability, but
do not explain the motives behind the workshop's water management. In all likelihood,
the occupants' decisions were purely the result of local conditions. As mentioned, the
workshop was installed into a residential building within a heavily built-up area, which
would have hindered the regulation of its water supply. Cistern no. 4 was built when
the Therippides Street, running along the southwestern end of the workshop (see Figure
5.5), was still in use. This created only a small amount of space for a cistern, which
explains its small size. Later, the street was shut off completely by the construction of
rooms AQ, AP, BA, and Washery no. 3. Besides these impediments, the harvesting of
surface runoff was further restricted because the workshop's only catchment was its roof.
Although the water it collected would have been sufficient to support domestic needs,
it cannot meet the demand created by metallurgical activities.

Given these circumstances, we could consider the possibility of seasonal metallurgical
activities at Thorikos and perhaps also the surrounding area. Unfortunately, there are only
brief excavation reports of the workshops in this region, rendering hydrological analyses
impossible. Nevertheless, more general conclusions about their water supply are feasible.
The *ergasteria* in this region present the typical features of ore-processing workshops,
incorporating both living and working quarters. Just as in Thorikos, the cisterns are few
and small (Oikonomakou 1996:140) and washeries have small to average capacities of
three to four nozzles. Also, they seem to have been dealing with their water management
independently from one another. Most of the workshops, however, seem to have had
a rather heterogeneous water supply. The Euthydike site (Oikonomakou 1991:66–69;
1997:87–88), located on the foot of the hills facing the Velatouri, had a workshop with
four small washeries, all supplied by wells. The nearby Kavodokano workshop (Oikonomakou 1996a:133–139; 1996b:65) incorporated two average-sized washeries supplied
by a well and a small cistern (ground surface 6.5 × 5 m). The cistern was different
from most others in the Laurion, in the sense that its bottom part was not carved out
into the rock, thus drastically limiting its capacity. On the other side of the plain in
the Potami valley bed, the Zoridis workshop (Zoridos 1980:75–84) contains two small
three-nozzle washeries but no cisterns. It seems that this workshop relied on the Potami
stream flowing through this valley. It is unclear whether this stream flowed seasonally
or year-round. Today it is completely dry, but nineteenth-century maps of Curtius and
Kaupert (1889) suggest that a copious amount of water used to flow through it. Further
west, the Skitzeri workshops (Oikonomakou 1996a:125–132) contain two washeries (A
and T), accompanied by two small cisterns. Washery A's cistern was destroyed during

Roman times and cannot be accurately measured; Washery T's cistern measures 5.7 × 5.7 m. This workshop's domestic water supply relied on an elaborate system of drains and basins that caught water from its roof. Given the position of Washery T's cistern in the heart of the workshop, it is likely that a similar water catchment was used for the industrial reservoir as well.

Apart from a heterogeneous water supply, the archaeological evidence points to a diverse pattern of activities. Philokrates, the owner of the Kavodokano workshop, was known to have been involved in affairs other than silver processing, such as beekeeping (Oikonomakou 1991:68). Furthermore, grain mills were encountered in the Euthydike workshop, suggesting that agriculture and metallurgy were performed side by side. This image is further backed up by observations from Salliora-Oikonomakou (2004:123–126) and Lohman (1993), which point to evidence of farms in this area. In sharp contrast to the central Laurion valleys, farming would have been feasible in the Adami and Potami area because of fertile alluvial deposits. Also, the harbor of Thorikos created many business opportunities beyond agricultural ones. This evidence, together with the small cistern sizes and low water availability at Thorikos, make the possibility of seasonal mining and agricultural activities a likely scenario.

THE LAURION HEARTLAND

The Laurion heartland presents a crucially different image than the Adami and Potami plain. The amount of archaeological remains in the central Laurion valleys is overwhelming. This is neatly illustrated by a survey performed in the Soureza Valley by Petropoulakou and Pedazou (1973), indicating no less than 60 to 70 cisterns. The most remarkable features in the valleys are related to water supply. Surface runoff was harvested in large cisterns according to two methods: the first is a central water catching and distribution system, built by a group of workshops alongside ephemeral gullies, which are consolidated with waterproof mortar. Cisterns tapped these gullies through artificial supply channels that led to decantation basins. Evidence of this method is clearly visible in the excavations of Kakavoyiannis in a side-branch of the Soureza Valley. Mining engineer E. Ardaillon (1897) demonstrated that this method was also applied in the nearby Botsari valley (Figure 5.8 on page 102), which is now incorporated in a military domain inaccessible to the public (Figure 5.9 on page 102). His map shows a central supply channel with side branches, around which dozens of workshops cluster. The second method was to use microcatchments, a technique used by individual workshops. The case studies of the Asklepiakon, Compound C, and Negris workshops present examples of both techniques.

COMPOUND C, AGRILEZA VALLEY (FIGURE 5.10, ON PAGE 103)

The Agrileza valley is divided into Lower- and Upper-Agrileza. Lower-Agrileza lends itself to agriculture because of alluvial deposits, whereas the steep slopes in the upper valley are exquisite places to harvest water. Not incidentally, most metallurgy workshops are situated in the upper branches. Between 1977 and 1983 J. Ellis Jones executed five exca-

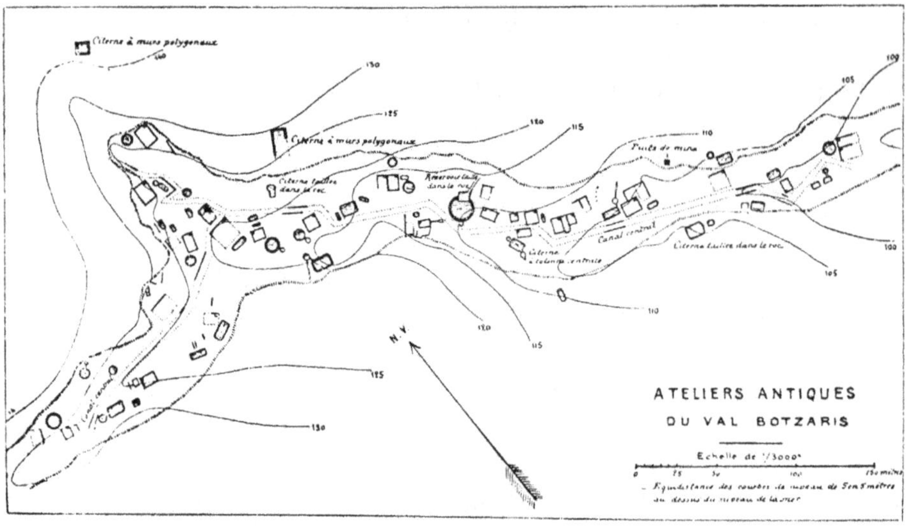

FIGURE 5.8 The Botsari Valley (Map by Ardaillon 1887).

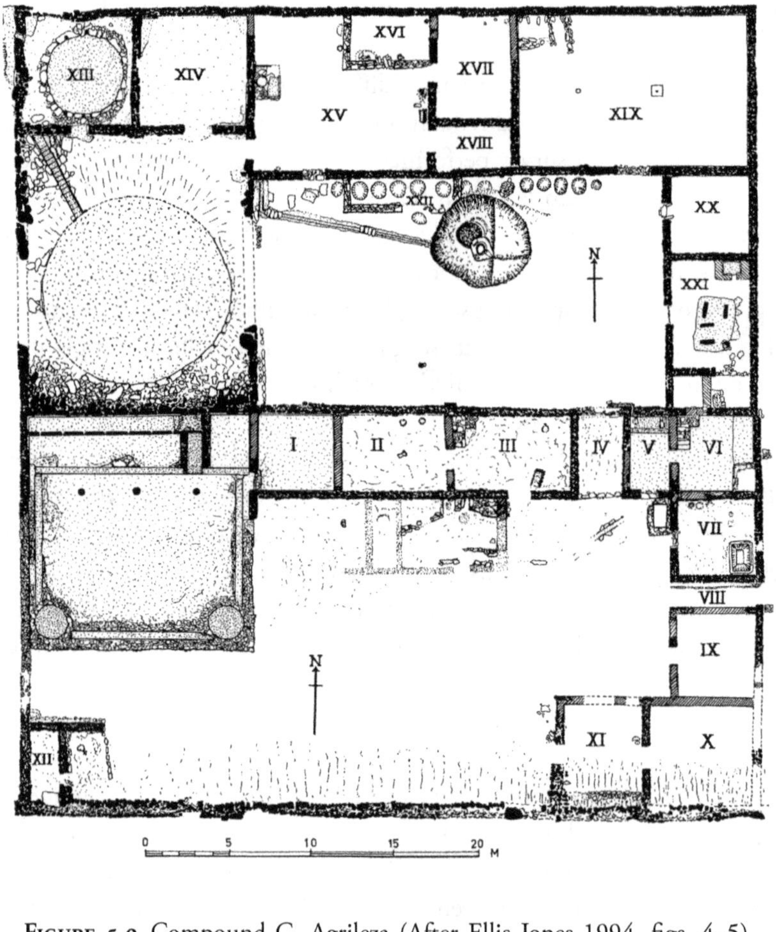

FIGURE 5.9 Compound C, Agrileza (After Ellis Jones 1994, figs. 4–5).

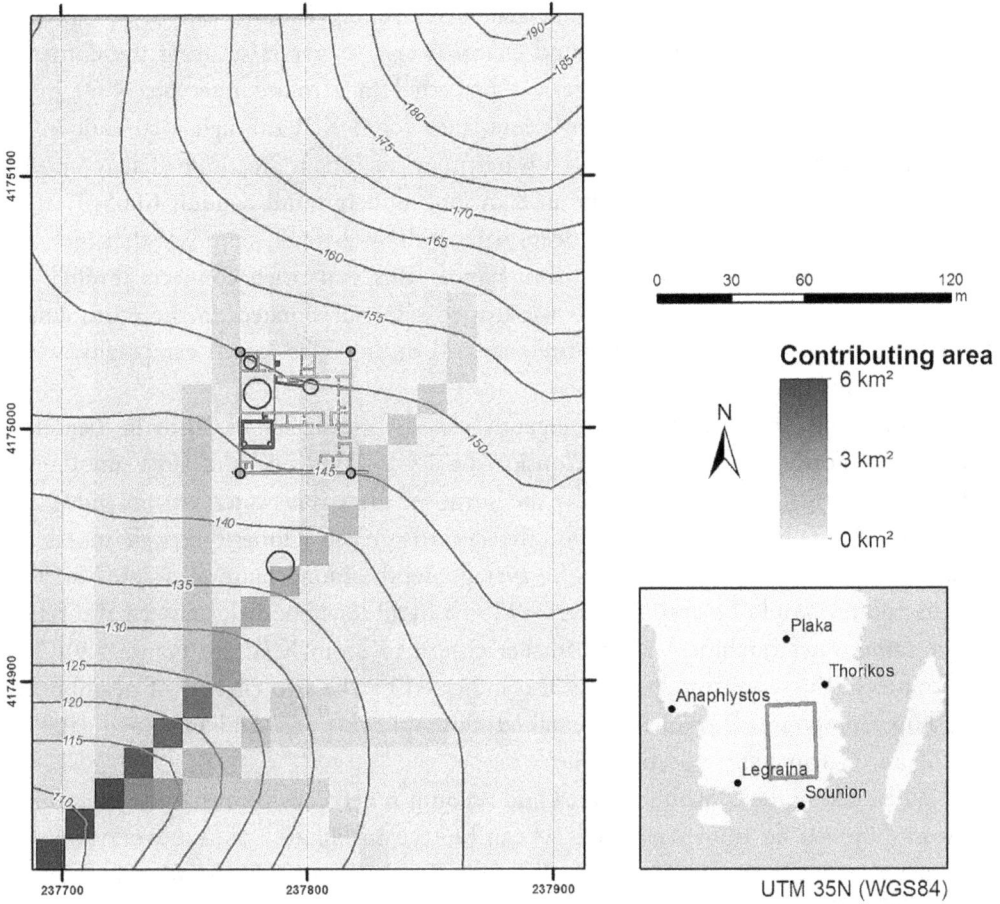

FIGURE 5.10 Detail of the contributing area map, showing Compound C (Map by C. Stal and K. Van Liefferinge).

vation campaigns at a complex of ore-washing installations on the south slope of Mount Michaeli, situated in a northern branch of the Agrileza Valley (Ellis Jones 1985, 1994).

The best-studied workshop of this complex is Compound C, a well-organized and nearly square building measuring 45 × 48 m. The workshop is organized around two interconnected courtyards, which seem to have had different functions: domestic activities took place in the northern courtyard and metallurgy in the southern one. In the northwest corner of the south courtyard, Ellis Jones revealed a huge ore washery (13.5 × 14 m) with seven funnels in its stand tank. There are three column bases on the northern end of the drying table, indicating that this washery was partly covered by a roof to protect the workers against the sun and prevent evaporation. At least 12 rooms were installed around this courtyard, many of which contain features such as crushing tables, fragments of grinding stones, a limestone trough, and a network of channels for discharging waste water—all of which point to industrial activities. Room III also contains evidence of iron working in the form of small hearths.

Directly north of this washery, several water supply features can be recognized. First, there is a network of underground channels and reservoirs securing the domestic water supply of the workshop. Water was harvested in a round reservoir (4.60 m in diameter, 5.30 m deep; volume 88 m³) sunk into room XIII through a conduit in its west wall. The conduit is connected to a waterproof catchment area immediately outside of the workshop. From this reservoir, an 8 m long underground conduit (0.65–1.10 m wide × 1.62 m high) leads to a 6 m deep, narrow draw-shaft in room XV that includes hand and foot holes for use during maintenance. This shaft then connects through an overflow channel to a subterranean, bottle-shaped reservoir situated on the north court. The cistern collapsed and was not entirely cleared during Ellis Jones's campaigns, so its volume remains unknown.

Besides this network, there is a gigantic cistern (measuring 11.20 m in diameter) immediately north of the washery. Considering its location and the large amount of water required for ore washing, it can be surmised that this water was intended for metallurgical activities. The collapse of the cistern's massive limestone wall makes its volume immeasurable, but if we use the average depth among Laurion cisterns of 5 m then its volume would be approximately 492 m³. In all likelihood this cistern also relied on the same water catchment as the smaller cistern in room XIII (see Figure 5.9). The importance of this water catchment is also indicated by the two cisterns of neighboring workshop Compound B, which were raised alongside this area and measured 10.2 m and 7.5 m in diameter, respectively.

When taking the contributing area into account it becomes clear that the location of the workshop was far from accidental. As can be seen in Figure 5.10, the workshop was constructed between two small gullies. The contribution area in this location indicates a water catchment of 3312 m³ for the large cistern (light gray curve on Figure 5.11), which would have been sufficient for yearlong metallurgical activity plus extra for domestic use.

It is clear that workers at this site were aware of the importance of a proper water management. The water supply was guaranteed by a range of factors including the location of the workshops, the large capacity of the cistern, the meticulous waterproofing of surfaces, and the carefully laid-out network of channels and reservoirs for the domestic water supply. In this discussion, an additional factor should be taken into account. Approximately 40 m south of Compound C is situated a large freestanding cistern with an estimated volume of 392.5 m³. As can be seen in Figure 5.10, this cistern is oriented immediately next to a large gully and has a catchment of no less than 13.824 m³. Unsurprisingly, the water balance model demonstrates that this reservoir was ample the entire year through. Considering the fact that this cistern does not seem to be part of a larger workshop, it is possible that the workers of Compound C and/or the other surrounding workshops relied on this cistern in case of water scarcity.

THE ASKLEPIAKON, SOUREZA VALLEY (FIGURES 5.12 ON PAGE 106 AND 5.13 ON PAGE 107)

In the late 1970s, Conophagos uncovered a group of four workshops in the south end of the Soureza Valley (Conophagos 1980; Tsaïmou 1979, 1988). Workshops 2 and 3,

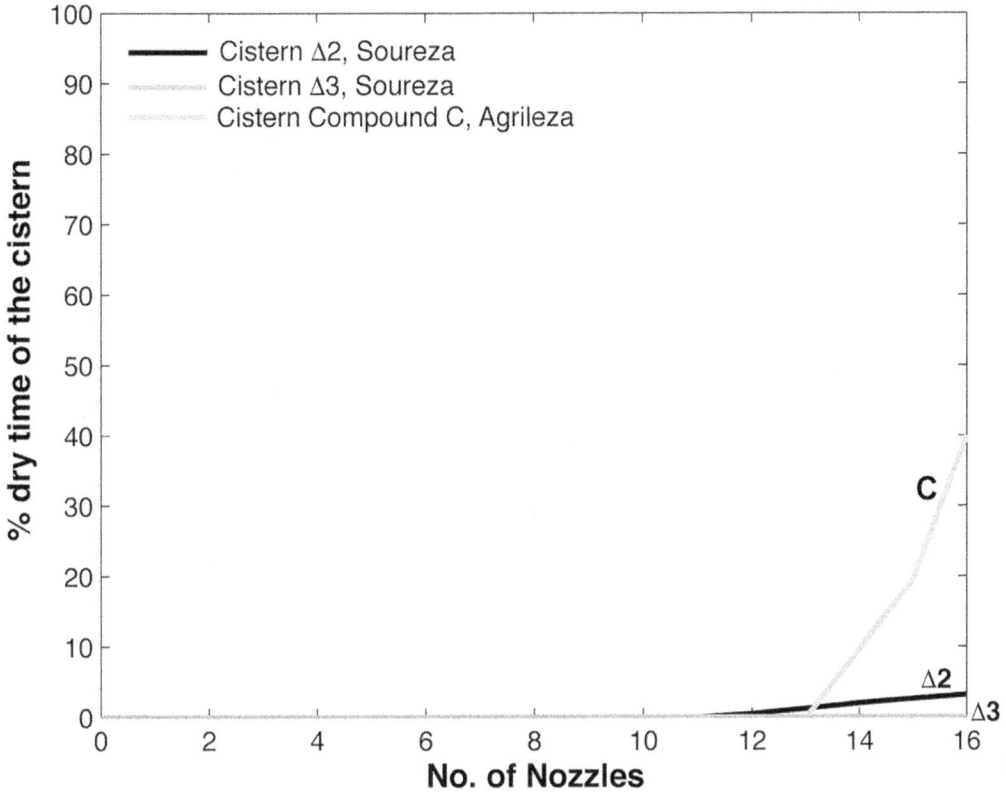

FIGURE 5.11 Water balance model of the cisterns in the Laurion heartland. The graph represents the percentage of dry time in relation to the number of nozzles/washery. The full gray curve shows the washery's use during the full-time series (Graph by M. van den Berg and K. Van Liefferinge).

dating to the second half of the fourth century BCE, will be discussed below. A partly preserved enclosure wall indicates that these workshops plausibly belonged to the same owner.

Workshop 2 is a complex organized around the four-nozzle washery Π2 (5.4 m × 9.19 m) and its cistern Δ2 (Δ2, diameter: 7.6 m; depth: 4.5 m; 204 m³). Water was harvested through a covered channel (0.40 m × 0.42 m) from a gully located east of the workshop. The conduit ran under the threshold of a door entrance in the most eastern room, then over the central courtyard Σ2 to the cistern's decantation basin (diameter: 2.25 m; depth: 1.3 m). Workshop 2 illustrates well how water was transported from cisterns to washeries: a stone plaque projecting from the cistern's rim acted as a sort of stepping stone, allowing water to be drawn from it with relative ease. Subsequently, the water would have been poured into an open channel connecting the cistern to the washery's reservoir. Around the central courtyard were situated 15 other rooms. A2, B2, and Γ2 were probably storage rooms. Two of these (B2 and Γ2) were coated with water-

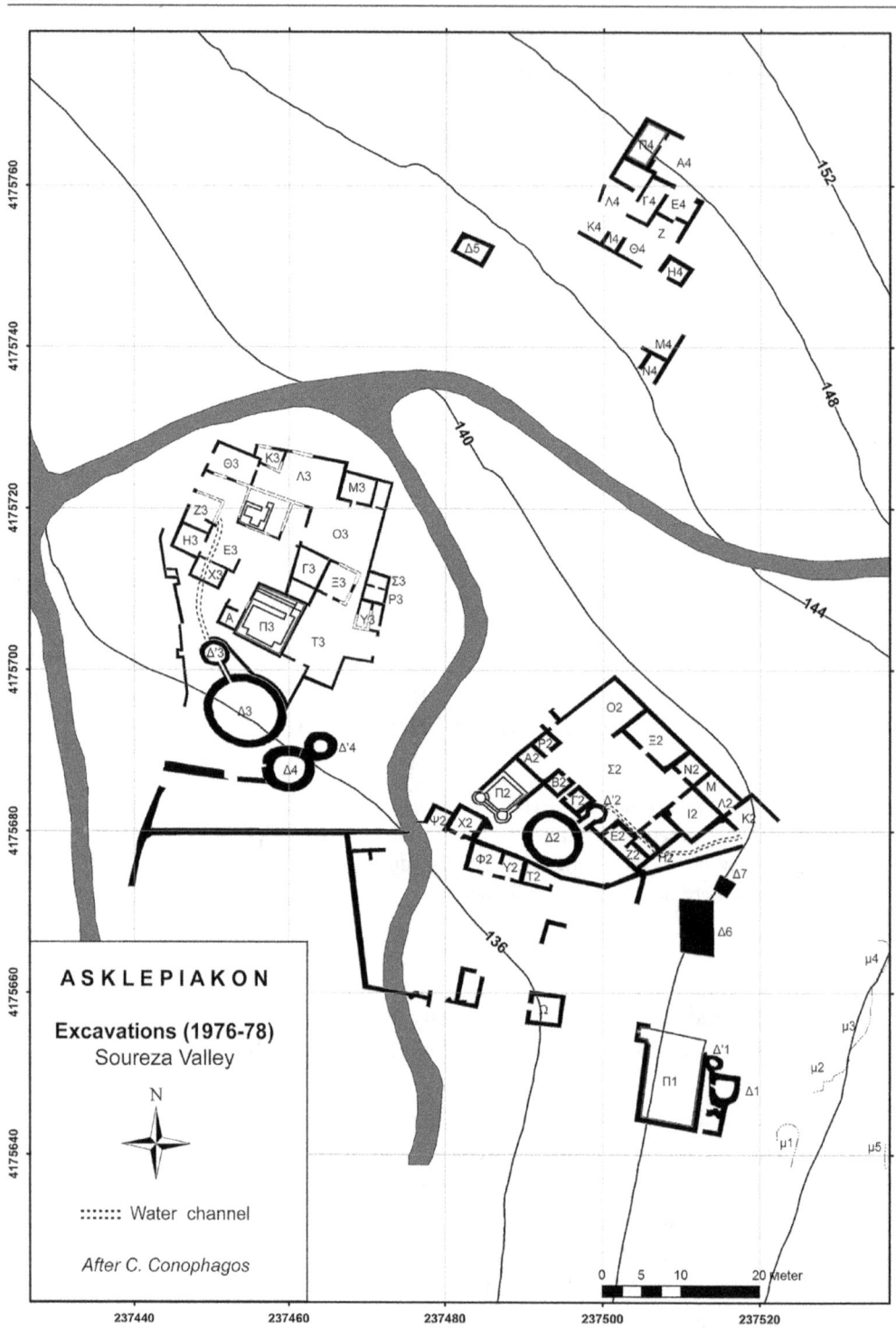

FIGURE 5.12 The Asklepiakon workshops in the Soureza valley (Map by C. Stal and K. Van Lefferinge. After Conophagos 1980:fig. 17.1).

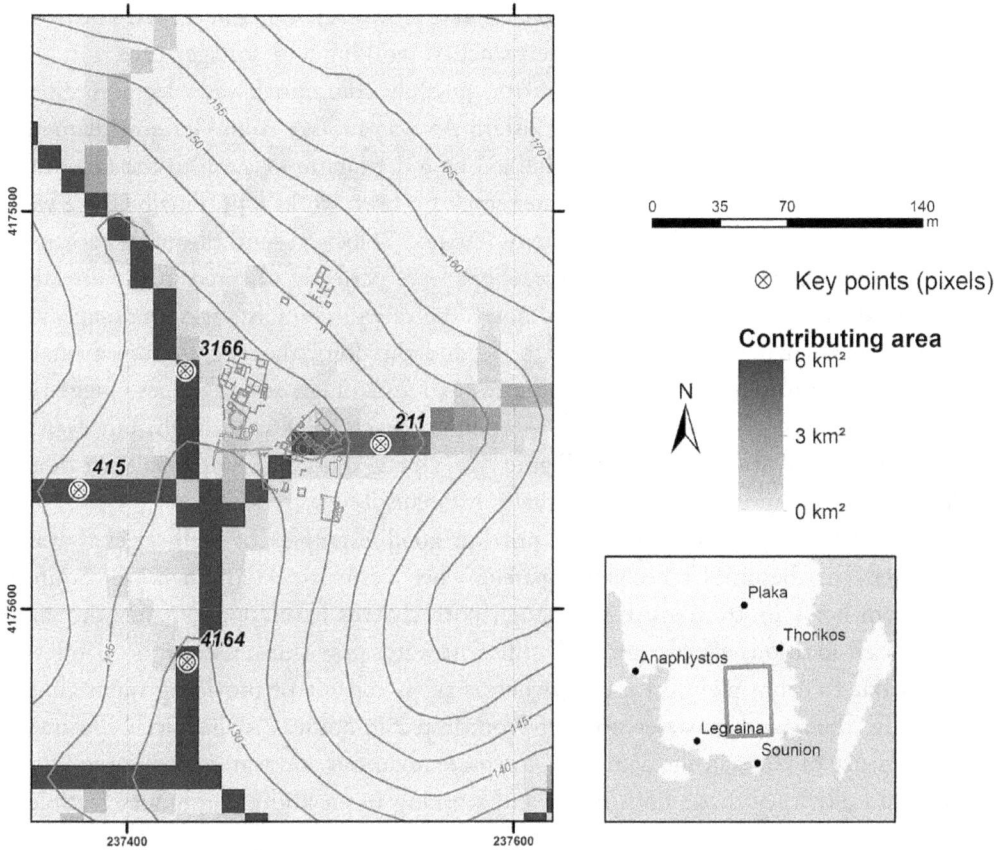

FIGURE 5.13 Detail of the contribution area map, showing the Asklepiakon workshop (Map by C. Stal. M. van den Berg, and K. Van Liefferinge; Van Liefferinge et al. 2014:fig. 13).

tight plaster. The bathroom area of the house (H2-Z2-E2), situated immediately east of the cistern, was connected with Π2 by a covered channel that recycled wastewater by leading it back to the washery's reservoir. Through this combination of measures—water recycling, and the meticulous waterproofing of rooms, surfaces, and devices—Workshop 2 demonstrates clear awareness of the importance of careful water management.

Workshop 3, the largest *ergasterion* of the complex, shows a similar yet less organized image. The workshop area was located south of the building, containing a large five-nozzle washery Π3 (12.22 m × 7.33 m; 5 nozzles) and a round cistern Δ3, located directly to its south (diameter: 11 m, depth: 5.2 m, capacity: 494 m³). Two column bases were encountered on the bottom of the cistern, suggesting the past presence of a roof to reduce evaporation. Water catchment was effected through a conduit, covered by stone plaques and leading right through the complex to the decantation tank located northwest of the cistern. The complex contained several rooms organized around three courtyards (O3, T3, and Ψ3), from which T3 and rooms A3, B3, and Y3, all lined with waterproof cement, comprised the washery's actual working and storage space.

Apart from these workshops, two extra, possibly communal water features should be mentioned. Immediately southeast of cistern Δ3 was another round cistern (diameter: 6 m; capacity approximately 141 m³) adjoined by a decantation cistern to the northeast. Possibly this cistern provided an extra water stock for both workshops. Finally, there were also two underground, interconnected cisterns (Δ6 and 7) located southeast of Workshop 2.

As shown on Figure 5.14, both workshops were perfectly oriented in the direction of ephemeral streams that were running through the valley, with Cistern Δ3 tapping water directly from the main stream and Cistern Δ2 and the domestic cisterns from a smaller tributary. The contributing area map indicates extremely high runoff values, suggesting that the workshops were not only able to operate the entire year through, but even to create a provisional water stock (see Figure 5.11 for graph). The water balance model confirms that this water supply was virtually inexhaustible.

The Asklepiakon workshops also provide good examples of well-selected water catchments. This becomes especially apparent when comparing Cistern Δ2 in Soureza with Cistern no. 1 in Thorikos. Even though both cisterns have approximately the same capacity, their locations effect completely different water provisions. Cistern no. 1 offers a sufficient but far from plentiful supply, whereas Δ2 is capable of providing water almost unlimitedly. The abundant water stock of Workshop 2 in Soureza is also nicely illustrated by the presence of baths in the complex, which are luxurious and water-consuming installations. Basically, they made both living and working in an arid environment feasible.

NEGRIS WORKSHOP, SPITHAROPOUSSI (FIGURE 5.14)

The Negris workshop, named after its excavator, remains unpublished to this day; however, the site is accessible and allows for the detection of several features.[8] The most impressive part of the workshop is undoubtedly its gigantic, nearly square cistern measuring approximately 11 × 12 m. Its basin is not entirely cleared, but with a presumed depth of 5 m, it would have had an approximate volume of 660 m³. The cistern was partly carved out of the rock and partly built of walls consisting of large polygonal blocks of marble measuring 1.60 m in width. A staircase on its south side would have aided maintenance. Another striking feature is the triangular structure or basin found south of the cistern. It is perfectly oriented toward the gully and coated with hydraulic mortar, suggesting that this space could have acted as a decantation tank for cleaning the turbid surface runoff. Northeast of the cistern, a large washery and several adjacent rooms with crushing tables and a limestone trough—reminiscent of one uncovered at Agrileza—can still be recognized. Finally, a mine shaft was incorporated into the workshop directly north of the cistern.

The location of the Negris workshop's cistern is particularly strategic: situated right in the middle of the valley bed, it would have intercepted the flow of surface runoff almost entirely. The contribution area points to a water catchment of no less than 75.744 m³ (526 pixels on the DEM), an amount that provides an inexhaustible water supply for metallurgical activities (Figure 5.11).

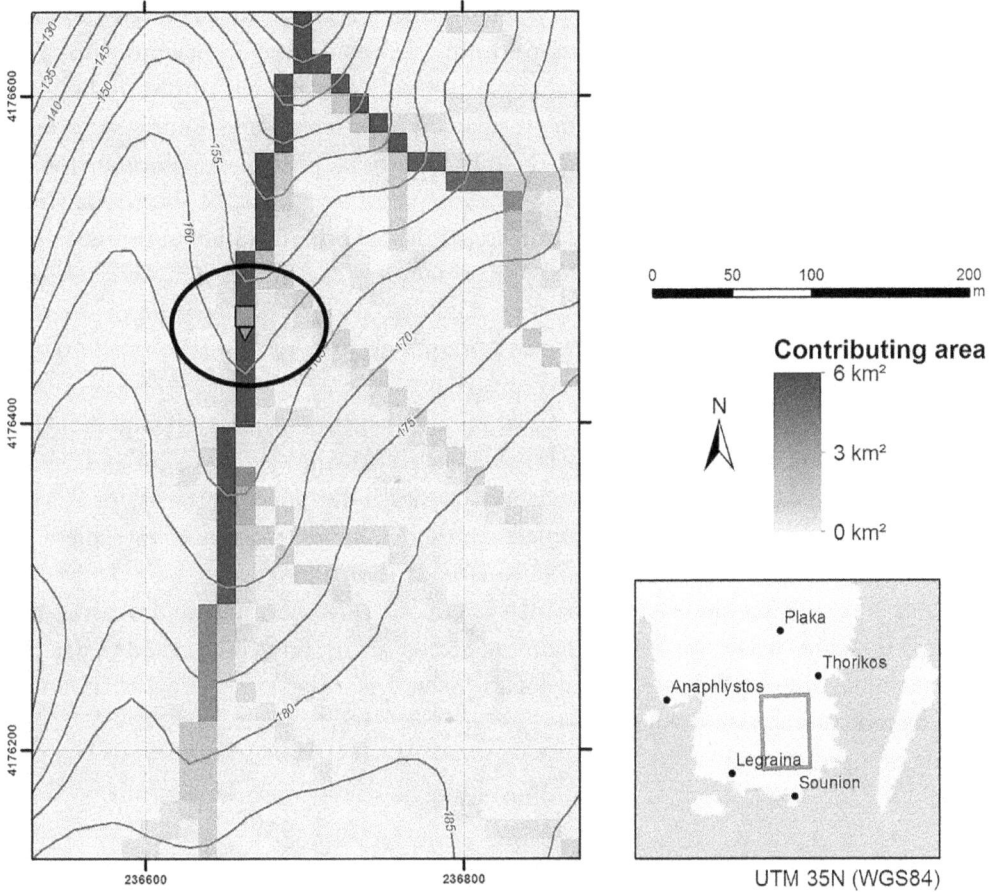

FIGURE 5.14 Detail of the contributing area map, showing the site of Thorikos (Map by C. Stal, M. van den Berg, and K. Van Liefferinge).

CONCLUSION

This paper has discussed regional inequality among Laurion mining sites through hydrological analyses and the archaeological interpretation of their results. Water availability in the Laurion differed both locally and regionally, affecting the water use of the workshops and consequently the operation of the silver industry. In the Adami and Potami area, washeries have modest dimensions and cisterns are few and small. At Thorikos, the location of favorable water catchments did not determine the location of workshops, thus hampering water collection. Water balance models suggest that miners generally did not harvest a reliable water stock to operate washeries throughout the year. Given the presence of alluvial plains and archaeological evidence for farming in the wider area, it can be suggested that metallurgy was performed as a side business and seasonal activity.

This image contrasts strongly with the mining activities in the central Laurion valleys. Although this area was semiarid, miners developed a sophisticated system of water management supported by barrages, supply channels, large cisterns, extensive waterproofing, and even water recycling. These efforts paid off: all the analyzed workshops display an almost inexhaustible water supply, enabling a full year operation of the workshops. In comparison to the Thorikos area, water availability was higher and miners were more aware of the importance of appropriate water catchments. This is neatly illustrated when comparing Cistern no. 1 at Thorikos with Δ2 at the Asklepiakon. Due to these environmental and social conditions, it can be concluded that Thorikos was not and could never have become the prominent player in the silver industry that the central valleys were.

ACKNOWLEDGMENTS

I am deeply indebted to Cornelis Stal, Martinus van den Berg, Niko Verhoest, and Alain De Wulf (Ghent University, Belgium) for their help with the topographical and hydrological modeling and Demetris Koutsoyiannis (National Technical University of Athens, Greece) for providing me with the rainfall time series. I would also like to express my appreciation to Roald Docter, Guy Dierkens and Thomas Pieters (Ghent University, Belgium) for enabling the excavations of Cistern no. 1 at Thorikos and assisting me during numerous fieldwalks in the Laurion area. Finally, I warmly acknowledge the logistic support of the Belgian Archaeological School at Athens and the 2nd Ephorate of Prehistoric and Classical Antiquities.

NOTES

1. Kraay 1958:1–2; Kraay and Emeleus 1962:15; Nicolet-Pierre et al. 1985:26, 31; Kroll 2009:195–196; Van Alfen 2012:91.
2. See Herodotos (*The Histories* 7.144) and Aristoteles (*Politeia Athenaion* 22.7) for Athenian involvement in the operation of the mines during the fifth century BCE; see the mine leases (Crosby 1941; 1950; 1957) and various ancient authors, principally Xenophon (*Poroi*), for fourth-century BCE evidence.
3. Negris (1881) and Conophagos (1980), contra Kakavoyiannis (2005) and Domergue (2008), who argue that ores were processed in the stand reservoir D instead of on E.
4. Sallares 2007. See also Theophrastos on the growth of plants (*Historia Plantarum* 8.6.6).
5. Purchased from the Hellenic Military Service at Athens http://web.gys.gr.
6. I am indebted to Prof. Demetris Koutsoyiannis for providing me this rainfall time series.
7. Average depth established during personal fieldwalks in the Laurion area.
8. Data recorded during a personal fieldwalk in August 2013. Also, the Hellenic Military survey has recorded the cistern on its topographical maps.

REFERENCES CITED

Ardaillon, E. 1897 *Les mines du Laurion*. Thorin et fils, Paris.

Conophagos, C. 1980 *Le Laurion antique et la technique Grecque de la production de l'argent*. Ekdotike Hellados, Athens.

Crosby, M. 1941 Greek Inscriptions. A Poletai Record of the Year 367/6. *Hesperia* 10:14–30.

Crosby, M. 1950 The Leases of the Laureion Mines. *Hesperia* 19:189–297.

Crosby, M. 1957 More Fragments of Mining Leases from the Athenian Agora. *Hesperia* 26:1–23.

Curtius, E., and J. A. Kaupert. 1889 *Karten von Attika*. Dietrich Reimer Verlag, Berlin.

Domergue, C. 2008 *Les Mines antiques, La production des métaux aux époques grecque et romaine*. Antiqua et Picard, Paris.

Ellis Jones, J. 1985 Laurion: Agrileza, 1977–1983: Excavations at a Silver-Mine Site. *Archaeological Reports* 31:106–123.

Ellis Jones, J. 1994 The Building and Industrial Remains at Agrileza, Laurion (Fourth Century BC) and Their Contribution to the Workings at the Site. *Annual of the British School at Athens* 89:307–358.

Foxhall, L., M. Jones, and H. Forbes. 2007 Human Ecology and the Classical Landscape. In *Classical Archaeology*, edited by S. E. Alcock and R. Osborne, pp. 91–117. Blackwell, Malden, MA.

Kakavoyiannis, E. C. 2005 Μέταλλα εργάσιμα και συγκεχωρημένα: η οργάνωση της εκμετάλλευσης του ορυκτού πλούτου της Λαυρεωτικής από την Αθηναϊκή Δημοκρατία. Archaeological Receipts Fund, Athens.

Kraay, C. M. 1958 Gold and Copper Traces in Early Greek Silver. *Archaeometry* 1:1–6.

Kraay, C. M., and V. M. Emeleus. 1962 *The Composition of Greek Silver Coins, Analysis by Neutron Activation*. Ashmolean Museum, Oxford.

Kroll, J. H. 2009 What about Coinage? In *Interpreting the Athenian Empire*, edited by J. Ma, N. Papazarkadas, and R. Parker, pp. 195–209. Dockworth, London.

Lohman, H. 1993 *Atene, Forschungen zu Siedlungs- und Wirtschaftsstruktur des klassischen Attika, Teil I*. Böhlau Verlag, Köln.

Mussche, H. F. 1967 Le Quartier Industriel: L'Insula 1. In *Thorikos II (1964), Rapport préliminaire sur la première campagne de fouilles—voorlopig verslag over de eerste opgravingscampagne*, edited by H. F. Mussche, J. Bingen, J. De Geyter, G. Donnay, and T. Hackens, pp. 48–62. Brussels.

Mussche, H. F. 1968. Le Quartier Industriel. In Thorikos I (1963), *Rapport préliminaire sur la première campagne de fouilles—voorlopig verslag over de eerste opgravingscampagne*. edited by H. F. Mussche, J. Bingen, J. Servais, R. Paepe, and T. Hackens, pp. 87–104. Comité des Fouilles Belges en Grèce, 1968–1971, Brussels.

Mussche, H. 1998 *Thorikos, a Mining Town in Ancient Attika*. Comité des fouilles belges en Grèce, Ghent.

Nicolet-Pierre, H., J.-N. Barradon, and J.-Y. Calvez. 1985 Monnaies archaïques d'Athènes sous Pisistrate et les Pisistratides (c.545–c.510). II. Recherches sur la composition métallique des Wappenmünzen. *Revue Numismatique* 6:23–44.

Negris, P. 1881 Laveries anciennes du Laurium. *Annales des mines* 20:160–164.

Oikonomakou, M. 1991 Οικοσμός Θορικού Λαυρείου (οικόπεδο Κωνστ. Μέξα), *Archaiologikon Deltion* 46:66–69.

Oikonomakou, M. 1996a Δύο αρχαία εργαστήρια στην περιοχή του Θορικού. *Archaiologikon Deltion* 51–52: 125–140.

Oikonomakou, M. 1996b Θορικός. Επαρχιακή οδός Καβοδόκανου-Θορικού. *Archaiologikon Deltion* 51:65.

Oikonomakou, M. 1997 Οικοσμός Θορικού (κτήμα Κωνστ. Μέξα). *Archaiologikon Deltion* 97:87–88.

Petropoulakou, M., and E. Pedazou. 1973 Αρχαίες Ελληνικές Πόλεις 21: Αττική. Οικιστικά στοιχεία, πρώτη έκθεση. Αθηναϊκός Τεχνολογικός Όμιλος, Athens.

Sallares, R. 2007 Ecology. In *The Cambridge Economic History of the Greco-Roman World*, edited by W. Scheidel, I. Morris, and R. Saller, pp. 15–38. Cambridge University Press, Cambridge.

Salliora-Oikonomakou, M. 2004 Ο αρχαίος δήμος του Σουνίου. Ιστορική και τοπογραφική επισκόπιση. Έκδοση Μιχάλης Τουμπή, Koropi.

Tsaïmou, C. G. 1979 Ο ανδρώνας του "πλυντηρίου του Σίμου" στην Σούρεζα της Λαυρεωτικής. Αρχαιολογικά Ανάλεκτα εξ Αθηνών 12:15–23.

Tsaïmou, C. G. 1988 Εργασία και ζωή στο Αρχαίο Λαύριο σε εγκατάσταση εμπλουτισμού μεταλλευμάτων τον 4ον αιώνα π.χ. Διδακτορική Διατριβή, Athens.

Van Alfen, P. G. 2012 The Coinage of Athens, Sixth to First Century BCE. In *The Oxford Handbook of Greek and Roman Coinage*, edited by W. E. Metcalf, pp. 88–104. Oxford University Press, Oxford.

Van Liefferinge, K., R. Docter, T. Pieters, and F. van den Eijnde. 2011 The Excavation of Cistern No. 1 at Thorikos. In *Thorikos 10, Reports and Studies*, edited by R. Docter, A. De Wulf, P. Monsieur, F. van den Eijnde, W. van de Put, and K. Van Gelder, pp. 57–74. Classical Archaeology, Department of Archaeology, Ghent University, Ghent.

Van Liefferinge, K., M. van den Berg, C. Stal, R. Docter, A. De Wulf, and N. Verhoest. 2014 Reconsidering the Role of Thorikos within the Laurion Silver Mining Area (Attica, Greece) through Hydrological Analyses. *Journal of Archaeological Science* 41:272–284.

Zoridis, P. 1980 Εργαστήριο εμπλουτισμού μεταλλεύματος στο Θορικό. *Archaiologike Ephemeris* 1980:75–84.

PART II

Waterscapes, Power Plays, and Display

Chapter Six

From Elite Villas to Public Spaces

The First Decorative Fountains in Ancient Rome

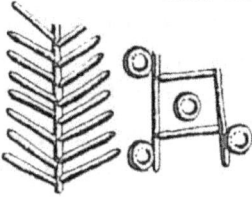

Brenda Longfellow

Abstract *In the second and first centuries BCE, wealthy Romans built opulent country homes in the suburbs around Rome, throughout Latium, and along the coast south of Rome that showcased ever more spectacular water features ranging from vaulted fishponds to artificial waterfalls in manmade caves. It was not until the last generation of the Republic that the arresting artistic water displays commonly found in elite dwellings began to be incorporated into public spaces. These hydraulic elements were intrinsically linked to larger spaces associated with an individual elite patron, from the theater complex of Pompey to the forum of Julius Caesar. This paper examines the elite origins of the first civic monumental fountains in ancient Rome and the social, political, and cultural expectations that accompanied the dramatic conversion of artistic water displays associated with villa culture into spectacles experienced by the entire Roman populace.*

An individual Roman's ability to harness nature was an essential expression of manly virtue and authority, and elite authors such as Pliny the Elder and Varro placed a high value on enhancing ecological resources through erudition and technology. These same writers linked the origins of the Roman state with cultivated nature, binding the Roman sense of self and civilization with the control of natural resources from the time of Romulus onward. Pliny the Elder (*Natural History* 50) reminisces about Romulus and the subsequent kings of Rome cultivating their gardens with their own hands, while Varro (*De re rustica* 1.10) records that Romulus granted each Roman as much land as could be ploughed by one man in a single day. These original allotments of land, which are estimated to be approximately two acres, could not be broken up or bequeathed outside the family, and thus these plots came to symbolize the ancestry and legitimacy of the patricians. The agrarian heritage of Rome informed an essential component of the Roman mindset that linked cultivated nature with the lifestyle of the elites, who were building private gardens and grandiose hydraulic displays in their villas long before monumental civic fountains were introduced to the cityscape of Rome. This essay focuses on the villa origins of monumental public fountains in Rome and the political and cultural expectations that accompanied the dramatic conversion of artistic water displays associated with the elite into resources open and accessible to the entire Roman populace.

In Roman society, where land ownership and political power went hand in hand, an individual's ambitious display of water could augment his authority while simultaneously confirming or challenging his place in the existing social hierarchy. By the second century BCE, powerful men frequently incorporated water and other aspects of the natural realm into their townhomes and villas but less often expressed their prowess at bending nature to their will with public works projects such as aqueducts. In Republican Rome, where the censors were charged with the care and maintenance of the water supply, these projects are notably few and far between. The first aqueduct to supply the city—the Aqua Appia—was built with tribute money by the censor Appius Claudius Crassus in 312 BCE, after his co-censor, Gaius Plautius, identified the spring that would feed the aqueduct (Frontinus, *On Aqueducts* 5). In 272 BCE, this aqueduct was joined by the Aqua Anio Vetus, which was contracted by the censor Manius Curius Dentatus to divert the waters of the Anio River to Rome. Two years later—and therefore after the 18-month censorship of Curius had ended—Curius was appointed by a senatorial decree to a two-man board to fulfill the contract. Because Curius died within days of this appointment, his co-appointee, Fulvius Flaccus, carried out the contract alone (Livy 9.29; Frontinus, *On Aqueducts* 6). In 184 BCE, the censor Marcus Porcius Cato repaired the aqueduct channels and dismantled the pipes that illegally diverted the aqueduct waters to private beneficiaries (Plutarch, *Cato the Elder* 19.1; Livy 39.44.5), but by 144 BCE, the Aqua Appia and the Aqua Anio Vetus were in such disrepair—and so much of their water supply was being illegally siphoned off for individual consumption—that the Senate tasked Quintus Marcius Rex, the *praetor urbanus,* with repairing and supplementing the lines. Given 180,000,000 sesterces from the sacks of Corinth and Carthage, Marcius repaired these lines and built the Aqua Marcia, the longest of all the aqueducts feeding Rome and the one with the reputation of delivering the coldest and most pure water to the city (Livy 39.44; Frontinus, *On Aqueducts* 7; Tacitus, *Annals* 14.22; Pliny, *Natural History* 36.121). In 125 BCE, the censors Gnaeus Servilius Caepio and Lucius Cassius Longinus contracted the Aqua Tepula, which would be last of the public aqueducts added to Rome before the Augustan period (Frontinus, *On Aqueducts* 8). These four aqueducts not only supplied civic hydraulic amenities but also provided a means for elites to legally or illegally claim water for their villas and *horti* located along the aqueduct routes.

By the early second century BCE, elites were building country homes throughout Latium, southern Etruria, along the coast south of Rome, and around the Bay of Naples. Tusculum, which is 25 kilometers southeast of Rome in the Alban Hills, and Tibur, which is about 30 kilometers northeast of Rome at the Anio Falls, were early favorites for villa owners. Indeed, 21 known villas at Tusculum and 16 at Tibur have archaeological remains dating the second century BCE; a further 23 villas at Tusculum and nine villas at Tibur have their earliest phases dated to the first century BCE (Marzano 2007:Appendix A). The popularity of these areas can be attributed in large part to these communities' relative proximities to Rome and abundant water sources, which included springs, rivers, and, in the case of Tibur, the aqueducts feeding Rome.

Over the course of the second century BCE, both the numbers of villas and their opulence grew. Contemporary pundits such as Cato the Elder reproached villa owners for their costly lifestyles while later writers characterized this period as the moment when the luxurious lifestyles associated with the Hellenistic East overtook traditional Roman austerity (e.g., Varro, *De re rustica* 2.1; D'Arms 1970:10; Wallace-Hadrill 1998:44). Soon after the Third Macedonian War ended in 168 BCE, Publius Cornelius Scipio Aemilianus Africanus Numantinus and Gaius Laelius Sapiens were conspicuous among the elites for owning more than one coastal villa, but this quickly became the new normal (Aulus Gellus 13.24.1; D'Arms 1970:15–17; Zarmakoupi 2014:7). At the same time as the villas were multiplying, so, too, were the amenities associated with the villa lifestyle. The dramatically escalating costs of such lifestyles in the late second and early first centuries BCE can be followed with the seaside villa at Misenum that Cornelia, mother of the Gracchi, purchased for 75,000 drachmas and to which she retired after her sons died in the 120s BCE (Plutarch, *Gaius Gracchus* 19.1–2; Valerius Maximus 4.4.1; D'Arms 1970:8–9). This villa was subsequently purchased by Lucius Lucullus for 2.5 million drachmas, and then by Gaius Marius in the early '90s BCE for an unknown, but presumably larger, amount. Seneca the Younger (*Epistulae* 51.11) compares Marius's villa, which was conspicuously located on top of a mountain ridge, to a military camp that effectively reminded those below of his martial prowess. According to Plutarch (*Marius* 34.2), however, the amenities of this house were "more luxurious and effeminate" than were suitable for a man with such a distinguished military career. Although Plutarch does not specify which accouterments in particular threatened the masculinity of Marius, the contemporary taste for ever more extravagant green spaces and hydraulic amenities such as baths and fishponds is well documented.

With such a relentless trend toward more lavish spaces and greater opulence in villa culture, a reliable water supply was a necessity for villa owners. For those with limited water supply from springs or wells, access to public, semiprivate, or private aqueducts was essential. In Tibur, the owner of a villa associated with Manlius Vopiscus in the Domitianic period and now located under the Villa Gregoriana built a private aqueduct to supply amenities that included vaulted fishponds, which were built in the late second or early first century BCE (Marzano 2007:582 L299). At the so-called Villa of Quintilius Varus at Tibur, which also dates to the end of the second century or beginning of the first century BCE, an enormous fishpond (62.8 × 24 m) was supplied by a cistern that in turn was fed by two aqueducts diverting water from the Anio River (Higgenbotham 1997:122–125; Mari and Boanelli 1991). Other waterworks, including a grotto nymphaeum discussed below, harmonized with this fishpond.

The Aqua Anio Vetus delivered water to Tibur and presumably the villas in the surrounding region before feeding Rome (Evans 1993; Frontinus, *On Aqueducts* 6). In some communities the need of elite landowners was so prioritized that aqueducts were built explicitly to supply private lands. The *municipium* of Tusculum, for instance, built the Aqua Crabra for local landowners such as Cicero, who paid a tax for its use on certain days and in certain quantities (Cicero, *Epistulae ad Familiares* 16.183; *De lege agraria* 3.2.9; Frontinus, *On Aqueducts* 9). Two surviving inscriptions from Latium illustrate how such services were regulated. One inscription, which may be associated with the Aqua Crabra (*CIL* XIV 3676), details the size of the connectors that could be used and indicates the hours when water was available. The other inscription (*CIL* VI 1261) not only gives the hours of operation but also provides a map of an aqueduct that names landowners and provides the number of pipelines they had connected to the aqueduct (Marzano 2007:167; Thomas and Wilson 1994:147; Wilson 1999:315–316). Presumably, it was up to the landowner whether they used the water for irrigation, animal needs, water mills, domestic use, stock piling, fishponds, baths, fountains, or any combination thereof. At villas, water would be needed for all of the above, with the increasing number of fountains and other hydraulic amenities requiring increasing amounts of water to be available to the landowner.

By the mid-first century BCE, Cicero, a man of comparatively modest means, owned at least eight villas, at least two of which were fed by water conduits and a third located at the confluence of two rivers. By multiplying Cicero's holdings by the number of men vying for power in the late Republic, it is possible to comprehend the vast number of villas that were being built across Latium and Campania. Indeed, many of the most famous Campanian villas date to the mid-first century BCE, including Villa A at Oplontis, Villa San Marco and Villa Arianna at Stabiae, the Villa at Boscoreale, and the Villa of the Mysteries at Pompeii. In fact, there were so many Campanian villas under construction during Cicero's lifetime that Horace (*Epistulae* 3.1.33–37) complained about the amount of trash from these projects being thrown into the sea.

Throughout this time period, villas and the time spent at villas were synonymous with pleasure, leisure, and escape from the pressures of Rome. These connotations of the villa lifestyle were as strong for broad segments of the population as they were for the fortunate elite who owned multiple country homes, where they entertained friends in a setting that framed their power to create spectacles of water and vegetation. These villas were designed with careful attention to the surrounding landscape, often built on slopes overlooking the sea, a river valley, or a waterfall. Peristyles, dining rooms, and other reception rooms were cleverly oriented to take advantage of particular vistas, effectively incorporating nature into the human realm. These villas also featured massive interior gardens, where groomed paths moved the visitor through ornamental and productive plantings. Water features ranging from pools to rectangular channels to fishponds to fountains enhanced the luxurious surroundings, and statues hidden among the vegetation transported the visitor to idyllic woodlands or the realm of Venus, Bacchus, or the nymphs.

Delighting in creating unexpected juxtapositions between nature and artifice, the Romans also took great joy in shaping the topography of the landscape, creating rivers, waterfalls, and hillsides where there were none before, and coercing natural features into architectural patterns (Purcell 1987:192). Over the course of the first century BCE, villas were luxurious retreats showcasing ever more spectacular water features that ranged from evocative canals to artificial waterfalls fed by aqueducts or channels directed into natural or man-made caves. One particularly influential referent point for villa fountains was the traditional shrines for nymphs that were set in caves with springs. The villa counterpart is a barrel-vaulted hall looking out over the sea, lake, or valley. One mid-first-century-BCE example is the Ninfeo Dorico at Castelgandolfo, which overlooked the Alban Lake (Figure 6.1). Water mimicked the effects of a spring as it flowed from the reservoir at the back into channels along the lateral walls, and the cave-like impression of the edifice was enhanced by the grotto stone used to face the niches and cover the lower parts of the wall (Letzner 1990:279; Neuerburg 1965:157; Tamm 1963:168).

This type of artistic water display, set within a barrel-vaulted room terminating in an axial niche or basin from which water poured forth, was particularly popular in first-century-BCE villas throughout Latium and Campania (Figure 6.2 on page 119). In the so-called Villa of Quintilius Varus at Tibur mentioned above, a small manmade chamber outfitted as a nymphaeum overlooked the falls of the Anio River (Letzner 1990:302; Mari and Boanelli 1991; Neuerburg 1965:250; Neuerburg 1968). In the so-called Villa of Cicero at Formia, the small nymphaeum faced onto the sea (Giuliani and Guaitoli 1972; Letzner 1990:362; Neuerburg 1965:146), while the basilica nymphaeum known as the Grotta di Paris at San Vittorino looked out over a valley (Letzner 1990:290; Neuerburg 1965:231; Quilici 1969). Partially cut into the shadowy side of a hill, the grotto effect of each is enhanced by pumice stone, shells, mosaic, and colored glass. Moreover, in each instance, water poured forth from the axial niche, enhancing not only the feel

FIGURE 6.1 Ninfeo Dorico at Castelgandolfo. Photo by Betsey A. Robinson.

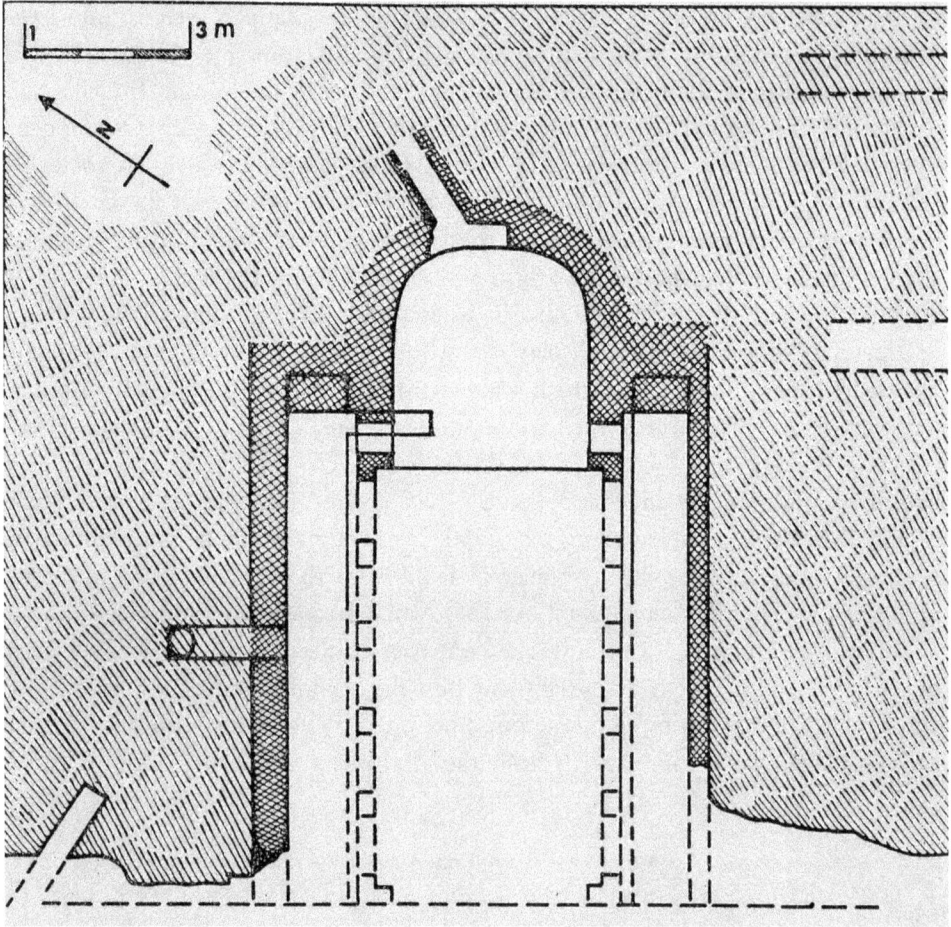

FIGURE 6.2 Plan of the Grotta di Paris at San Vittorino. After Quilici 1969:tav. IV.

of a grotto but also the axial effect. The desire to create axial displays that played with the visual and aural effects of water would prove to be an enduring impulse for Roman villa owners and patrons of monumental civic fountains.

By the mid-first century BCE, no villa was complete without pools, fishponds, and fountains. In contemporary Rome, a green belt of elite villas and *horti* on the Esquiline and Pincian hills, the southeast flank of the city in the Via Appia valley, and in Transtiberim showcased the mastery of elite landholders in the taming of raw nature. These walled spaces were irrigated and typically featured some kind of natural or artificial water display (von Stackelberg 2009:19). Among the most famous *horti* is that of Lucius Licinius Lucullus, a key general in the Third Mithradatic War (73–63 BCE). Laid out on the Pincian Hill, the Horti Lucullani overlooked the Campus Martius and provided a dramatic setting for the former military commander's famous feasts; this setting included an artificial lake for mock naval battles. According to the Augustan moralist Papirius Fabianus, the elites building these luxurious gardens and inhabiting these peri-urban spaces "copy even mountains and forests in their damp houses, and, in the sunless smog green places, coastlines, and streams" (Seneca *Controversiae* 2.1.3; trans. Purcell 1987:190). Because this manipulation of the larger landscape was taking place within sight of Rome, the act of transformation not only emphasized the wealth and power of the landholder but also helped cement elite claims of ancestral rights to these properties (Cook and Foulk 2013:182). Moreover, the power of such landholding privileges was enhanced by the fact that the general populace was excluded from all but the briefest glimpses of these displays, while the sound of water within the tall perimeter walls was probably audible to those passing by.

In contrast to the lavish water displays common to Republican villas, most second- and first-century-BCE civic fountains were functional edifices found along roads or in piazzas. These had minimal decorative embellishments and took a decidedly different architectural form from the evocatively ornamented grotto nymphaea repeatedly found in villas. For instance, the fountain along the Via Appia at Formia provides one of the few certain examples of a monumental street fountain dating to the Republican period (Figure 6.3). The fountain consists of a hypaethral rectangular basin fed by two waterspouts

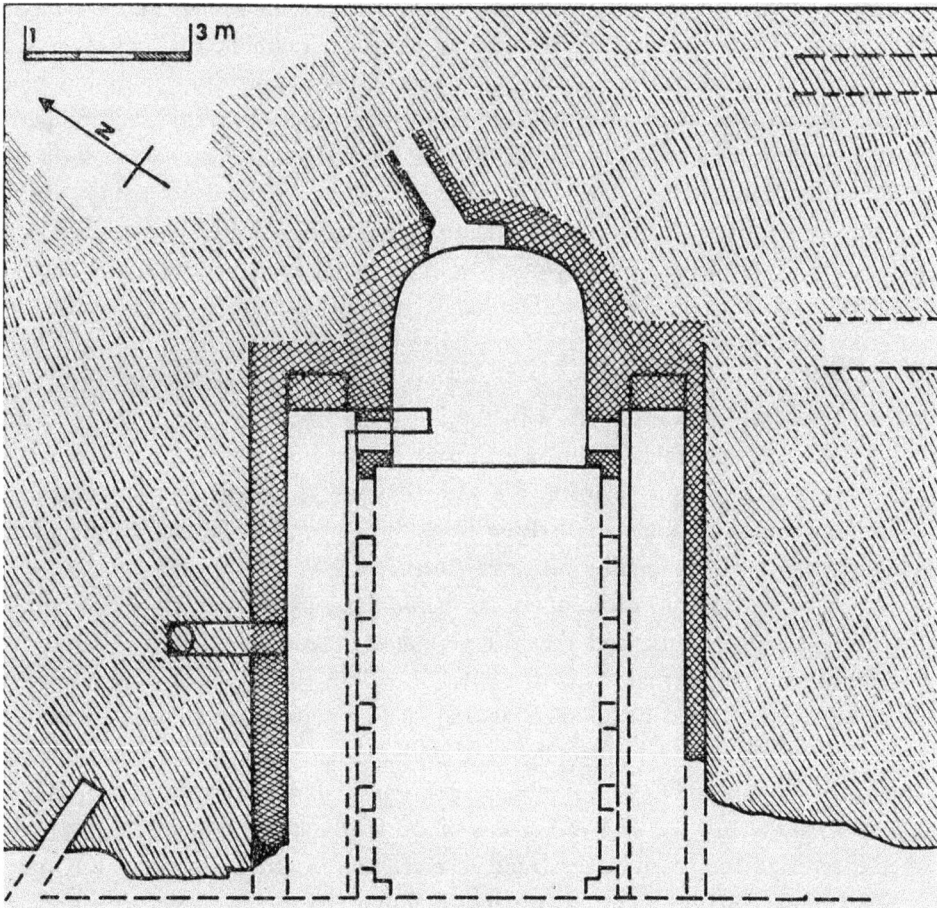

FIGURE 6.3 Late Republican fountain on the Via Appia near Formia. Photograph: Steingräber, DAI-Rom Neg. D-DAI-Rom 1982.0993.

set into a 22 meter ashlar wall. The waterspouts take the form of Oceanus masks and comprise the only decorative features of the edifice (Letzner 1990:438–439; Neuerburg 1965:147). Other Republican fountains in Italy are known at Assisi, Praeneste, and Paestum. In all three cities, these edifices share the basic form of the Formia fountain—a rectangular basin fed by one or more waterspouts—but are notably less monumental in scale (Letzner 1990:447–448; Neuerburg 1965:176; Schmölder-Veit 2009:34).

Livy provides the earliest reference to civic fountains in Rome: in 190 BCE, Scipio Africanus erected an honorific arch at the foot of the Capitoline Hill with two marble basins in front (37.3.7). The earliest archaeological evidence for a public fountain in Rome comes from the second half of the second century BCE. Standing in front of the Temple of Magna Mater on the Palatine Hill, this simple rectangular basin was filled by a waterspout set behind and above it in an ashlar wall. Fed by the Aqua Marcia, this public fountain went out of use when the piazza in which it stood was destroyed in 111 BCE (Pensabene 1988; Schmölder-Veit 2011:3). The simple rectangular forms of public fountains in Rome and other Italian cities stand in stark contrast to the opulent displays featured in contemporary villas. Even though the technology and urban water supply was available for monumental public water displays in Rome, utilitarian basins were the norm. It was not until the last generation of the Republic that grandiose water features began to be incorporated into public spaces. Moreover, those fountains placed in complexes associated with an individual elite patron, such as the theater complex of Pompey and the forum of Julius Caesar, took a decidedly more decorative form than other public fountains.

Although neither Pompey nor Caesar improved the water supply system of Rome, both took advantage of the power symbolism inherent in the aquatic displays that were encountered in elite dwellings but unfamiliar in the public domain. Pompey the Great dramatically changed the landscape of Rome when he appropriated the luxury and leisure associated with villa culture to create an enormous complex that included the first public garden in Rome, which was replete with the amenities associated with elite residences, including decorative fountains. Built on Pompey's private property in the marshy area of Rome known as the Campus Martius, Plutarch (*Pompey* 40.5) tells us that the complex gave the impression of a huge ship, rising from the empty, wet surface of the swamp, with Pompey's own house floating nearby as the dinghy.

Known as the porticus of Pompey, this garden was part of an enormous complex that included a senate house and the first permanent theater in the city (Figure 6.4). Built with the spoils of Pompey's victories over 14 nations spread across three continents, the complex was dedicated in 55 BCE as part of Pompey's triple triumph, which was celebrated with horseraces, elephant fights, and the slaughtering of lions in the Circus Maximus as well as musical and gymnastic contests in Pompey's new theater (Cicero, *Epistulae ad familiares* 7.1.2–4; Dio Cassius 39.38.1; Plutarch *Pompey* 52). Inspired by the theater at Mytilene, this theater could seat at least 11,000 people and was part of the most ambitious architectural undertakings in Rome. At the apex of the theater stood a temple to Venus Victrix—ostensibly the justification for the entire complex—as well as perhaps fourteen statues by Coponius personifying the nations conquered by Pompey

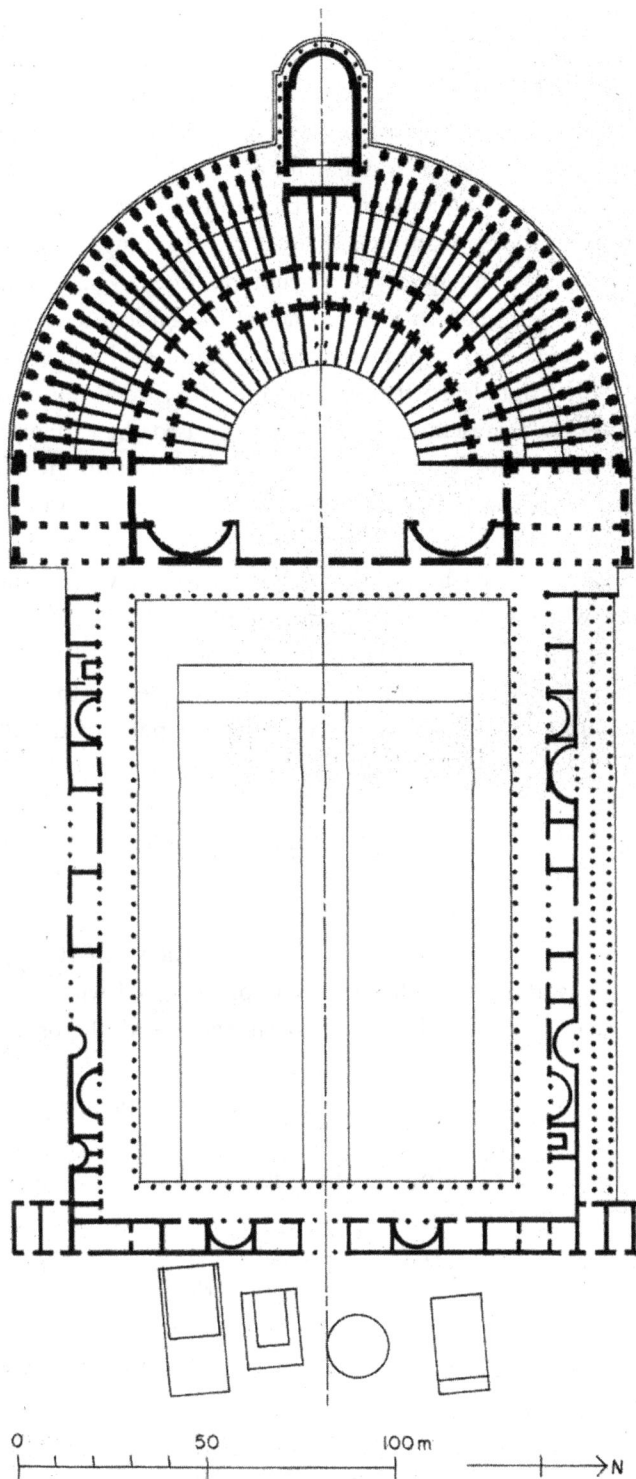

Figure 6.4 The theater and porticus complex of Pompey in Rome. Stamper 2005:fig 65. Reproduced with permission.

(Pliny, *Natural History* 7.3.34, 36.4.41; Plutarch, *Pompey* 45.2). Water flowed down channels built into the cavea of the theater, emphasizing the fertility associated with Venus and the power of Pompey who made waterfalls appear where there were none.

Unlike earlier public porticoes that housed manubial treasures, such as the porticus of Metellus in the Campus Martius, a major focal point of the porticus of Pompey was its garden and the accompanying amenities. The porticus shared many features with the gardens of the wealthy, including shaded walkways, Greek paintings and sculpture, luxurious fabrics, artificial waterways, and symbolic vegetation (Pliny, *Natural History* 12.54.111, 35.35.59, 35.37.114, 35.40.126). In every corner of the garden, references were made to Pompey's victories, references that promoted and legitimized Pompey's desired position as undisputed ruler. The double portico surrounding the garden not only served as covered walkway but also as a museum gallery that showcased the extraordinary war booty brought to Rome by Pompey (Stamper 2005:89). This collection included a portrait of Alexander the Great by Nicias the Younger, which was protected from the sun by heavy gold curtains taken from the Hellenistic capital of Pergamon. In the central garden area, low ground cover was provided by myrtle, a plant sacred to Venus, and laurel, a plant symbolic of victory, while avenues of plane trees imported by Pompey from Asia Minor provided shade. Kathryn Gleason (1994:14–17) has noted that the plane tree not only was a new type of tree for Rome but also that these examples probably were arranged in columnar rows, imitating the regularity of the manmade portico surrounding the green space, if not soldiers in rank and anticipating battle.

Limited excavations in the area of the porticus have revealed concrete platforms of monumental fountains and an associated channel with waterproof concrete (Gianfrotta, Mazzucato, and Polia 1968–69:34). These fountains have been reconstructed as either lining or dotting the main axis of the complex, where they cooled the air and provided soothing background noise (e.g., Gleason 1994:fig. 5; Packer 2010:fig. 5.25). Like the garden plants and trees, these water features were orchestrated within this larger display arena to promote and legitimize Pompey's social and political position. An elegy of Propertius (2.32.11–16) describes one of these fountains as depicting Maron, the satyr who supplied Odysseus with the heady wine offered to Polyphemos:

> Pompey's portico, I take it, is not good enough for you,
> with its shady columns, resplendent with brocaded awnings,
> or the dense avenue of plane-trees rising evenly,
> the streams which issue out of the slumbering Maron,
> or the sound of the water which splashes all round the basin,
> when Triton suddenly pours forth a fountain from his lips. (trans. Goold 1990)

The elegy suggests Maron is sprawled on his unsealed wine flask and thus unknowingly emptying it, providing the public with a comical image similar to those of inebriated followers of Dionysus frequently found in villa gardens. In this public arena, however, the humor is merged with Pompey's palpable political ambitions. Ann Kuttner (1999:357–358) has suggested that the sleeping Maron echoes the statue of Marsyas with his wine sack that stood before the Senate house in the Roman Forum, and thus it underscores how Pompey moved the political center of Rome from the Roman Forum and to a garden complex attached to his private house. Together with the plane trees and the water flowing through the theater's cavea, the Maron fountain highlighted Pompey's ability to manipulate nature to theatrical effect.

This first urban park, with its shady green spaces and entertaining fountains, quickly became one of the most popular places in Rome. Built at the height of Pompey's rivalry with Julius Caesar, Pompey offered spectacles to the average Roman that they had heard of but perhaps never experienced firsthand. And now, thanks to Pompey, they had access to the amenities and life of leisure associated with villa culture. Indeed, the association of leisure with gardens transferred to the newly conceived public area, causing elites such as Martial (11.1.11) to grumble that the idlest crowds could be found in the porticus of Pompey.

With Pompey's development of the public garden, the urban portico as well as the natural elements contained within became a popular way for elites to competitively emphasize and augment their power and authority. During his election campaign, Pompey used his gardens as a staging ground for paying off votes (Plutarch, *Pompey* 44), the environs serving to remind voters of the benefits of his leadership. Perhaps in response to this, Julius Caesar invited the general public to a feast in his private gardens to celebrate his Spanish triumph (Valerius Maximus 9.15.1). Usually, such feasts were held in the Roman Forum where the victorious general was surrounded by monuments making reference to the history of great men in Rome (Wickham 2012:21). By inviting the public to enter his garden, Caesar was able to stage his celebration in a space entirely focused on his own elite status. Plus, he fostered goodwill by allowing the general public to experience the opulent elite lifestyle in a privileged setting.

Caesar also responded to Pompey's extensive complex by building a complex of his own, the Forum of Caesar. Buying the land for this purpose within a year of Pompey's spectacular dedicatory celebrations for his complex, Caesar began to plan the complex after he defeated Pompey at the Battle of Pharsalus in 48 BCE (Ulrich 1993:51). This complex, which originally featured a temple dedicated to Venus Victrix, the patron deity of Pompey, eventually was dedicated to Venus Genetrix in order to celebrate Caesar's divine lineage. Like Pompey, Caesar used his complex to display paintings and other manubial treasures that emphasized the extent of the Caesarian victories. Unlike Pompey's complex, however, Caesar's complex did not feature a green space with the amenities associated with elite gardens. The major exception is the prominent inclusion of a monumental fountain known as the Appiades fountain (Figure 6.5 on page 126). The fountain is singled out by Ovid (*Ars amatoria* 1.79–83, 3.451–452) for its sculptural display of the Appian nymphs, a theme that calls to mind the grotto nymphaea that continued to be popular retreats in villas. But the appearance and positioning of the Appiades fountain suggest new ambitions are on display, perhaps in a concerted effort to fuse the decorative impact of private fountains with public functions. The fountain consisted of two long, narrow, brick-faced concrete walls set 1.35 m in front of the temple podium (Ulrich 1986:414). These walls, which perhaps displayed the Appian nymphs singled out by the ancient

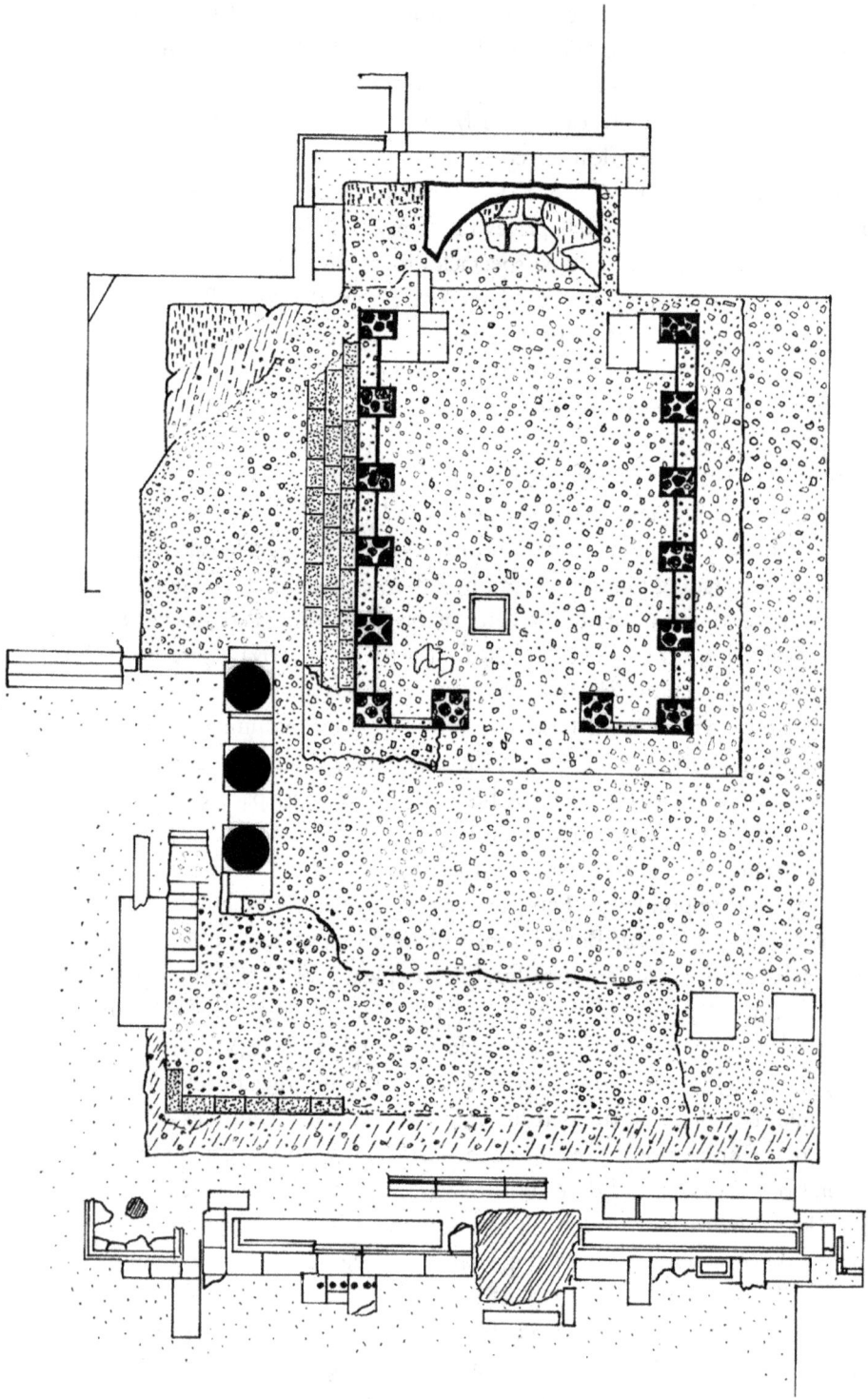

FIGURE 6.5 Temple of Venus Genetrix with the Appiades fountain in front: present state plan. © Roger B. Ulrich, by permission.

authors for attention, flanked a large central basin set into the pavement and terminated in shallow, square marble basins set into the pavement. As Roger Ulrich (1986:421–422; 1993:77) has aptly noted, the proximity of the fountain to the unusually tall temple podium effectively transformed the fountain into a security barrier for those addressing the crowd from the podium of the Temple of Venus Genetrix.

Both the Appiades Fountain in the Forum of Caesar and the fountain described by Propertius in the Porticus of Pompey borrow elements from elite residential gardens, including sculptures of nymphs, axial water displays, and the element of surprise and humor. These fountains introduced the Roman public to a new type of civic water display, one connected with the luxury of elite residences. Similar to fountains in villas, these civic fountains were experienced as one element within a much larger complex focused on the patron.

Upon his death, Caesar willed his gardens to the Roman people, and this transfer of an elite space to the Roman populace increased the goodwill and political support for Caesar's adopted son and heir, Octavian. Octavian, who took the title of Augustus in 27 BCE, shrewdly took advantage of the well-established link between political power, public green spaces, and water works. Under Augustus, three aqueducts were added and public gardens proliferated; these gardens were as carefully planted as the porticus of Pompey for impressing the public community and justifying the new emperor's authority. The walkways of the porticus of Livia were shaded by a vine famed for its wine production, while the porticus Vipsania was planted with laurels, a victory plant associated with Augustus's patron deity, Apollo (Martial, *Epistulae* 1.108.3; Pliny, *Natural History* 14.1). In addition to planted porticoes that continued the garden type begun by Pompey, Augustus transformed the Campus Martius into a public recreational area, the size of which rivaled the massive parks incorporated into country villas. Augustus's new green space in Rome included the groves around his mausoleum and those surrounding the baths of Agrippa, the first imperial bath complex in Rome. These green spaces focused attention on the transformed city of Augustus and were filled with the amenities associated with the leisure and extravagance of elite gardens. For instance, the gardens near the baths of Agrippa featured a mile-long canal that ran from an artificial basin, the *stagnum Agrippae,* to the Tiber (Lugli 1938:158–159; Strabo 13.1.19). This canal was large enough to float Nero's pleasure barge for a dinner party and was called the Euripus after the straits between Eubeoa and Greece, where the tide changes direction four times a day (Tacitus, *Annals* 15.37). This naming of the canal after a feature of the Greek landscape further associates this public area with elite amenities, for elites named parts of their villas after Greek sites. Cicero, for instance, evocatively named his peristyle at Tusculum the Academy, after Plato's Academy in Athens. Thus, the Euripus provided yet another way for the imperial circle to bestow the trappings of elite culture on the general populace of Rome.

For the Romans, where land ownership and political authority went hand in hand, cultivated nature could be used as a political tool. The venerable connection between political power, nature, and artifice created an atmosphere in which Pompey and Caesar could use gardens, both public and private, to announce their ambitions and further their respective political careers. Augustus recognized the public appeal of green spaces and associated artistic water displays, and, as part of his efforts to create a new political stability in Rome, he sanctioned civic green spaces dotted with water spectacles for the leisure activities for the general public. Moreover, it was under Augustus that the monumental decorative civic fountain was transformed from being one amenity among many set within a large space to a monumental stand-alone edifice that could telegraph the ideology of the emperor. For instance, a 16-meter-tall conical fountain stood near the birthplace of Augustus and marked the convergence of at least four of the fourteen Augustan regions of the city. Its shape recalls the baetyl, which Augustus adopted as a symbol of Apollo (Panella 1990:53). The connection between Augustus and a conical monument at this juncture would have been self-evident for any and all Romans steeped in Augustan ideology.

REFERENCES CITED

Cook, K., and R. Foulk. 2013 Gardens and the Larger Landscape. In *A Cultural History of Gardens in Antiquity* vol. 1, edited by K. Gleason, pp 177–196. Bloomsbury Academic, London and New York.

D'Arms, J. 1970 *Romans on the Bay of Naples: A Social and Cultural Study of the Villas and Their Owners from 150 B.C. to A.D. 400*. Harvard University Press, Cambridge.

Evans, H. 1993 *In Tiburtium usum*: Special Arrangements in the Roman Water System (Frontinus, *Aq.* 6.5). *American Journal of Archaeology* 97:447–455.

Gianfrotta, P. A., O. Mazzucato, and M. Polia. 1968–69 Scavo nell'area del teatro Argentina (1968–1969). *BullCom* 81:25–36.

Giuliani, C. F., and M. Guaitoli. 1972 Il ninfeo minore della villa detta di Cicerone a Formia. *Mitteilungen des Deutschen Archäologischen Instituts. Römische Abteilung* 72:191–219.

Gleason, K. 1994 *Porticus Pompeiana*: A New Perspective on the First Public Park of Ancient Rome. *Journal of Garden History* 14:13–27.

Goold, G. P. 1990 *Propertius Elegies*. Harvard University Press, Cambridge.

Higgenbotham, J. 1997 Piscinae: *Artificial Fishponds in Roman Italy*. The University of North Carolina Press, Chapel Hill and London.

Kuttner, A. 1999 Culture and History at Pompey's Museum. *Transactions of the American Philological Association* 129:343–373.

Letzner, W. 1990 Römische Brunnen und Nymphaea in der westlichen Reichshälfte. Lit, Münster.

Lugli, G. 1938 *I monumenti antichi di Roma e suburbia*. Vol. 3. G. Bardi, Rome.

Marzano, A. 2007 *Roman Villas in Central Italy: A Social and Economic History*. Brill, Leiden and Boston.

Mari, Z., and F. Boanelli. 1991 La villa di Quintilio Varo. *Bollettino di archeologia* 10: 37–50.

Neuerburg, N. 1965 *L'architettura della fontane e dei ninfei nell'Italia antica*. Gaetano Macchiaroli, Naples.

Neuerburg, N. 1968 The Other Villas of Tivoli. *Archaeology* 21:288–297.

Packer, J. 2010 Pompey's Theater and Tiberius' Temple of Concord: A Late Republican Primer for an Early Imperial Patron. In *The Emperor and Rome: Space, Representation, and Ritual*, edited by B. Ewald and C. Noreña, pp. 135–168. Cambridge University Press, Cambridge.

Panella, C. 1990 La valle del Colosseo nell'antichità. *Bollettino di Archeologia* 1–2:34–88.

Pensabene, P. 1988 Scavi nell'area del tempio della Vittoria e del santuario della Magna Mater sul Palatino. *Archeologia Laziale* 9:54–67.

Purcell, N. 1987 Town in Country and Country in Town. In *Ancient Roman Villa Gardens*, edited by E. B. MacDougall, pp. 187–203. Dumbarton Oaks, Washington, DC.

Quilici, L. 1969 *La Grotta di Paris a S. Vittorino.* 'L'Erma' di Bretschneider, Rome.

Schmölder-Veit, A. 2009 *Brunnen in den Städten des westlichen Römischen Reichs.* Dr. Ludwig Reichert, Wiesbaden.

Schmölder-Veit, A. 2011 Aqueducts for the *Urbis Clarissimus Locus*: The Palatine's Water Supply from Republican to Imperial Times. *The Waters of Rome* 7:1–26.

Sear, F. 1977 *Roman Wall and Vault Mosaics.* F. H. Kerle, Heidelberg.

Stamper, J. W. 2005 *The Architecture of Roman Temples: The Republic to the Middle Empire.* Cambridge University Press, Cambridge and New York.

Tamm, B. 1963 *Auditorium and Palatium: A Study on Assembly-Rooms in Roman Palaces during the 1st Century B.C. and 1st Century A.D.* Almqvist & Wiksell, Stockholm.

Thomas, R., and A. Wilson. 1994 Water Supply for Roman Farms in Latium and South Etruria. *Papers of the British School in Rome* 62:139–196.

Ulrich, R.B. 1986 The Appiades Fountain of the Forum Iulium. *Mitteilungen des Deutschen Archäologischen Instituts, Römische Abteilung* 93:405–423.

Ulrich, R. B. 1993 Julius Caesar and the Creation of the Forum Iulium. *American Journal of Archaeology* 97:49–80.

Von Stackelberg, K. 2009 *The Roman Garden: Space, Sense, and Society.* Routledge, London and New York.

Wallace-Hadrill, A. 1998 The Villa as Cultural Symbol. In *The Roman Villa:* Villa Urbana, edited by A. Frazer, pp. 43–53. Philadelphia, University of Pennsylvania Museum.

Wickham, L. 2012 *Gardens in History: A Political Perspective.* Oxbow Books, Oxford.

Wilson, A. 1999 Deliveries *extra urbem*: Aqueducts and the Countryside. *Journal of Roman Archaeology* 12: 314–331.

Zarmakoupi, M. 2014 *Designing for Luxury on the Bay of Naples: Villas and Landscapes (c. 100 BCE–79 CE).* Oxford University Press, Oxford.

CHAPTER SEVEN

From Urban Oasis to Desert Hinterland

The Decline of Petra's Water System. The Case of the Petra Garden and Pool Complex

Leigh-Ann Bedal

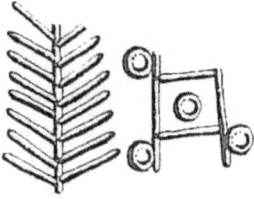

Abstract *During the height of the Nabataean kingdom (late first century BCE–first century CE), its capital city, Petra, reflected its increasing wealth and status with all of the trappings of power and prestige exhibited in political and ceremonial centers in the Hellenistic-Roman World. To convert a dry wadi valley in southern Jordan into an urban center, the Nabataeans developed engineering skills to construct a complex hydraulic system that exploited local springs and water runoff to serve the practical needs of Petra's population, but also to supply installations of water display. The Petra Garden and Pool Complex, a luxury garden with a monumental pool located in the city center, exemplifies the conspicuous consumption of water as a symbol of abundance and prosperity. As Petra's economy began to wane in Late Antiquity, transforming from capital city to hinterland, maintenance of its elaborate hydraulic system ceased. While the springs continued to flow, channels, cisterns, and pools fell into disrepair. Remnant seminomadic populations and periodic settlers constructed small-scale localized systems and re-used old elements of the Nabataean water system, but the potential of its spring resources were never again fully exploited. This paper reviews the decline of Petra's hydraulic infrastructure with special attention to evidence from the Petra Garden and Pool Complex, which transformed into an agricultural plot from Late Antiquity through the modern era.*

A TALE OF TWO AQUEDUCTS

A century ago, local folklore was documented by explorers and scholars who visited the site of Petra in southern Transjordan. One tale relates the story of two men who competed for the Nabataean princess' hand in marriage. The princess was confined to the palace and needed to quench her thirst. In order to accomplish this, each man set out to procure water by building conduits from two different spring sources—'Ain Brak and 'Ain Musa ('Ain Abu Haroun). While accounts of the story vary as to who won the contest and why,[1] the prevailing theme preserved in this folktale is the necessity of the construction of channels to transport spring water into Petra's city center.

Petra and Its Environment

Petra is located approximately 80 kilometers southeast of the Dead Sea in modern Jordan (30°19'N, 35°28'E). It is situated on the northwestern edge of the Arabian Desert, in Jordan's Western Highland/Western Mountain geological region (Macumber 2001:19–26), which forms the eastern border of the Wadi 'Araba, a section of the Great Rift Valley. The ancient city is situated on the western slopes of the Sharā Mountain Range, in a wide basin surrounded by deeply eroded mountainous ridges of sandstone, with outcrops of limestone and porphyry that form a natural fortification. Wadis that cut through the canyon walls functioned as communication routes between the eastern plateau and Wadi 'Araba (Figure 7.1).

The development of Petra as an important political, economic, and cultural center in the Near East during the Hellenistic-Roman period (first century BCE–second century CE) was ultimately the result of its strategic position on the crossroads of the major trade and communication routes that crossed the region. At Petra, the major north-south route (the King's Highway), which created a link between the Gulf of Aqaba and Syria, intersected with the trans-Arabian routes (to southern Yemen and the Arabian Gulf) and the trans-Negev route (to Gaza and the Mediterranean Sea). Wadi Musa, the narrow valley along which Petra developed, provided one of the few convenient and negotiable routes through the mountainous barrier allowing caravans to pass between the high desert plateau to the east and Wadi 'Araba to the west. This strategic position on the crossroads of the desert trade routes made it possible for the inhabitants of Petra to establish control over the caravans that traveled between Arabia and the Mediterranean (Erickson and Israel 2013; Graf and Sidebottom 2003; Hammond 1973:66–68).[2]

Recent studies of the world's water resources rank Jordan as one of the most water-deprived countries in the world. In 2003, Jordan ranked eleventh of water-poor countries by the United Nations Food and Agriculture Organization (FAO) (2003:table 4). By 2008, Jordan was ranked fourth (Denny et al. 2008:2). In 2014, Jordan placed second with water per capita cited at 88 percent below the international water poverty line of 1,000 cubic meters (Namrouqa 2014). The climate of modern Jordan is classified as Mediterranean, with hot, dry summers and cool, arid winters, although its elevation and distance inland from the Mediterranean Sea result in more extreme temperature fluctuations. Precipitation is limited to a rainy season, October through April, with variations in the annual rainfall from year to year. Much of Jordan receives less than 250 mm of precipitation annually, and much of the water is lost to evaporation and drainage into the Jordan Valley, Dead Sea, and Wadi 'Araba. Between 1980 and 2007, the annual

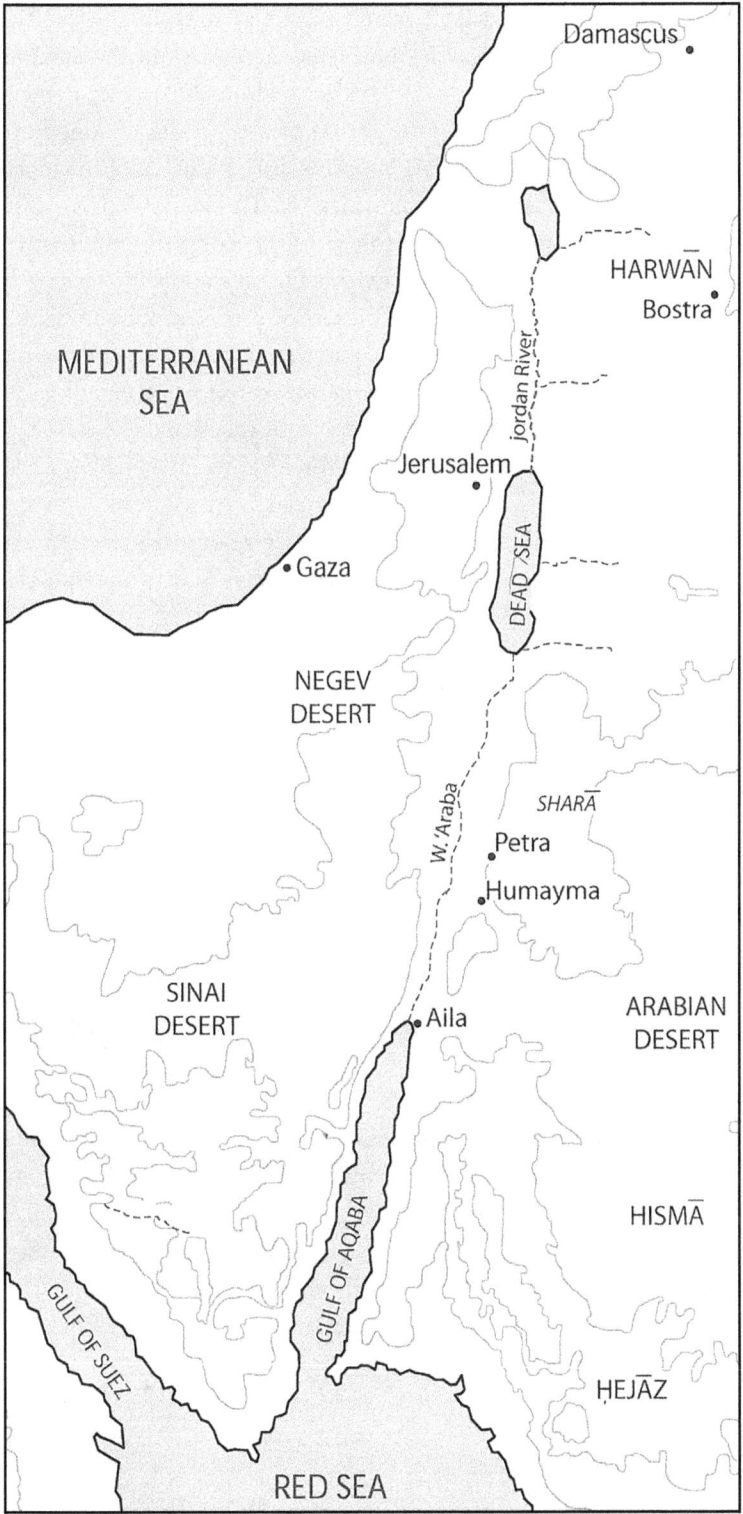

Figure 7.1 Map showing the location of Petra.

rainfall in Petra averaged around 150 mm (Al-Farajat and Salameh 2012:328–329). At least 300 mm of rainfall per year is considered necessary for sustainable agriculture (Macdonald 2000:21–43; MacDonald 2001:596; Oleson 2001:603; Parker 2006:518). Studies indicate that the climate during the period of the Nabataean kingdom was similar to current conditions with slightly wetter conditions during the Late Roman and Byzantine periods, between the second and sixth centuries (cf. Parker 2006:518). Remnants of a wooded forest of oak and juniper can be found today along the mountain range north of Petra, stretching between Hisha and Shawbak. Deforestation in the area began in the Bronze Age with copper mining and other intensive forms of human exploitation such as charcoal production, firewood harvesting, and land clearing (Macdonald 2000:38).

Most of the agricultural activity for Petra was carried out along wadis that drain into the Wadi 'Araba valley during the short winter rainy season. The soils are particularly good for cultivation, but irrigation is required for a more sustainable intensive production due to the low rainfall (Alcock and Knodell 2012; Al-Muheisin 1992; Beckers and Schütt 2013; Macdonald 2000:35). Since local water resources are often insufficient to sustain life in this region, settled populations have always had to manipulate the natural hydrology to the best of their ability.

The Water System of Nabataean Petra

The Nabataeans' knowledge of water sources and water-harvesting skills are observed in contemporary Classical sources. As early as the fourth century BCE, Hieronymus of Cardia is credited for noting their use of subterranean concrete-lined cisterns concealed below narrow openings to conserve and protect their watering holes.[3] However, the ancient texts lack detailed descriptions of the complex hydraulic technology that served Petra. The modern study of Nabatean water systems began with Nelson Glueck (1959:90–97, 72–73), who described surviving features in his survey of the southern Levant in the early to mid-twentieth century, and intensified over the next few decades, substantiating the designation of the Nabataeans as "Masters of the Desert."[4] A systematic study of the hydraulic installations in Petra was initiated in the early 1980s by Zeidoun Al-Muheisin (1983, 1986) and has been greatly enhanced by survey and excavation conducted over the last three decades.[5] Of particular importance is the excavation of the *Siq* (the narrow gorge entrance to Petra) in the 1990s, under the auspices of the Petra National Trust, which revealed valuable information about the transport and storage of water in the *Siq* as well as the floodwater diversion system (Bellwald et al. 2003), and allowed for a more comprehensive understanding of Petra's hydraulic infrastructure (Bellwald 2008) upon which the following description is based.

Hydraulic Infrastructure

In a description of Petra dated to the late first century BCE, the Greek geographer Strabo noted two factors significant to the establishment of Petra as an urban settlement despite its arid desert environment: its natural fortification and reliable water sources:

The capital of the Nabataeans is called Petra. It is situated on a spot which is surrounded and fortified by a smooth and level rock, which externally is abrupt and precipitous, but within there are abundant springs of water both for domestic purposes and for watering gardens. Beyond the enclosure the country is for the most part a desert, particularly towards Judea. (*Geog.* XVI.4.21)[6]

The primary source of Petra's water was a chain of natural springs that arise along a continuous elongated recharge mound formed in the Sharā mountain range in the vicinity of Petra (Al Atteyat et al. 2013:6; Al-Farajat and Salameh 2012:327–328). In order for the city's inhabitants to benefit fully from the nearby perennial springs, the Nabataeans designed a complex system of aqueducts and pressure pipelines, using bridges and arches to transport water across rough terrain and deep ravines to strategic locations within the city. Reservoirs, cisterns, and dams collect every available drop of water from these perennial springs supplemented by runoff catchment of the meager rainfall in order to provide a reliable water resource for the demands of a growing urban population (commonly estimated at 30,000). Nabatean stonecutters, known for carving monumental facades into the cliff faces, applied their stonecutting skills to the engineering challenges of Petra's hydraulic works (Hammond 1967:37–38). The dating of the construction of the spring aqueducts corresponds with the height of Petra's prosperity in the late first century BCE through the mid-late first century CE.[7]

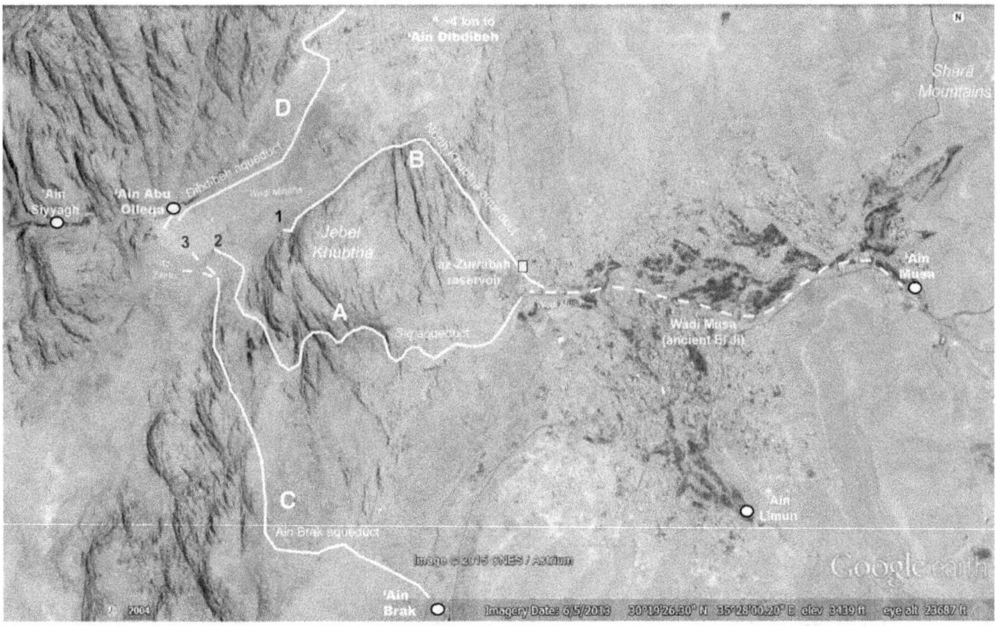

FIGURE 7.2 Map showing the locations of the spring sources, the major aqueducts (A–D), and their termini (1–3) in the city center. Display of water system by L. Bedal, based on Bellwald (2008: Fig. 3). Google Earth satellite image accessed 6/5/2013.

The main water source for ancient Petra was 'Ain Musa located on the western slope of the Sharā range approximately 5 kilometers east of the city center (3.50 km from the entrance to the *Siq*). Its water feeds two of Petra's major conduits: the Khubtha North aqueduct led around the north edge of the Khubtha Mountain, terminating at the east edge of the Petra basin; the *Siq* aqueduct led down through the *Siq* gorge and into the city center (Figure 7.2). In the *Siq,* a channel was cut first along the north wall and installed with interlocking ceramic water pipes. Later, a channel was cut along the south wall and covered with stone slabs (Bellwald et al. 2008:49–55) (Figure 7.3).

Despite these efforts to bring water into Petra, the narrow *Siq* and its multiple inlets presented a serious threat of dangerous and destructive flash floods during the rainy season.[8] To prevent such events, the Nabataeans designed a flood prevention system that included a diversion dam and tunnel (40 m long) to direct most of the water north to empty into Wadi Mataha, ultimately converging with Wadi Musa in the city center, where walls and diversion channels kept the water flow in check. Several smaller dams were built across the small wadis that empty into the *Siq* (Bellwald 2008:69–76; Gunsam 1980; Hammond 1967:42; Al-Muheisin and Tarrier 1995, 1996). Their reservoirs created useful water storage for the dry months. Numerous rock-cut cisterns are found throughout Petra for catching and storing water runoff to supplement the spring water supply (Hammond 1967).

South channel

North channel

FIGURE 7.3 Water channels cut into the north and south walls of the *Siq* gorge entrance onto Petra (Photo by L. Bedal, 2001).

A second major spring source that served Petra in antiquity was 'Ain Brak, located in the Sharā range 3.50 kilometers southeast of the city center. The 'Ain Brak aqueduct entered Petra from the south, terminating at the southern edge of the city center (Bellwald 2008:56–58; Lindner 1997) (Figure 7.2). 'Ain Abu Olleqa, located at the west end of the city proper, could not have been a primary water distribution source due to its low elevation. Its water serviced facilities in the temenos area at the west end of the city (Bellwald 2008:58) (Figures 7.2 and 7.7 C). Remnants of both the 'Ain Brak (Figure 7.4) and 'Ain Abu Olleqa aqueducts show that they were finely constructed of ashlar masonry—each composed of double channels—one open flow, one pipeline—crossing difficult terrain, with arches to span gulleys and ravines (Bellwald 2008:58). When the demands of the thriving city outgrew the output of the three local springs, probably in the late first century CE, an aqueduct was constructed from 'Ain Dibdibeh, six kilometers northeast of Petra, terminating at a reservoir at the west end of the city center, opposite the Qasr al-Bint (Bellwald 2008:60–61) (Figures 7.2 and 7.7 B). The spring in Wadi es-Siyagh probably never played a major role in supplying Petra's civic needs due to its location at a significantly lower elevation west of the city center. The total length of the aqueduct channels and pipelines associated with the four spring sources has been calculated to measure more than 55,000 meters, with the potential volume of water supplied to Petra estimated to be approximately 132 million cubic meters (MCM) per year (Bellwald 2008:61–64, Tables 1 and 2).

FIGURE 7.4 A section of the 'Ain Brak aqueduct, heading west from the source (Photo from Petra Garden Feasibility Study, 2001).

Water Display

As stated, the purpose of the aqueducts was to transport water from external springs over several kilometers to strategic points in the city center. It was here that the Nabataeans accentuated their achievement with prominent water installations that demonstrated the Nabataeans' control over their water sources, so much as to produce a surplus that could be wasted in displays of conspicuous consumption. The Khubtha North aqueduct terminated at a large rock-cut apsidal nymphaeum with terraced basins adjacent to the monumental rock-cut façades known as the "Royal Tombs" that dominate the east face of the Petra Valley (Figures 7.5 and 7.7 N–O). Bellwald's survey demonstrates that the aqueduct feeds into a pool at the base of the nymphaeum (2008:52, fig. 8). However, this does not explain the purpose of the prominent apse behind the pool. Laureano incorrectly reconstructs the aqueduct to feed into the top of the nymphaeum so that the water would cascade down as a waterfall (1994:76). It is worth noting that the large rock shelf immediately above the nymphaeum (Figure 7.5) remains uncleared and could potentially hold a basin to catch runoff from the precipice above, its overflow washing over as a waterfall to join the aqueduct water in the basins below. Therefore, while the Khubtha nymphaeum may have featured a waterfall, its existence remains to be proven.[9]

Figure 7.5 The Khubtha Nymphaeum, far left, adjacent to the "Royal Tombs" (Photo by L. Bedal. 1998).

FIGURE 7.6 The South Nymphaeum, with Jennifer Ramsay as scale (Photo by L. Bedal, 2011).

The *Siq* aqueduct terminated at the South Nymphaeum (Figure 7.6) at the east end of the Colonnaded Street, opposite the confluence of Wadi Musa and Wadi Mataha (Bellwald 2008:54, fig. 10) (Figure 7.7 I). The South Nymphaeum remains unexcavated and so the details of its waterworks remain unknown. However, its location marked the entrance into the city center proper, and would have served as a public assembly area and place to find a refreshing splash of water for locals and visitors alike as they carried out their activities in the city.

The 'Ain Brak aqueduct terminates at the very heart of the city at a small reservoir perched on the edge of a rock cliff that provides water to a monumental pool and garden, a kind of *paradeisos* that is one component of a larger complex that occupies the Southern Terrace of Petra's city center, including the Great Temple, and the as yet unexplored "Middle Market" and "Upper Market" (Bedal 2004:171–178) (Figure 7.7 J–M).[10] The Petra Garden and Pool Complex (PGPC) is the only example of a Nabataean garden known in the archaeological record, and is one of the few ancient garden sites to be excavated and studied in the region.[11] Close parallels found in the excavated gardens and pools of contemporary palaces at Jericho, Herodium, Masada, and Caesarea Maritima (Gleason and Bar-Nathan 2013; Netzer 2001), and at Ramat Hanadiv (Hirschfield 2000) in neighboring Judaea dated to the reign of the Hasmonean Dynasty (168–40 BCE) and

A. Qasr al-Bint
B. 'Ain Dibdebeh aqueduct terminus
C. 'Ain Abu Olleqa
D. Temple of the Winged Lions
E. Petra Church

F. Temenos Gate
G. Colonnaded Street
H. North Nymphaeum
I. South Nymphaeum
J. Great Temple

K. Garden and Pool Complex
L. "Middle Market"
M. "Upper Market"
N. "Royal Tombs"
O. Khubtha Nymphaeum

FIGURE 7.7 Locations of the major monuments and features in the Petra valley. Map by L. Bedal, Google Earth satellite 2004, image accessed 6/5/2013.

Herod the Great (37–4 BCE) support the author's interpretation of the PGPC as part of an elite/palace complex laid out on the Southern Terrace.[12]

Excavations over eight field seasons have revealed the remains of a monumental swimming pool[13] with an island-pavilion that was decorated in imported marble and painted stucco (Al-Bashaireh and Bedal 2015; Bedal 2004:50–59; Bedal et al. 2007:159–162). The complex was constructed early in the reign of the Nabataean king, Aretas IV (9 BCE–40 CE) and continued in use for a period of time after the Roman annexation of Petra in 106 CE (Bedal et al. 2007:163–165). The garden terrace has a series of built features (two stone platforms and a pergola-like structure) laid out along its central north-south axis, which is bisected by a stone-lined (possibly colonnaded) pathway along its central east-west axis (Bedal et al. 2011:325–326). Evidence for plantings in the form of tree pits, root cavities, and ceramic planting pots, *olla perforate,* allow the identification of some of the locations for plants on the garden terrace (Bedal et al. 2007:158; 2011:324–326; Macauley Lewis 2006)[14] (Fig. 11).

An elaborate water distribution system was incorporated into the design and construction of the pool and garden. As described above, the 'Ain Brak aqueduct transported water to the southern terrace, terminating at a reservoir ("East Cistern") perched more than ten meters above the pool. Based on findings in the 2013 field season, it appears that water flowed down to the pool level—probably in a controlled manner—via an apsidal cut in the bedrock escarpment (a smaller version of the rock-cut apse of the North Khubtha nymphaeum) in the southeastern corner of the pool complex (Figures 7.8 and 7.9 on page 142).[15] The pool's capacity is estimated at 2,122 cubic meters of water based on its dimension, 43 × 23 meters, 2.5 meters deep (calculating the space occupied by the island). The inlet to fill the pool from the ʿAin Brak source has not yet been uncovered. A subterranean cistern (capacity of 327 cubic meters) cut into the

FIGURE 7.8 Map of the water system of the Petra Garden and Pool Complex (Photo by S. K. Reid, 2001).

FIGURE 7.9 View of the "East Cistern" and rock-cut apse, a possible nymphaeum/ waterfall, in the southeastern corner of the PGPC pool complex (Photo by L. Bedal, 2013).

bedrock of the Great Temple's East Plaza (Joukowsky and Cloke 2007:433–435) likely provided supplemental water to the pool complex when needed. A channel directing water to the pool from the west side may be connected to the cistern. Additionally, pipelines—both ceramic and lead—laid under the pavement on the west promenade also appear to originate from the direction of the Great Temple cistern.[16] While the pipelines may belong to the original water system, they more likely were laid during renovations carried out soon after Roman annexation (Bedal et al. 2007:164–165). Excavations have exposed large sections of a channel that was originally covered by the pavement of the promenade that circumscribes the pool. This channel transported water around the pool's perimeter, and flowed into a tank (*castellum*), which fed into stone conduits, part of an irrigation system for the expansive (65 × 53 meters) garden laid out on the adjoining earthen terrace. A 2001 geophysical survey of the garden terrace using ground-penetrating radar (GPR) detected evidence for a large, underground cistern in the southeastern area of the terrace (Conyers et al. 2002). Two large subterranean channels cut into the bedrock along the east border of the terrace indicate the existence of a separate system that bypassed the pool and garden, perhaps to direct wastewater from the Az-Zantur residences or destructive floodwater into the wadi (Bedal et al. 2009:322–323).

To complete the review of the spring aqueducts, 'Ain Abu Olleqa and the terminus of the 'Ain Dibdibeh aqueduct coincide with the sacred area of Petra's temple to Dushara, the Qasr al-Bint (Figure 7.7 A, B, and C). While no installations of prominent water display are identified in this area, remnants of a channel and pool found in an earlier phase of an apsidal monument dedicated to the late-second-century-CE emperors Marcus Aurelius and Lucius Verus demonstrate the presence of some form of water feature (Auge et al. 2014:72–73). Its location suggests the 'Ain Abu Olleqa aqueduct as its most likely source and fits the pattern of water display features marking the terminus of aqueducts in Nabataean Petra. On the other hand, the reservoir at the terminus of the 'Ain Dibdibeh aqueduct is poorly preserved and shows no evidence for display. However, this may be easily explained by the fact that the Dibdibeh aqueduct as a later addition toward the end of Nabataean rule was constructed to serve purely practical purposes, at a time in which water display was perhaps impractical or at least did not take priority.

The use of extravagant water display marking the terminus of Petra's major aqueducts is astonishing when one considers the amount of wasted water due to evaporation from waterfalls and open-air pools. It contradicts the assumption of desert inhabitants as inherent conservators of their most precious resource. But it is exactly this contradiction that would have compelled the Nabataean rulers to commission such public works: that fountains, pools, expansive gardens, and (perhaps) waterfalls are unexpected spectacles in a desert. Only at very productive oases might desert travelers expect to see lavish displays of water usage and waste. But Petra was not an oasis. The Nabataean ruler who commissioned these waterworks (symbolized by the princess in our folktale) must have seen a benefit to gambling precious resources. For him to develop and maintain a hydraulic system that provided sufficient water to the inhabitants of this desert city was accomplishment enough to earn the respect and acknowledgment of his citizens, but to exploit and command the natural resources in such a way as to be able to supply multiple nymphaea and a recreational swimming pool and to water a *paradeisos* was truly remarkable. The creation of an urban oasis delivered a powerful statement to merchants and foreign delegates entering the city after a long journey through the harsh desert environment, impressing them with a gratuitous display of conspicuous consumption, a symbol to observant rivals of the Nabataean king's power and Petra's wealth and status.[17]

DECLINE AND TRANSFORMATION AFTER THE NABATAEANS

What has been described thus far is the water system of Petra, as currently understood, during its "Golden Age," the first century BCE–first century CE. In CE 106, the kingdom was annexed into the Roman Empire and Petra maintained its status as capital of what was now called *Provincia Arabia* (Bowersock 1971). Initially, under the Romans, the city flourished politically and economically. There is evidence for renovations of several monuments and the North Nymphaeum was erected at the entrance to the Colonnaded Street (opposite the South Nymphaeum) (Figure 7.7 H), evidence that the practice of water display continued for some time under the Romans whose aqueducts, fountains, pools, and gardens served as symbols of luxury and prestige (i.e., Berg 1994:92ff; Hodge 1992:5–6; Jashemski 1996; Jones and Robinson 1998; Wilson 1995). An additional pipeline was installed in the *Siq* to convey water to a cistern at the far eastern end of the city, opposite the theater. However, by the third century CE, the buildup of lime deposits threatened to burst the pipes in the *Siq* system and so the tops were cut off, transforming it to an open flow system (Bellwald 2008:53). This example of an unsophisticated solution to a significant threat to Petra's water system reflects a decline that is evidenced elsewhere in the city.

By the third century CE, Petra experienced a loss of privileged economic status as its position in the long-distance caravan trade system changed (trade routes shifted to the north and south). No new public buildings were being built and some residential areas (Az-Zantur, Katute) show evidence of abandonment (Fiema 2002:199, 239; Khairy 1990:3–8; Kolb 1998:267). In the PGPC, a deep stratum of soil and debris (chock-full of pottery and animal bones) was deposited along the pool bottom (Figure 7.11 A), showing a lack of maintenance over a long period of time, extending into the fourth century. It is probably during this time that a wall of reused stones was built up against the face of the pool's north wall and a ceramic pipeline running east-west across the site was installed into the face of the new wall and inside the decorative moulding along the base of the pool façade, using mortar and chinking to hold it in place (Figure 7.10). The orientation of the bell and socket pipe segments show that the water was being transported from west to east (from the Great Temple toward the "Middle Market"), and it may be related to the Late Roman Bath complex west of the Great Temple (Joukowsky 2007:88–98), although the pipeline is not preserved beyond its encasement in the pool façade moulding.

FIGURE 7.10 The pool's façade (north wall), with the *castellum* at center. The Late Roman wall against the face of the pool wall is on the left. The dashed line traces the bottom of the pipeline installed in the LR wall and the pool wall moulding (Photo by L. Bedal, 1998).

The purpose of the Late Roman wall is unclear as the pool's north wall's façade appears to be well preserved behind the Late Roman wall, but answers may come with future removal of the Late Roman wall.[18] These new installations, which can only be described as an unsightly blemish against the finely built, monumental Nabataean architecture, is testimony to the decline of Petra and its infrastructure during this period. It is clear that the site of the PGPC was no longer a representation of abundance and wealth.

In 363, a major earthquake struck the region, causing damage to cities from northern Palestine to the Gulf of Aqaba. A Syriac text describes the destruction, noting for Petra that "a third of the city was destroyed," which is evidenced by vast rubble deposits from structural collapse found throughout Petra (Russell 1980).[19] In the PGPC, a layer of stone rubble, the collapse of the upper courses of the island-pavilion and the walls of the pool's promenade, immediately overlying deposits of the third through mid-fourth century CE is testimony to earthquake destruction (Bedal 2004:76–79, Bedal et al. 2007:165) (Figure 7.11 B). In addition to the major monuments and residences, serious damage suffered by

FIGURE 7.11 A deep trench inside the pool reveals (A) a stratum of debris collected on the pool bottom prior to (B) the deposit of earthquake rubble dated to 363 CE, followed by (C) a long period of disuse, followed by (D) a second earthquake event in the Late Byzantine period (Photo by L. Bedal, 2001).

the 'Ain Brak and Dibdebeh aqueducts are attributed to the 363 earthquake, and there is no evidence that they were ever rebuilt (Bellwald 2008:58, 61). Damage to the *Siq* water system—including the flood prevention system—put much of it permanently out of commission. Only the south channel was repaired to working order, but the repair was shoddy and the channel no longer covered (Bellwald 2008:54). The lack of repair to the monuments and water system demonstrates the decline of Petra's political and economic infrastructure at the onset of its Byzantine Christian era (mid-fourth to seventh centuries), after more than two and one-half centuries of Roman rule. A destructive earthquake has greater impact on a city that is already not thriving.

During the fifth and sixth centuries CE, Petra's settlement was mostly restricted to the northern area of the city, with some domestic occupation at Katute in the south (end of the sixth century only), and in the shops at the east end of the Colonnaded Street (Fiema 2002:221). It is difficult to estimate the population size of this Byzantine community inside Petra, but it was large enough and prosperous enough to boast three churches, the largest of which (The Petra Church, Figure 7.7 E) possessed marble furnishings and finely worked figural mosaics (Bikai 2002; Waliszewski 2001), which stood in contrast to the ruins of the former Nabataean capital that lay around them. The historical record tells us that Byzantine Petra was endowed with the status of "metropolitan see" and the honorifics *Palaestina Salutaris* and *Palaestina Tertia* during this period (Fiema 2002:193, 213). The Petra scrolls inform us that much of the local population was settled in agricultural villages outside of Petra, to the east (El Ji, modern Wadi Musa) and hinterlands, in closer proximity to the spring sources and slightly more rainfall (Fiema 2002:207; Nasarat et al. 2012). However, the destruction of the spring water aqueduct system in 363 meant that the Byzantine community inside the Petra valley was reliant on the one internal spring, 'Ain Abu Olleqa, and rainwater catchment. A channel dating to the Late Roman building underlying the Petra Church is described by the excavators as a "well-built, solid, masonry construction" that would have been suitable as a conduit connected to the Dibdebeh aqueduct (bringing water into city from the north) (Fiema 2001:15–16). However, this channel was intentionally blocked up when the church was constructed—probably due the fact that the aqueduct was long ago destroyed and the channel no longer of use. Instead, the church's enclosed atrium was designed for efficient rainfall catchment from the surrounding rooftops with a large cistern for storage (Fiema 2001:50). The Late Roman and Early Byzantine residences on Ez-Zantur (the southern ridge) also show a reliance on rainwater catchment (Kolb and Stucky 1993:422) as maintenance of the city's water system declined and the spring aqueducts were ultimately destroyed. The need for reliance on rainwater harvesting may have benefited from the region's proposed slightly wetter conditions during the Roman and Byzantine periods (Issar 1995:351–352; MacDonald 2001:599; McCormick et al. 2012:203–205).

Another indication of the demise of the basic infrastructure that had supported the construction and maintenance of the city's water system is the evidence for unrepaired damage to the Nabataean flood prevention system following the 363 earthquake. Excavations of the "shops" along the street revealed that alluvial deposits in this area began to build up in the late fourth century, and damage continued over the next few centuries as the flood prevention system was no longer maintained (Fiema 1998:420; 2002:198–199).

Geoscientist Tom Paradise documented extensive alluvial deposits that indicate a major flood event in the fourth-fifth century to which he attributes the destruction of the North Nymphaeum and washing away of much of the street pavement (Paradise 2011).

In the PGPC, a stratum of grayish-brown soil covers the entire terrace, including the remains of architectural elements of the Nabataean period garden. The soil has characteristics of cultivation, including a heavy inclusion of ash, which is used as fertilizer. It is apparent that, as early as the end of the Late Roman period and continuing through the Byzantine period, the expansive garden terrace was converted into an agricultural field. Although little attention has been given to the post-363 soil deposits on the terraces along the southern side of Nabataean Petra's city center, from the Upper Market to the Qasr al-Bint (Figure 7.7), it appears that, while their monuments continued to lie in ruins, the terraces filled with natural soil deposits and much of the area to the east and west of the PGPC garden terrace was, as well, likely used for agriculture.[20] The pavers that had covered the water channels on the pool promenade were robbed out (probably for reuse in the Byzantine period structures), and the open channels reused to catch water runoff to irrigate the fields on the terrace. Remnants of plastering suggest the creation of a shallow basin to catch the water that flowed from the channels through the *castellum*. A basin created from a reused column drum and a pipeline installed on top of the paved walkway along the north edge of the garden terrace illustrate efforts to contain and direct water collected from the reused channels (Bedal et al. 2007:165–166) (Figure 7.12). In

FIGURE 7.12 Byzantine period basin and pipeline illustrate continued efforts to use the pool's water system in the Byzantine period (Photo by L. Bedal, 1998).

the meantime, the pool continued to fill with soil and debris washed down from the Az-Zantur hillside behind it, an indication of the decline of the residential quarter in that area (Fiema 2002:234; Kolb and Stucky 1993:422). A second earthquake, probably the seventh-century earthquake that caused partial collapse of the Petra Church (Fiema 2001:111; 2002:200), caused further destruction to the pool's monumental architecture (Bedal et al. 2007:166) (Figure 7.7 C and D). Over the following centuries, the pool filled in completely, and the soil and debris that washed down from Az-Zantur built up, creating an overburden measuring five to fourteen meters above the pool. A series of walls, functioning as catch dams, were erected to control the flow of water runoff and to give support to the earthen slope (Bedal et al. 2007:167), presumably to protect the fields from mud slides and damaging floods during the rainy season (Figure 7.13). The

FIGURE 7.13 Photo sequence of the pool complex, looking west toward the Great Temple, taken in 1998 (top) and 2013 (bottom), showing features revealed with the removal of overburden covering the pool (Photos by L. Bedal).

destructive potential of water runoff on the site has been observed by the author upon return to the site after a wet winter, necessitating the strategic placement of sandbags to divert water from excavation trenches and architectural features. Flooding over the winter of 2014 caused a trench excavated at the base of the south escarpment during the 2013 field season to be completely filled in with soil carried down from Az-Zantur.

By the eighth century CE, with the arrival of Islam, Petra was politically and economically isolated from the thriving agricultural and trade activity in the region (Fiema 2002:237). The Petra valley was essentially rural, with agricultural plots on the flatter land, and clusters of domestic habitation and squatters (some engaged in looting) spread among the ruins (Bikai 2002:76; Fiema 2001:95; 2002:222). Based on the amount of water available today from the 'Ain Abu Olleqa spring, the only source of drinking water other than rainfall catchment, Bikai estimates the population inside Petra to be no more than a few hundred (Bikai 2002:276). In the twelfth century, Petra regained some importance due to its strategic location with the arrival of a Frankish garrison and construction of two fortress in what they dubbed *Li Vaux Moise* ("The Valley of Moses") as part of a defensive system against the Saracen forces (Kennedy 1994:24–30). Both fortresses, Wu'ayra and Al-Habis, relied on the collection of rainwater in cisterns (Hammond 1970:27; Vannini and Tonghini 1997:373). Artifacts representing the Early Islamic and Crusader period turn up in small numbers in excavations around Petra, but the valley remained undeveloped—its role as a political, cultural, and economic center in the past. In 1276, Sultan Baybars passed through what is described as a desolate and empty Petra on his way to Kerak (Zayadine 1985:164–168).

Conclusion

In closing, we return to the folktale presented at the beginning of this paper. The princess resided securely in her well-fortified but parched valley. She demanded water to quench her thirst, but even more imperative was the need to demonstrate her wealth and status with conspicuous displays of water consumption. She challenged her subjects to construct the sophisticated aqueduct systems needed to transport water from reliable spring sources to feed her nymphaea, fountains, and pools, and to irrigate her luxurious *paradeisos*—an urban oasis in the desert. By this means, she presented herself to her rivals (the competing rulers of the Hellenistic-Roman world) as a legitimate and powerful authority. Upon the demise of the Nabataean monarchy and decline of trade revenue under the Romans (symbolically, the death of the princess), the demand for such conspicuous displays waned. With no new public monuments being built, the demand for stonemasons and engineers with the knowledge and skill to properly repair damaged aqueducts and construct new ones abated. As the aqueduct systems fell into disrepair, the incentive and support for its repair was no longer present. The inhabitants of the Petra valley returned to the practices of traditional desert inhabitants, efficient and conservative exploitation of the local water resources.

The perennial springs that supplied the water that gave life to the Nabataean capital still flow today. 'Ain Musa ("Spring of Moses") is a popular tourist stop where visitors are told the local folktale, of Crusader origin, that this is the spring that burst forth from the rock when Moses struck it with his staff (*Exodus* 17:1–7; *Surat al-Baqarah* 2:60). The flow of 'Ain Brak was reduced significantly in the 1990s as the result of construction of a modern road and five star hotels. The spring water is used by the local populations of modern Wadi Musa and its suburbs for domestic needs and irrigation of fields.

ACKNOWLEDGMENTS

I wish to acknowledge the support of the staff of the Department of Antiquities of Jordan (DOA), the American Center of Oriental Research (ACOR) staff and its director Barbara Porter, and the staff of the Petra Archaeological Park (PAP). Funding for the field seasons referenced in this paper came from the National Science Foundation (No. 0317706), ACOR-CAORC Senior Research Fellowship, Dumbarton Oaks Project Grants, Samuel H. Kress Foundation Research Fellowship, Penn State Behrend's H&SS Endowment Grant and Global Fund, Cornell University's Midas-Croesus Fund and Hirsch Fund for Archaeology, a University of Minnesota Grant-in-Aid, and the Macauley Fund. Further institutional support was provided by The College at Brockport-SUNY. Much gratitude is also due to the dedicated field staff, in particular Kathryn L. Gleason, James G. Schryver, Jennifer H. Ramsay, Fawwaz Ishaqat, John Rucker, Pamela Koulianos, Sarah Wenner, Alex Zarley, and our field school students whose hard work and talents produced the material upon which this research is based. Special gratitude is owed to the Bedoul of Umm Sayhoun, especially the family of Dakhilallah Qoblan, for their valued contributions to the project and warm hospitality.

NOTES

1. The two earliest reports of the tale have different outcomes. In one, the man who procured water from 'Ain Abu Haroun is the winner (Musil 1907:108). In the other, it is the man who procured water from 'Ain Brak who marries the princess (Dalman 1912:16). A third version, recorded more than a decade later, again has the builder of the 'Ain Abu Haroun conduit as the winner, but it is attributed to his acknowledgment of God's assistance in his accomplishment, and the divine intervention of a locust wing that irreparably blocks the 'Ain Brak conduit and seals the deal (Canaan 1929:9–10). Canaan equates 'Ain Abu Haroun with what is today called 'Ain Musa.

2. For further reading on the geography of Petra, see Bowersock 1983:1–11; Hammond 1973a:41ff; Horsfield and Horsfield 1938:1–4; Kennedy 1925; Smith 1931:573–575.

3. Cited in a secondary account by Diodorus of Sicily, *Bibliotecha Historica* II:48:1–2, XIX:94:6–8 in Oldfather 1933.

4. For general studies and discussions of Nabataean hydraulics, see Al-Farajat and Salameh 2010; Daviau and Foley 2007; Eadie and Oleson 1986; Evenari and Koller 1956; Evenari et al. 1982:95–190; Hillel 1982; Kloner 1975; Lindner 2003, 2005; McKenzie 1990:109–110; Negev 1983; Oleson 1995, 2007, 2010.

5. Gustaf Dalman (1912:15–18) was the first modern explorer to describe some of Petra's hydraulic installations in some detail. For studies and discussions of Petra's extensive water

collection and supply system, see Akasheh 2004; Al-Muheisin 1990, 1992, 2009; Al-Muheisin and Tarrier 1995, 1996; Bellwald 2004, 2008; Bellwald et al. 2003; Gunsam 1980; Hammond 1967, 1973:72–73; Laureano 1994:76–82; Lindner and Hübl 1997; Ortloff 2005. For studies of the water systems associated with specific monuments and sites within Petra and its suburbs, see 'Amr and Al-Momani 2001; Bedal 2001, 2002; Drap et al. 2006; Joukowsky 2004; Joukowsky and Cloke 2007; Lindner and Gunsam 1995; Schmid 2008; Twaissi et al. 2010:35–36; Urban et al. 2012, 2013.

6. As with the other Classical sources, Strabo's *Geography*, dated to the end of the first century BCE, provides a secondary account of others' reports on Petra and the Nabataeans.

7. Bellwald dates the construction of the North Khubtha, *Siq*, and 'Ain Brak aqueducts and the flash flood prevention system to the late first century BCE, with the addition of the *Siq*'s south channel and the 'Ain Dibdebeh aqueduct in the first century CE (Bellwald 2008:48–87; Bellwald et al. 2003:59). However, Parr 2008 raises questions about some of these dates based on other archaeological evidence and methodology, placing the earliest date for the *Siq* aqueduct in the first century CE (Parr 2008).

8. In the 1960s, a group of French tourists was killed during a visit to Petra when a wall of water crashed through the *Siq* following a rainstorm. Since then, the restoration and reuse of the ancient Nabataean water control system has prevented similar tragic events (Hammond 1967:40–41; 1973:72).

9. The author's discussions of a waterfall adjoining the "Royal Tombs" in previous publications were based on Laureano's (1994) reconstruction of Petra's waterworks. Bellwald's survey of Petra's hydraulic infrastructure provide a comprehensive reconstruction based on empirical data.

10. Two other structures in Petra have been convincingly proposed as possible palaces. The proposed palace on top of Umm al-Biyārah is comparable to the hilltop palaces of Herod the Great, while the palatial structure in the northeast, near the "Royal Tombs," is compared with Seleucid *basileia* (Schmid et al. 2012). I propose that the complex on the Southern Terrace would serve more of an administrative function due to its location inside the city center.

11. The PGPC is a case study in the *Sourcebook for Garden Archaeology: Methods, Techniques, Interpretations, and Field Examples* (Bedal et al. 2013).

12. The Petra Garden and Pool Complex (PGPC) excavation is an ongoing, multiyear, interdisciplinary archaeological research project under the direction of Dr. Leigh-Ann Bedal (Director), Dr. James G. Schryver (Associate Director), and Dr. Jennifer H. Ramsay (Associate Director). Dr. Kathryn L. Gleason acts as a consultant on garden archaeology. For excavation reports on the PGPC, cf. Bedal 2004, Bedal et al. 2007 and 2011.

13. Swimming pools in association with gardens had become a fashion in Hellenistic palaces, especially those in Judaea, during the late second-first centuries BCE (Bedal 2002:232–233; Bedal 2004:154–155; Netzer 2001:21–25, 36–37, 57, 107–113, 118–122; Nielsen 1994:156–160). A second known Nabataean swimming pool (Structure no. 63) is found at Humayma (Oleson 2010:187).

14. For a report on the archaeobotanical findings in the PGPC, see Ramsay and Bedal 2015.

15. In prior publications, it was proposed that a waterfall was located at the north end of the East Cistern, dropping to the uppermost of the Eastern Terraces to the east of the pool. Excavations in 2011 uncovered a cave in that location with no evidence for water catchment. In 2013, an apsidal cut in the southeast corner was revealed that parallels the

rock-cut nymphaeum of the North Khubta aqueduct (Bedal, "The Petra Garden and Pool Complex, 2011 and 2013," *ADAJ*, in preparation). Further excavations will determine if there is a water catchment system at the base of the apse.

16.   Joukowsky and Cloke 2007.

17.   A more thorough treatment of the role of water display in Hellenistic and Roman East gardens is presented in Bedal 2004:104–105.

18.   Excavations around the east half of the pool's north wall, where the Late Roman wall was built, are currently not possible due to logistics of removing excavated soils from the pool area.

19.   For a more updated review of the archaeological evidence for the 363 destruction in Petra and its aftermath, see Fiema 2002:195–199.

20.   Excavators identify an area to the west of the Qasr al-Bint that functioned as an agricultural terrace during the Byzantine period (Auge et al. 2014:79).

References Cited

Abbreviations

ADAJ   *Annual of the Department of Antiquities of Jordan*
AJA   *American Journal of Archaeology*
BASOR   *Bulletin of the American Schools of Oriental Research*
NEA   *Near Eastern Archaeology*
PEQ   *Palestine Exploration Quarterly*
QDAP   *Quarterly of the Department of Antiquities in Palestine*
SHAJ   *Studies in the History and Archaeology of Jordan*

Akasheh, T. S. 2004 Nabataean and Modern Watershed Management around the Siq and Wadi Musa in Petra. In *Men of Dikes and Canals. The Archaeology of Water in the Middle East*, edited by H.-D. Bienert and J. Häser, pp. 109–120. Leidorf, Rahden.

Al Atteyat, N., N. Al Jahed, and J. Khataibeh 2013 *Geophysical Studies in Petra Region: Wadi Al Bayda Area*. The Hashemite Kingdom of Jordan Natural Resources Authority, Geology Directorate, Geophysical Studies Division, Amman.

Al-Bashaireh, K., and L.-A. Bedal 2015 Provenance of white and colored marbles from the Petra garden and pool complex, Petra, South Jordan. *Archaeological and Anthropological Sciences* 9/5:817–829.

Alcock, S. E., and A. R. Knodell 2012 Landscapes North of Petra: The Petra Area and Wadi Silaysil Survey (Brown University Petra Archaeological Project, 2010–2011). In *The Nabataeans in Focus: Current Archaeological Research at Petra*, edited by L. Nehmé and L. Wadeson, pp. 5–16. Supplement to Proceedings of the Seminar for Arabian Studies, 42. Archaeopress, Oxford.

Al-Farajat, M., and E. Salameh 2010 Vulnerability of the Drinking Water Resources of the Nabataeans of Petra—Jordan. *Jordan Journal of Civil Engineering* 4:321–335.

Al-Muheisen, Z. 1983 L'alimentation en Eau de Pétra. Unpublished PhD dissertation, Université de Paris, Sorbonne.

Al-Muheisen, Z. 1986 Techniques hydrauliques dans le Sud de la Jordanie en particulier à l'époque nabatéennes. Unpublished PhD dissertation, Université de Paris, Sorbonne.

Al-Muheisen, Z. 1990 Maîtrise de l'eau et Agriculture en Nabatène: L'Exemple de Pétra. *Aram* 2:205–220.

Al-Muheisen, Z. 1992 Modes d'installations agricoles nabatéenes dans la région de Pétra et dans le Wadi 'Arabah. *SHAJ* IV:215–219.

Al-Muheisen, Z. 2009 *The Water Engineering and Irrigation System of the Nabataeans.* Yarmouk University, Irbid.

Al-Muheisen, Z., and D. Tarrier. 1995 La Protection du Site de Pétra à L'époque Nabatéenne. *SHAJ* V:721–725.

Al-Muheisen, Z., and D. Tarrier. 1996 Menace des Eaux et Mesures Préventives à Pétra à L'époque Nabatéenne. *Syria* 73:107–204.

'Amr, K., and A. Al-Momani. 2001 Preliminary Report on the Archaeological Component of the Wadi Musa Water Supply and Wastewater Project. *ADAJ* 45:253–285.

Augé, Ch., L. Borel, J. Dentzer-Feydy, C. March, F. Renel, and L. Tholbeq. 2014 Pétra—Le sanctuaire du Qasr al-Bint et ses abords: un état des lieux des travaux de la Mission archéologique française à Pétra, Jordanie (1999–2013). In *De Pétra à Wadi Ramm: Le Sud Jordanien Nabatéen et Arabe: Rapport des campagnes archéologiques 2013,* edited by L. Tholbecq, pp. 19–86. Mission Archéologique Française, Bruxelles.

Beckers, B., and B. Schütt. 2013 The Chronology of Ancient Agricultural Terraces in the Environs of Petra. *In Men on the Rocks: The Formation of Nabataean Petra,* edited by M. Mouton and S. G. Schmid, pp. 313–322. Supplement to the Bulletin of Nabataean Studies, 1. Logos Verlag, Berlin.

Bedal, L. 2001 A Pool Complex in Petra's City Center. *BASOR* 324:23–41.

Bedal, L. 2002 Desert Oasis: Water Consumption in the Nabataean Capital. *NEA* 65(4):225–234.

Bedal, L. 2004 *The Petra Pool-Complex: A Hellenistic Paradeisos in the Nabataean Capital (results from the Petra Lower Market Survey and Excavation, 1998).* Gorgias Dissertations: Near Eastern Studies, 4, Gorgias Press, Piscataway, NJ.

Bedal, L., K. L. Gleason, and J. G. Schryver (with reports by J. H. Ramsay and J. Bowsher). 2007 The Petra Garden and Pool Complex, 2003–2005. *ADAJ* 51:151–176.

Bedal, L., J. G. Schryver, and K. L. Gleason. 2011 The Petra Garden and Pool Complex, 2007 and 2009. *ADAJ* 55:313–328.

Bedal, L, L. B. Conyers, J. E. Foss, and K. L. Gleason. 2013. The Petra Garden and Pool Complex, Ma'an Jordan. In *Sourcebook for Garden Archaeology: Methods, Techniques, Interpretations, and Field Examples,* edited by A. Malek, pp. 625–641. Peter Lang/Fondations des parcs et jardins de France, Berne.

Bellwald, U. 2004 Streets and Hydraulics: The Peta National Trusts Siq Project in Petra 1996–1999 The Archaeological Results. In *Men of Dikes and Canals: The Archaeology of Water in the Middle East,* edited by H. Bienert and J. Häser, pp. 73–94. Leidorf, Rahden.

Bellwald, U. 2008 The Hydraulic Infrastructure of Petra—A Model for Water Strategies in Arid Land. In *Cura Aquarum En Jordanien. Proceedings of the 13th International Conference on the History of Water Management and Hydraulic Engineering in the Mediterranean Region Petra/Amman, 31 March–09 April 2007,* edited by C. P. J. Ohlig, pp. 47–94. Schriften Der Deutschen Wasserhistorischen Gesellschaft, 12, DwHG, Sieberg.

Bellwald, U., M. al-Huneidi, A. Salihi, D. Keller, R. Naser, and D. al-Eisawi 2003 *The Petra Siq: Nabataean Hydrology Uncovered.* Edited by I. Ruben. Petra National Trust, Amman.

Berg, D. 1994 Fountains and Artistic Water Displays in Classical Antiquity: Origins and Development from 700 to 30 B.C. Unpublished PhD dissertation, University of Texas at Austin.

Bikai, P. M. 2002 The Churches of Byzantine Petra. *NEA* 65(4):271–276.

Bowersock, G. W. 1971 A Report on Arabia Provincia. *Journal of Roman Studies* 61:219–242.

Bowersock, G. W. 1983 *Roman Arabia*. Harvard University Press, Cambridge, MA/London.

Canaan, T. 1929 Studies in the Topography and Folklore of Petra. *Journal of the Palestine Oriental Society* IX:136–218.

Conyers, L. B., E. Ernenwein, and L. Bedal. 2002 Ground-Penetrating Radar Discovery at Petra, Jordan. *Antiquity* 76 (292):339–340.

Dalman, G. 1912 *Neue Petra-Forschungen und der Heilige Felsen von Jerusalem*. Palästinische Forschungen zur Archäeologie und Topographie, II. Hinrich, Leipzig.

Daviau, P. M. M., and C. M. Foley. 2007 Nabataean Water Management Systems in the Wadi Ath-Thamad. *SHAJ* IX:357–365.

Denny, E., K. Donnelly, R. McKay, G. Ponte, and T. Uetake. 2008 *Sustainable Water Strategies for Jordan*. International Economic Development Program, Gerald R. Ford School of Public Policy, University of Michigan, Ann Arbor, http://www.umich.edu/~ipolicy/Policy%20 Papers/water.pdf; accessed March 16, 2015.

Drap, P., R. Franchi, and R. Gabrielli. 2006 Integrated Application of Laser Scanning Techniques and Close Range Photogrammetry. The Case Study of the Ancient Water Supply System of Petra. *Archaeological Computing Newsletter* 64:12–18.

Eadie, J. W., and J. P. Oleson. 1986 The Water-Supply Systems of Nabataean and Roman Humayma. *BASOR* 262:49–76.

Erickson-Gini, T., and Y. Israel. 2013 Excavating the Nabataean Incense Road. *Journal of Eastern Mediterranean Archaeology and Heritage Studies* 1(1):24–53.

Evenari, M., and D. Koller. 1956 Ancient Masters of the Desert. *Scientific American* 194(4):39–45.

Evenari, M., L. Shannan, and N. Tadmor. 1982 *The Negev: The Challenge of the Desert*. Harvard University Press, Cambridge, MA.

Fiema, Z. T. 1998 The Roman Street of the Petra Project, 1997: A Preliminary Report. *ADAJ* 42:395–424.

Fiema, Z. T. 2001 Reconstructing the history of the Petra Church—data and phasing. In *The Petra Church*, edited by Fiema et al., pp. 7–137. American Center of Oriental Research, Amman.

Fiema, Z. T. 2002. Late Antique Petra and Its Hinterland. Recent Research and New Interpretations. *The Roman and Byzantine Near East* 3:191–252.

Fiema, Z. T., C. Kanellopoulos, T. Waliszewski, and R. Schick. 2001 *The Petra Church*. American Center of Oriental Research, Amman.

Food and Agricultural Organization 2003 *Review of Water Resources by Country*. Water Reports 23. Rome, Food and Agricultural Organization (FAO) of the United Nations. http://www. fao.org/docrep/005/y4473e/y4473e00.HTM; accessed March 16, 2015.

Gleason, K. L., and R. Bar-Nathan. 2013 The Paradeisoi of the Hasmonean and Herodian Palace Complex at Jericho: A Preliminary Report on the Palace Gardens and Ollae Perforata. In *Hasmonean and Herodian Palaces at Jericho. The Finds from Jericho and Cypros*, edited by R. Bar-Nathan and J. Gärtner, pp. 317–366. Israel Exploration Society, Jerusalem.

Glueck, N. 1959 *Rivers in the Desert: A History of the Negev*. Farrar, Straus, and Cudahy, New York.

Graf, D. F., and S. E. Sidebotham. 2003 Nabataean Trade. In *Petra Rediscovered: Lost City of the Nabataeans*, edited by G. Markoe, pp. 65–74. Harry N. Abrams, New York.

Gunsam, E. 1980 Die nordliche Hubta-Wasserleitung in Petra. In *Petra und das Königreich der Nabatäer*, edited by M. Lindner, pp. 302–312. Auflage, Munich.

Hammond, P. C. 1967 Desert Waterworks of the Ancient Nabataeans. *Natural History* 7(9):36–43.

Hammond, P. C. 1970 *The Crusader Fort on El-Habis at Petra: Its Survey and Interpretation.* University of Utah, Salt Lake City.

Hammond, P. C. 1973. *The Nabataeans—Their History, Culture, and Archaeology.* Studies in Mediterranean Archaeology 37. Paul Åströms Forlag, Gothenburg.

Hammond, P. C. 1980 New Evidence for the 4th-Century A.D. Destruction of Petra. *BASOR* 238:65–67.

Hillel, D. 1982 *Negev, Land, Water, and Life in a Desert Environment.* Praeger, New York.

Hirschfield, Y. 2000 *Ramat Hanadiv Excavations: Final Report of the 1984–1998 Seasons.* Israel Exploration Society, Jerusalem.

Hodge, A. T. 1992 *Roman Aqueducts and Water Supply.* Duckworth, London.

Horsfield, G., and A. Horsfield. 1938 Sela-Petra, the Rock of Edom and Nabatene, I–II. *QDAP* 7:1–42.

Issar, A. 1995 Climate Change and the History of the Middle East. *American Scientist* 83:350–355.

Jashemski, W. F. 1996 The Use of Water in Pompeian Gardens. In *Cura Aquarum in Campania. Proceedings of the Ninth International Congress on the History of Water Management and Hydraulic Engineering in the Mediterranean Region. Pompeii, 1–8 October 1994,* edited by N. de Haan and G. C. M. Jansen, pp. 51–58. Annual Papers on Classical Archaeology, Suppl. 4, Babesch, Leiden.

Jones, R., and D. Robinson. 1998 Water Wealth and Status at Pompeii: The House of the Vestals in the First Century AD. *AJA* 109(4):695–710.

Joukowsky, M. S. 2004 The Water Installations of the Petra Great Temple. In *Men of Dikes and Canals: The Archaeology of Water in the Middle East,* edited by H. Bienert and J. Häser, pp. 121–141. Leidorf, Rahden.

Joukowsky, M. S. 2007 Exciting Developments: The Brown University 2006 Petra Great Temple Excavations. *ADAJ* 51:81–102.

Joukowsky, M. S., and C. F. Cloke. 2007 The Petra Great Temple's Water Strategy. *SHAJ* IX:431–437.

Kennedy, A. B. W. 1925 *Petra. Its History and Monuments.* Country Life, London.

Kennedy, H. 1994 *Crusader Castles.* Cambridge University Press, Cambridge.

Khairy, N. 1990 *The 1981 Petra Excavations, Vol. I.* Abhandlungen Des Deutschen Palästinavereins, Band 13. Harrassowitz, Weisbaden.

Kloner, A. 1975 Ancient Agriculture at Mamshit and the Dating of the Water-Diversion Systems in the Negev. *Eretz-Israel* 12:167–170 (Hebrew), 124 (English translation).

Kolb, B. 1998 Swiss-Liechtenstein Excavations at Ez-Zantur in Petra 1997. *ADAJ* 42:259–77.

Kolb, B., and R. A. Stucky. 1993 Preliminary Report of the Swiss-Liechtenstein Excavations at Ez-Zantur in Petra 1992: The Fourth Campaign. *ADAJ* 37:417–423.

Laureano, P. 1994 Abitare il deserto: il giardino come oasi. In *Giardino Islamico: Architettora, Natura, Paesaggio,* edited by A. Petrucciolo, pp. 63–84. Electa, Milano.

Lindner, M. 2003 Hydraulic Engineering and Site Significance in Nabataean-Roman Southern Jordan: Ba'ja, as-Sadah, Sabra, Umm Ratam. *ADAJ* 47:183–194.

Lindner, M. 2005 Water Supply and Water Management at Ancient Sabra, Jordan. *PEQ* 137(1):33–52.

Lindner, M., and E. Gunsam. 1995 A Newly Described Nabataean Temple near Petra: The "Pond Temple." *SHAJ* V:199–214.

Lindner, M., and H. Hübl 1997 Where Pharao's Daughter Got Her Drinking Water From. The 'En Brak Conduit to Petra. *Zeitschrift Deutschen Palaestina-Vereins* 113:61–67.

Macaulay-Lewis, E. 2006 Planting Pots at Petra: A Preliminary Study of Ollae Perforatae at the Petra Garden Pool Complex and at the "Great Temple." *Levant* 38:159–170.

MacDonald, B. 2000 *East of the Jordan: Territories and Sites of the Hebrew Scriptures.* ASOR Books 6. American Schools of Oriental Research, Boston.

MacDonald, B. 2001 Climate Change in Jordan through Time. In *The Archaeology of Jordan,* edited by MacDonald et al., pp. 595–601. Sheffield Academic Press, Sheffield.

MacDonald, B., R. Adams, and P. Bienkowski (editors). 2001 *The Archaeology of Jordan.* Sheffield Academic Press, Sheffield.

Macumber, P. G. 2001 Evolving Landscape and Environment in Jordan. In *The Archaeology of Jordan,* edited by MacDonald et al., pp. 1–30. Sheffield Academic Press, Sheffield.

Malek, A. (editor). 2013 *Sourcebook for Garden Archaeology: Methods, Techniques, Interpretations, and Field Examples.* Peter Lang/Fondations des parcs et jardins de France, Berne.

McCormick, M., U. Büntgen, M. A. Cane, E. R. Cook, K. Harper, P. Huybers, T. Litt et al. 2012 Climate Change during and after the Roman Empire: Reconstructing the Past from Scientific and Historical Evidence. *Journal of Interdisciplinary History* 43 (2):169–220.

McKenzie, J. S. 1990 *The Architecture of Petra.* British Academy Monographs in Archaeology, No. 1. Oxford University Press, London.

Musil, A. 1907 *Arabia Petraea, Vol. II: Edom.* Hölder, Wein.

Namrouqa, H. 2014. Jordan World's Second Water-Poorest Country. *The Jordan Times,* October 22. http://jordantimes.com/jordan-worlds-second-water-poorest-country; accessed March 16, 2015.

Nasarat, M., F. Abudanh, and S. Naimat. 2012 Agriculture in Sixth-Century Petra and Its Hinterland, the Evidence from the Petra Papyri. *Arabian Archaeology and Epigraphy* 23:105–115.

Negev, A. 1983 *Tempel, Kirchen und Zisternen: Ausgrabungen in der Wüste Negev, die Kultur der Nabatäer.* Calwer, Stuttgart.

Netzer, E. 2001 *The Palaces of the Hasmoneans and Herod the Great.* Israel Exploration Society, Jerusalem.

Nielsen, I. 1994 *Hellenistic Palaces: Tradition and Renewal.* Studies in Hellenistic Civilization V. Aarhus University Press, Aarhus.

Oldfather, C. H. (translator). 1933 *Diodorus of Sicily.* Loeb Classical Library 10. G.P. Putnam's Sons, New York.

Oleson, J. P. 1995 The Origins and Design of Nabataean Water-Supply Systems. *SHAJ* V:707–719.

Oleson, J. P. 2001 Water Supply in Jordan through the Ages. In *The Archaeology of Jordan,* edited by B. MacDonald, R. Adams, and P. Bienkowski, pp. 603–614. Sheffield Academic Press, Sheffield.

Oleson, J. P. 2007 Nabataea Water Supply, Irrigation, and Agriculture. In *The World of the Nabataeans: Volume 2 of the International Conference The World of the Herods and the Nabataeans held at the British Museum, 17–19 April 2001,* edited by K. D. Politis, pp. 217–250. Oriens et Occidens, Band 15, Franz Steiner Verlag, Munich.

Oleson, J. P. 2010 *Humayma Excavation Project, 1: Resources, History, and the Water-Supply System.* American Schools of Oriental Research, Boston.

Ortloff, C. R. 2005 The Water Supply and Distribution System of the Nabataean City of Petra (Jordan), 300 B.C.–A.D. 300. *Cambridge Archaeological Journal* 15(1):93–109.

Paradise, T. 2011 The Great Flood of Petra: Evidence for a 4th–5th AD Century Catastrophic Flood. *ADAJ* 55:43–56.

Parker, S. T. 2006 History of the Roman Frontier East of the Dead Sea. In *The Roman Frontier in Central Jordan: Final Report on the Limes Arabicus Project, 1980–1989*, edited by S. Th. Parker, pp. 517–575. Dumbarton Oaks Studies, 40. Dumbarton Oaks, Washington, DC.

Parr, P. J. 2008 Dating the Hydraulic Installations in the Siq. *PEQ* 140(2):81–86.

Ramsay, J. H., and L. Bedal. 2015 Garden Variety Seeds? Botanical Remains from the Petra Garden and Pool Complex. *Vegetation History and Archaeobotany* (March). DOI 10.1007/s00334-015-0520-4.

Russell, K. W. 1980 The Earthquake of May 19, AD 363. *BASOR* 238:47–64.

Schmid, S. G. 2008 L'eau À Pétra: L'exemple Du Wadi Farasa Est. *Syria* 85:19–31.

Schmid, S. G., P. Bienkowski, Z. T. Fiema, and B. Kolb. 2012 The Palaces of the Nabataean Kings at Petra. In *The Nabataeans in Focus: Current Archaeological Research at Petra*, edited by L. Nehmé and L. Wadeson, pp. 73–98. Supplement to Proceedings of the Seminar for Arabian Studies, 42, Archaeopress, Oxford.

Smith, G. A. 1931 *The Historical Geography of the Holy Land*. 25th edition. Hodder and Stoughton, London.

Twaissi, S., F. Abudanh, and Q. Twaissi. 2010 The Identity of the Nabataean "Painted House" Complex at Baidha, North-West Petra. *PEQ* 142(1):31–42.

Urban, T. M., S. E. Alcock, and Ch. A. Tuttle. 2012 Virtual Discoveries at a Wonder of the World: Geophysical Investigations and Ancient Plumbing at Petra, Jordan. *Antiquity* 86 (331). http://www.antiquity.ac.uk/projgall/urban331/; accessed August 14, 2014.

Urban, T. M., E. Bocancea, C. Vella, S. N. Herringer, S. E. Alcock, and Ch. A. Tuttle. 2013 Investigating Ancient Dams in Petra's Northern Hinterland with Ground-Penetrating Radar. *The Leading Edge* 32:190–192.

Vannini, G., and C. Tonghini. 1997 Medieval Petra. The Stratigraphic Evidence from Recent Archaeological Excavations at Al-Wu'ayra. *SHAJ* VI:371–384.

Waliszewski, T. 2001 Mosaics. In *The Petra Church*, edited by Z. T. Fiema, C. Kanellopoulos, T. Waliszewski, and R. Schick, pp. 219–270. American Center of Oriental Research, Amman.

Wilson, A. 1995. Running Water and Social Status in North Africa. In *North Africa from Antiquity to Islam*, edited by M. Horton and T. Weidemann, pp. 52–56. CMS Occasional Paper, 13, Center for Mediterranean Studies (University of Bristol), Bristol.

Zayadine, F. 1985 Caravan Routes between Egypt and Nabataea and the Voyage of Sultan Baibars to Petra in 1276 A.D. *SHAJ* II:159–174.

CHAPTER EIGHT

Spatial Archaeology, Hydrology, and the Historical Dynamics of Water in Ancient Southern Arabia (Yemen and Oman)

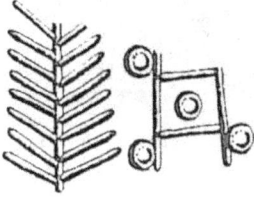

Michael J. Harrower

Abstract *Environmental and political circumstances and variability are essential components of water and power in past societies. This chapter compares spatial patterning of water in Southwest Arabia (Yemen) and Southeast Arabia (Oman) and examines how differing environmental and political dynamics shaped the origins of agriculture and rise of complex societies in these two very different regions. The flashflood (sayl) irrigation systems that supported the rise of pre-Islamic kingdoms of ancient Yemen during the early first millennium BCE differ widely from the oasis (falaj) irrigation systems that sustained early complex polities in Oman as early as the mid-third millennium BCE. These technologies and their various social, logistical, and ideological involvements offer a range of insights on ancient water use worldwide.*

Spatial variability of landscapes and politics are central to water and power in past societies. Environments are often defined by the timing and periodicity of precipitation; water is often a foundational theme of religious traditions and a common point of politics. This chapter compares and contrasts the long-term role of water in ancient Southwest Arabia (Yemen) with Southeast Arabia (Oman) with a particular focus on agricultural origins and state formation (Figure 8.1 on page 160). I concentrate on two general perspectives—water histories and spatial archaeology—that are well suited to help clarify similarities and differences in the long-term geographic and historic influences of water in these two adjacent but different regions.

The spatial and historical dynamics of water in Southwest and Southeast Arabia were shaped by a wide range of social, cultural, political, and environmental factors. Distinct topographies and geologies receive seasonal patterns of precipitation that vary widely

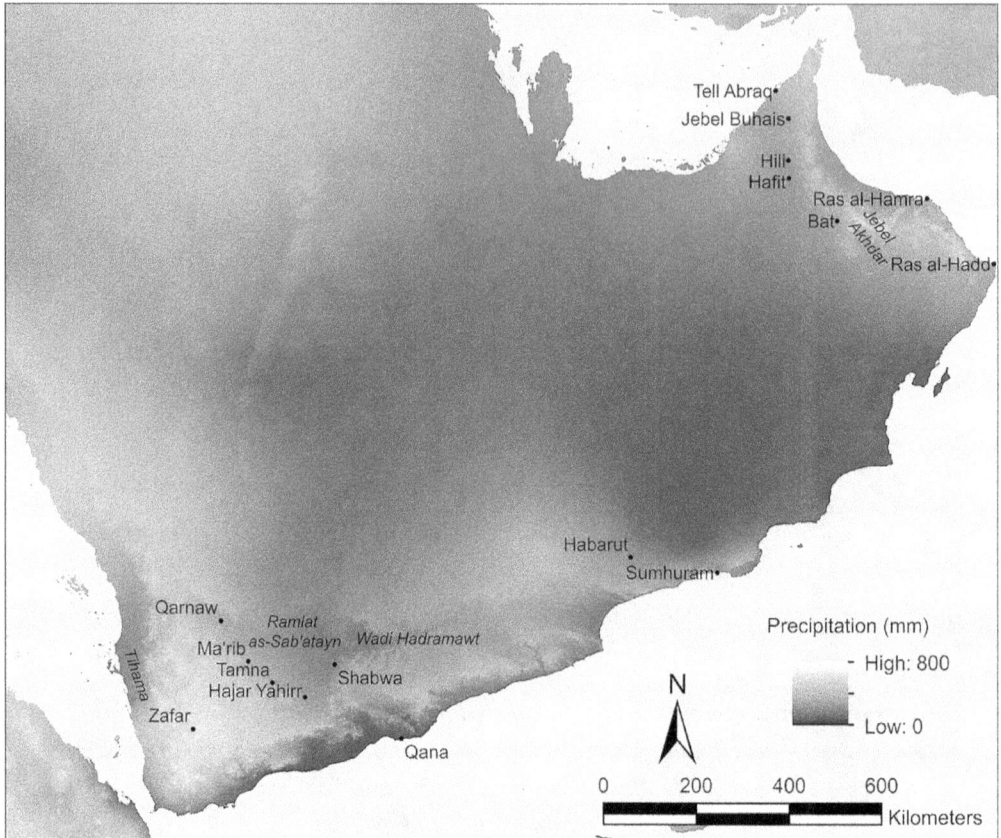

FIGURE 8.1 Map of major archaeological sites overlaid on average annual precipitation (data from Hijmans et al. 2005).

through space and time—mostly summer monsoon rainfall in Yemen, with predominantly winter rains in northern Oman. Domesticated plants and animals appear across the Fertile Crescent region (i.e., Israel, Jordan, Lebanon, Syria, Turkey, Iraq, and Iran) substantially earlier than in Yemen or Oman. Southern Arabia is thus often overlooked in reviews of agricultural origins in the Near East (Zeder 2011); and it is frequently presumed that agriculture must have spread through migration or diffusion from north to south (Dreschsler 2007, 2009). However, portrayals of Arabia as a peripheral recipient of agriculture that originated elsewhere undermines recognition of the unique technological and social reconfigurations necessary in regions such as Yemen and Oman (Harrower et al. 2010). From the beginnings of food production, increasingly sophisticated technologies and elaborate strategies diversified in different locales. The flashflood (*sayl*) irrigation systems that eventually supported pre-Islamic kingdoms of ancient Yemen greatly differ from the *falaj* irrigation systems that sustained early complex polities in Oman. Distinct identities were formed in part through the spectacle of desert water control and accompanying political rhetoric and social logic that rationalized and perpetuated particular ways of thinking and interacting.

Our understanding of ancient geographies greatly benefits not only from applications of new spatial technologies, but similarly from new ways of analyzing and theorizing histories. Beginning in the 1950s, radiocarbon dating revolutionized archaeologists' analyses of time; spatial technologies are now similarly revolutionizing archaeologists' analyses and understandings of space. Spatial technologies, including satellite imagery, Global Positioning System (GPS), and Geographic Information System (GIS) software, have increasingly transformed archaeological research, and these tools hold wide utility in understanding water. New technologies, including airborne and space-borne Synthetic Aperture Radar (SAR), LiDAR (Light Detection and Ranging), 3-Dimensional (3D) Modeling, and Unmanned Aerial Vehicles (UAVs), are enabling dramatically new ways of analyzing the ancient past. Given their wide impacts, these technologies also require new spatial theory, multiscalar modes of analysis that challenge the conventional boundaries and categories by which we divide, organize, and understand histories (Harrower 2016). Vastly different scales, from individual lives in villages over seasons and years, to population level changes over millennia across continents, lead to very different interpretations of the past that are often, unnecessarily, viewed as entirely distinct and incomparable.

Physical Geographies and Climates

Moving from west to east across southern Arabia, physical circumstances and water geographies differ dramatically. From the Tihama coastal plain of Yemen along the Red Sea, deeply dissected volcanic mountains rise abruptly to over 3,600 m in Yemen's western highlands (Figure 8.1). Rain, which falls mostly in the summer, increases with elevation from a low of about 50 mm along the coast to a high of nearly 800 mm per annum near the modern cities of Ta'iz and Ibb. These high-elevation areas are marked by far cooler average temperatures and correspondingly lower evapotranspiration contributing to the far wider prevalence of agriculture. Major drainages fed by vast watersheds flow intermittently from western mountains into the Red Sea, the Gulf of Aden, and Yemen's Ramlat as-Sab'atayn Desert interior. As further discussed below, only the latter group of inward draining wadis gave rise to early kingdoms. One factor that may have contributed to this pattern—slope across the watersheds of outward draining wadis tends to be, on average, far steeper than inward draining wadis so that some of the most dangerously powerful flash floods run outward, and the inward draining wadis generate comparably less abrupt and less treacherous flash floods (Harrower 2016:table 5.1). These conditions make the water flows of inward draining wadis easier to capture, less destructive, and more likely to deposit rather than erode valuable arable sediments. Moving east, Wadi Hadramawt—Southwest Arabia's largest catchment—flows into a deep canyon inscribed into eastern Yemen's limestone highlands and (after being renamed Wadi Masila once it passes the city of Tarim) drains eventually into the Indian Ocean. Topographically, a plethora of wadis drain from western Yemen into the Ramlat as-Sab'atayn Desert interior toward Wadi Hadramawt. In recent times almost all of the flow from the western highlands infiltrates into desert sands before reaching Wadi Hadramawt forming a massive endorheic basin. However, paleolake sediments at Al-Hawa (Lézine et al. 2010) reveal that in the distant past some overland flow from the desert did occasionally reach Wadi Hadramawt (see also Cleuziou et al.

1992). A number of the tributaries of Wadi Hadramawt farther downstream, including Wadi 'Amd, Wadi Daw'an, Wadi Idm, Wadi Sana, and Wadi Washa'a, show substantial evidence of human activity from Paleolithic through the Iron Age but none of these somewhat smaller wadis were home to ancient state capitals.

In Oman, vast sandy desert areas that receive as little as 65 mm of rainfall per year contrast with the rugged Jebel Akhdar "Green Mountain" highlands that reach up to 3,000 m and receive as much as 300 mm of precipitation per annum (Kwarteng et al. 2009). From west to east, the drylands of the southern region of Dhofar are uniquely punctuated by a rugged cloud-forest escarpment surrounding the modern coastal city of Salalah. This unique microecology is immersed in monsoonal fog during the summer, yet spans only about 100 km along rugged coastal mountains. The ancient port city of Sumhuram (25 km east of Salalah) marked the maximum of extent of the ancient Yemeni Kingdom of Hadramawt (Avanzini 2008). Moving to the northeast, expansive deserts afforded few opportunities for dense populations until reaching the al-Hajar Mountains more than 600 km north. The al-Hajar (rocky) range stretches in a north-south band more than 500 km long and 100 km wide from the Musandam Peninsula to Oman's easternmost point at Ras al-Hadd. The highest point—Jebel Shams—reaches just over 3,000 m and the surrounding Jebel Akhdar region is uniquely cool and verdant, even in summer. Much of the al-Hajar range is composed of the geologically famous Samail Ophiolite—a layer of oceanic crust from the Earth's mantle thrust over the Arabian Plate—that forms substantially smaller and more permeable watersheds than those of Yemen. Some of Oman's agriculturally most productive areas are fed by water from aquifers reachable relatively near the surface along the base of mountainous uplands. Oman's irrigation systems are correspondingly very different than those of Yemen. Omani systems tend to rely far more on groundwater in comparison with the flash flood (sayl) systems that sustained ancient Yemen's pre-Islamic kingdoms (Charbonnier 2012, 2015).

WATER IN HISTORICAL TRAJECTORIES OF YEMEN AND OMAN

Patterning of water in space and time played an important role in changing foodways across Arabia, including during the first appearance of domesticates, and during the rise of the earliest complex polities. A wide range of paleoclimatic records show early Holocene pluvial conditions substantially wetter than today with a precipitation maximum near 6000 BCE. Rainfall then declines with an abrupt shift toward aridity near 3500 BCE and oscillating arid conditions thereafter (Fleitmann et al. 2011; Van Rampelbergh et al. 2013). Long-term histories are to a substantial degree connected to differing topographies, climatic, and environmental changes and the ways in which different populations adapted, reacted, and transformed their surroundings.

WATER, PASTORALISM, AND AGRICULTURE

In both Southwest and Southeast Arabia, the earliest animal and plant domesticates appear at roughly the same time in very different contexts. Populations of hunter-gatherers grew substantially through the late Pleistocene, increasing most dramatically during wetter early Holocene pluvial conditions (Wilkinson 2009). Domestic sheep, goats, and cattle appear near 6000 BCE at sites including Al-Buhais in the UAE (Uerpmann et al. 2013) and Manayzah in Yemen (Martin et al. 2009). Although outward stylistic similarities between Pre-Pottery Neolithic B (PPNB, 8500–6250 BCE, Kuijt and Goring-Morris 2002) projectile points of the Levant and Fasad projectile points found across southern Arabia have long been used as evidence for diffusion from northern into southern Arabia (Uerpmann et al. 2009), such connections have proven difficult to substantiate because of the very different knapping techniques used in production (Charpentier and Crassard 2013).

Domesticated plants follow a few thousand years later, near 3000 BCE, with some of the earliest evidence including wheat and barley (and other crops) at Hili, UAE (Tengberg 2003), and in Yemen at Hayt al-Suad and Jubabat al-Juruf (Ekstrom and Edens 2003). Many key domesticates were imports to the region, and finds such as fifth-millennium Mesopotamian 'Ubaid ceramics at sites along the coast of UAE attest to early connections with surrounding regions (Uerpmann and Uerpmann 1996). However, conceiving of agriculture as an invention that merely diffused from elsewhere in the Near East neglects local contingencies. Food production in both Southwest and Southeast Arabia was adjusted to fit very different social and environmental contexts, including availabilities of water, and involved a complex range of local and foreign influences. Transitions from hunting and gathering to animal husbandry required new settlement strategies and exclusionary rights to valuable water sources and grazing territories (Fedele 2013; McCorriston et al. 2012). Small-scale (dolmen) monument building in eastern Yemen (McCorriston et al. 2011) and cemeteries in the UAE and Oman were among the means that established communal rights to territories, with evidence from sites such as Al-Buhais 18 (de Beauclair et al. 2006; Uerpmann et al. 2000) and Ras al-Hamra 5 (Salvatori 1996) that valuables such as jewelry differentiated members of early communities. After approximately two millennia of forager-pastoralism, most of the fourth millennium, which M. Uerpmann (2003) deems the "dark millennium," sees a relative paucity of settlement activity across inland areas of Southeast Arabia. However, human activity appears to have been comparably more abundant in coastal areas where numerous fishing settlements, including Ras al-Hamra, Ras al-Hadd and Ras al-Jinz, show occupation along the Gulf of Oman (Charpentier 2008; Cleuziou and Tosi 2007).

Near the end of the fourth millennium, a major societal transformation is evident as innumerable small circular tower tombs (often referred to as Hafit tombs in the UAE and Oman) appear across southern Arabia (Figure 8.2 on page 164). It is difficult to conclusively attribute the onset of tomb building to a population increase, as a plentitude of tombs could have been built by relatively small numbers of highly mobile people over a very long period of time. Indeed, radiocarbon dates show a long period of use and reuse even extending in rare cases into the early first millennium CE (de Maigret 1996; McCorriston et al. 2011, 2014). However, the resemblance of tombs over a vast area, which at a minimum includes Yemen and Oman, demonstrates that a genre of small circular tomb building spread widely during the late fourth to mid-third millennium BCE (e.g., Giraud 2010; McCorriston et al. 2011, 2014; Williams and Gregoricka 2013).

FIGURE 8.2 Circular tower tombs at Al-Ain, Oman. Comparable tombs that vary in style, construction, and contents can be found across southern Arabia as early as the late fourth millennium BCE and they extend in considerable numbers throughout the third millennium.

Although tombs vary in construction and contents within subregions and there is substantial stylistic change over time, comparable tomb forms demonstrate sustained contacts and an element of shared mortuary practices over a vast swath of Arabia. Environmentally, the onset of tomb building approximately follows heightened aridity during the mid to late fourth millennium BCE (Lézine et al. 2010), which may have led to increased residential mobility and/or population dispersion. The first Hafit tombs also roughly coincide with the Late Uruk and Jemdat Nasr periods in Mesopotamia. Indeed, Jemdet Nasr ceramics (bi-conical jars sometimes painted with distinctive geometric designs) are quite often found in Hafit tombs in UAE and Oman (Potts 1986) indicating contact and trade with Mesopotamia along the Persian Gulf (Méry and Schneider 1996). As of yet, very little evidence of settlements has been discovered in connection with small circular tombs, either in Yemen or Oman, which suggests those who built these tombs were highly mobile and may have often lived in temporary encampments, tents, or palm frond houses that left few enduring archaeological remains. Claims to arable, water-rich areas were ever more crucial during arid intervals and tombs along cliff lines likely served as a highly visible means of pronouncing claims to water (Harrower 2008). However, there is relatively little evidence to support pronounced social hierarchy during this early time period since most Hafit tombs are alike in terms size and contents with few clear markers of vastly differential wealth (e.g., Salvatori 2001).

WATER AND COMPLEX POLITIES IN OMAN

From the mid-third millennium onward, water histories of Southwest and Southeast Arabia diverge dramatically. Prominent similarities in lithic technologies and tombs that span Yemen and Oman during earlier periods diminish; and new, locally distinctive patterns of social and political life begin to distinguish different parts of southern Arabia.

In Oman, dense congregations of people start to cluster around oases during the Umm an-Nar period (ca. 2700 to 2000 BCE, Cleuziou 2002; Potts 2012). Earlier Hafit tombs develop into much larger collective Umm an-Nar tombs that hold tens and even sometimes hundreds of individuals. The spatial patterning of tombs across landscapes also changes dramatically; while Hafit tombs are more widely scattered and located atop cliff lines, Umm an-Nar tombs are most often located in low-lying areas (Giraud 2012). Rather than constructions for particularly wealthy or privileged individuals, Umm an-Nar tombs inter a wide cross-section of populations, including women and men, old and young, ill and healthy (Weeks 2010). Indeed, there are surprisingly few definitive indicators of differential wealth or differential access to resources and a general lack of evidence for hereditary inequality and hierarchy. Current evidence instead suggests communality-dominated social relations with water playing a substantial role. Massive towers 20 m or more in diameter are found around oases during the Umm an-Nar period with three to five towers scattered throughout larger sites such as Bat and Bisya (Cable and Thornton 2013; Cleuziou and Méry 2002; Orchard 2000). Research and debate continues on the purpose and use of Umm an-Nar towers. They may have played a role in defense, storage, rituals, or as residences; but their role as monuments is undeniable and many contain a carefully constructed well near their center (Harrower et al. 2014). A dualistic human/animal motif appears on artifacts and monuments during the Umm an-Nar period signaling social logic founded upon partnership (Cleuziou 2003). Access and rights to water, which in Oman is most readily available at oases where groundwater often percolates to the surface, appear to have been similarly predicated on equitable allocation and community sharing.

There has been considerable, long-running debate on the origins of *qanat* irrigation systems and their precursors in regions surrounding the Gulf (e.g., Boucharlat 2003; Cleuziou 1996). This innovative technology taps water from underground aquifers via a horizontal tunnel connected to a series of vertical access shafts (Figure 8.3 on page 166). The traditional view that such "underground infiltrations galleries" originated in Iran during the first millennium BCE and then diffused to Southeast Arabia (J. C. Wilkinson 1977) has been strongly challenged, with some maintaining evidence of underground waterworks at least that early in Southeast Arabia (Magee 2005; al-Tikriti 2011). Importantly, since crop domesticates are present in Southeast Arabia as early as the third millennium BCE

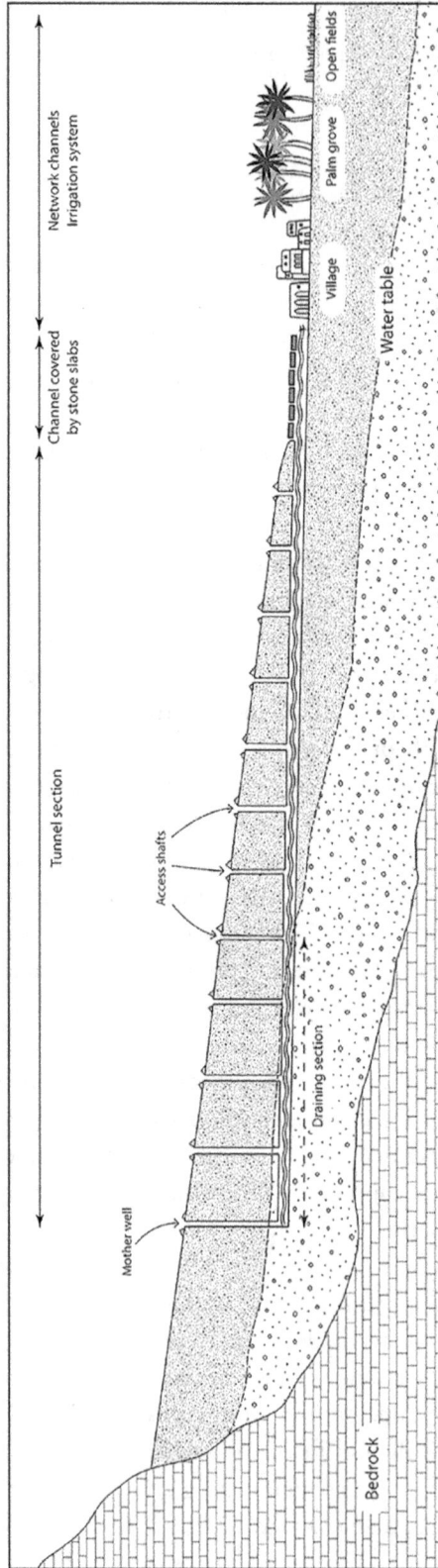

Figure 8.3 Schematic drawing of a *qanat* underground infiltration gallery (figure adapted from Charbonnier 2015).

(Potts 1994; Tengberg 2003), some form of irrigation must have been practiced long before the appearance of underground galleries since the region is simply too dry to support cultivation without irrigation. The precise nature of technologies used during the earliest stages of cultivation is a matter of considerable ongoing research. Less technologically complex diversion of spring water and/or use of water from wells likely predominated during the third and second millennia BCE, and small channels have been identified at numerous oases including Hili (Cleuziou 1997) and Bat (Frifelt 2002). These early systems and the social logistics of harnessing, distributing, and allocating water played a major long-term role in population growth, changing social relations and conceptions of water. As increasingly sophisticated techniques for channeling water (including underground water) emerged during the Iron Age, new techniques interconnected with changing social relations, ritual practices, and public life, as evidenced, for example, by snake cult motifs on pottery of the era (Benoist 2007).

WATER AND COMPLEX POLITIES IN YEMEN

In Yemen, complex polities developed very differently with patterns of settlement and water use that bear scant resemblance to those of Oman. Pastoralism and early cultivation first centers at natural (*ain* and *ghayl*) springs as in Oman, but later groups came to rely on hillslope runoff, terrace building, and eventually massive flash floodwater (*sayl*) irrigation systems. Many of these differences are a function of very different topographies, spatiotemporal availabilities of water, and widely disparate ways in which people and polities adapted to and harnessed water through time. As in Oman, a fourth millennium shift toward aridity played a substantive role, but should not be viewed as a unicausal determinant of change (Cleuziou 2009). Near 3200 BCE small circular tombs begin to appear, and the earliest evidence of crops and irrigation is evident in the region at nearly the same time (Ekstrom and Edens 2003; Harrower 2008; Wilkinson 1999). During the third millennium, large fortified hilltop settlements were established in the highlands of western Yemen (Edens et al. 2000). In eastern Yemen, mobile agro-pastoralism appears to have prevailed for a longer period, but sedentary settlements were certainly well established in a number of areas by the second millennium BCE (Breton 2003; McCorriston 2000; Steimer-Herbet et al. 2006).

Thousands of years of experience capturing water in Yemen eventually led to advanced flash floodwater irrigation systems that sustained ancient desert kingdoms (Brunner 1997; Mouton 2004; Wilkinson 2006). Alongside frankincense trade to the eastern Mediterranean, the historical and technological development of irrigation systems has long been a major topic in Southwest Arabian archaeology (Breton 1999). Five major kingdoms, Ma'in, Saba, Qatabān, 'Awsan, and Hadramawt, emerged around the margins of Yemen's Ramlat as-Sab'atayn Desert. This expansive desert—part of the Rub al-Khali (Empty Quarter) of Arabia—forms a massive endorheic basin into which Yemen's inward-draining wadis flow before disappearing beneath desert sands. By the late second millennium BCE, the major towns, irrigation technologies, and writing system that laid the foundations of Yemen's ancient kingdoms began to coalesce around the outlets of major wadis along the desert (de Maigret 2002).

In conjunction with topography, the timing of summer monsoon precipitation played a major role in Southwest Arabian irrigation. Unlike in Oman, where rain mostly falls in the winter, in Yemen sudden bursts of rain concentrate in a bimodal late-spring and summer pattern that generates powerful flash floods. Diversion of these floods thorough massive barrage headworks into primary, secondary, and tertiary distributary canals to earthen-banked fields enabled cultivation of cereal crops and date palms over vast areas. In Oman, water tapped from aquifers flows gradually and relatively continuously for much of the year; but in Yemen, powerful, sporadic floods arrive only a few times a year and require technologies devised many months in advance. Large work crews are needed to build massive diversion structures that can withstand flash floods. When floods arrive, quick coordination (sometimes in the middle of the night) is often required to regulate the diversion of flows into fields while redirecting excess back to natural channels to prevent damage and erosion. Large aggregations of laborers are then periodically required to make repairs and remove sediments that accumulate behind dams and along canals.

The irrigation works of the Sabaean state capital of Ma'rib are by far the most well-known and extensively studied of Southwest Arabian irrigation systems (Brunner 2000; Brunner and Haefner 1986; Francaviglia 2000; Kühn et al. 2010; Pietsch et al. 2010). At its apogee, the Great Dam at Ma'rib stood at least 19 m high and spanned 600 m between bedrock outcrops where it captured and redirected water from an enormous 11,598 sq km watershed (Brunner 2000; Nebes 2004). It irrigated an area up to 9,600 hectares that can be readily identified by the geometric patterns of canals and earthen banked fields visible in air photos and satellite imagery (Brunner and Haefner 1986, 1990). This system was clearly a massive engineering, organizational, and operational undertaking that borrowed on thousands of years of experience with floodwater irrigation technologies. Some of the earliest definitive evidence of a major dam at Ma'rib comes from inscriptions at Temple of Almaqah at Sirwah (RES 3945 and 3946) that describe construction of waterworks built by Karibil Watar during the early seventh century BCE (Avanzini 2016: 112, 301–302). Many centuries of construction and reconstruction (sometimes involving many thousands of workers) followed until the Great Dam at Ma'rib finally collapsed during the late sixth century CE just prior to the rise of Islam (Vogt 2005).

CONCLUDING REMARKS:
COMPARATIVE DYNAMICS OF WATER AND POWER IN YEMEN AND OMAN

A broad range of factors contributed to widely differing dynamics of water and power in ancient Yemen and Oman. As shifts in perspective that realign thinking, water histories and spatial archaeology hold considerable potential to advance our understanding of these and other regions. In both Yemen and Oman, natural water geographies (including topographies, structural geologies, and patterns of precipitation) contributed to wide spatial heterogeneity. Adapting to and exploiting this heterogeneity, by capturing water that made agriculture possible even in hyper-arid areas, became a key factor that generated wide historical and cultural diversity. Interestingly, the first appearance of animal (early sixth millennium BCE) and then plant (mid-fourth millennium BCE) domesticates occurred at roughly comparable times in Southwest and Southeast Arabia. Broad similarities in stone tools, including among Fasad-type projectile points, shows interaction that may have contributed to experimentation with animal husbandry. The appearance of small circular tombs across southern Arabia during the late fourth millennium similarly shows correspondence over vast areas linked to changing patterns of land and water use.

From the early third millennium BCE onward, water histories of Southwest and Southeast Arabia diverge dramatically as new irrigation technologies and sociopolitics diversify and differentiate in different locales. In Oman, near-surface aquifers offered relatively continuously flowing water so that devising and coordinating equitable arrangements for sharing water (commonly by allocations of time) was critically important (Charbonnier 2014). In Yemen, where abrupt flash floods arrive sporadically over the summer months, the primary challenge for ancient states was not so much sharing water (as once floods arrived there was far more water than could be utilized), but rather coordinating the labor necessary to construct massive diversion systems to make flash floods useful rather than destructive. In both cases, the spectacle and grandeur of water control was critically important, yet differing natural circumstances contributed to very different modalities of power. In Oman, the need for sharing of continuous flows contributed to emphasis on equity and communality. In Yemen, centralization of design, construction, operation, and production contributed to far more hierarchical dynamics of power.

The future holds an enormous range of opportunities to reexamine water and power in the past in ways that inform understanding of the present and the future. The distressing breadth of contemporary conflict in Yemen and more broadly across the Middle East makes it even more important to study and better understand how water shapes politics. Air photos and satellite imagery have made major contributions to the study of ancient water use, and new spatial technologies have a critical role to play in understanding water geographies and spatial heterogeneity. Patterns of water flow across rugged terrain can be examined with increasingly detailed topographic models, and irrigation-deposited sediments can be mapped with increasingly high spectral resolution satellite imagery. However, it is not simply new technologies but more importantly their interface with new spatial theory and new ways of thinking about geographies that offer the most promising opportunities to better understand the dynamics of water and power. Even though Yemen and Oman share some basic commonalities, it is through comparison and juxtaposition that their differences begin to clarify patterning of human societies and their diverse and creative interrelations with water.

REFERENCES CITED

Avanzini, A. 2008 The History of the Khor Rori Area: New Perspectives, in *A Port in Arabia Between Rome and the Indian Ocean (3rd C. BC to 5th C. AD)*, edited by A. Avanzini, pp. 13–27. L'erma di Bretschneider, Rome.

Avanzini, A. 2016 By Land and By Sea: A history of South Arabia before Islam recounted from inscriptions. L'erma di Bretschneider, Rome.

Benoist, A. 2007 An Iron Age II Snake Cult in the Oman Peninsula: Evidence from Bithnah (Emirate of Fujairah). *Arabian archaeology and epigraphy* 18(1):34–54.

Breton, J.-F. 2003 Preliminary Notes on the Development of Shabwa. *Proceedings of the Seminar for Arabian Studies* 33:199–213.

Breton, J.-F. 1999 *Arabia Felix from the Time of the Queen of Sheba: Eighth Century B.C. to First Century A.D.* University of Notre Dame Press, Notre Dame.

Boucharlat, R. 2003 Iron Age Water-Draining Galleries and the Iranian "Qanat," in *Archaeology of the United Arab Emirates*, edited by D. T. Potts, H. Al-Naboodah, and P. Hellyer, pp. 162–72. Trident Press, Abu Dhabi.

Brunner, U. 1997 Geography and Human Settlements in Ancient Southern Arabia. *Arabian archaeology and epigraphy* 8:190–202.

Brunner, U. 2000 The Great Dam and the Sabean Oasis of Ma'rib. *Irrigation and Drainage Systems* 14:167–182.

Brunner, U., and H. Haefner. 1986 The Successful Floodwater Farming System of the Sabeans: Yemen Arab Republic. *Applied Geography* 6:77–86.

Brunner, U., and H. Haefner. 1990 Altsüdarabische Bewässerungsoasen. *Die Erde* 121:135–152.

Cable, C. M., and C. P. Thornton. 2013 Monumentality and the Third Millennium "Towers" of the Oman Peninsula. In *Connections and Complexity: New Approaches to the Archaeology of South Asia*, edited by S. A. Abraham, P. Gullapalli, T. P. Raczek, and U. Z. Rizvi, pp. 375–399. Left Coast Press, Walnut Creek, CA.

Charbonnier, J. 2012 L'irrigation et les débuts de l'agriculture sur les marges arides du Rub' al-Khâlî: IVᵉ–IIᵉ millénaires av. J. C. In *Aux Marges de L'archeologie: Hommage à Serge Cleuziou*, pp. 241–252. De Boccard, Paris.

Charbonnier, J. 2014 In the Shadow of Palm Trees: Time Management and Water Allocation in the Oasis of Adam (Sultanate of Oman). *Proceedings of the Seminar for Arabian Studies* 44:83–98.

Charbonnier, J. 2015 Groundwater Management in Southeast Arabia from the Bronze Age to the Iron Age: A Critical Reassessment. *Water History* 7:39–71.

Charpentier, V. 2008 Hunter-Gatherers of the "Empty Quarter of the Early Holocene" to the Last Neolithic Societies: Chronology of the Late Prehistory of South-Eastern Arabia (8000–3100 BC). *Proceedings of the Seminar for Arabian Studies* 38:93–116.

Charpentier, V., and R. Crassard. 2013 Back to Fasad . . . and the PPNB Controversy. Questioning a Levantine Origin for Arabian Early Holocene Projectile Points Technology, *Arabian archaeology and epigraphy* 36:28–36.

Cleuziou, S. 1996 The Emergence of Oases and Towns in Eastern and Southern Arabia. In *The Prehistory of Asia and Oceania*, edited by G. E. Afanas'ev, S. Cleuziou, J. R. Lukacs, and M. Tosi, pp. 159–165. UISPP, Forli.

Cleuziou, S. 1997 Construire et protéger son terroir : les oasis d'Oman à l'Âge du Bronze. In *La dynamique des paysages protohistoriques, antiques, médiévaux et modernes. XVIIe Rencontres Internationales d'Archéologie et d'Histoire d'Antibes*, edited by J. Burnouf, J.-P. Bravard, and G. Chouquer, pp. 389–412. APDCA, Antibes.

Cleuziou, S. 2002 The Early Bronze Age of the Oman Peninsula from Chronology to the Dialectics of Tribe and State Formation. In *Essays on the Late Prehistory of the Arabian Peninsula*, edited by S. Cleuziou, M. Tosi, and J. Zarins, pp. 191–236. Istituto Italiano Per L'Africa e L'Oriente, Rome.

Cleuziou, S. 2003 Early Bronze Age Trade in the Gulf and the Arabian Sea: The Society behind the Boats. In *Archaeology of the United Arab Emirates*, edited by D.T. Potts, pp. 133–150. Trident Press, London.

Cleuziou, S. 2009 Extracting Wealth from a Land of Starvation by Creating Social Complexity: A Dialogue between Archaeology and Climate. *C.R. Geoscience* 341:726–738.

Cleuziou, S., M.-L. Inizan, and B. Marcolongo, 1992 Le Peuplement pré- et protohistorique due système fluviatile fossile du Jawf-Hadramawt au Yémen (d'après l'interprétation d'images satellite, de photographies aériennes et de prospections). *Paléorient* 18(2):5–29.

Cleuziou, S., and S. Méry. 2002 In-Between the Great Powers: The Bronze Age Oman Peninsula. In *Essays on the Late Prehistory of the Arabian Peninsula*, edited by S. Cleuziou, M. Tosi, and J. Zarins, pp. 273–316. Istituto Italiano per L'Africa e l'Oriente, Roma.

Cleuziou, S., and M. Tosi. 2007 *In the Shadow of the Ancestors: The Prehistoric Foundations of the Early Arabian Civilization in Oman*. Ministry of Heritage and Culture, Muscat.

de Beauclair, R., S. A. Jasim, and H.-P. Uerpmann. 2006 New Results on the Neolithic Jewellery from al-Buhais 18, UAE. *Proceedings of the Seminar for Arabian Studies* 36:175–187.

de Maigret, A. 1996 New Evidence from the Yemenite "Turret Graves" for the Problem of the Emergence of the South Arabian States. In *The Indian Ocean in Antiquity*, edited by J. Reade, pp. 321–338. Kegan Paul, London.

de Maigret, A. 2002 *Arabia Felix: An Exploration of the Archaeological History of Yemen*. Stacey International, London.

Drechsler, P. 2007 The Neolithic Dispersal into Arabia. *Proceedings of the Seminar for Arabian Studies* 37:93–109.

Drechsler, P. 2009 *The Dispersal of the Neolithic over the Arabian Peninsula*. Archaeopress, Oxford.

Edens, C., T. J. Wilkinson, and G. Barratt. 2000. Hammat al-Qa and the Roots of Urbanism in Southwest Arabia. *Antiquity* 74:854–862.

Ekstrom, H., and C. Edens. 2003 Prehistoric Agriculture in Highland Yemen: New Results from Dhamar. *Yemen Update: Bulletin of the American Institute for Yemeni Studies* 45:23–35.

Fedele, F. G. 2013 Neolithic Settlement of the Eastern Yemen Plateau: An Exploration of Locational Choice and Land Use. *Arabian Archaeology and Epigraphy* 24:44–50.

Fleitmann, D., S. J. Burns, M. Pekala, A. Mangini, A. Al-subbary, M. Al-aowah, J. Kramers, and A. Matter. 2011 Holocene and Pleistocene Pluvial Periods in Yemen, Southern Arabia. *Quaternary Science Reviews* 30(7–8):783–787.

Francaviglia, V. M. 2000 Dating the Ancient Dam of Ma'rib (Yemen). *Journal of Archaeological Science* 27:645–653.

Frifelt, K. 2002 Bat, a Centre in Third Millennium Oman. In *Essays on the Late Prehistory of the Arabian Peninsula*, edited by S. Cleuziou, M. Tosi, and J. Zarins, pp. 101–110. Istituto Italiano per L'Africa e l'Oriente, Roma.

Giraud, J. 2010 Early Bronze Age Graves and Graveyards in the Eastern Ja'alan (Sultanate of Oman): An Assessment of the Social Rules Working in the Evolution of a Funerary Landscape. In *Death and Burial in Ancient Arabia and Beyond: Multidisciplinary Perspectives*, edited by L. Weeks, pp. 71–84. Archaeopress, Oxford.

Giraud, J. 2012 Les espaces du passé. L'exemple du Ja'alan à la période Hafit. In *Aux marges de l'archéologie*, edited by J. Giraud and G. Gernez, pp. 133–151, De Boccard, Paris.

Harrower, M. 2008 Hydrology, Ideology, and the Origins of Irrigation in Ancient Southwest Arabia (Yemen). *Current Anthropology* 49(3):497–510.

Harrower, M., J. McCorriston, and A. C. D'Andrea, 2010. General/Specific, Local/Global: Comparing the Beginnings of Agriculture in the Horn of Africa (Ethiopia/Eritrea) and Southwest Arabia (Yemen). *American Antiquity* 75(3):452–472.

Harrower, M. J. 2016 *Water Histories and Spatial Archaeology: Ancient Yemen and the American West.* Cambridge University Press, Cambridge.

Harrower, M. J., K. M. O'Meara, J. J. Basile, C. J. Hickman, J. L. Swerida, I. A. Dumitru, J. L. Bongers, C. J. Bailey, and E. Fieldhouse. 2014 If a Picture is Worth a Thousand Words . . . 3D Modeling a Bronze Age Tower in Oman. *World Archaeology* 46(1):43–62.

Hijmans, R. J., S. E. Cameron, J. L. Parra, P. G. Jones, and A. Jarvis. 2005 Very High Resolution Interpolated Climate Surfaces for Global Land Areas. *International Journal of Climatology* 25(15):1965–1978.

Kühn, P., D. Pietsch, and I. Gerlach. 2010 Archaeopedological Analyses around a Neolithic Hearth and the Beginning of Sabaean Irrigation in the Oasis of Ma'rib (Ramlat as-Sab'atayn, Yemen). *Journal of Archaeological Science* 37:1305–1310.

Kuijt, I., and N. Goring-Morris. 2002 Foraging, Farming, and Social Complexity in the Pre-Pottery Neolithic of the Southern Levant: A Review and Synthesis. *Journal of World Prehistory* 16(4):361–440.

Kwarteng, A. Y., A. S. Dorvlo, and G. T. V. Kumar. 2009 Analysis of a 27-Year rainfall Data (1977–2003) in the Sultanate of Oman. *International Journal of Climatology* 29:605–617.

Lézine, A. M., C. Robert, S. Cleuziou, M. L. Inizan, F. Braemer, J. F. SaliF, F. Sylvestre, J. J. Tiercelin, R. Crassard, S. M. S., V. Charpentier, and T. Steimer-Herbet. 2010 Climate Change and Human Occupation in the Southern Arabian Lowlands during the Last Deglaciation and the Holocene. *Global and Planetary Change* 72:412–428.

Magee, P. 2005 The Chronology and Environmental Background of Iron Age Settlement in Southeastern Iran and the Question of the Origin of the Qanat Irrigation System. *Iranica Antiqua* 40:217–231.

Martin, L., J. McCorriston, and R. Crassard. 2009 Early Arabian Pastoralism at Manayzah in Wadi Sana, Hadramawt, *Proceedings of the Seminar for Arabian Studies* 39:285–296.

McCorriston, J. 2000 Early Settlement in Hadramawt: Preliminary Report on Prehistoric Occupation at Shi'b Munayder. *Arabian archaeology and epigraphy* 11:129–153.

McCorriston, J., M. Harrower, T. Steimer-Herbet, K. Williams, M. Senn, M. Al-Hadhari, M. Al-Kathiri, 'A. A. Al-Kathiri, J.-F. Saliege, and J. Everhart. 2014 Monuments and Landscape of Mobile Pastoralists in Dhofar: The Arabian Human Social Dynamics (AHSD) Project, 2009–2011. *Journal of Oman Studies* 18:117–143.

McCorriston, J., Harrower, M., L. Martin, and E. Oches. 2012 Cattle Cults of the Arabian Neolithic and Early Territorial Societies. *American Anthropologist* 114(1):45–63.

McCorriston, J., T. Steimer-Herbet, J. Kemang, M. Harrower, and K. Williams. 2011 Gazetteer of Small-Scale Monuments in Prehistoric Hadramawt, Yemen : A Radiocarbon Chronology from the RASA-AHSD Project Research 1996–2008. *Arabian Archaeology and Epigraphy* 22:1–22.

Méry, S., and G. Schneider. 1996 Mesopotamian Pottery Wares in Eastern Arabia from the 5th to the 2nd Millennium BC: A Contribution of Archaeometry to Economic History. *Proceedings of the Seminar for Arabian Studies* 26:79–96.

Mouton, M. 2004 Irrigation et Formation de la Societe Antique dan les Basses-Terres du Yemen: un essai de modele. *Syria* 81:81–104.

Nebes, N. 2004 A New Abraha Inscription from the Great Dam of Marib. *Proceedings of the Seminar for Arabian Studies* 34:221–230.

Orchard, J. 2000 Oasis Town or Tower Hamlets? Bisya during the Al-Hajar Period. *Proceedings of the Seminar for Arabian Studies* 30:165–175.

Pietsch, D., P. Kühn, T. Scholten, U. Brunner, H. Hitgen, and I. Gerlach, 2010 Holocene Soils and Sediments around Ma'rib Oasis, Yemen : Further Sabaean Treasures? *The Holocene* 20(5):785–799.

Potts, D. T. 1986 Eastern Arabia and the Oman Peninsula during the Late Fourth and Early Third Millennium BC. In *Gamdat Nasr Period or Regional Style?*, edited by U. Finkbeiner and W. Röllig, pp. 121–170. Ludwig Reichert Verlag, Wiesbaden.

Potts, D. T. 1994 Contributions to the Agrarian History of Eastern Arabia II: The Cultivars. *Arabian archaeology and epigraphy* 5:236–275.

Potts, D. T. 2012 *In the Land of the Emirates: The Archaeology and History of the UAE*. Trident Press, Abu Dhabi.

Salvatori, S. 1996 Death and Ritual in a Population of Coastal Food Foragers in Oman. In *The Prehistory of Asia and Oceania*, edited by G. E. Afanas'ev, S. Cleuziou, J. R. Lukas, and M. Tosi, pp. 205–222. UISPP, Forli.

Salvatori, S. 2001 Excavations at the Funerary Structures HD 10-3.1, 3.2, 4.1, 4.2, and 2.a at Ra's al-Hadd (Sultanate of Oman). *Rassegna di Archeologia* 25:67–77.

Steimer-Herbet, T., G. Davtian, and F. Braemer. 2006 Pastoralists' Tombs and Settlement Patterns in Wadi Wash'ah during the Bronze Age (Hadramawt, Yemen). *Proceedings for the Seminar for Arabian Studies* 36:1–9.

Tengberg, M. 2003 Archaeobotany in the Oman Peninsula and the Role of Eastern Arabia in the Spread of African Crops. In *Food, Fuel, and Fields: Progress in African Archaeobotany*, edited by K. Neumann, A. Butler, and S. Kahlheber, pp. 229–238. Heinrich-Barth Institut, Koln.

al-Tikriti, W. Y. 2011 *Archaeology of the Falaj: A Field Study of the Ancient Irrigation Systems of the United Arab Emirates*. Abu Dhabi Culture and Heritage, Abu Dhabi.

Uerpmann, H.-P., D. T. Potts, and M. Uerpmann. 2009 The Holocene (Re-)Occupation of Eastern Arabia. In *Evolution of Human Populations in Arabia*, edited by M. D. Petraglia and J. I. Rose, pp. 205–214. Springer, Dordrecht.

Uerpmann, H., M. Uerpmann, A. Kutterer, and S. A. Jasim. 2013 The Neolithic Period in the Central Region of the Emirate of Sharjah (UAE). *Arabian Archaeology and Epigraphy* 108:102–108.

Uerpmann, M. 2003 The Dark Millennium—Remarks on the Final Stone Age in the Emirates and Oman. In *Archaeology of the United Arab Emirates*, edited by D. T. Potts, H. Al-Naboodah, and P. Hellyer, pp. 74–81. Trident Press, London.

Uerpmann, M., and H. P. Uerpmann. 1996 'Ubaid Pottery in the Eastern Gulf—New Evidence from Umm al-Qaiwain (U.A.E.). *Arabian archaeology and epigraphy* 7:125–139.

Uerpmann, M., H.-P. Uerpmann, and S. A. Jasim. 2000 Stone Age Nomadism in SE-Arabia—Palaeo-economic Considerations on the Neolithic Site of Al-Buhais 18 in the Emirate of Sharjah, U.A.E. *Proceedings of the Seminar for Arabian Studies* 30:229–234.

Weeks, L. 2010 *Death and Burial in Ancient Arabia and Beyond: Multidisciplinary Perspectives*. Archaeopress, Oxford.

Wilkinson, J. C. 1977 *Water and Tribal Settlement in South East Arabia: A Study of the Aflaj of Oman*. Oxford University Press, Oxford.

Wilkinson, T. J. 1999 Settlement, Soil Erosion and Terraced Agriculture in Highland Yemen: A Preliminary Statement. *Proceedings of the Seminar for Arabian Studies* 29:183–191.

Wilkinson, T. J. 2006 From Highland to Desert: The Organization of Landscape and Irrigation in Southern Arabia. In *Agricultural Strategies*, edited by J. Marcus and C. Stanish, pp. 38–70. Cotsen Institute of Archaeology, University of California, Los Angeles.

Wilkinson, T. J. 2009 Environment and Long-Term Population Trends in Southwest Arabia. In *The Evolution of Human Populations in Arabia*, edited by M. D. Petraglia and J. I. Rose, pp. 51–66. Springer Netherlands, Dordrecht.

Williams, K. D., and L. A. Gregoricka. 2013 The Social, Spatial, and Bioarchaeological Histories of Ancient Oman Project: The Mortuary Landscape of Dhank. *Arabian archaeology and epigraphy* 24:134–150.

Van Rampelbergh, M., D. Fleitmann, S. Verheyden, H. Cheng, L. Edwards, P. De Geest, D. De Vleeschouwer, S. J. Burns, A. Matter, P. Claeys, and E. Keppens. 2013 Mid- to Late Holocene Indian Ocean Monsoon Variability Recorded in Four Speleothems from Socotra Island, Yemen. *Quaternary Science Reviews* 65:129–142.

Vogt, B. 2005 The Great Dam, Eduard Glaser, and the Chronology of Ancient Irrigation at Ma'rib. In *Sabaean Studies: Archaeological, Epigraphical, and Historical Studies*, edited by A. M. Sholan, S. Antonini, M. Arbach, pp. 501–520. Naples-Sanaa: University of Sanaa, Yemeni-Italian Centre for Archaeological Researches, Ṣanʾāʾ.

Zeder, M. 2011 The Origins of Agriculture in the Near East. *Current Anthropology* 52(S4): 221–235.

PART III

Coastal Water

CHAPTER NINE

The Sea and Bronze Age Transformations

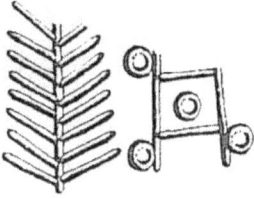

Christopher Prescott,
Anette Sand-Eriksen,
and Knut Ivar Austvoll

Abstract *Along the western Norwegian coast, in the northwestern region of the Nordic Late Neolithic and Bronze Age (2350–500 BCE) there is cultural homogeneity but variable expressions of political hierarchy. Although new ideological institutions, technology (e.g., metallurgy and boat building), intensified agro-pastoral farming, and maritime travel were introduced throughout the region as of 2350 BCE, concentrations of expressions of Bronze Age elites are intermittently found along the coast. Four regions—Lista, Jæren, Karmøy, and Sunnmøre—are examined in an exploration of the establishment and early role of maritime practices in this Nordic region. It is argued that the expressions of power and material wealth concentrated in these four regions are based on the control of bottlenecks, channels, portages, and harbors along important maritime routes of travel. As such, this article is a study of prehistoric travel, sources of power, and maritime landscapes in the Late Neolithic and Early Bronze Age of Norway.*

The Nordic Bronze Age (1700–500 BCE) is an exceptionally vibrant cultural and social expression in European prehistory. Although the term often generates geographic connotations to Northern Germany, Denmark, and Scania, the cultural region extends into much of the Scandinavian Peninsula and the Baltic. One sphere of interaction within the Nordic region is found along the western Norwegian coast from Lista in southwestern Norway to Troms in Northern Norway. Though the cultural expression within this 1,200 kilometer stretch is similar, there seem to be variable expressions of political hierarchy—localized chiefdoms—within the region. Such expressions are found in Lista, Jæren, and Karmøy in southwestern Norway, the islands of Sunnmøre in northwestern Norway, and the Trondheimsfjord area in central Norway (Figure 9.1 on page 178).

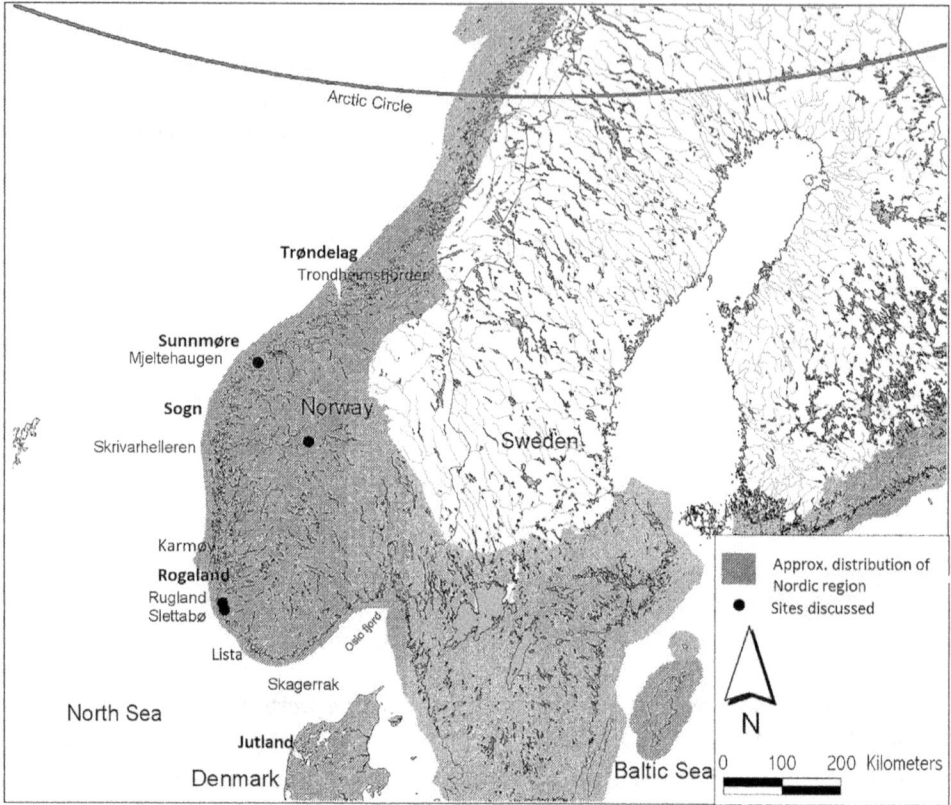

FIGURE 9.1 The Nordic region in the Late Neolithic and Bronze Age. Sites and regions discussed in the text are marked (after Prescott and Glørstad 2015:fig. 1).

Traditionally, the rise of an elite in these regions has been seen in light of agricultural potential, as especially Lista, Jæren, and Trøndelag are among the most agriculturally productive regions in Norway. In recent years it has been more common to argue that the roots of the Nordic Early Bronze Age are to be found in the preceding Nordic Late Neolithic (2400/2350–1700 BCE), which was instigated by the Bell Beaker Culture in western Scandinavia (e.g., Prieto-Martínez 2008). New ideological institutions, technology (e.g., metallurgy and boat building), intensified agro-pastoral farming, maritime travel, warriors, and elite interaction were introduced at this time, and represent the basis for the rise of Bronze Age society in the Nordic region.

The present article explores the establishment and early role of maritime practices in the Nordic Late Neolithic (2400/2350–1700 BCE) and Early Bronze Age (1700–1100 BCE) in the Nordic region along the western coast of Norway. Four regions with concentrations of Late Neolithic and Early Bronze Age material, and expressions of hierarchy and chiefdoms along the western Norwegian coast—Lista, Jæren, Karmøy, and Sunnmøre—are examined. Though practices and institutions such as warrior ideals, technology, exchange, maritime travel, hierarchy, intensified farming, and metal are fundamental for Bronze

Age society along the Norwegian coast, expressions of power are concentrated in the four regions, and it was probably tied to controlling bottlenecks, channels, portages, and harbors along important maritime routes of travel. As such, this article is an exploration of prehistoric travel, sources of power, and maritime landscapes in the Late Neolithic and Early Bronze Age of Norway.

THE SEA AND SCANDINAVIAN ARCHAEOLOGY

The sea is always present in Scandinavia. Since the Kitchen Midden Commissions—two multidisciplinary projects that ran from 1848 to 1895 to investigate Late Mesolithic shell midden deposits along the Limfjord in Jutland—the sea has held a recurring presence in Scandinavian archaeology. The sea has served a multitude of purposes in archaeological study and discourse. Shoreline displacement was the basis for absolute and relative dating, the study of subsistence is often the study of marine resources, and the sea as a route of communication and mobility permeates discourse about, for example, postglacial colonization, Bronze Age rock carvings, or Viking Age expansion.

Still, a terrestrial perspective that emphasizes agrarian production and land rights permeates the broader narratives of prehistory in Norway from the Neolithic to the Iron Age. The role of the maritime sphere has an aura of passiveness, and is often taken for granted (Kvalø 2007), entailing that the historicity of the role of the sea has been understated (Glørstad 2013). Agriculture and pastoralism are often ascribed the dynamic role in history—to the extent that Bronze Age rock art, which in western Norway is dominated by figures of boats, is traditionally labelled "agrarian rock art" (e.g., Hagen 1990; Marstrander 1978). Fortunately, the agricultural perspective has in the last ten years been complemented by a suite of factors such as maritime technologies (Glørstad 2012; Kvalø 2007; Østmo 2012), metallurgy (Melheim 2012; Melheim and Prescott 2016), exchange networks, and migration (Prescott 2012).

In Scandinavia, and particularly the southern part of the region, the Nordic Late Neolithic (LN) and Early Bronze Age (EBA) are associated with a spectacular archaeology that includes bifacially worked flint (such as the LN fishtail dagger from Hindsgavl), bronze weapons (the EBA Rørby sword with a boat figure on the blade), and personal items of metal, monumental graves (like the EBA oak coffin graves), rock carvings (where the boat commonly is a central motif), and settlements with long houses. These and a host of other archaeological objects and sites are the basis for interpretations concerning the establishment of metallurgy, intensified agro-pastoral production, warfare, monumentality and associated rituality, social hierarchy, political economy, and integration with Northern European and indeed continental networks (e.g., Jensen 2002; Kristiansen and Larsson 2005).

Though the rich archaeological materials from present-day Northern Germany, Denmark, and southerly Sweden usually come to mind in discussions of the Nordic LN and EBA, the rapid establishment and reproduction of Nordic LN-EBA–type societies, spheres of interaction and culture had a much wider dispersion into the Baltic Sea region and north into Norway (Figure 9.1). In some ways, history in the more peripheral regions is all the more dramatic, as hunter-gatherer groups with deep regional culture traditions were rapidly replaced by LN societies. Archaeologically, in Norway this transition, around 2400–2350 BCE included the establishment of the farm as the fundamental social and economic entity, concurrent establishment of transhumant exploitation of the uplands, bifacial lithic technologies, European artefact forms, weaponry, early copper metallurgy, regular crossings of open stretches of sea, regional patterns of interaction (Prescott and Glørstad 2012).

CHANGING MARITIME PRACTICES IN PREHISTORY?

Maritime mobility has been an essential factor in the human settlement of Norway since deglaciation. The initial postglacial settlement was profoundly tied to the sea, and the maritime orientation continued throughout most of the Mesolithic and Neolithic. The structure of human-sea interaction can be seen in the spread of cultural elements that generally follows the coast in a southeastern to northwestern direction. Though the cumulative outcome was widespread communication and diffusion of cultural elements, the individual trips in the Mesolithic, Early, and Middle Neolithic seem to have been small-scale and coast-bounded—not long sea journeys between alliance partners (Glørstad 2012, 2013).

A major cultural horizon in easterly Northern Europe is represented by the Corded Ware Culture (CWC). Representing a substantial break with older Funnel Beaker, Pitted Ware, and hunter-gatherer traditions, the CWC is probably the result of migration, represents the first spread of Indo-European languages, and had a strong pastoral orientation. The CWC in Norway (or Battle Axe Culture, 2750–2400/2350 BCE) is primarily represented in Eastern Norway, with a patchy settlement pattern along the Oslo fjord's coast through the inland valleys to Trøndelag in Central Norway (Hinsch 1956). The CWC represents an enigmatic period in Norwegian prehistory (Hinsch 1956; Østmo 1988:227–231; Prescott and Walderhaug 1995; Shetelig 1936); however the data at the moment suggests the following patterns:

- Migration: The CWC was the result of a small-scale immigration, but did not trigger substantial change.

- Eastern and limited impact: The CWC was primarily located in small settlement patches in eastern Norway.

- Terrestrial: In terms of maritime practices, the CWC does not represent a significant break from older traditions, though it seems to have a more pronounced terrestrial bearing. It is conceivable that pastures and hunting grounds were a more important political-economic resource than waterways.

The mid-third millennium in Norway, around 2400 BCE, represents a significant reorientation. Bell Beaker Culture (BBC) settlements in western Denmark and Norway archaeologically mark the instigation of the Nordic LN, though much of the historical process leading from the Bell Beaker to the Late Neolithic, 2500 to 2350 BCE, remains unclear (Prescott 2012; Prescott and Melheim 2009; Prieto-Martinez 2008:116; Sarauw 2007:66; Vandkilde 2001, 2005). Still, the outcome is the establishment of the Nordic region of interaction in the Baltic, Northern Germany, Sweden, Denmark, and Norway. The distribution of artifact materials such as Bell Beakers and flint daggers attests to the far-flung network of regular exchange and communication. This general region of interaction was reproduced through the Late Neolithic and Bronze Age.

The type 1 Nordic flint dagger of the LN1 was produced in Northern Jutland; however, approximately 10 percent of the recovered daggers are found in southwestern Norway (Apel 2001:295). The distribution of the daggers demonstrates two new and important institutionalized practices:

- A substantial number of Jutish daggers (and other objects) are exported across the 130 km-wide Skagerrak strait between Jutland and Norway (Figure 9.2). There were regular and intensive movements across open stretches

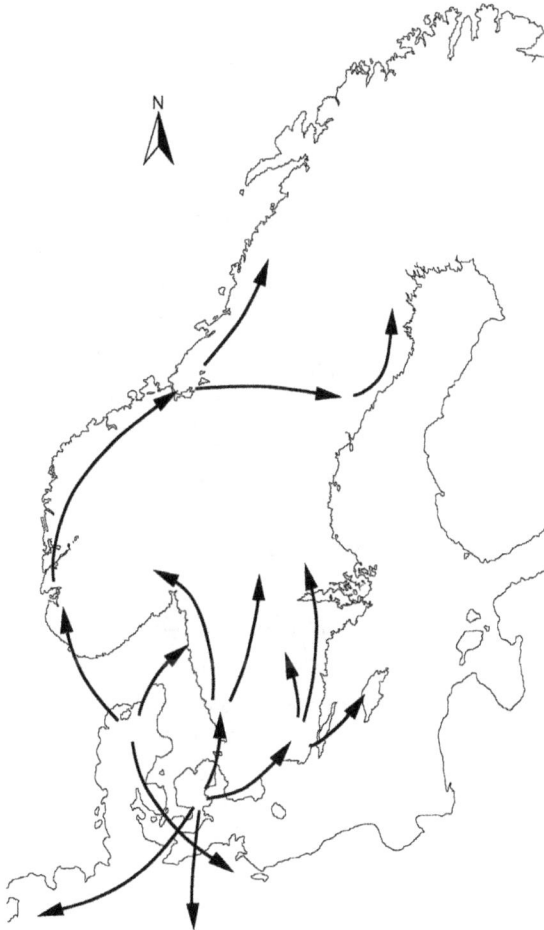

FIGURE 9.2 Distribution routes for LN1 flint daggers type 1 suggesting communication routes and networks. (Redrawn after fig. 9, Apel 2001:17).

of sea (compared to the predominantly small-scale coastal mobility of the preceding eras).

- The daggers help to define the western Norwegian subregion within the Nordic region (Bakka 1976, Prescott and Glørstad 2015:79). This subregion stretches from Lista in the south to Troms above the Arctic Circle, bound together by the sea.

The development in maritime capacity is certainly a dynamic factor in the development of the Nordic region, as well as a premise for the rapid and continuous dispersion of a range of social, technological, and cultural innovations that characterize the LN and EBA. Unfortunately, apart from petroglyphs demonstrating large seafaring vessels parallel to the Early Iron Age Hjortspring war boat (Crumlin-Pedersen and Trakadas 2003; Østmo 2012:66; Rosenberg 1937), we do not have much direct archaeological evidence of boat technology in the LN and EBA (Kvalø 2007:52; Østmo 2012). What leads up to the creation of the Nordic region, intensified interaction, and new exchange practices is subject to discussion (Prescott 2012). Einar Østmo (2012:67) argues that new boat technology, specific to the Nordic region, developed in Denmark and was a precondition for the LN and EBA distribution patterns. An adjustment or elaboration on Østmo's idea is that establishing social institutions, for instance, alliance networks, intensified exchange and an ideology emphasizing elite travel (cf. Kristiansen and Larsson 2005:32ff; Kvalø 2007:81ff) in the wake of Bell Beaker expansion, created the social basis for the establishment and maintenance of networks (Prescott 2012). In practical terms, this allowed boats to sail and land far from their home territory. In all probability, developments represent a situation typical of the mid-third millennium: technology, politics, and ideology combine to generate new practices. Thus, having boats and knowledge to navigate open stretches of challenging sea, and being welcomed by people perceived as kin at your destination harbor were probably both necessary and new to the third millennium.

INTEGRATING WATERWAYS INTO BRONZE AGE HISTORY OF NORWAY

The above focuses on the sea as a medium of transportation, the boat as the technology to exploit the sea, alliances as the social mechanism that permits communication, and ideology that encourages travel and exchange. However, to adopt a more historical approach, the next half of this article will deal with the rise of the sea as a source of power, how a maritime landscape of power evolved and how the maritime landscape indicates the sources of power that created localized chiefdoms at advantageous places along the western Norwegian coast.

A number of interpretations, theoretical concepts, and empirical observations are useful when attempting to understand the role of sea travel. These include application of Anthony's (1990, 2007:108ff) models for the process of migration, and Mary Helms's (1988) ethnographic concept of the social role of travel, to contextualize exchange and alliance maintenance but also in the legitimization of an elite's position "at home" (i.e.,

Kristiansen and Larsson 2005; Kvalø 2007). In empirical terms, the growingly diverse data from European isotope and aDNA studies underscore widespread and diverse mobility in third and second-millennium Northern Europe (Allentoft et al. 2015; Chenery et al. 2011; Frei et al. 2015, 2012; Haak et al. 2015; Ling et al. 2013; Malmström et al. 2009; Skoglund et al. 2012). Antonio Gilman (1981) emphasized a materialist approach to the rise of the Bronze Age, pointing out the requirements and long-term effects of investments such as permanent clearances and houses. By applying the terms *maritime realization* and *ritual mobilization,* Frode Kvalø (2007) brings together the material qualities of Gilman's approach with Helms's anthropology, to situate overseas contact in the capacity to build and sail boats, have power over coastal bottlenecks, and have knowledge of the sea and ports as well as alliance partners. This is partially echoed by Rowlands and Ling (2013), in their discussion of amber, metal, trading networks, and the advantages of maritime ideology and praxis for the Nordic region. The growing number of studies of materials and human remains demonstrate that, throughout Europe, people and materials were on the move throughout the third millennium, supporting the idea that maritime travel and exchange were fundamental to the Bronze Age societies of Northern Europe, and fundamental to explaining the archaeological record.

To historically explore the role of the sea, three scenarios based on recent studies from Norway are explored below. These scenarios explore the region's BA-history: the opening of western Norway to Northern Europe's oldest Bronze Age culture (the BBC) around 2400 BCE, the establishment of a BBC-elite around 2350 BCE, and maintenance of chiefdoms in the Early Bronze Age.

DISCOVERY: WATERWAYS, BELL BEAKER PROSPECTING AND THE THIRD MILLENNIUM TRANSITION

As noted above, in the mid-third millennium a series of new practices and institutions were rapidly adopted along the western Norwegian coast. This can be described as the establishment of the Nordic Late Neolithic and Bronze Age region and a fundamental transformation of the fabric of life in the region. The transition from the preceding Neolithic period hunter-gatherer societies was rapid and represents a dramatic termination of hunter-gatherer traditions. It has been argued that the transformation is tied to initial migrations of people to the western coast of Norway from BBC areas, possibly from northern Jutland (Prescott 2011; Prescott and Walderhaug 1995:273). Bifacial tanged-and-barbed points, often referred to as "Bell Beaker points," probably represent an early, short phase of the BBC-transition around 2400 BCE. In Norway these points have a predominantly western and coastal distribution (Østmo 2012:64), underscoring the maritime nature of the initial BBC-expansion.

A number of resources have been mentioned as the "pull factor" drawing Bell Beaker people to western Norway, for example, hunting grounds, pastures, and copper resources. In terms of copper ores there is no unequivocal evidence concerning pre-Medieval exploitation of the many copper sources in Norway. Attempts at utilizing the ores can neither be proven nor ruled out. However, there are circumstantial indications of attempts at exploiting ores, such as a number of co-occurrences of BBC elements, LN and/or EBA sites, and copper sources (Melheim 2015:161–202). In response to the question about what attracted people from Bell Beaker groups to western Norway, responses have hypothesized hunting products, political power, pastures, and metals. Particularly the latter has been emphasized by Lene Melheim (2012, 2015:37ff).

A recent study by Melheim and Prescott (2016) integrated maritime exploration with metal prospecting to explain initial excursions of BBC-people along the western coast and into the fjords. Building on the archaeological concept of traveling metal prospectors as an element in the expansion of the Bell Beaker phenomenon, in combination with anthropological perspectives on prospecting, the article explores how prospecting for metal would have adjusted to the landscapes of western Scandinavia. Generally speaking, prospecting seldom leads to successful metal production, and it is difficult to study archaeologically. However, it will often create links between the prospectors' society and indigenous groups, opening new territories, and have a significant transformative impact—on both the external and indigenous actors and societies. Two archaeological sites in western Norway are relevant in terms of initial BBC exploration: the Slettabø in Rogaland (Skjølsvold 1977) and the LN1 layers at Skrivarhelleren in Sogn (Prescott 1991).

Slettabø is a settlement site in southwestern Norway (Figure 9.1). The BBC-phase at the site seems to represent a short visit. The single bell beaker found in Norway is from Slettabø. The phase with the bell beaker also yielded five tanged-and-barbed points and is dated to around 2400 BCE, that is, around the Middle to Late Neolithic transition. The site would have been located on a small patch of land between a strait and a barren rock knoll, on the protected inward side of an island (Figures 9.1 and 9.3) on the outer coast of Rogaland. It has been interpreted as a harbor, potentially related to the first phase of BBC-expansion (Prescott and Glørstad 2015).

The site could have served well as a bridgehead into the region for BBC explorers or immigrants with ties to Jutland. Along the coast north of Slettabø there are several copper deposits (Melheim 2015:164). A likely scenario is that BBC-boats would have followed the coast looking for the telltale signs of copper deposits, for example, in Egersund, at Karmøy, Bømlo, and Årdal. One of the most promising areas would have been found by following the Sognefjord 150 kilometers into the interior to Årdal (Figures 9.1 and 9.5). The Skrivarhelleren rock shelter (Figure 9.4 on page 186) site in Årdal is archaeologically important (Prescott 1991). The rich finds of BBC-related materials in this peripheral environment suggest that there are particular reasons for this seasonal settlement. Both this site and other parts of Årdal have long traditions of copper metalworking: the LN2 layers (1950 BCE) contain the oldest in situ copper alloy casting in Scandinavia, Skrivarhelleren and another site (Kalvebeitet) demonstrate bronze metallurgy in the ensuing Bronze Age deposits, the Årdal region has several occurrences of readily exploitable copper, and there has been extensive copper mining since 1700 CE (Melheim and Prescott 2016).

There are several low-lying copper deposits in Årdal easily accessed from the fjord, and with higher sea levels in the Late Neolithic, several of these would have been situated along the mid-third-millennium shoreline (Figure 9.5). Other substantial deposits are located in the mountain sides along the fjord, and would have been visible from the

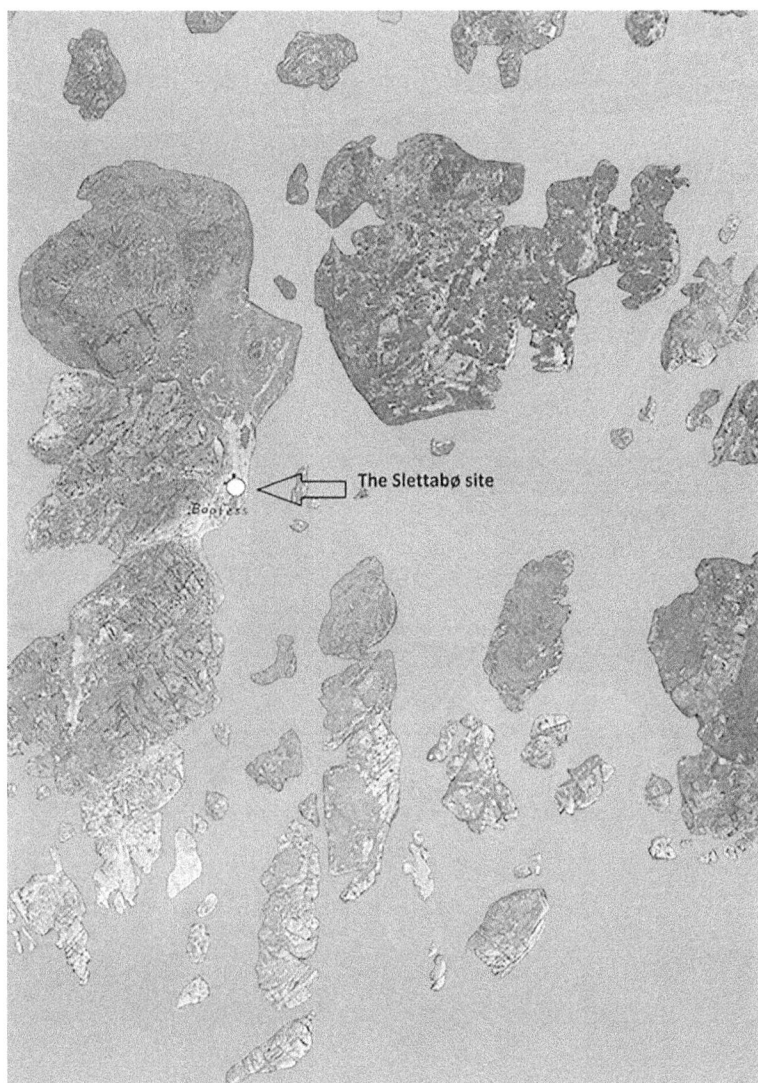

FIGURE 9.3 Map showing the location of the Slettabø site 2400 BCE and today (underlying shadowing). The site's position, on the protected side of an outer coastal island, indicates its role as a harbor (based on Prescott and Glørstad 2015).

water (as they are today). Not even having to leave his boat, an experienced prospector would have discovered the potential for finding copper ores—instigating an investigation of the region. This might be an explanation for the lowest levels (with Bell Beaker related finds) in the Skrivarhelleren site, 790 m asl and a few hours' walk from the fjord.

Prospecting is extremely difficult to archaeologically study, and as the evidence now stands there is no conclusive evidence for the exploitation of Norwegian ores in the third millennium BCE. However, most prospecting expeditions do not lead to successful metal production, but they can spearhead other processes of contact and migration. Bell Beaker

FIGURE 9.4 The Skrivarhelleren rock shelter (790 m asl. In the center of the picture, indicated by circle) in the interior of Norway lies in an area rich in copper deposits and easily accessed from the Sognefjord (photo: Christopher Prescott).

FIGURE 9.5 View from the Moa valley, in which the Skrivarhelleren site is located toward Øvre Årdal and the eastern end of the Sognefjord. In the Late Neolithic and Bronze Age the fjord would have covered today's built-up areas. Known copper deposits, prospecting sites, and mines visible from this vantage point are marked with arrows (photo: Christopher Prescott).

prospectors may have played the role of David Anthony's "scouts" (Anthony 1990), the first explorers into an area, starting a migration process. There is strong evidence of a maritime exploration of or expansion along the Norwegian coast around 2400 BCE, and it is worth considering whether boat-based scouts were initially searching for metals, but ended up changing the course of history.

ESTABLISHING A NORDIC ELITE:
THE MJELTEHAUGEN MONUMENT AND SAHLIN'S "STRANGER KING"

The Mjeltehaugen mound is one of the most enigmatic prehistoric monuments in Norway. Located on the island of Giske on the coast of Sunnmøre (Figures 9.1 and 9.6), the mound was excavated in 1847, 1867, and 1878. The mound is monumental in size, estimated to originally have been 25 m in diameter and 7 m high. It contained a large chamber, or set of eight chambers, made of stone slabs. Importantly, the slabs were decorated with geometric motifs, boats, and a dagger (Figure 9.7 on page 188).

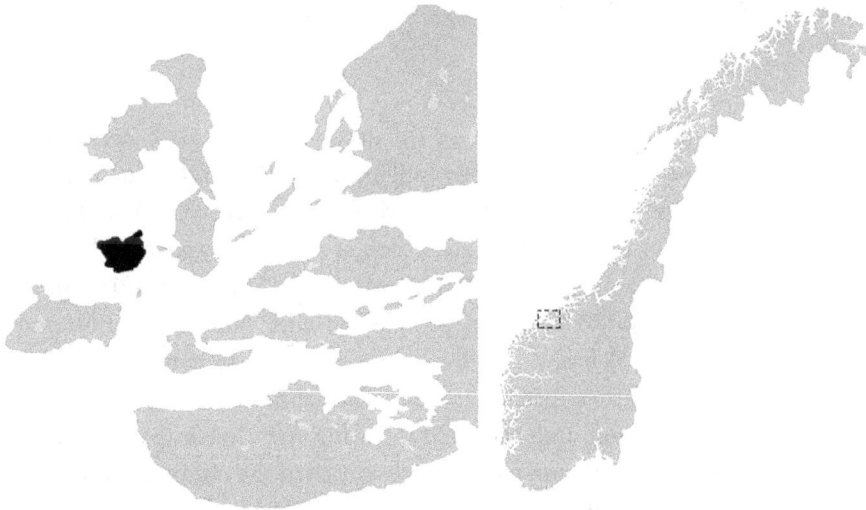

FIGURE 9.6 Map and photo of Giske demonstrating how the island and the mound are situated in the seascape. The Mjelthaugen mound's position is indicated (photo: Frode Inge Helland, map from Sand-Eriksen 2015).

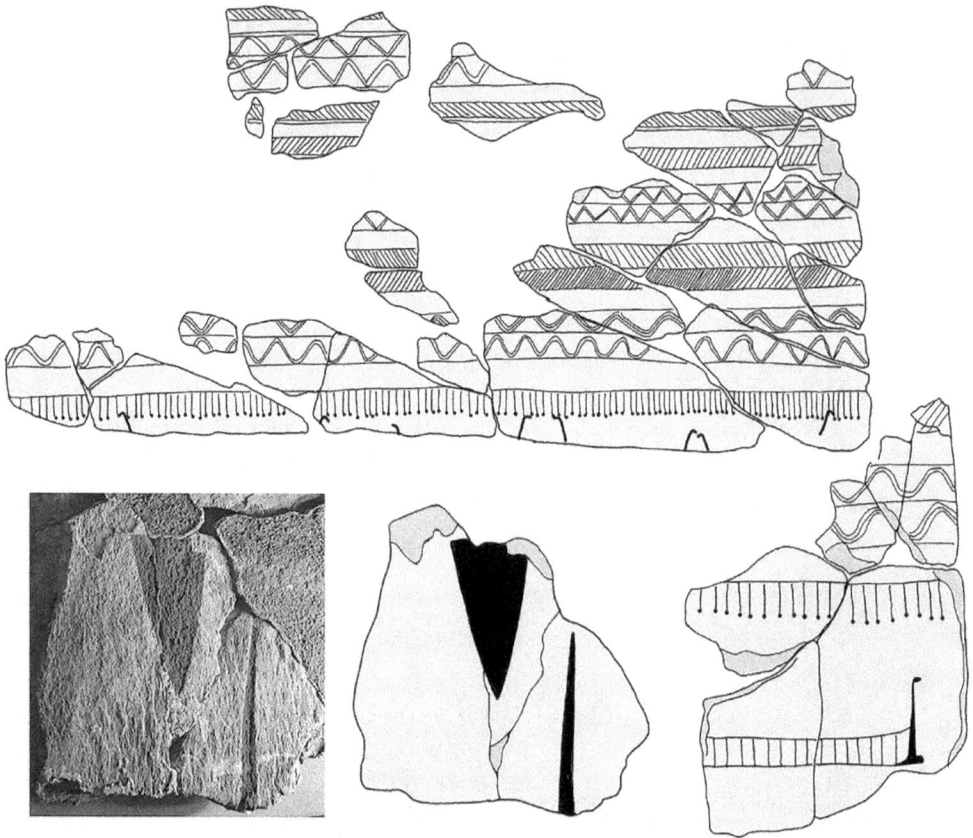

FIGURE 9.7 Fragments of the decorated Mjeltehaugen slabs. Top: the geometric design pieced together. Bottom right: depiction of a boat. Bottom left; the dagger blade (from Sand-Eriksen 2015).

The age and cultural context, based on the decorated slabs, have been subjected to debate for over a century, with suggestions ranging from the Middle or Late Neolithic (based on comparison with the Göhlitzsch grave in Halle, Germany) to Early Bronze Age (based on comparison with Nordic graves such as Kivik in Sweden and Skjølingstad, Steine, and Rege in Norway) (Linge 2007; Mandt 1983; Marstrander 1978). A recent study of the figures and context based on comparison with Nordic and European grave contexts (Sand-Eriksen 2015) found that the figures had little in common with the Nordic EBA graves, but had clearest parallels in Bell Beaker monuments, Le Petit-Chasseur in Sion, Switzerland (Harrison and Heyd 2007) being the clearest parallel. Typological studies of the dagger and boat figures partially substantiated the chronological and cultural conclusions of a Bell Beaker affiliation (Sand-Eriksen 2015).

The Mjeltehaugen slabs demonstrate many similarities with, among others, Le Petit-Chasseur, but the boats articulate an adaptation to the local maritime context. In context with the mound and grave's position overlooking the sea lane and the other motifs on the slab, the boats express the referential importance of the sea and seafaring as the important Nordic mode of communication and source of power for the elites.

The practical and referential importance of the sea, and the sea as a long-term source of the elite's power, is demonstrated by how the mound is situated in the landscape—or rather *seascape*. Giske is a flat island and the Mjeltehaugen mound would have towered above the fields and bogs around it, visible to everyone sailing by on the east side of the island. Giske is one island in a row of outer islands that protects the islands and mainland to the east from the powerful waves, currents, and storms of the North Atlantic. The open sea along the western Norwegian coast is difficult to sail, with treacherous currents and winds, heavy waves, and frequent storms. Predictable communication along the coast is dependent upon long stretches of protected routes behind the protective string of islands along the coast. Controlling these, especially at bottlenecks such as narrow straits, staging grounds for crossing open stretches (when conditions permitted), or harbors is a potential source of power in a chiefdom type of society. The Mjeltehaugen mound is on the inner side of Giske, looking over the protected north-south sea lane and the east-west lanes into the fjords leading into the interior (Figure 9.6). Virtually all traffic in the area would have passed Giske.

Tying all these strands of evidence and interpretation together, the Mjeltehaugen mound is an early expression of monumentality, most likely from the mid-third millennium. The decorative scheme of the slabs ties it to the exclusive suite of elite graves in Europe at this time, and the context should be fixed within the Bell Beaker expansions. The Bell Beaker development has been interpreted as the result of migration and the influx of a new elite. An important source of power for this elite was symbolically in reference to its foreignness—a parallel to Sahlin's (2009) concept of the stranger king, where an outsider may ascend to power in reference to being outside local indigenous conflicts. As "the elementary forms of kinship, politics and religion are all one" (Sahlins 2009:197), the Bell Beaker elite brought robust networks to Sunnmøre based on their kinship with groups in the area of their origin. The elite's power was symbolically and in real terms linked to control of the sailing route, but also its capacity to realize maritime endeavors through boat technology. This entails the knowledge and capacity to get suitable boats built, knowledge of sailing conditions, and the vital networks and alliances of kin that allowed them to travel safely to distant harbors and settlements. This elite probably held a warrior identity that communicated a capacity to use force, if necessary. Mjeltehaugen is potentially the oldest monumental materialization of new institutions of power that in time would characterize the EBA in central areas. Based on maritime capacity (especially the power to control the local sea lanes and expressed through strategically positioned monuments), networks, and alliances with elites in Northern Europe, the sources of the power of the Bronze Age elites along the western Norwegian coast can be discerned. Though Mjeltehaugen stands alone in the archaeology of the LN of Norway and Scandinavia in terms of its size and decorated chamber, it is not a unique expression of new, externally provided (Bell Beaker) burial customs. An LN1 cairn with a cremation and tin awl at Farsund in Vest-Agder and an LN2 mound with a gold *Noppenring* at Klokkhamar in Lista (Melheim 2015:31–35), as well as several *hocker* burials in rock shelters, convey some of the same cultural message. These graves represent the new era of hierarchy and the Bronze Age.

BRONZE AGE SEAWAYS—A SOURCE OF CHIEFLY POWER

The Mjeltehaugen mound has often been viewed as an isolated and enigmatic anomaly in Scandinavian prehistory, but interpreting it as a result of the establishment of a Bell Beaker elite and dating it to the early Nordic LN creates a consistent and logical cultural historical context. If this monumental mound is seen in light of LN and EBA trends, instead of viewing it as an isolated incident the mound should be seen as an incipient expression of a "marinescape of power." This interpretation creates a meaningful structural and historical context. The ensuing developments demonstrate that Mjeltehaugen represents the start of a Bronze Age praxis.

Within the Nordic Bronze region along the western Norwegian coast a handful of areas stand out with concentrations of EBA bronzes, petroglyphs, and monumental mounds and cairns (Hagen 1983; Johansen 2000). These include, from north to south, the Trondheimsfjord area, the islands of Sunnmøre (where the Mjeltehaugen mound is situated), the area around the Karmsund sound, the Jæren region in Rogaland, and Lista in Vest-Agder.

In modern times these are among the most productive agricultural districts in Norway. Though the contemporary landscape is largely the result of artificial draining of wetlands and industrial agriculture, these areas were probably relatively productive in the Bronze Age as well. The concentration of EBA material, and the interpretation that these areas held more hierarchical and larger-scale political entities, has largely been explained in reference to their agro-pastoral potential, though the premises and implications of this agrarian perspective have not been explored in depth. Agro-pastoral production and the farm economy is certainly an important economic, demographic, and cultural factor in the Bronze Age. Still, it does not seem to explain the concentration and expressions of power in these regions at various times of the Bronze Age, nor their role in the networks of exchange and interaction.

The main advantage of long distance transportation by boat, as opposed to movement on land, is that it is relatively fast, it is difficult to control and moderately safe from predatory attacks. Still, climate, wind, and currents render the open and unprotected sea outside the islands dotting large parts of the Norwegian coast difficult and perilous to navigate with open boats (Kvalø 2007:62–64). However, large stretches of the coast can be navigated through protected lanes between the mainland and the outer line of islands. A number of difficult sea stretches can be avoided altogether by pulling boats over portages (e.g., articles in Westerdahl 2006). Harbors, where travelers can rest and wait for beneficial weather conditions just before crossing difficult stretches like the mouth of a fjord or open sea, such as Skagerrak are vital. Natural conditions can thus force boat traffic into bottlenecks and harbors, and controlling and protecting these are readily a source of social, political, economic, and military power. Several recent studies (Austvoll 2014; Kvalø 2007) demonstrate that the areas where expressions of Early Bronze Age power and wealth accumulate coincide with bottlenecks or harbors.

THE MARINESCAPES OF BRONZE AGE POWER IN SOUTHWESTERN NORWAY

The southwestern peninsula of Norway, Lista, is a flat and delimited area of about 70 sq km. The peninsula is situated between rocky uplands and the sea, and in the Bronze Age would have offered a varied landscape of wetlands, tillable glacial soils, lakes, and inlets favorable for settlement. Routes along the western coast of Norway to the Baltic, over Skagerrak to Jutland and Germany, pivot around Lista. The sea outside of Lista being one of the two most difficult stretches to sail along the Norwegian coast, weather conditions change quickly and vary seasonally, while wave climate is usually difficult. Not surprisingly, this area is host to a high concentration of shipwrecks.

Lista has one of the most concentrated accumulations of prestigious Late Neolithic and Early Bronze Age finds in Norway (Johansen 1986:164), and 90 percent of the metal finds in the county of Vest-Agder are found on the small Lista-peninsula. In terms of monuments, the low coastal zone and the inlets into bays are dotted with monumental mounds and cairns from the Bronze Age and Iron Age. Against the low-lying terrain, these monuments form a chain along the sea/land interface that is readily visible from the sea. The construction of these mounds started with a moderate-sized burial at Lundevaagen in the LN1, but evolved into the large mounds of the Bronze Age and Iron Age (Figure 9.8).

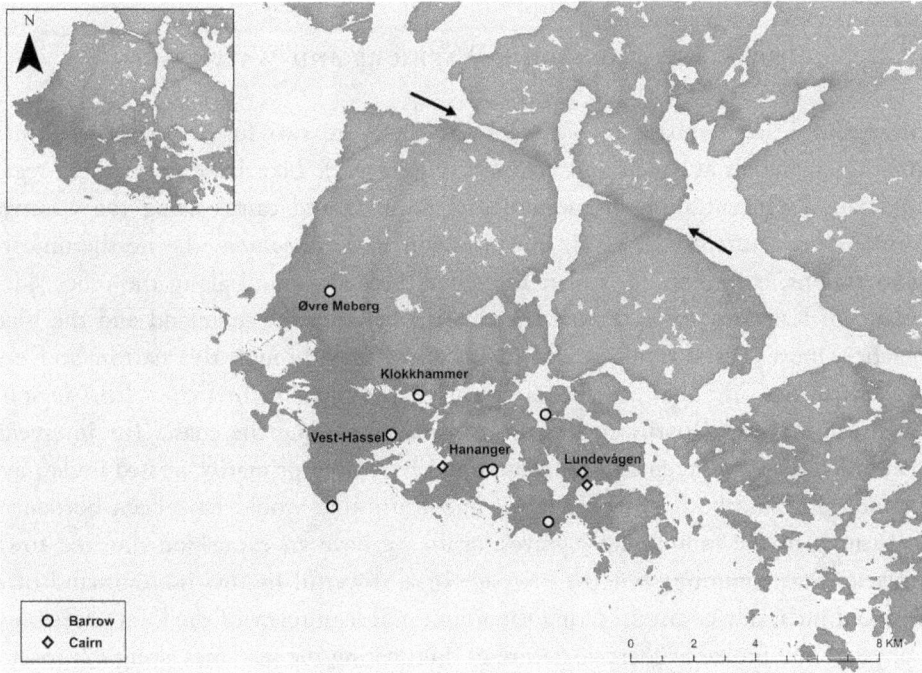

FIGURE 9.8 Distribution of Bronze Age mounds and cairns on the Lista peninsula. The shoreline is adjusted for a 5 meter higher sea level and before modern draining of inlets and wetlands, and demonstrates that the grave mounds and cairns would have been located in relation to the sea. Portages (indicated with arrows) are located at the foot of the peninsula (after Austvoll 2014).

The mounds can thus be viewed as expression of the power of the controlling elite directed out toward those sailing these waters. For domestic use, the mounds demonstrated the source of and legitimacy of power—sea travel and networks—as well as a lineage's "deed" to the sea lanes. The importance of the sea, boats, and maritime communication is further demonstrated by the many ship figures that dominate petroglyphs from between 1500–700 BCE in Lista (Hagen 1990:143ff; Mandt and Lødøen 2005:242ff).

If the landscape is examined in more detail, the source of power is not solely the position along important Nordic sea routes, but the bottleneck feature of the landscape. Along the Lista-peninsula's 20 nm (37 km) long coast there are virtually no harbors and no refuge from bad weather. However, the difficult conditions can be avoided, and access to harbors attained, by using an 800 m portage from the western inlet into a series of inland waterways (Figure 9.8). Indeed, this portage is in use today, allowing boats up to 35 feet to be pulled overland. A number of large "inland" grave monuments are explained by their association with this route (Kvalø 2007:69).

Lista's Late Neolithic and Bronze Age materials and the monumental grave monuments represents the historical rise and reproduction of an elite that is probably best understood in reference to power based on controlling a bottleneck at a critical passage along one of the most important maritime communication routes along the Scandinavian peninsula (Austvoll 2014:83).

JÆREN AND KARMSUND, WARRIORS AND WATERWAYS

Northwest of Lista, but still in SW Norway, there are two further concentrations of Bronze Age materials at Jæren and Karmøy (Figure 9.1). Like Lista, both these regions demonstrate a concentration of monumental mounds and cairns along the waterways (Figure 9.9; see Austvoll 2014:69). The situation in Karmsundet, the northernmost of the two regions, is interesting in that the graves here are found along the inner side of the island of Karmøy, facing the narrow channel between the mainland and the island. In practice, most coastal traffic would have had to pass through this narrow and easily controlled passage. The marinescape along the coast of Jæren, the richest EBA region in Norway, can be related partly to harbors and passages along the coast. The intervening Boknafjorden between Jæren and Karmøy would have been primarily crossed under favorable conditions, and both northern Jæren and Karmsund would have been bottlenecks.

Turning to the monumental graves, again we have an expression directed toward the traveler that communicates the presence of a powerful lineage in command of the seaway, and internally communicating the source and legitimacy of the local elite's power. The physical and probably coercive nature of dominating the sea lanes along the coast are illustrated by the nature of the materials in the graves at Karmsund and Jæren. All the graves directly located along the Karmsund channel contain weapons, as do a majority of the graves along the coast or at critical points in Jæren (Figure 9.9)—all these graves contain male burials. On a general level the weapon graves communicate to us that there was a military side to these societies, that control of the waterways was important and

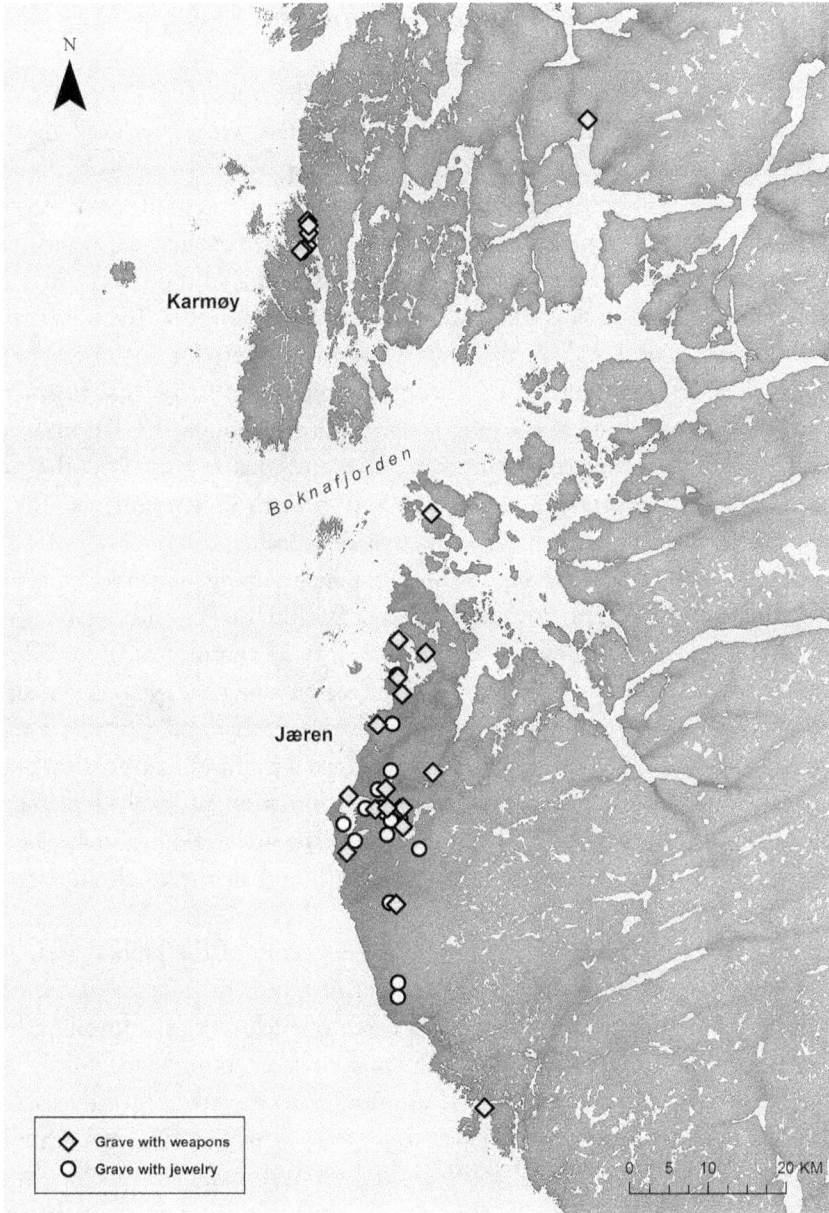

FIGURE 9.9 Distribution of cairns and mounds with graves containing either weapons or jewelry, Karmøy and Jæren (after Austvoll 2014).

that there is a tie between warriors and the waterways. What connotations these monuments (and the weapon graves they contained) communicated to the traveler seeking leave to pass through these controlled waters is difficult to ascertain. It is reasonable that the presence of power and a threat of force permeated the message.

MARITIME CHIEFDOMS?

Around 2400 BCE, a field of interaction arose along the western Norwegian coast. This region was part of the Nordic Late Neolithic world that was reproduced through the Bronze Age. The transition to the LN along the coast represented a dramatic breach with older hunter-gatherer economies, and it would seem most aspects of life were transformed. The driving force for this transformation is probably a Bell Beaker expansion into this northern part of Europe. The initial "pull factor" was probably the search for resources, and the search for copper ores was conceivably one of these resources. The waterways along the coast and fjords were probably the most important means for exploring the coast.

The Bell Beaker expansion led to the establishment of an elite that began to mark its presence with monumental grave mounds and cairns. Though the European cultural background is readily recognized in the material expressions at this time, the new elite also communicated its maritime orientation in and through its monuments. The Mjelte-haugen mound is probably an expression of this Bell Beaker elite.

Sea travel was an all-important medium for maintaining networks, alliances, and exchange within the Northern European sphere. Within the Nordic region there is a remarkably homogeneous cultural expression that also communicates wider Nordic and European affiliations. However, within the Nordic region along the Norwegian coast there are also concentrations of monuments and metal objects that indicate that wealth and power were unevenly distributed. Such concentrations are found at places such as Lista, Jæren, Karmøy, and the islands of Sunnmøre. This situation probably represents local, small-scale chiefdoms during the Early Bronze Age. The archaeological material suggests that the material base for this power and wealth is found in the local elite's control of bottlenecks and other strategic places.

Though the sea has always been present in the history of the Nordic area, as of the mid-third millennium it binds the region together in a field of interaction. The capacity to realize maritime practices was probably essential to elites, as was controlling maritime traffic. This is expressed archaeologically in the many references to boats and the sea. The social capacity to interact with Northern European elites has roots in the establishment of alliances. As politics, kinship, and religion are one, as of the Late Neolithic the sea, travel, and boats were thus very real sources of power and integral to social institutions, but they also permeated the fabric of thought and symbols. To paraphrase Lévi-Strauss, the sea and boats are not only useful in communication and politics, they are chosen as symbols because they embody central elements of society—they are "good to think" (Lévi-Strauss 1966:89).

REFERENCES CITED

Allentoft, M. E., M. Sikora, K.-G. Sjögren, S. Rasmussen, M. Rasmussen, J. Stenderup et al.
2015 Population Genomics of Bronze Age Eurasia. *Nature* 522:167–172.
Anthony, D. W. 1990 Migration in Archeology: The Baby and the Bathwater. *American Anthropologist* 92(1):896–914.

Anthony, D. W. 2007 *The Horse, the Wheel, and Language. How Bronze-Age Riders from the Eurasian Steppes Shaped the Modern World.* Princeton University Press, Princeton.

Apel, J. 2001 *Daggers of Knowledge and Power. The Social Aspects of Flint-Dagger Technology in Scandinavia 2350–1500 cal. BC.* Coast to Coast Book 3. Uppsala University, Uppsala.

Austvoll. K. I. 2014 Constructing Identities. Structure and Practice in the Early Bronze Age—Southwest Norway. Master's thesis, University of Oslo. https://www.duo.uio.no/handle/10852/40888.

Bakka, E. 1976 *Arktisk og nordisk i bronsealderen i Nordskandinavia.* DKVNS Miscellenea 25, Trondheim.

Chenery, C. A. og J. A. Evans. 2011 A Summary of the Strontium and Oxygen Isotope Evidence for the Origins of Bell Beaker Individuals Found near Stonehenge. In *The Amesbury Archer and the Boscombe Bowmen. Bell Beaker Burials at Boscombe Down, Amesbury, Wiltshire*, edited by A. Fitzpatrick, pp. 185–191. Wessex Archaeology Report 27, Salisbury.

Crumlin-Pedersen, O., and A.Trakadas. 2003 Hjortspring: a Pre-Roman Iron-Age Warship in Context. The Viking Ship Museum, Roskilde.

Frei, K. M., R. Frei, U. Mannering, M. Gleba, M-L. B. Noschog, H. S. Lyngstrøm. 2009 Provenance of Ancient Textiles: A Pilot Study Evaluating the Sr Isotope System in Wool. *Archaeometry* 51(2):252–276.

Frei, K. M., U. Mannering, K. Kristiansen, M. E. Allentoft, A. S. Wilson, I. Skals, S. Tridico, M. L. Nosch, E. Willerslev, L. Clarke, and R. Frei. 2015 Tracing the Dynamic Life Story of a Bronze Age Female. *Scientific Reports* Volume: 5, Art. nr:10431doi:10.1038/srep10431.

Gilman, A. 1981 The Development of Social Stratification in Bronze Age Europe. *Current Anthroplogy* 22(1):1–23.

Glørstad, H. 2012 Historical Ideal Types and the Transition to the Late Neolithic in South Norway. In *Becoming European. The Transformation of Third Millennium Europe and the Trajectory into the Millennium BC*, edited by C. Prescott and H. Glørstad, pp. 82–99. Oxbow Books, Oxford.

Glørstad, H. 2013. Where Are the Missing Boats? The Pioneer Settlement of Norway as Long-Term History. *Norwegian Archaeological Review* 46(1):57–80.

Haak, W., O. Balanovsky, J. J. Sanchez, S. Koshel, V.Zaporozhchenko, C. J. Adler, C. S. I. D. Sarkissian, G.Brandt et al. 2010 Ancient DNA from Ancient European Neolithic Farmers Reveals Their Near Eastern Affinities. *PloS Biol* 8(11), e1000536.doi:10.1371/journal. pbio.1000536.

Haak, W. H., I. Lazardis, N. Patterson, N. Rohland, S. Malllick, B. Llamas, G. Brandt et al. 2015 Massive Migration from the Steppe was a Source for Indo-European Languages in Europe. *Nature* 522:207–211.

Hagen, A. 1983 *Norges Oldtid.* Cappelen, Oslo.

Hagen, A. 1990. *Helleristningar i Noreg.* Det norske samlaget, Oslo.

Harrison, R., and V. Heyd. 2007 The Transformation of Europe in the Third Millennium BC: The Example of "le Petit-Chasseur I+III" (Sion, Valais, Switzerland). *Praehistorische Zeitschrift* 82:129–214.

Hinsch, E. 1956 *Yngre steinalders stridsøkskulturer i Norge.* Årb. Univ. i Bergen, hum.ser.1954/1. University of Bergen, Bergen.

Jensen, J. 2002 *Danmarks Oldtid. Bronzealder 2.000–500 f.Kr.* Gyldendal, Copenhagen.

Johansen, Ø. 1986.*Tidlig metallkultur i Agder.* Univ. Oldsaksamlings Skr. 8. Universitetets Oldsaksamlings, Oslo.

Johansen, Ø. 2000. *Bronse og makt.* Andresen & Butenschøn, Oslo.

Kristiansen, K., and T. B. Larsson. 2005 *The Rise of Bronze Age Society. Travels, Transmissions, and Transformations.* Cambridge University Press, Cambridge.

Kvalø, F. 2007 Oversjøiske reiser fra Sørvest-Norge til Nordvest-Jylland i eldre bronsealder—En drøfting av maritim realisering og rituell mobilisering. In *Sjøreiser og stedsidentitet. Jæren/ Lista i bronsealder og eldre jernalder,* edited by L.Hedeager, pp. 11–134. Oslo Academic Press, Oslo.

Lévi-Strauss, C. 1966 *The Savage Mind.* Weidenfeld & Nicolson, London.

Ling, J., Z. Stos-Gale, L. Grandin, K. Billström, E. Hjärthner-Holdar, P.-O. Persson. 2014 Moving Metals II: Provenancing Scandinavian Bronze Age Artefacts by Lead Isotope and Elemental Analyses. *Journal of Archaeological Science* 41:106–132.

Linge, T. 2007 Mjeltehaugen—fragment frå gravritual, i Østigård, T. (red.) *UBAS—Universitetet i Bergen Arkeologiske Skrifter. Hovedfag/Master 3.* Arkeologisk institutt, Universitetet i Bergen. Bergen.

Malmström, H., M. T. P. Gilbert, M. G. Thomas, M. Brandstöm, J. Storå, P. Molnar, P. K. Andersen,C. Bendixen, G. Holmlund, A. Götherstöm, og E. Willerslev. 2009 Ancient DNA Reveals Lack of Continuity between Neolithic Hunter-Gatherers and Contemporary Scandinavians. *Current Biology* 19(20):1758–1762.

Mandt, G. 1983 Tradition and Diffusion in West-Norwegian Rock Art. Mjeltehaugen Revisited. *Norwegian Archaeological Review* 16(1):14–32.

Mandt, G., and T. Lødøen. 2005 *Bergkunst. Helleristningar i Noreg.* Det norske Samlaget, Oslo.

Marstrander, S. 1978 The Problem of European Impulses in the Nordic Area of Agrarian Rock Art. In *Aspects of the International Symposium on Rock Art,* edited by S. Marstrander, pp. 45–67. Universitetsforaget, Oslo.

Melheim, L. 2012 Towards a New Understanding of Late Neolithic Norway—The Role of Metal and Metal Working. In *Becoming European. The Transformation of Third Millennium Europe and the Trajectory into the Second Millennium BC,* edited by C. Prescott and H. Glørstad, pp. 70–81. Oxbow Books, Oxford.

Melheim, L. 2015 *Recycling Ideas: Bronze Age Metal Production in Southern Norway.* BAR intl ser 2715. Archaeopress, Oxford.

Melheim, L., and C. Prescott. 2016 Exploring New Territories—Expanding Frontiers: Bowmen and Prospectors on the Scandinavian Peninsula in the 3rd Millennium BCE. In *Comparative Perspectives on Past Colonisation, Maritime Interaction and Cultural Integration,* edited by L.Melheim, H. Glørstad, and Z. Glørstad, doi: 10.1558/equinox.24608. Equinox, Sheffield.

Østmo, E. 1988 Etableringen av jordbrukskultur i Østfold i Steinalderen. Universietets Oldsak-samlings Skrifter. Ny rekke 10. Universitetet i Oslo, Oslo.

Østmo, E. 2012. Late Neolithic Expansion to Norway. The Beginning of a 4000 Year-Old Ship-building Tradition. In *Becoming European. The Transformation of Third Millennium Europe and the Trajectory into the Second Millennium BC,* edited by C. Prescott and H. Glørstad, pp. 63–69. Oxbow Books, Oxford.

Prescott, C. 1991 *Kulturhistoriske undersøkelser i Skrivarhelleren.* Arkeologiske rapporter 14. Historisk museum, University of Bergen, Bergen.

Prescott, C. 2012. Third Millennium Transformations in Norway: Modeling an Interpretative Platform. In *Becoming European. The Transformation of Third Millennium Northern and Western Europe,* edited by C. Prescott and H. Glørstad, pp. 115–127. Oxbow Books, Oxford.

Prescott, C., and H. Glørstad. 2012 Introduction: Becoming European. In *Becoming European. The Transformation of Third Millennium Northern and Western Europe*, edited by C. Prescott and H. Glørstad, pp. 1–11. Oxbow Books, Oxford.

Prescott, C., and H. Glørstad. 2015 Expanding 3rd Millennium Transformations: Norway. In *The Bell Beaker Transition in Europe*, edited by M. P. Prieto-Martínez and L. Salanova, pp. 77–87. Oxbow Books, Oxford.

Prescott, C., and L. Melheim. 2009 The First Bronze Age Communities in Scandinavia. Comments on M. Pilar Prieto-Martínez: "Bell Beaker Communities in Thy: The First Bronze Age Society in Denmark." *Norwegian Archaeological Review* 42 (1):89–93.

Prescott, C., and E. Walderhaug. 1995 The Last Frontier? Processes of Indo-Europeanization in Northern Europe: The Norwegian Case. *Journal of Indo-European Studies* 23 (3/4):257–281.

Prieto-Martínez, M. P. 2008 Bell Beaker Communities in Thy: The First Bronze Age Society in Denmark. *Norwegian Archaeological Review* 41(2):115–158.

Prieto-Martínez, M. P. 2012. Perceiving Changes in the Third Millennium BC in Europe through Pottery: Galicia, Brittany, and Denmark as Examples. In *Becoming European. The Transformation of Third Millennium Northern and Western Europe*, edited by C. Prescott and H. Glørstad, pp. 30–47. Oxbow Books, Oxford.

Rosenberg, G. 1937 *Hjortspringfundet*. Nordiske fortidsminder III. Bb, 1. Hft. Det Kgl. Nordiske Oldskriftselskab. Copenhagen.

Sahlins, M. 2007 The Stranger-King or, Elementary Forms of the Politics of Life. *Indonesia and the Malay World* 36(105):177–199.

Sand-Eriksen, A. 2015 *Mjeltehaugen—et klokkbegeruttrykk? Stil som uttrykk for social identitet.* Master's thesis. University of Oslo, https://www.duo.uio.no/handle/10852/88.

Sarauw, T. 2007 Male Symbols or Warrior Identities? The "Archery Burials" of the Danish Bell Beaker Culture. *Journal of Anthroplogical Archaeology* 26:65–87.

Shetelig, H. 1936 [1947] Germanerenes avstamning under arkeologisk synspunkt. *Kunst og Kultur* 1936. Reprinted in Shetelig, H., 1947 *Arkeologi, historie, kunst, kultur. Mindre avhandlinger*, pp. 262–269. Johan Griegs Forlag, Bergen

Skjølsvold, A. 1977 *Slettabøboplassen. Et bidrag til diskusjonen om forholdet mellom fangst-og bondesamfunnet i yngre steinalder og bronsealder.* AmS Skrifter 2. Arkeologisk museum i Stavanger, Stavanger.

Skoglund P., H. Malmstöm, M.Raghavan, J. Storå, P.Hall, E. Willerslev, M.T.P. Gilbert, A. Götherstöm, and M. Jakobsson. 2012 Origins and Genetic Legacy of Neolithic Farmers and Hunter-Gatherers in Europe. *Science* 336:466–469.

Vandkilde, H. 2001 Beaker Representations in the Danish Late Neolithic. In *Bell Beakers Today. Pottery, People, Culture, Symbols in Prehistoric Europe. Proceedings of the International Colloquium, Riva del garda, 11–16 May 1998*, edited by F. Nicolis, pp. 333–360. Ufficio Beni Archeologici, Trento.

Vandkilde H. 2005 A Review of the Early Late Neolithic Period in Denmark: Practice, Identity, and Connectivity. *Offa* 61/62:75–109.

Westerdahl, C. 2006 *The Significance of Portages*. BAR International Series 1499. Archaeopress, Oxford.

CHAPTER TEN

Southeast Asian Maritime Power, Seventeenth-Century Spice Wars, and Tiworo's Neglected Fortifications

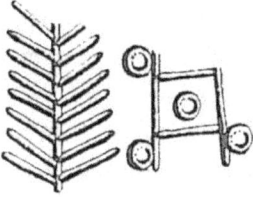

Jennifer L. Gaynor

Abstract *Seventeenth-century Dutch East India Company (VOC) documents reveal the importance of unstudied fortifications in the Straits of Tiworo region of Sulawesi, Indonesia. The fortresses belonged to the realm that VOC sources called "Tiworo" (also: Tivora, Tibore), which included settlements both in the straits and along its fringing shores. These VOC sources indicate that the first fortress, located at the northwest end of Muna (Pangesane) Island, was "often mentioned," and hence well known to the Dutch, although exactly who mentioned them remains unclear. Nevertheless, recent research in these sources has clarified why Tiworo gained notoriety at the time as a "nasty pirate's nest." Tiworo's fortresses supported its role as a nonurban maritime hub during conflicts over control of the archipelago's spice trade. The maritime-oriented people of the straits buoyed the trade and military endeavors of the powerful polity of Makassar, which lay more than two hundred miles to the west, and provided its fleets with a safe haven and a staging area for engagements farther east. While the "oft-mentioned" fortress at Tiworo was torn down in 1655 during the Great Ambon War, it was replaced by two others, in turn demolished in 1667, at the time of the Makassar War. Tiworo's two defeats in these conflicts present a striking contrast. In the Great Ambon War, when Tiworo was allied with Makassar, Tiworo suffered the slaughter of more than two hundred men and the seizure of three hundred women and children, as well as incineration of its boats. However, twelve years later, in the lead-up to the Makassar War, the bulk of Tiworo's people took flight, forewarned of the naval advance of the VOC and its allies. Yet, sixty of Tiworo's men were also incorporated, with rank, into the forces of the VOC's foremost ally, Arung Palakka, who had seized Tiworo's boats and barred the VOC's highest authority from* *taking them. These divergent outcomes: slaughter, capture, and the destruction of boats, versus flight, the preservation of nautical capacity, and incorporation into a former enemy's forces, illustrate how land-based powers built social and political connections with maritime-oriented people and severed the ties of their foes.*

In Eastern Indonesia's Moluccas, famed as "the Spice Islands," fortifications found on the islands of Ternate, Tidore and Ambon testify to a well-known part of the early modern archipelago's colonial legacy: the effort by European companies and their allies to dominate the trade in cloves and nutmeg. This chapter highlights the existence of additional fortifications whose part in this history has only recently come to light. Located in the Straits of Tiworo, a nonurban maritime hub, these fortifications fit into a larger story about the dynamics of politics, trade, littoral society, and military cooperation in the seventeenth-century maritime world of Southeast Asia (Gaynor 2016).

Two wars frame Tiworo's chapter in the larger story: the Great Ambon War, and the Makassar War. At the center of the series of conflicts from 1651–1656 known as The Great Ambon War lay the clove-growing areas on islands in the vicinity of Ambon. Arnold de Vlaming van Oudshoorn, as "superintendent," led the forces of the VOC, the United Dutch East India Company (*Vereenigde Oost-Indische Compagnie*), to victory in this war with the help of local allies. These allies operated primarily under Ternate's Sultan Mandarsyah, who claimed numerous islands in the region as part of his dependencies (see Figure 10.1).

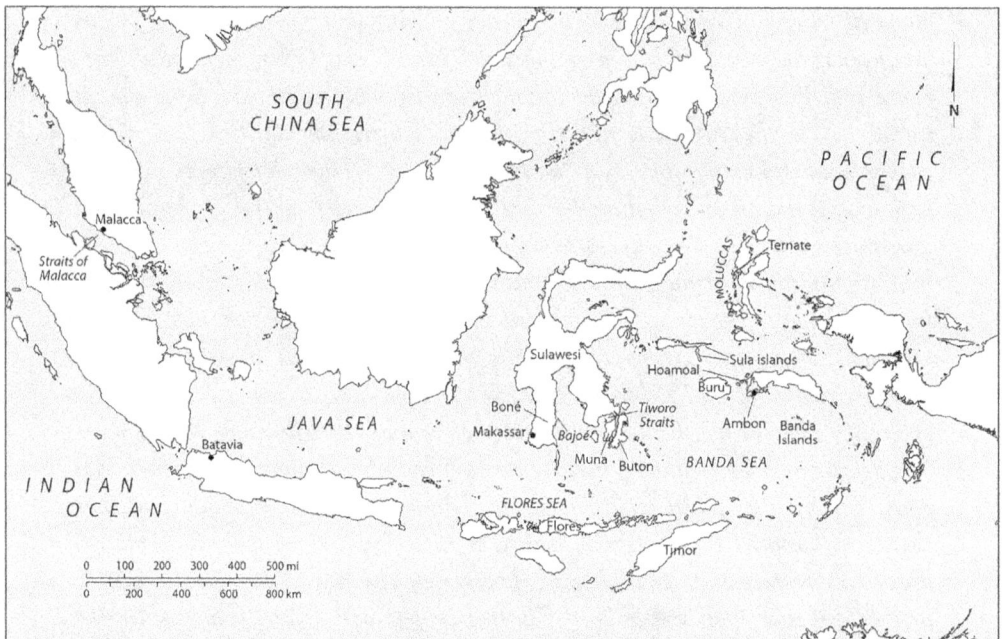

Figure 10.1 Sulawesi (Celebes) and the eastern archipelago of what is now Indonesia. Cartography by Bill Nelson.

At the time, a rival of Ternate's, the powerful port of Makassar on the southwest peninsula of Sulawesi (formerly Celebes), stood out as the primary transshipment point for goods from the eastern archipelago, including Moluccan spices. Many of the spices and other goods transshipped through Makassar went to western archipelago ports, such as Malacca, from which merchants shipped them to other parts of the world. The Portuguese had taken Malacca in 1511, thus undermining Venice's hold on the European branch of the spice trade, which had previously flowed to the Eastern Mediterranean through the Levant. The 1641 seizure of Portuguese Malacca by VOC forces drove members of the Portuguese, Malay, and other merchant communities to relocate, some to the already cosmopolitan port of Makassar, which lay closer to the source of the goods they so desired (Reid 2000:100–125). Makassar, ruled by the dual realms of Gowa and Talloq, supported clove-growing regions in the eastern archipelago, such as the Hoamoal peninsula, in their struggle against the VOC during the Great Ambon War (Bor 1663:288–298, 301–303; Hägerdal 2012:115; Knaap 2003:179, 180–181). Although by the conflict's end in 1656, the VOC eventually managed to subdue the places that Makassar had supported, during the decade that followed, Makassar set out to replenish its clients and satellites in the eastern archipelago (Andaya 1981:60–72, Knaap 2012:178–183). Makassar's resurgent influence, along with its continued primacy among regional trading ports, contributed to the VOC's decision to join forces once again with Makassar's rivals. This time, however, while Ternate lent assistance, the VOC partnered closely with a famous foe of Makassar's from Boné, a neighboring Bugis region of Sulawesi. This man, Arung Palakka, led allied forces alongside the VOC in the Makassar War. Together they defeated Makassar in 1667, yet, after what the VOC claimed was a breach of the resulting treaty, Makassar was effectively reconquered in 1669 (Speelman 1669:684v–685v).

The Makassar War and the earlier Great Ambon War, separated by more than a decade, usually form the focus of separate studies. Their main areas of conflict were also separated by great distances. Between Makassar and the Hoamoal peninsula stretched an archipelagic expanse of 600 miles as the crow flies. Yet, both conflicts were fundamentally concerned with control of the spice trade, and their connections also reached beyond this shared concern with spices. Causal ties between these wars run through the Straits of Tiworo. Tracing Tiworo's involvement with the conflict and competition over the spice trade reveals how its relationship with Makassar, and its defeat in the first war, led Makassar's Sultan Hasanuddin—according to his own words—to reassert his claims in the eastern archipelago. This re-expansion threatened Dutch interests, among others, precipitating the second war.

On what was Tiworo's relationship with Makassar based? Tiworo offered Makassar a number of geographic advantages. It provided a shorter route to the eastern archipelago that bypassed political rivals, a safe haven for Makassar's fleets, and, importantly, a nautical staging area for trade and military engagements farther east. In addition, Tiworo's boats and mariners supported Makassar's endeavors. Dutch sources characterize Tiworo as subject to Makassar, yet also portray their leaders at the time as close friends. This picture fits with political structures common to precolonial Southeast Asia, in which subordinate polities demonstrated their allegiance within center-weighted segmentary political structures. Allegiance between segments was commonly secured and cemented through marriage ties, which was likely the case between Makassar and Tiworo, as well.

In my book *Intertidal History in Island Southeast Asia* (2016) I offer a more detailed analysis of maritime-oriented Tiworo's history and its connections with Makassar, as well as scrutinize new evidence that reveals the close relations between Makassar and local leaders of the regionally dispersed Sama "sea people." Sama leaders were active in the inner circles of seventeenth- and eighteenth-century Makassar's political, military, and kin structures. Whatever the nature of the bonds between Makassar and Tiworo, whether a triad of political alliance, shared economic interest, and friendship, or all these together with kinship, these ties among allies in this complex littoral society undergirded the dynamics of archipelagic politics, and, in particular, the vehemence of Sultan Hasanud-din's vengeance—his stated rationale for re-expansion.

TIWORO'S GEOGRAPHIC ADVANTAGES

One might think that the best route from Makassar to the eastern archipelago would entail keeping a safe distance from nearshore hazards by sailing through the open waters of the Flores and Banda Seas. Yet, a more direct route to Hoamoal passed through the Straits of Tiworo, which lay about one-third of the distance there from Makassar. During the Great Ambon War, Makassar's fleet traveled via Tiworo to reach eastern archipelago growers in need of Makassar's support—growers whose products were, presumably, marketed in Makassar (on provisions apparently bound for Asahudi at Tiworo, see: Generale Missieve, July 12, 1655:543r, and de Vlaming and Maetsuyker 1655:99; on Makassar's fleets taking the route through Tiworo, see Bor 1663:263; de Vlaming 1655b:87; de Vlaming and Maetsuyker 1655:97). The shorter route through Tiworo was not, however, the only reason why mariners under Makassar plotted their course through the straits.

In addition to avoiding natural hazards, these sailors also had to navigate political hazards. If, instead of traveling through Tiworo, Makassar's boats sailed eastward past the southern tip of Buton island, near Buton's center in Bau Bau, they risked attracting Buton's notice. Circumventing Buton was tactically wise since Buton was a close ally of the VOC. Although Buton lacked substantial naval power of its own during the 1650s, it effectively managed this shortcoming by pleading with the VOC for assistance. The VOC helped to defend Buton, while Buton begged the VOC's forgiveness for its own lack of boats.

For instance, in April 1654, a Dutch *chialoup*, which had been chasing five of Makassar's boats, got rather far from the main ship in its group and suddenly found itself the target of its erstwhile prey. The boats it had been chasing turned and ran it down, resulting in the deaths of all but five Dutchmen, who were taken captive. In retaliation, the VOC burned fifteen of Makassar's junks. The 500-odd crew who had sailed on these vessels fled, some into forests and some to Tiworo, with the five captured Dutchmen. Buton's king sent two ships with envoys and slaves to Tiworo in order to try to gain the Dutchmen's release, but without success. In a letter to Admiral Arnold de Vlaming and Governor Willem Van der Beecq, the king of Buton explained that he did not have the power to take the men back by force since the place was full of Makassar's supporters. Moreover, his realm was, he added, "not strong enough, save by the force of the Company, and we have not enough boats (*praauwe*) with which we would have been able to get the Dutchmen with guns" (King of Buton *in* de Vlaming 1654:892r–894r). Buton's limited naval capacity left them unable to address the five Dutchmen's capture on the VOC's behalf. Still, if Makassar's vessels sailed past Buton's southern point they might be sighted and reported to the VOC. Rather than take such a risk, it was safer to avoid Buton by traveling eastward via Tiworo, where those sailing under Makassar found shelter.

In addition to offering a shorter route and one that bypassed Buton, Tiworo's location provided a staging ground, or rather, a nautical staging area. From this base, away from prying eyes, men loaded boats with stores gathered for the long haul 400 miles to Hoamoal. Proof of this came after the VOC and its allies took Tiworo in 1655, with no small amount of luck.

After erecting and manning two small forts on Buton's beach to help protect their staunch ally, Admiral de Vlaming set off north up the Buton Straits to the Pangesane Narrows—also known as the Straits of Tiworo—to meet up with Vice Admiral Roos. Roos had just burned and decommissioned enemy ships he encountered on the east coast of Buton, including three of Makassar's junks loaded with threshed and unthreshed rice (*padi*) (Bor 1663:259). Preceding de Vlaming and Roos's arrival at the mouth of the Straits of Tiworo, Sultan Mandarsyah and his Ternatan forces had, a few days earlier, taken the initiative to head into the straits toward Tiworo's main settlement. This move inspired de Vlaming to urge his vice admiral to take eleven row yachts and 300 Dutchmen to find Sultan Mandarsyah and to look together for the Makassar fleet. He advised Roos, if it were not too dangerous, to undertake something violent against Tiworo (Bor 1663:260–262; de Vlaming 1655a:76–77).

THE ATTACK ON TIWORO IN THE GREAT AMBON WAR

There could hardly have been a less dangerous moment to attack. Makassar's fleet was not at Tiworo when they arrived. Moreover, a contingent of about 300 of Tiworo's most courageous men had been sent out with their weapons to subdue neighboring regions, while a second troop, around 150 strong, had gone off to hunt buffalo. As a result, although the VOC's own complement had only "150 white and as many Ternaten" men, they were able to take Tiworo's villages and fortress by storm. After they rowed up the river about a mile, they landed and took two captives who led them to the main village. Bursting upon the settlement at the hottest point of the day, they caught the frightened villagers unawares, causing them to flee hither and yon, some to the fortress, into which VOC forces followed, and after scant resistance overpowered them. The VOC sustained a mere three casualties and a few lightly wounded, mostly from accidents caused by their own recklessness. Considering the trifling casualties on the VOC side, the other side's losses seem especially high. More than two hundred people were killed at five different locations in Tiworo (Bor 1663:260–262; Generale Missieve, July 12, 1655:543r; de Vlaming 1655a:76–77; de Vlamingh 1655b:88–89).

A vast store of provisions including rice, plus quality merchandise such as clothing and other goods, lay ready to be shipped, apparently to Asahudi, a site of conflict in the Hoamoal peninsula. These provisions and goods were stolen, burned, or destroyed by the VOC forces. Moreover, the VOC incinerated fifty "beautiful ships": junks, galleys, and *kora-kora* (Generale Missieve, July 12, 1655:543r; de Vlaming and Maetsuyker 1655:99–100; de Vlaming 1655b:88–89). Another 10 to 30 boats may have escaped this fate, since, given Tiworo's geography, the 300 men sent to subdue neighboring regions would likely have taken boats to do so. In any case, the destruction of these fifty junks, galleys and *kora-kora* by the VOC implies that Tiworo's boats aided, or joined, Makassar's fleets. The composition of its fleets therefore included people with affiliations to more than just Makassar, a matter about which more will be said below.

The VOC and its allies took Tiworo's fortress, some six miles from the river, on the third of January, 1655. A sturdy stone structure reinforced with distinct bulwarks, the fortress's walls reached five fathoms high, that is, between 33.5 and 37 feet (10.2– 11.28 m), based on the variations of a seventeenth-century fathom noted by Parthesius (2010:178, note 56). De Vlaming's secretary claimed the fortress was reinforced with seven round towers. The Dutch dismantled it before they departed, leveling it to the ground. However, archival documents record two other fortresses at Tiworo a dozen years later. The fortress dismantled in 1655 had been an important structure. In remarking on the VOC's lucky success in defeating Tiworo, de Vlaming proclaimed that "the name and weapons of the Company will without doubt gain a reputation in these parts, since the oft-mentioned fortress was reputed to be very strong and the capital place of Pangesane [Muna] Island." Exactly who had mentioned the fortress with any frequency is a mystery, but de Vlaming's comment makes it clear that the fortress marked Tiworo as the island's most significant place (Bor 1663:262; de Vlaming 1655c:79–81, 1655b:88; de Vlaming and Maetsuyker 1655:97 and 100). This is particularly remarkable given the negligible notice Tiworo has received from historians.

Tiworo, it must also be noted, was not simply located on Muna Island. The northwest part of Muna was merely Tiworo's most substantive landward margin. Other parts of Tiworo were located in the straits. Since we are so accustomed to associating polities and historical events with places on land, this point may be easy to overlook. One might be tempted, moreover, to consider the nautical orientation an artifact of the historical source material, for, after all, much of it consists in ship-to-ship and ship-to-shore correspondence. However, this watery view on the straits was not simply due to the manner in which the VOC conducted its affairs. While de Vlaming singled out Tiworo's fortress as the capital place of Pangesane or Muna Island, he also portrayed Tiworo's main sites as located in the straits. Writing with news of its defeat to Governor Jacob Hustaert and the Council in the Moluccas, he stated, "We have fought the enemy's villages and the fortress at Tiworo (*Tibore*) situated in the Straits of Pangesane" (de Vlaming and Maetsuyker 1655:97). That Tiworo was located in the straits, with areas both on dry ground and in the littoral, seems less surprising given other period evidence of communities constructed on tidal flats, and Tiworo's own later settlement patterns in which villages of pile dwellings were erected in the shallows of its coasts and offshore islands (Gaynor 2016). While this particular fortress was located a few miles inland, Tiworo's energies coalesced in the littoral.

Among those killed in the 1655 attack were Tiworo's king (*raja*), the greater number of his entourage or notables, as well as his sons. De Vlaming viewed this as a serious blow to Makassar, "to lose their friend, the king, with most of his peers," as he was "a man on whom a lot was riding and in this region was greatly esteemed" (Generale Missieve, July 12, 1655:543r; de Vlaming 1655b:89; de Vlaming and Maetsuyker 1655:99–100). Like his comment about Tiworo's "oft-mentioned" fortress marking the importance of its location, de Vlaming's words about Makassar's reliance on, and high regard for, Tiworo's raja indicated the raja's prominence. Although de Vlaming may not have been cognizant of all the ways in which Tiworo and Makassar were tied, his comments show an awareness that, in addition to the spice trade's high stakes, other features of social relations sustained interactions between his foes.

In addition to the "great number" of people, more than 200, killed at Tiworo, around 300 were taken alive (Generale Missieve, July 12, 1655:543r). One might expect they would have been taken to Batavia to be sold as slaves, but this, at least initially, was not their fate. Indeed, the largest circuit of Dutch slavery in the seventeenth-century Indian Ocean world was centered in Southeast Asia (Vink 2003:143–144, 146–149). Yet, not all people captured in conflicts wound up as slaves in the largely urban-dominated market for them. Some were kept or bestowed as war spoils. For instance, earlier during the Great Ambon War, in the 1654 storming of Laala on the Hoamoal peninsula, the VOC's forces killed 700 people, both locals and reinforcements under Makassar who were "capable of bearing arms." Yet they also took another 400 people captive: women, children, and the indigent elderly. These were granted as spoils to the victors, that is, to the VOC's allies, in order to foster or stimulate bravery among them in the future (Bor 1663:236–240).

The VOC likewise gave the roughly 300 women and children taken at Tiworo over to those who fought for them, "amounting to a good number of them falling into the hands of the Ternatans and Mardijkers" (de Vlaming and Maetsuyker 1655:99). "Mardijker," from "*orang merdeka*" or "free man," was a term originally used in Ambon for free Moluccans baptized and educated by the Portuguese, who generally adopted the language and lifestyle of their colonial masters. In Batavia, the term was used as a collective noun to refer to Asians of varying social status and origin, who had in common the Christian religion and use of the Portuguese language. Most were freed slaves from the Coromandel and Malabar coasts or from Ceylon. Some had been captured by the Dutch on board Portuguese vessels, while others came on their own initiative from formerly Portuguese settlements such as Pulicat and Malacca after these were taken by the Dutch (Blussé 1986:165. There was also some overlap with the term *Topass*. See Hägerdal 2012:46).

The women and children captured at Tiworo were given over to the VOC's Ternatan and Mardijker allies, de Vlaming wrote to Governor Hustaert, "in order to get them off our hands, regarding which Your Lordship will respect the special nature." De Vlaming did not clarify what he meant by their "special nature." However, he did explain that allowing him, the Governor's delegate, "to please them [their allies] to be treated," was "so that they, for the time being, stay calm and contented to continue with the work." In other words, the captives were apparently granted as an incentive to boost the willingness of fighters to undertake further combat (de Vlaming and Maetsuyker 1655:99).

VOC reports also made note of the fact that the women and children taken alive at Tiworo included most of the king's wives and daughters, and that "the king's real wife and daughters, as well as a good number of concubines, were left to the conquerors" (Generale Missieve December 24, 1655:6r; de Vlaming 1655b:89, 99). While the division into "real wife" and "concubines" may reflect the projection of European notions about elite social organization onto Southeast Asian social realities, this sort of capture and keeping by foes in the context of colonial conflicts, given little attention in the scholarly literature, was not a novel phenomenon within the region. Indeed, while de Vlaming apparently bestowed the captives, claiming that he allowed them to be kept as spoils by his allies, such captures built on long-standing practices of raiding in archipelagic Southeast Asia (Junker 1999).

Three days after the VOC captured Tiworo's fortress, as some Dutch boats lay in the Tiworo river getting fresh water, a fleet from Makassar appeared in the river, some forty or fifty ships strong. Upriver they were sure to discover the bodies of the slain, "among whom were also many Macassars" (Bor 1663:263; de Vlaming 1655b:87; de Vlaming and Maetsuyker 1655:97). The fortuitous timing of their arrival was not lost on de Vlaming, who noted that had they come a few days earlier, it would have been impossible for the Dutch "to have been there alone to carry out the job and our people undoubtedly would have perished and been beaten" (de Vlaming 1655b:88). Delighted by this new development, de Vlaming urged Vice Admiral Roos to use caution to evade the fleet, "since they may be too strong for you." They entertained ideas for taking on the fleet, yet in the end, caution won out and they abandoned their plans to deal with the Makassar fleet at Tiworo itself (de Vlaming 1655a:76–77, 1655b: 91).

Instead, hoping to intercept Makassar's ships as they headed toward Hoamoal and other sites, the Dutch stationed boats at the eastern points of egress from the Tiworo Straits and in front of Buton's main town. They also set up patrols in parts of the eastern archipelago. (Bor 1663:260; Generale Missieve, December 24, 1655:6v; de Vlaming 1655a:77, 1655c:79–81, 1655d:78, 1655e:81–82). However, Makassar's fleet apparently stayed put in Tiworo through early April. With all the VOC's careful monitoring and patrolling, it was "absolutely disheartening" when the fleet slipped out of their sanctuary, eluding the Dutch in a very dense fog (Bor 1663: 273–274).

With the bulk of its fighting men away, Tiworo was depopulated, politically decapitated, and socially diminished by the attack during the Great Ambon War. The boats moored there were burned, the remaining men slain, and its women and children were taken. Still, it provided a safe haven for Makassar's fleet. Although no record exists of what the absent men thought when they either came back from hunting buffalo and subduing neighboring regions, or learned why they should delay such a return, it would be no great stretch to imagine their shock and outrage.

BETWEEN THE WARS

Clarifying the above events, the geography in which they took place, and the networks of political relations on both sides of the conflict makes it possible to grasp the significance of a remark Sultan Hasanuddin made about his motivation for conducting a campaign of re-expansion in the eastern archipelago. His remark, discussed further below, appeared in a report by a Commissioner van Wesenhagen, who had been sent by the Dutch in 1666 ostensibly to preserve the peace. The peace, such as it was, had been tried by a series of events during the first half of the 1660s. These included the Dutch occupation of a fort near Makassar at Paqnakkukang in 1660, Gowa's use of 10,000 Bugis corvée laborers to dig a canal cutting off the fort from the Makassar mainland, and the eventual rebellion of these laborers whose leaders then fled back to their Bugis homelands. Among them was Arung Palakka, who removed himself, his family and other Bugis leaders to the island of Buton—a journey that likely passed through the Straits of Tiworo. Then with Dutch assistance Arung Palakka relocated to Batavia (Andaya 1981:59, 65–68, 316 note 17; Cummings, ed., 2010:90 and note 233).

This series of events called forth diplomatic efforts. After the VOC took the fort at Paqnakkukang, the Sultan's representative went to Batavia to negotiate a treaty with the Company. When Dutch envoys came to Makassar to deliver the treaty, the Sultan welcomed them, asked when they would be giving back his fort, and proceeded to ignore the treaty provisions. During their visit, the Dutch envoys noticed major defensive preparations underway in Makassar. They did not realize that the preparations were as much in case of a rumored Buton-Bugis-Ternate invasion as they were a precaution for the possibility of hostilities with the Dutch. With the treaty's implementation still stalled, it concerned the VOC that at this time, in 1661, Makassar was busy fortifying its harbor region. In addition, they learned that large quantities of gunpowder were being put by and defenses constructed, and moreover heard that 1,200 to 1,500 boats in different areas were said to be in a state of readiness (Andaya 1981:59–61; Heeres 1931:171 in Andaya 1981:65).

Yet another set of incidents caused friction in 1662 after a Dutch ship foundered in Makassar's waters. Sixteen cannons and other goods were seized from the ship, and the negotiations and concessions that followed resulted in the return of only half the cannons. When another Dutch vessel shipwrecked on an island off Makassar's coast, the Dutch were angered by the Sultan's refusal to allow them access to it, and when the Sultan sent his own people to retrieve the ship's money chest, the Dutch considered it piracy. Members of a Dutch party who were sent out to the island to investigate were murdered there. Efforts to resolve the situation broke down and the entire Dutch post in Makassar sailed to Batavia in June 1665. While Sultan Hasanuddin seemed unperturbed by the prospect that the Dutch might wish to start a war, the Company, for its part, tried to dispel the impression that this was its aim with a mission sent to Makassar in 1665. However, the mission's envoy was not permitted to land (Andaya 1981:62–63; Stapel 1922:83–85 in Andaya 1981:63).

On top of these incidents, Makassar was busy re-establishing its authority in areas of the archipelago to its east. In 1665, Gowa's forces invaded the Sula Islands east of

Sulawesi with more than 200 ships, and took the cannon from the fortress at Ternate, along with more than 2,000 people. According to Admiral Cornelis Speelman, who led VOC forces in the Makassar War, this

> put all the eastern provinces in turmoil, and not without reason, since, certainly encouraged by this booty, one saw with what incredible power they equipped and furnished (a fleet) the following year under (Karaeng) Bontomarannu, consisting of, according to musterings done in the Bay of Boné, more than 700 vessels and 20,000 people, no doubt with the intention to bring Buton to her fealty, and then subsequently to concentrate first on Maluku, or closer, on the Sula islands. (Speelman 1669:684r–684v)

Attentive to Makassar's military preparations and maneuvers, the VOC sent a new mission to Makassar after the previous one had been barred from landing, in order to seek satisfaction for the Dutch murders, and, as mentioned above, to preserve the peace. Arriving in April 1666, Commissioner van Wesenhagen learned that the Harbormaster (*sabannaraq*), Daeng Makulle of Gowa, had recently returned after being away with a fleet sent to Sulawesi's east coast and the Sula Islands. English, Portuguese, and Indian Muslim merchants in Makassar informed van Wesenhagen that the reason for this first expedition was to assert Gowa's suzerainty over lands contested by Ternate, lands that had been seized by Gowa during the first half of the seventeenth century. Makassar's fleet also attacked Ambon and Buton but was unable to conquer them. Hence, it was rumored that a second fleet was being prepared for an expedition aimed at Buton and Ternate, both staunch allies of the VOC. Although the rumors at the time estimated that the second fleet would contain 300 boats, Speelman later recorded, as noted above, a mustering of 700 vessels (Andaya 1981:64; Stapel 1922:86; van Wesenhagen 1666:511, 514; Makassar invaded the Sula Islands in 1665, as noted by Speelman 1669:684r).

In Admiral Speelman's assessment, the inspiration for Makassar's gathering such an impressive force was to acquire booty and to bring Buton to heel, as well as, perhaps, parts of the eastern archipelago. However, plunder and prostration were not the sole motivations. At least, Sultan Hasanuddin offered another rationale for re-expansion: avenging the attack on Tiworo in 1655. As Commissioner van Wesenhagen reported in 1666, Sultan Hasanuddin would be inclined toward peace with the Dutch if the rebel Bugis leaders who had fled from Buton to Batavia were returned—meaning, especially, Arung Palakka—and also if the Dutch would condone Makassar's occupation of the lands disputed by Ternate. Sultan Hasanuddin explained, "*that he would never have had to maintain his rights to these lands in question if Ternate had not attacked the Makassar territory of Pancana*" (Andaya 1981:65; my emphasis; van Wesenhagen 1666:521).

Pancana, Panstiano, Pangesane (among others) are variant spellings for the island now known as Muna. As discussed above, during the Great Ambon War, Tiworo, "with its oft-mentioned fortress," had been considered the capital place of this island. The Tiworo Straits were also sometimes referred to as the Pangesane Straits or Narrows. In 1655 during the Great Ambon War, when Admiral de Vlaming had counseled Vice Admiral Roos to undertake some violence against Tiworo, the VOC's boats literally followed the lead of Ternate's Sultan Mandarsyah, who had already entered the straits with his men to advance on Tiworo. Although Ternate's role does not feature prominently in the reports from de Vlaming about Tiworo's 1655 defeat, Ternate clearly played a major role. It both led the way and joined the VOC fighters with an equal complement of men, who came away with women and children captured from Tiworo.

MAKASSAR'S TIES WITH MARITIME-ORIENTED PEOPLE

The slaughter at Tiworo of many people, including the king, his notables, and sons, the burning of Tiworo's boats and main settlement, as well as the dismantling of its fortress, all surely mattered. Yet the ignominy was compounded by the capture and redistribution of women and children from Tiworo to a foe, including the raja's wives and daughters. Their capture and relocation plays an integral part in making sense of Sultan Hasanuddin's statement about what motivated his campaign of re-expansion in the eastern archipelago. The significance of this forced redistribution derives less from anything supposedly inherent about women, than from the contrast this action posed vis-à-vis an array of other practices such as negotiated unions and alliance-making between elite families. Part of a dynamic social system of rank and status that stretched across the littoral regions of Southeast Asia, capture and redistribution, like negotiated unions, affected individuals and kin groups, here reproducing and there altering their social positions relative to others.

Marital unions negotiated between members of high status lineages form a common and well-known part of regional politics. Yet capture and relocation, also an important part of political relations, remain less well-studied. Better represented numerically in the limited work on regional slaving and raiding, capture and relocation pose challenges for qualitative approaches. The reasons seem obvious, given the impetus in highly status-conscious societies to downplay, hide, or forget about the historical degradations and ruptures they produce. Ethnographic and historical evidence from across the region suggests that while marrying within social class (rank-endogenous marriage) was weakly proscribed, both individuals and whole kin groups moved vertically within the social hierarchy through a single fortuitous or ill-advised marriage (Junker 1999:142).

How much more so, then, with capture. To have high-ranking daughters and wives simply taken during conflict issued a flagrant affront that signaled the opposite of efforts to forge connections between status peers. Whereas practices of negotiating alliances by linking lineages and kin groups through marriage produced mutual recognition between them, the capture of women of rank breached such expectations of mutual recognition. While colonial conflict may have fostered captures, it nevertheless contributed, perhaps unwittingly, to an already extant dynamic, building on earlier practices of maritime raiding endemic to the region—part of, not apart from, the mechanisms driving the production of social class, in ways that cut across ethnic groups. Instead of negotiations followed by reciprocal exchanges with an eye toward building politically strategic alliances, abduction created subordination through conquest and the violent acquisition of dependents. This not only increased dependent followings, but also disrupted the alliances forged by foes.

In south Sulawesi, strategic marriage played a role in both the development and strengthening of tributary relationships, part of the multicentered and highly decentralized political structure of the peninsula's kingdoms from at least 1600, and probably earlier. Like other polities in the south Sulawesi peninsula, Makassar used marriage to maintain political alliances. This was a world in which lineage provided the better part of descendants' social rank. Hence, not only rulers, but other individuals also maneuvered to use marriage within and between ethnic groups to their own advantage and their progeny's. For instance, Sultan Hasanuddin's sister, Karaénta ri Bontojéqnéq, maneuvered between a series of four marriages to ensure not only her influence in the present but also reverence in the future by becoming an ancestor who would link later generations with influential forebears (Bulbeck 1996:280–315, esp. 311–312; Chabot 1996[1950]; Cummings, ed., 2010:19–20; 2005:40–62; Druce 2009:23, 26–27, 30; Mangemba 1975:53–57). Strategic marriage thus involved a relation with the past through lineages that determined ascribed status in the present, as well as efforts to secure ennobling futures.

According to VOC sources, Tiworo was a political subordinate of Makassar and their rulers were close friends. Yet, a relevant comparison from the same time may prove instructive, suggesting that their ties probably ran deeper than this. Just as Makassar relied on access to Tiworo, and on the skills and boats of its mariners, it also relied on the maritime-oriented Sama "sea-people" closer to home. As with historians' disregard of Tiworo, evidence of the actual depth of Makassar's ties with Sama people has received surprisingly little notice. Sama people were not just apparently present in the legendary birth of Makassar, as is well known. They also played vital roles at the center of the polity during the seventeenth century. Women and men who traced their descent through chiefly or royal Sama lineages moved among Makassar's elite, intermarried with its royalty, and held strategically important positions such as Harbormaster (sabannaraq) (Gaynor 2016:87–97). Since Makassar's trade and military might relied so heavily on the skills and cooperation of regional mariners, it cultivated close connections with Sama people from high-status lineages through kinship ties and the conferral of rank.

Some harbormasters or sabannaraq were unmistakably Sama, while for others this is less easy to determine. For instance, as mentioned in the previous section, when the VOC sent Commissioner van Wesenhagen to Makassar in 1666, he obtained news about the sabannaraq Daeng Makkulle of Gowa (in Makassar's diarchy of Gowa and Talloq). Daeng Makkulle had recently returned from being off with a fleet, the first expedition sent to reassert Gowa's suzerainty. His marriage and the birth of a child are recorded in the Makassar Annals, showing that he was part of the inner circle of Makassar's ruling families. Installed as sabannaraq in 1661, he would have played a role in the fortification of Makassar's coastal defenses, in addition to the campaign reported by van Wesenhagen (Cummings, ed., 2010:91, 122, 126).

Daeng Makkulle (also known as I Mappaq) was succeeded in the position of sabannaraq by Daeng Buraqne, and the latter was replaced in 1710 by Daeng Makkulle's namesake and presumably his son, Daeng Makkulle Ahmad. In addition to being sabannaraq, Daeng Makkulle Ahmad also occupied another rank that was apparently not Makassar's to confer, a specifically Sama leadership position called the Papuq. "Daeng" is an honorific commonly used in Makassar language contexts. One cannot always reliably determine a person's ethnicity by the use of such honorifics, since people in south and southeast Sulawesi were sometimes known by different titles and names, depending on the sociolinguistic context. In contrast, "Papuq" is not merely an honorific, but a Sama-language title for a specifically Sama paramount chief or noble. References to three people who held the position of Papuq in Makassar during the late seventeenth and early eighteenth centuries appear in the *Makassar Annals*: Daeng Numalo, Daeng Makkulle Ahmad, and Daeng Manggappa (also known as "Mommiq") (Cummings, ed., 2010:139 note 358, 156, 176, 186, 223–224).

After the death of the Papuq Daeng Numalo on March 12, 1703, Daeng Makkulle Ahmad was then "installed as Papuq by his family" on June 12, 1703. This wording implies that he was installed as Papuq not by any of Makassar's rulers or councils, but rather by "his family," that is to say, by his Sama kin. In other words, members of this high-status lineage of maritime-oriented Sama people interacted closely with Makassar's ruling family, and apparently intermarried with them, yet, as was also common for land-based tributaries on the peninsula, they maintained the ability to choose their own leader. Hence, while members of this Sama lineage maintained tight ties with Makassar's rulers and were considered part of the social and political elite at the center of the polity, their appearance in the *Annals* proof of their stature in Makassar, they were at the same time socially and politically distinct (Cummings, ed., 2010:7, 176).

Daeng Makkulle Ahmad served as the Sama Papuq for seven years before he was made Makassar's harbormaster. Like him, Daeng Manggappa, born in 1688, also served both as the Sama Papuq and as Makassar's *sabannaraq*. As the *Annals* do not record whether Daeng Makkulle the elder ever held the title of Papuq, it is slightly less certain that he was Sama. Yet that possibility is certainly strong, for if his son Daeng Makkulle Ahmad was chosen "by his kin" to be Papuq, then, given bilateral descent reckoning in these societies, either the elder Daeng Makkulle was Sama, or he married into a high-status Sama lineage. In either case—but perhaps more so if he himself had Sama descent—he would have had many Sama followers, especially since, as *sabannaraq*, he was in charge of the harbor, where Sama would have lived in houses and boats at estuaries and other spots along the intertidal zone.

The implications of this politically distinct, yet tightly cooperative and kin-mediated relation ran deep. Clearly, the rulers of Makassar saw advantages in putting Sama leaders in charge of maritime affairs. The *sabannaraq* oversaw the port and had his finger on the pulse of comings and goings. Yet, the *sabannaraq* had much more authority than simply overseeing the harbor. He had some punitive powers within Makassar and also led military expeditions on its behalf. As *sabannaraq*, the elder Daeng Makkulle led, or was among the leaders of, Makassar's first expedition of re-expansion to the eastern archipelago in 1666. During the early eighteenth century, *sabannaraq* Papuq Daeng Makkulle Ahmad and his son-in-law, Daeng Manassaq, led military campaigns across the Flores Sea. With such tight connections to Sama leaders, who undoubtedly had numerous Sama followers, it appears that Makassar flexed its naval might with the sinews of Sama strength. Indeed, this fact was remarked on in a Dutch report from 1733 (Makassar to Batavia 1733:119).

Did Makassar, through its Gowa or Talloq lineages, have direct kin links to people in Tiworo? And did the prominent Sama in Makassar have such kin links with people of prominent lineages in Tiworo (whether they were Sama, or, less likely, some other ethnicity)? What Makassar-language sources reveal about kin and political ties between Makassar's royalty and the high-ranking Sama at the highest echelons of its polity suggests that kin ties played a part in cementing the loyalties of those who sailed for Makassar from other bases. The role of kin ties seems especially likely for people in the Straits of Tiworo, who played such a crucial role in supporting Makassar against the VOC and its allies during the 1650s and 1660s. Kin links between Makassar and Tiworo would have made Tiworo's defeat and the capture and redistribution of so many women and children that much more grievous, an offense not just against allies and friends, but against family and the wider kin group. The prominent rank of the Tiworo king's captured wives and daughters compounded the offense, affecting their own and their relatives' standing. Taking into account the likelihood of kin ties between allies, alongside the importance of status competition and lineage precedence in archipelagic politics, lends particular credence to the rationale Sultan Hasanuddin offered for Makassar's expansionary campaign, that is, to avenge Tiworo's defeat.

TIWORO, THE MAKASSAR WAR, AND BAJOÉ

Tiworo rebuilt between the wars and continued to serve as a haven for fleets under Makassar. In 1667, before Admiral Speelman and Arung Palakka regrouped to sally forth across the Gulf of Boné and attack Makassar, they made Tiworo the target once again. Yet, forewarned by Daeng Mangaga (probably Daeng Mangagaang of the *Makassar Annals*), who with 60 boats under Makassar was busy evading the Dutch, Tiworo's people this time managed to flee (Cummings 2010, ed., 219; Gaynor 2016:97–106; Speelman 1667:46r). Hence it was that Tiworo fell into the hands of the VOC's ally, Arung Palakka. This was once again extraordinarily lucky and unexpected, to take Tiworo without a fight.

After further unsuccessful searching for Daeng Mangaga, Arung Palakka returned to Buton, where he was not warmly welcomed, and in March Admiral Speelman sent him to Tiworo to take up the watch. When Captain Lieutenant David Steijger joined him six days later with ships and supporters, curiously, he found Tiworo's ruler in his fortress in a wooded area on elevated ground situated six miles from Tiworo's settlement (Speelman 1667:51v–52r). This fortress, "Lapadacca" was probably built on the site of the one torn down twelve years before.

The remains of a stronghold may still be found at Lapadaku. In the nineteenth century, A. Ligtvoet referred to the place Lapadaku, in the Tiworo area, when he traced part of the genealogy of a Tiworo princess married with Aru Bakung (or Arung Baku, probably To Palettéi) (See Gaynor 2016:17–22; Ligvoet 1878:22). "Lapadaku" may derive from the Sama term *padakau*, meaning "unity," from the root *dakau*, which in Sama means "one" (personal communication, July 24, 2013, Kamaruddin Thamzibar and Nasir, the Sapati of the current realm [*kerajaan*] of Tiworo). "*La*," an honorific, was applied to the name of the fortress, much as regalia receive names and honorifics. The "unity" may originally have referred to the political alliance between different descent groups, for instance, an alliance between Sama and Makassar lineages, perhaps also including those of the northwest Muna subgroup, recently called "Muna-Tiworo." Alternatively, Lapadak(a)u could simply be a nominalization of "one," meaning "(the) first (thing)," in other words, the first fortress, memorializing the one that had been torn down in 1655.

When Captain Lieutenant David Steijger rejoined Arung Palakka at Tiworo in 1667, Tiworo's king bought time by offering to negotiate. But in the end, the two sides engaged, and the Raja of Tiworo and his men were pursued to another fortification, "Ollenbacca"—probably what is now known as the "Tiworo fortress" near the mouth of the Tiworo river. In the skirmish, Arung Palakka was wounded with an arrow and visibly shaken by it. However, eventually, with threats backed by force of arms, Steijger and Palakka's men took the fortress and detained Tiworo's king there with another notable. Then, while Steijger was called away on orders elsewhere, Arung Palakka gave his permission for the prisoners to wash, and on this pretext of needing to bathe they escaped, despite some 1,000 men in chase. Before departing for the South Sulawesi peninsula, the VOC tore down most of "the overgrown fort" and set fire to the village (Speelman 1667:52r–54r).

Admiral Speelman spared no kind words for Tiworo, calling it "a nasty pirate's nest" (Speelman 1669:684v). Yet his closest ally, Arung Palakka, appropriated Tiworo's boats rather than burn them as had been done twelve years prior. Moreover, Arung Palakka hand-picked and armed sixty of Tiworo's men to fill half of his Guard of Prime Commanders. Sources are silent about what happened to the women and children from the torched settlement, but they were apparently not treated as spoils. Instead, the rank bestowed on the 60 Tiworo men would likely have redounded to the benefit of their female kin.

This illustrates a major unanswered historical question about maritime people in the archipelago: How did they come to shift allegiances from one center to another? The process sketched above illustrates the shift of allegiances from Makassar to the Bugis center, Boné. The advent and rapid expansion of Bajoé, the littoral settlement that served as Boné's harbor, dates from shortly after this time (Gaynor 2016:27–28; Makassar to Batavia 1714:103). In the Bugis language, "Bajoé" means "the Bajo," an exonym for the maritime-oriented "Sama." The timing suggests that the large number of prominent figures from Tiworo who left there with new allegiances to the Bugis leader Arung Palakka—and thus implicitly also to Boné—were Sama people.

Boné may have had connections with the Sama before Bajoé's rise. However, the political arrangement with Bajoé entailed cooperation between Boné's rulers and members of an elite Sama lineage. This fruitful cooperation between land-based and maritime-oriented people was part of a wider pattern that repeated the earlier successful approach of other polities, such as Makassar. The ties between elite Boné and Sama lineages are memorialized in substantial detail in rare Bugis-language manuscripts inherited through Sama lineages. These manuscripts attest to the long history of interconnections between the Bugis polity of Boné and Sama people, who, while often living at some distance from Bajoé, nevertheless maintained loyalty to it (Gaynor 2016:107–166).

Conclusion

Although a rather sleepy backwater now, Tiworo achieved a certain infamy among the Dutch during the seventeenth century, and its fortresses were integral to its nautical significance. The role it played as a nonurban maritime hub led the VOC forces under Arnold de Vlaming and their Ternatan allies to take it, with no small amount of luck, during the Great Ambon War. In the war against Makassar, Admiral Cornelis Speelman and his ally Arung Palakka neutralized the threat Tiworo posed before moving to attack Makassar and its supporters on Sulawesi's southwestern peninsula.

While European overseas maritime power has received a great deal of attention, the archipelago was, of course, rife with boats of many kinds. This look at Southeast Asian maritime power contributes to our understanding of the social and political world into which boats from elsewhere sailed. The challenge has not been to show that water under-pinned power in this world, but rather to show how maritime power was inextricably tied to social and political networks of people with the skills and knowledge to work the waves.

Acknowledgments

I would like to thank IEMA, Peter Biehl, and Emily Holt for the wonderful conference and the opportunity to contribute to the volume from which it springs. I gratefully acknowledge a grant from the Baldy Center for Law and Social Policy at the University at Buffalo, SUNY, in support of this research.

References Cited

Abbreviations

VOC	Dutch East India Company (Vereenigde Oost-Indische Compagnie)
JESHO	Journal of the Economic and Social History of the Orient
RIMA	Review of Indonesian and Malaysian Affairs
KITLV	Koninklijk Instituut voor Taal-, Land- en Volkenkunde (Royal Netherlands Institute of Southeast Asian and Caribbean Studies)
BKI	Bijdragen tot de Taal-, Land- en Volkenkunde/Journal of the Humanities and Social Sciences of Southeast Asia (viz., Bijdragen van het Koninklijk Instituut / Proceedings of the Royal Institute)

Archives

VOC, 1602–1799. Archive of the Vereenigde Oost-Indische Compagnie (VOC), access number 1.04.02. National Archives of the Netherlands.

Unpublished Manuscripts

King of Buton. 1654 Letter from the King of Buton to Admiral Arnold de Vlaming and Governor Willem Van der Beecq, in Dachregister bij d'Hr. Arnold de Vlamingh van Outshoorn,

VOC 1205, pp. 892r-894r. (The letter was copied into Arnold de Vlaming's *dagregister* (journal or ship's log) on the day it was received, April 5, 1654.)

Generale Missieve (Originele). 1655 (12 July), VOC 1208.

Generale Missieve (Originele). 1655 (24 December), VOC 1209.

Makassar to Batavia. 1714 (23 September), VOC 1853.

Makassar to Batavia. 1733 (21 May), VOC 2285.

Speelman, Cornelis. 1667 Letter of 18 to Joan Maetsuijker and the Council of the Indies, VOC 1264.

Speelman, Cornelis. 1669 Notitie dienende voor eenen corten tijt, en tot naeder last van de Hooge Regeringe op Batavia, tot naerrichtinge voor den ondercoopman Jan van Opijnen bij provisie gestelt, tot Opperhooft en Commandant int Casteel Rotterdam op Maccassar, en van den Capitain Jan France als hooft over de melitie mitsgaders die van den Raede, VOC 1276.

Vlaming, Arnold de. 1655a Letter of January 9, from aboard the *Erasmus*, delivered express to the Authorities before Tiworo (*Tibore*), VOC 1211.

Vlaming, Arnold de. 1655b Letter of 17 January, to Simon Cos, Provis. President in Ambon, from Arnold de Vlaming van Outshoorn in the ship *Erasmus* lying at anchor by the east end of the Buton Straits, VOC 1211.

Vlaming, Arnold de. 1655c Letter of 16 January, to Marten Doane, Skipper of the *Concordia*, sent with the Post to *Het Haesjen*, from Arnold de Vlaming van Outshoorn, in the ship *Erasmus* at anchor by the (fresh) waterplace in the Buton Straits, VOC 1211.

Vlaming, Arnold de. 1655d Order of January 16, for the Post and Haes to dispense rules, from Arnold de Vlaming van Outshoorn, on board the ship *Erasmus*, VOC 1211.

Vlaming, Arnold de. 1655e Order of January 17, for Commander Gerrit Roos, to instruct him further, from Arnold de Vlamingh van Outshoorn in the ship *Erasmus* at anchor by the waterplace in the Buton Straits VOC 1211.

Vlaming, Arnold de, and Willem Maetsuyker. 1655 Letter to Governor Jacob Hustaert and the Council in Molucco, with the Yacht *Dromedaris*, February 2, written from Batoij, signed on the chaloup *Sumatra*, lying at anchor off the coast of Celebes opposite Chassea Island, VOC 1211.

Wesenhagen, Commissioner van. 1666 Report of July 16 on mission to Makassar and Ternate, VOC 1257.

Books and Articles

Andaya, L. 1981 *The Heritage of Arung Palakka: A History of South Sulawesi (Celebes) in the Seventeenth Century*. Nijhoff, The Hague.

Blussé, L. 1986 *Strange Company: Chinese Settlers, Mestizo Women, and the Dutch in VOC Batavia*. Foris Publications, Dordrecht and Providence.

Bor, L. 1663 *Amboinse Oorlogen door Arnold de Vlaming van Oudshoorn als superintendent over d'Oosterse gewesten oorlogaftig ten eind gebracht*. Bon, Delft.

Bulbeck, F. D. 1996 The Politics of Marriage and the Marriage of Polities in Gowa, South Sulawesi, during the 16th and 17th Centuries. In *Origins, Ancestry, and Alliance*, edited by J. J. Fox and C. Sather, pp. 280–315. Department of Anthropology Comparative Austronesian Project, Research School of Pacific and Asian Studies, and Research School of Pacific and Asian Studies, The Australian National University, Canberra.

Chabot, H. Th. 1996 [1950] *Kinship, Status, and Gender in South Celebes*. KITLV Press, Leiden.

Cummings, W. 2005 Historical Texts as Social Maps: *Lontaraq bilang* in Early Modern Makassar. *BKI* 161(1):40–62.

Cummings, W. (translator and editor). 2010 *The Makassar Annals*. KITLV Press, Leiden.

Druce, S. C. 2009 *The Lands West of the Lakes: A History of the Ajattapareng Kingdoms of South Sulawesi 1200–1600 CE*. KITLV Press, Leiden.

Gaynor, J. L. 2016 *Intertidal History in Island Southeast Asia: Submerged Genealogy and the Legacy of Coastal Capture*. Cornell University Press, Ithaca and London.

Hägerdal, H. 2012 *Lords of the Land, Lords of the Sea: Conflict and Adaptation in Early Colonial Timor, 1600–1800*. KITLV Press, Leiden.

Heeres, J. E. (editor). 1931 *Corpus Diplomaticum Neerlando-Indicum; Verzameling van politieke contracten en verdere verdragen door de Neerlanders in het Oosten gesloten, van privilegebrieven aan hen verleend, enz., vol. 2: 1650–1675*. Nijhoff, The Hague.

Junker, L. L. 1999 *Raiding, Trading, and Feasting: The Political Economy of Philippine Chiefdoms*. University of Hawai'i Press, Honolulu.

Knaap, G. 2003 Headhunting, Carnage, and Armed Peace in Amboina, 1500–1700. *Journal of the Economic and Social History of the Orient* 46(2):165–192.

Ligtvoet, A. 1878 Beschrijving en Geschiedenis van Boeton. *BKI* 26: 1–112.

Mangemba, H. D. 1975 Le statut des femmes bugis et makassar vu par leur propre société. *Archipel* 10:153–157.

Parthesius, R. 2010 *Dutch Ships in Tropical Waters: The Development of the Dutch East India Company (VOC) Shipping Network in Asia, 1595–1660*. Amsterdam University Press, Amsterdam.

Reid, A. 2000 The Rise of Makassar. In *Charting the Shape of Early Modern Southeast Asia*, pp. 100–125. ISEAS, Singapore. Originally published in *RIMA* 17 (1983).

Stapel, F. W. 1922 *Het Bongaais Verdrag*. J. B. Wolter's, Groningen.

Vink, M. 2003 "The World's Oldest Trade": Dutch Slavery and Slave Trade in the Indian Ocean in the Seventeenth Century. *Journal of World History* 14(2):131–177.

CHAPTER ELEVEN

The Power of Coastal Resources

Assessing Maritime Economic Opportunity in the Roman Mediterranean

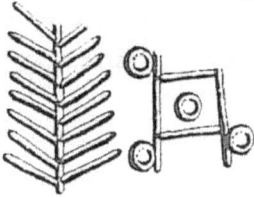

Justin Leidwanger

Abstract *Clustered along its sinuous shores, the inhabitants of the ancient Mediterranean harnessed the power and potential of the sea to widely varying degrees. For the Roman era, considerable emphasis has been placed on the expansive port networks and large-scale directed exchange that linked cities across its tamed waters, yet the extent and practical impact of direct maritime access and opportunity beyond urban centers remains a critical question for a population that was still overwhelmingly rural. Using Cyprus as a case study, this paper incorporates GIS-based analysis of marine and terrestrial topography as a means of exploring the spatial patterning of settlements and activity areas, providing a clearer picture of how simple coastal facilities and easy mobility on and around the island allowed for a distinctively regional scale of maritime economic activity. Centered around what might be considered generally as coastal landing sites, the rise in exchange, fishing, and probably market activities during the Roman (ca. 50 BCE–350 CE) and especially the late Roman (350–700 CE) period suggest that new maritime opportunities counterbalanced the earlier social and economic centrality of the island's cities, and in doing so restructured the rhythms of rural economic prosperity and connectivity.*

The inhabitants of the ancient Mediterranean famously clustered along its sinuous shores, according to Plato (*Phaedo* 109b), like "ants or frogs around a pond." The sea brought tremendous social and economic potential, yet this basic proximity need not imply that everyone used the sea in the same manner or to the same extent. Like other of the larger islands, Cyprus often looks inward rather than outward, whether for natural resources or for food and recreation. That is, Cyprus is an island that does not always conform to modern notions of "island life," choosing to exploit and to ignore its sea to varying degrees throughout its history and even today.[1] While Plato's passage is nearly always excerpted for its amphibious frogs, most leave aside his landlubber ants.[2] This contribution explores how ancient Cypriots variously acted both as ants and frogs within the context of a changing maritime landscape, evolving local power structures, and shifting regional political and economic centralities of the Roman and late antique worlds.

Recent paradigms of the Mediterranean have generally centered on the notion of connectivity, particularly seaborne connectivity, as a fundamental and defining component of past cultural development. For Fernand Braudel (1972), the Mediterranean is time-less, definite, and central. Peregrine Horden and Nicholas Purcell (2000) emphasize the power of the sea to connect communities across the roughly two millennia spanning the Iron Age, Greco-Roman, and Medieval worlds. At no point prior to the early modern period was this sea more a focus of sustained and intense activity than the long Roman era, roughly 50 BCE to 700 CE. Horden and Purcell explore this distinctive flavor of classical Mediterranean maritime connectivity that has fostered parallel "Mediterranean-ization" paradigms across the globe (Abulafia 2005; Morris 2003). Cyprian Broodbank's (2013) compelling recent tome explores the formation of this particular connectivity in the much deeper Holocene and pre-Holocene past. For the later end of antiquity, Michael McCormick (2001) and Chris Wickham (2005) offer contrasting models for how seaborne connectivity, communication and commerce temporarily abated, or at least transformed, before reviving centuries later in proto–early modern forms.

However persuasive the conceptual framework of connectivity might be, to some degree it leaves a spatially and temporally unchanging maritime Mediterranean; it allows for a seemingly infinite range of connections, but lacks dynamism. The sea was a source of power, peace, and prosperity for Rome, reflected in the rather unsubtle title of "mare nostrum" (Sallust *Jug.* 17). From a spatial perspective, it is certainly the case that never before had this sea been so unified politically, had its waters been so freely crossed, or had key social and economic institutions so fully spanned the whole of the region. Growth in the number of shipwrecks is the most commonly cited evidence—but not without important caveats—in support of flourishing maritime communication and exchange during the height of the Roman empire (Parker 1992; 2008; cf. Wilson 2011:33–39). But beyond the sheer intensity of the situation, these figures can hardly tell the whole story since studies based on broad quantification tend to mask the diversity of local and regional responses to this new Roman reality. The Roman Mediterranean clearly offered unprecedented opportunity for the exploitation of maritime space, yet the question remains of how different communities chose to capitalize on such new prospects. In fact, understanding Roman power is perhaps impossible without studying the many facets of its varied interaction with the sea. While we can and should engage with the models so elegantly described by Braudel and others, we should not be constrained by a chrono-logically and geographically static Roman maritime landscape. The inhabitants of the ancient Mediterranean, like the modern denizens of Cyprus and so many other islands (Ilves 2011:4), harnessed the power and potential of the sea to widely varying degrees.

For the Roman maritime world, emphasis has long been placed on the expansive port networks and large-scale directed exchange that linked "consumer cities" across its tamed waters. The remarkable accomplishments of the empire's engineers in providing safe haven along any shore has been an important focus of recent work (Brandon et al. 2014; Keay and Paroli 2011), and such technological studies offer a critical window into the broader social and economic dynamics of harbor infrastructure in the ancient Mediterranean. But most importantly, it is the often bewildering density of mobility and connectedness evident in the archaeological record of exchange that has captured scholarly attention. Rich assemblages of imported ceramics can sometimes mislead us to the assumption that the sea brought everyone together in an undifferentiated network: whether through the grandest long-distance trade or the shortest coast-hopping cabotage, all communities around the sea were tied into a "Med Wide Web," or so a simple story might go.[3] Yet differential exploitation of the sea was probably as real in antiquity as it is today.

With the sea never far away for most Romans, the practical impact of this direct maritime access remains a critical factor for understanding daily life in antiquity. This issue is all the more acute beyond large urban ports given that even in this famous "world of cities" (Finley 1977:305) the ancient Mediterranean population was still overwhelmingly based in smaller towns and rural areas. From a socioeconomic standpoint, the most celebrated mode of interaction with the sea during the Roman era is certainly exchange, and this theme forms the central focus of concern for the present study. Trade and exchange rose to an unprecedented scale under Rome, and their social and economic importance must not be downplayed. Even so, seaborne commerce has long been assumed as the default raison d'être behind any coastal facility, or for that matter the economic livelihood of any coastal site. Drawing on case studies from the Baltic Sea region, Kristin Ilves (2011:6) has observed that "[t]he pronounced emphasis on trade has created a simplistic and almost deterministic understanding of landing sites," and this certainly seems applicable for Mediterranean contexts as well. Although the focus of the present study on economic opportunity created by maritime access in the Roman world necessarily looks deeply at seaborne exchange, it seeks to place this and other maritime economic activities—particularly fishing—within a broader contextual view of their spaces and material records.

How did the agricultural communities that formed a productive backbone of the Roman empire engage with the sea? To what extent were their economic impact and social connections mediated through large city centers and harbor networks? What role did smaller, secondary, and opportunistic ports play in structuring maritime interaction and socioeconomic life in their hinterlands? Were different communities in different localities tied into different seafaring practices and seaborne networks? In what ways, if any, did coastal access change the structure of rural socioeconomic life? Seminal contributions three decades ago by Geoffrey Rickman (1985; 1988) called for critical inquiry into the broader social context of small—sometimes ephemeral or seasonal, and often multiuse—coastal landing sites in the Roman world, but still our understanding of their function, and even our ability to identify them systematically within the broader landscape, remains limited (Houston 1988; Rogers 2013). The discussion that follows aims to explore and to evaluate the economic potential of the maritime landscape for these communities during the peaceful prosperity of the Roman era, from the resources and livelihoods it provided to the exchange opportunities it afforded.

APPROACHING ROMAN COASTAL ACTIVITIES

The eastern Mediterranean island of Cyprus provides an intriguing vantage point for this sort of archaeological exploration. Maritime survey fieldwork off its coasts over the past two decades has brought to light a series of simple coastal landing sites littered with artifacts but lacking built harbors and, at times, even the most basic infrastructure in the water or on the adjacent shore (Figure 11.1).[4] While Cyprus is known for its extensive harbor network associated with the larger coastal cities (Leonard 1995b; Theodoulou 2012), such small coves and inlets can be found every 5–10 km for much of the island's coast beyond these urban centers. Precisely when and by whom these spaces were utilized, and how they functioned within their local contexts of extensive settlement across the island, though, are unresolved questions. They remain largely outside the realm of urban-focused literary and historical records, and while comparative and ethnographic approaches hold some potential, archaeology must provide the ultimate testing for any maritime landscape models.

A fundamental methodological problem immediately arises in seeking answers to these questions through material culture: without durable built structures, the spaces are

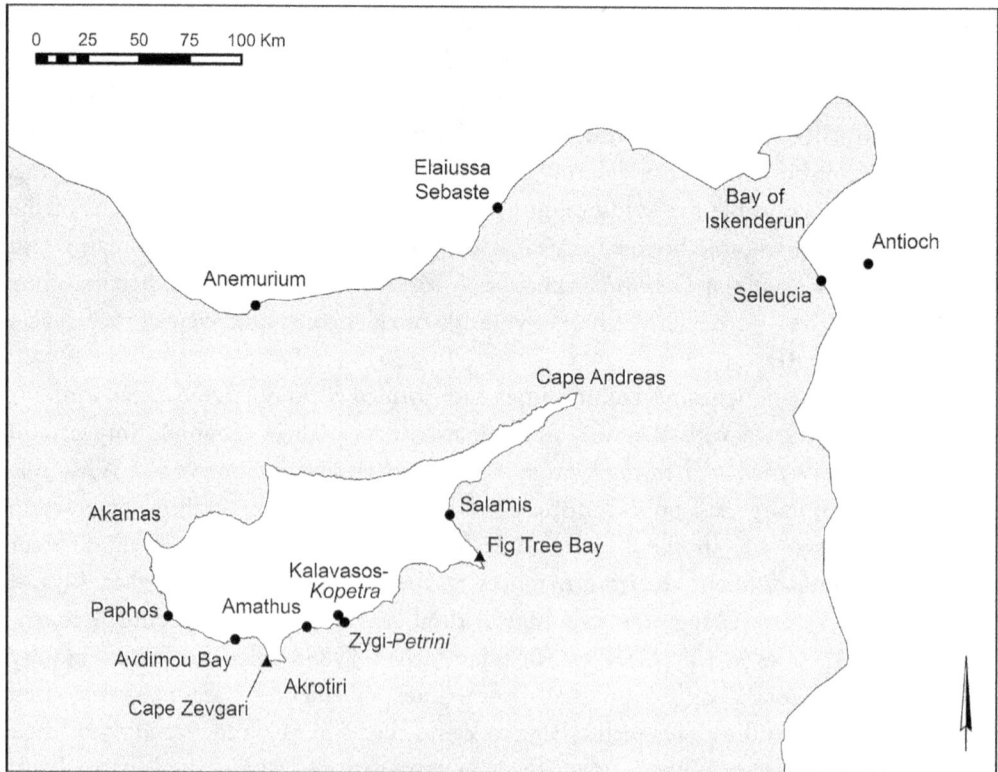

FIGURE 11.1 Map of Cyprus and the neighboring mainland showing sites mentioned in the text.

obviously difficult to recognize and their functions challenging to distinguish. A broad but clear and well-defined terminology is fundamental for embracing the rich assemblage of smaller secondary maritime sites with widely ranging functions within the maritime landscape. Here, Ilves's (2011) description, though drawing on Baltic Sea examples, applies well also within the Mediterranean world where the water was an ever-present resource for economic and social opportunity: "a landing site as a contact zone where movements and meetings on land and by watercraft take place and are facilitated by the locality as such." Best refined here to coastal landing sites—since our interest is seafaring activity on the Mediterranean rather than rivers, etc.—this definition shifts the emphasis away from the traditional scholarly preoccupation with harbors and provides a level baseline on which the various economic and social processes as well as their material culture signatures can be evaluated.

The transfer of goods is therefore not a safe assumption for all coastal landing sites, but it does provide a handy first context for exploring the material remains of certain spaces. Rome built the most extensive and complex port infrastructure of its day, yet the routine activities of loading and unloading goods and people can be undertaken, at least on a small scale, from nearly any strip of coast that is accessible in some capacity from both sea and land (Karmon 1985). Durable indicators such as a path or road to the interior, storage facilities, and a source of fresh water seem likely in some instances, but may not have been necessary in others. So long as vessels can stop—even temporarily— and goods can be maneuvered through the shallows, simple unadorned beaches might suffice in antiquity as they do in modern times. Temporarily grounding small vessels in the intertidal zone or pulling them up along the beach can require little manpower and no real infrastructure. The famous early-third-century CE mosaic from Sousse (Tunisia) appears to show a small boat rowed or towed into the shallows and unloaded by hand, accompanied by two figures with a balance scale, suggesting that trading activity could immediately take place at beachside locations (Figure 11.2 on page 222). Such distinctive archaeological signatures of exchange—scales, weights, coins, recording tablets, etc.—may be few, and are unlikely to be found through surface survey. Ceramic and other material remains may be more plentiful, but identifying an exchange context can be more problematic. Lost anchors, abandoned moorings, and discarded ballast may be associated with exchange, but could equally point to vessels simply seeking shelter at anchor rather than communication on shore. The casual debris—on and off shore—of transport jars (amphoras) broken at sea or during handling, and the worn or broken cooking and table wares that once served ships' crews, could likewise serve as indicators of an opportunistic port of exchange; but they could also be markers of jettison or other maritime activity.

Fishing shelters provide a less celebrated but still critical context for understanding Roman interaction with the sea. Probably the most detailed evidence at hand comes from the maritime villa installations created along the Italian coast to satisfy wealthy tastes for fine fish (Marzano 2007:161–166, 2015), but certainly numerous other sites served fishermen outside these elite contexts. A simple wooden dock, improvised several decades ago by resourceful locals, effectively created a small seasonal fishing shelter at an otherwise unpromising inlet below the precipitous cliff west of ancient Kourion along

FIGURE 11.2 Roman mosaic, now in the Bardo Museum in Tunis but originally from Sousse (Hadrumetum), showing beachside merchant activity. The merchant vessel is being unloaded directly in the shallows without port infrastructure while two others at left are engaged in measuring goods for exchange (Scala/Art Resource, NY).

Cyprus's south coast (Figures 11.1, 11.3, 11.4). Even this basic jetty would in many cases have been unnecessary, and landing sites for fishermen today in the coastal communities of the Mediterranean sometimes lack this basic infrastructure. John Leonard's (1995a:150,

FIGURE 11.3 Overview of the inlet situated beneath the cliffs west of Kourion, with simple wooden docks of the fishing port created in modern times.

FIGURE 11.4 View of the boats and docks in the opportunistic fishing port located below the cliffs west of Kourion.

fig. 25) interview with a single fisherman moored in the shallows of the small cove at Drousha-*Kioni*, off the west of Cyprus's Akamas peninsula (Figure 11.1), underscores the adaptability of spaces for small-scale fishing operations. Proper natural shelter from the spectrum of possible winds and waves may also be overrated if one considers the reliability of prevailing conditions for what was most often probably a seasonal occupation restricted to the calmer late spring through early autumn months. For the coast of southern Cyprus, winds from directions other than the west are highly unusual during the major seafaring season (Heikell 2006:316–317; UKHO 2008:194), meaning that any basic shelter from these westerlies could do; the several fishermen moored seasonally in the shallows of south-facing Avdimou Bay, about 10 km west of Kourion, move their vessels into more protected harbors or bring them ashore during the stormy winter months. While nets, lines, and floats are unlikely to survive, any weights, fittings, and tools for their repair are possible markers; at the same time, such implements have been found in small quantities routinely on board transport vessels as a source of provisioning the crew (Beltrame 2010). Discarded ceramics for temporary storage, preparation, and consumption of food could signal such a fishing site assemblage. Water and a path or road to the interior are again advantageous, but by no means necessary for small-scale operations where equipment, supplies, and catch could be carried by hand.

The modern makeshift fishing shelter west of Kourion underscores several critical issues in the interpretation of these ancient sites. Reports hint at metal anchors removed from the water in the twentieth century, though at present no firm evidence points to this area's use in antiquity as a landing site. Reliable access to the inlet in the modern era only became possible for vehicles with the cutting of a road to facilitate retrieval of sand for a nearby construction project. Once this initial purpose was satisfied, the durability of a path intended to be temporary allowed the area to be repurposed as a basic fishing shelter through the addition of the wooden jetty. While sand removal is unlikely to have been a substantial activity for ancient coastal communities, the example here points to another critical factor: the shifting or overlapping material manifestations associated with changing uses or multiple contemporaneous uses can further complicate the interpretation of local maritime landscapes. In many cases, these spaces could have simultaneously accommodated exchange, fishing, and likely other activities, some on a more routine basis, others only occasionally. Disentangling these complementary local uses may be difficult, and for good reason since their material culture, and in many instances the personnel involved, might be identical. Distinguishing the residue of coastal landing sites from those in shallow waters produced by seafaring activities that had little or no contact on shore (e.g., overnight anchoring) may likewise be problematic. Can we differentiate between contact and active engagement with coastal landing sites and their associated resources on the one hand, and passing traffic on the other? Many sites on Cyprus and elsewhere were topographically appropriate for a wide range of functions—loading zones, exchange ports, fishing coves, shipbuilding and repair, or overnight anchorages—and as mentioned above, even some topographically unlikely sites could serve any of these purposes as necessary. Their material assemblages may at times be quite similar, at least to surface survey, but the economic and social implications for their nearby residents are drastically different. Archaeological investigations of maritime landscapes in the Baltic Sea have revealed remarkable diversity of the sort we might expect to see also in the Mediterranean: seasonal or temporary fishing shelters, yards for the repair and breakup of vessels, and opportunistic anchorages with only minimal and constrained connections onshore (Ilves 2004, 2009, 2011; Westerdahl 1992, 2011). The process of identifying these maritime landscapes and their mercantile, fishing, and other seafaring communities must proceed from a ground-level evaluation of material and topographical signatures; in the end, any plausible identifications will depend on the cumulative weight of many otherwise equivocal factors.

How did these coastal landing sites function within their local contexts? What practical social and economic effects did they have for their communities? To what extent did they empower those living outside urban centers to develop their own economic resources and seaborne connections? In pursuing these questions, we must also examine not only the relationships among different types of sites—fishing, commerce, anchorage, boatyards, etc.—but the connections among different scales of each site, particularly for the ports of exchange that specifically looked outward across the water: in general, the largest Roman urban harbors probably drew traffic more widely and operated logistically differently from minor outlying coastal ports, and also from the small but well-built shelters or simple jetties associated with maritime villas (Schörle 2011). Should we imagine these as participating in the same sorts of maritime structures and networks proposed for larger-scale facilities? These should be questions of central importance in light of recent network theory studies of maritime connectivity (Leidwanger et al. 2014; Preiser-Kapeller and Daim 2015).

Network approaches have tended to evaluate the Mediterranean system broadly, stressing not only the complexity and expansiveness of sea routes in the Roman world, but the integrity and coherence of an overall maritime network. Walter Scheidel's (2013, 2014) ORBIS geospatial network uses costs in travel times to evaluate the structure and performance of connectivity across the whole of the Roman world. Pascal Arnaud (2005:107ff) characterizes Roman commerce as "navigation segmentée," in which larger warehouse ports typically located four to five days apart served as central hubs from which goods continued along smaller, more localized routes between secondary urban ports. It is perhaps most natural to think in such "dendritic"—or, to borrow riverine terminology, "tributary" and "distributary"—terms; Carol Smith's (1974, 1976) pioneering economic geography work on early markets speaks to the appeal of such models for understanding and representing politically centralized and complex urban societies such as Rome. Such a system would have been broadly the most efficient maritime network solution *if* efficiency and transaction costs across the whole system are the key criteria and *if* the maritime activity that contributes to connectivity is limited solely to economic exchange. If so, we should expect "local ports" to be connected to "regional ports" of nearby city centers, which in turn were linked to larger emporia, and so on until one reaches the gates of Rome.

Such a model, however, tends to obscure the true range and diversity of coastal landing sites and associated activities evident in the maritime material record. It also largely eschews the multivalent social factors that contribute to the formation of maritime traditions in favor of a purely economic motive and exchange-dominated model. Yet neither exchange nor economy in general can be disentangled from their social context, which is crucial for understanding the local function and broad implications of such sites for daily life. Along Cyprus, small facilities served a range of purposes, and local exchange was often part of this activity. Yet even this function as opportunistic locations for import and export could itself reflect a complex interplay of primary shipment from countryside to nearby port cities, cabotage or coast-hugging exchange, and direct overseas exchange around the island and beyond. In focusing on the social importance of these spaces within the busy and dynamic Cypriot countryside, I would like to draw attention to the role of coastal landing sites in fundamentally shifting the geography of distribution during the Roman and late Roman eras. Dense maritime opportunity and ease of mobility—both on and around the island—created a low threshold for seaborne connectivity. Easy maritime access allowed communities to forge new links, widen local economic horizons, launch a new, distinct, and regionally integrated economic sphere, and in turn transform socioeconomic life more generally across parts of the countryside. Some coastal landing sites may themselves have become spaces of community gathering for markets and the like. Beyond exchange, growing and diversifying utilization of these maritime sites may also have helped to foster parallel seafaring activities such as fishing that naturally expanded the maritime reach of these communities. This sort of maritime landscape model would reflect significant power transference, and an inversion of the typical core-periphery relations that still underlie most discussions of town-country economic dynamics around the urban centers of Cyprus and beyond. As such, it has important implications for how we understand the relationship between water and power across the ancient Mediterranean.

EXPLOITING THE COASTS OF ROMAN CYPRUS

Along Cyprus's south coast, Avdimou Bay provides a useful first case study (Figures 11.1, 11.5). Once the outlet for the Avdimou River, the cove today serves as a seasonal base for a few fishermen, and its deep history of maritime use is quickly apparent. A small shrine on shore here is said to commemorate the landing and first martyr of the Mamluk invasion of the island in the early fifteenth century, and until 1974 the area was primarily Turkish-Cypriot (Swiny 1982:161). Ruined carob stores stand prominently just to the east, where the remains of a simple iron pier attest to maritime export (and perhaps import) activity of this important island commodity over the last few centuries (Leonard 2005:570–571). Clearly, ancient mariners also recognized Avdimou Bay's potential as a temporary shelter against the prevailing westerly winds. A scatter of ceramics and various simple weight anchors in stone rest on the sandy seabed near the western edge, currently only 3–4 m deep, suggesting small vessels with shallow draught. This western edge of the bay behind the headland, though small, was among the most naturally protected landing sites in the area. If use of the bay in antiquity extended farther to the east, in

FIGURE 11.5 View of the beach and cove at Avdimou Bay from the east. Scattered ceramics have been observed on the headland at the far end of the bay as well as around the low hill from which the picture is taken.

the area of the river mouth or beyond, any associated cultural material is likely buried by substantial sediment and longshore drift. The beach near the western edge is narrow but low, facilitating the easy dragging of small vessels onto shore. Pottery scattered on shore, particularly eroding out of the headland to the west and around the hill near the shrine at the center of the bay, includes a few probable Hellenistic and Roman wares, but the record is dominated by late Roman amphoras, particularly from Cilicia and the Gaza/Ashkelon regions, and perhaps some southern Cypriot products as well. A small and much-disturbed assemblage in the shallows here likely reflects all that remains of a shipwreck of similar late antique date (Leidwanger 2007:311–313). Despite substantial pottery and a well-eroded context, the site shows no discernible architecture that can be connected to port infrastructure. Nonetheless, a simple earthen road has been traced branching off from the main coastal circuit and leading down to the bay (Bekker-Nielsen 2004:218), suggesting some integration of this coastal feature with the inland local landscape and beyond.

How, then, was this bay utilized in antiquity? The anchors could point to any number of activities, although their size and simple technology are most appropriate for small-scale vessels.[5] The scattered late Roman shipwreck and pottery of similar date and origin onshore seem most easily explicable by some level of basic commercial activity. Yet just as today, fishing may have been a key component of the local maritime economy. The bay may then have served well as an easy multipurpose fishing shelter and transshipment point for local agricultural produce from around the Avdimou River valley, particularly during late antiquity.

East of Avdimou, Zygi-*Petrini*, situated near the Vasilikos Valley mouth, may have served as another such multipurpose site (Figure 11.1). The beach is only minimally sheltered from predominant easterly winds. No proper port infrastructure appears in the sea, but a series of buildings are evident just above the water level eroding from the scarp, and more may have been lost in recent years to these devastating coastal processes. Ceramic evidence on shore as well as pottery and anchors underwater point to maritime activity along this coastal stretch since the Late Bronze Age (Manning et al. 2002), but the late Roman period seems particularly prominent in the local material record (Manning 2002:77–78; Todd 2004:183–184, 2013:106–108). The structures on shore are best connected to this late flourish, and seem to include workshops with kilns for the production of Late Roman 1 transport amphoras (Manning et al. 2000). Marcus Rautman (2003:241) has reasonably concluded that "[t]he seaside setting and period of occupation suggest that *Petrini* was one of many small commercial points along the [south] coast that prospered as ships anchored offshore to take on and unload their cargoes." Located approximately 1 km east of the Vasilikos River mouth, *Petrini* was well-situated to take advantage of traffic across the coastal plain, up the Vasilikos Valley, and perhaps as far as the adjacent Maroni Valley, which also saw substantial settlement and economic activity during the late Roman centuries and probably had a second rudimentary anchorage nearby (Manning 2002:77–78; Manning et al. 2002:119–121). Fishing may again have been part of the local maritime activity, and the low-lying beach would have offered an ideal setting for boat construction, repair, and storage.

A key rationale behind selecting *Petrini* as a case study is its comparatively well-documented and well-published hinterland that offers glimpses into the daily life of those whose social and economic activities may have intersected with the use of this local maritime facility. Survey in the Vasilikos Valley brought to light at least 32 sites during the prosperous early Roman period, a number that rises to 44 during the unprecedentedly prosperous late Roman centuries (Rautman 2003; Todd 2004, 2013). The most prominent local town, with some 600 residents during late antiquity, was located 4 km up the river at Kalavasos-*Kopetra*. The rich ceramic repertoire and range of imports point to its flourish and probable function as a local redistribution center. Rautman's work at *Kopetra* offers an outstanding window into the overseas products—at least those that arrived in durable transport amphoras—that found their way to such a rural market town (Rautman 2003:168–175, 169 tbl. 5.5; Rautman et al. 1999; Rautman 2013). Three-fifths (59.3 percent) of the transport amphora assemblage is comprised of Cilician and northwest Syrian imports. Other imported jars are relatively few, but include southern Levantine, Egyptian, and Aegean types (1.3 percent, 0.1 percent). Imports here reflect an enormous percentage of the overall assemblage, larger even than local amphoras, yet they were drawn almost exclusively from a restricted area along the neighboring mainland. During this same period, Cyprus's larger port cities record substantial numbers of imports as well, including Amathus, the nearest major harbor to *Petrini* (Kaldeli 2008). Assemblages there, however, exhibit a range of materials drawn more widely from not only the island but the whole of the Mediterranean, with extraregional links not seen at *Petrini*. The material evidence points to two distinct spatial networks of maritime exchange centered on different ports and commodities, and probably also different ships and agents.[6]

Just how convenient were coastal landing sites for day-to-day life in their hinterlands? How easily and reliably reached were *Petrini*, Avdimou Bay, or other similar locations? A basic sense of mobility and human geography can be achieved through GIS-based estimates of travel times derived from local topography.[7] Results of such analyses are always tentative, reflecting in general an average figure under good conditions, and not without a variety of caveats regarding data and interpretation (Connolly and Lake 2006:253–256; Kantner 2012). Nonetheless, these figures can give a general picture of each site's catchment community and allow comparability across landscapes (Figure 11.6). In the case of *Petrini*, analysis suggests that none of the major towns, and even very few of the smaller sites up the Vasilikos Valley, were more than a four-hour trip—and many a two-hour trip—away from *Petrini* on foot or by cart. Contrast this with approximately eight hours for a trip from most of these locations to the nearest major harbor at Amathus. The latter journey would have been easier given the coastal road, but hardly practical on a routine basis for such activities as daily buying and selling of wares in the market. On the other hand, *Petrini* was easily reachable for routine day trips, an ideal candidate for the collection and redistribution of agricultural produce, marine and other goods by sea, and perhaps even as an occasional place of market activity itself.

What sorts of mariners used these coastal landing sites? Certainly, these spaces appear to have been the domain of small vessels. Very few archaeological remains have

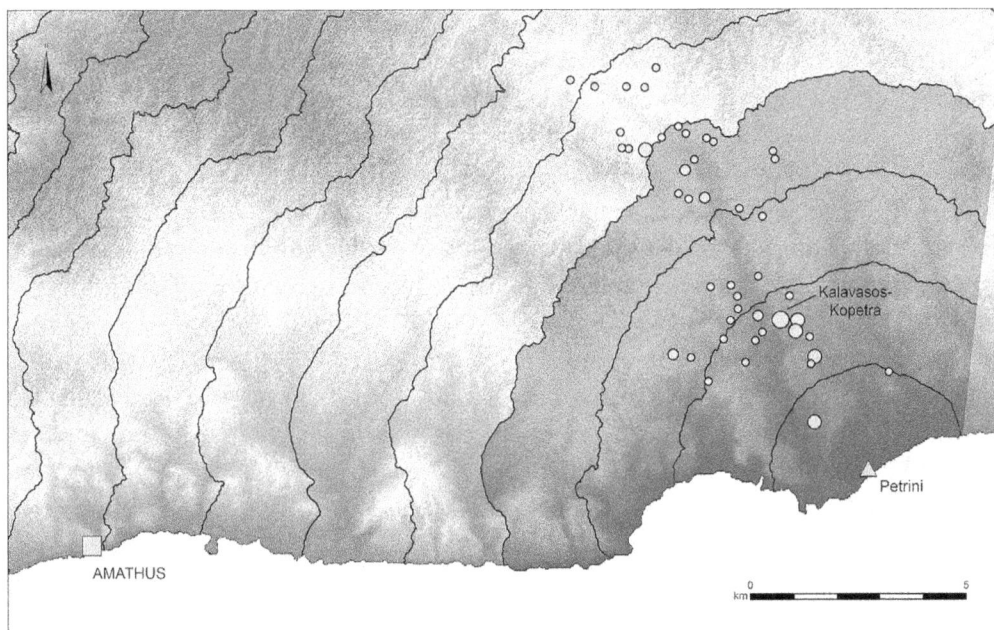

FIGURE 11.6 Approximate travel times, represented as 1-hour contours, from Zygi-*Petrini* throughout the Vasilikos Valley and as far as Amathus. Sites in the Vasilikos Valley are based on data from Rautman 2003, with Kalavasos-*Kopetra* shown most prominently.

been persuasively classified as fishing boats, and all belong to vessels no longer than 10 m. The best identification to date of a Roman fishing craft—made on the basis of a peculiar tank within the hull intended for carrying live fish—is only 5.6 m in length, Fiumicino 5 from Portus near Rome (Boetto 2006, 2010). Such distinctive archaeological signatures, however, are rare within a group of vessels that are otherwise simply nondescript small boats. Certainly this is part of the reason why fishing boats feature so rarely in the scholarly literature, where small vessels—often only found thanks to their cargos—are generally assumed (by archaeologists interested in exchange) to be coastal traders. The interdependence of small-scale movements of goods and people along the coast no doubt meant that vessels of similar size could variously be called fishing boats, local merchant craft, or simply multipurpose boats, used for fishing, trade, or the transfer of people depending on need. Two small early Roman craft found without cargos at Herculaneum and along the Sea of Galilee may reflect just these multifaceted processes at work (Steffy 1985; Wachsmann 2000). Merchant ships frequenting such landing sites probably also were quite small, much like the one that sank in Avdimou Bay. Only a few wrecks around the island have been surveyed in sufficient detail to provide estimates of cargo size, but study of the second-century CE Fig Tree Bay shipwreck off the southeast coast brought to light four to five tons of agricultural goods carried in fewer than

150 amphoras, the overwhelming majority of which were produced on the neighboring mainland of Cilicia and northwest Syria (Leidwanger 2013a). One late Roman shipwreck explored at Cape Zevgari foundered while carrying its agricultural load in just 150 or so diverse amphoras, perhaps of eastern Cilician manufacture, amounting to no more than five tons (Leidwanger 2007:308–311).

Hand in hand with these simple and small craft went short sailing distances. We might once again imagine small-scale fishermen largely relegated to their own known coastal waters. Boetto (2006, 2010) argues that the construction and propulsion of the Fiumicino 5 wreck would have limited its operations to the Tiber River and delta, nearby lagoons, and perhaps limited near-shore ventures. For merchantmen, understanding the duration of journeys is fundamental to gauging how routine activities might have established the basic socioeconomic patterns of coastal landing sites such as *Petrini* and Avdimou Bay. Geographic Information Systems (GIS) can again provide some sense of journey times and perhaps the rhythm of a maritime landscape (Leidwanger 2013).[8] Trips such as those indicated in the Fig Tree Bay and Cape Zevgari wreck assemblages need not have included extensive open-water voyages or long durations at sea. In average winds, the short crossing between southern Cyprus and the adjacent mainland of eastern Cilicia and northwest Syria could have been accomplished in perhaps two days (Figures 11.7, 11.8). A trip from nearly

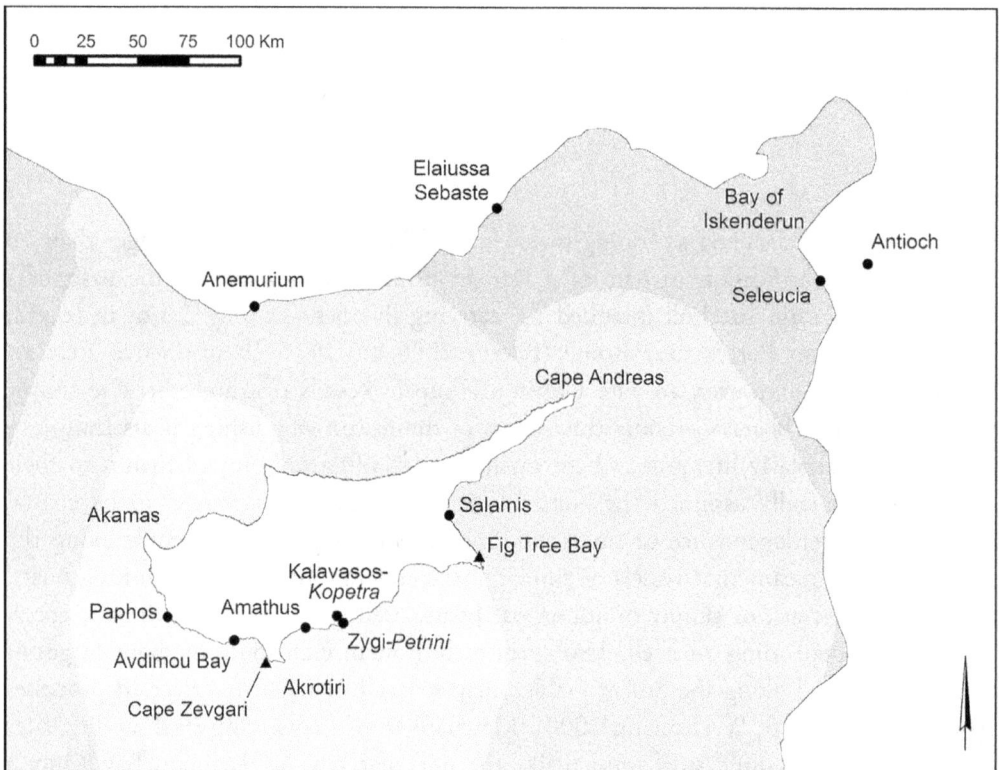

FIGURE 11.7 Approximate sailing times, represented as 1-day contours, from Cyprus to the opposite mainland, based on an origin at Paphos.

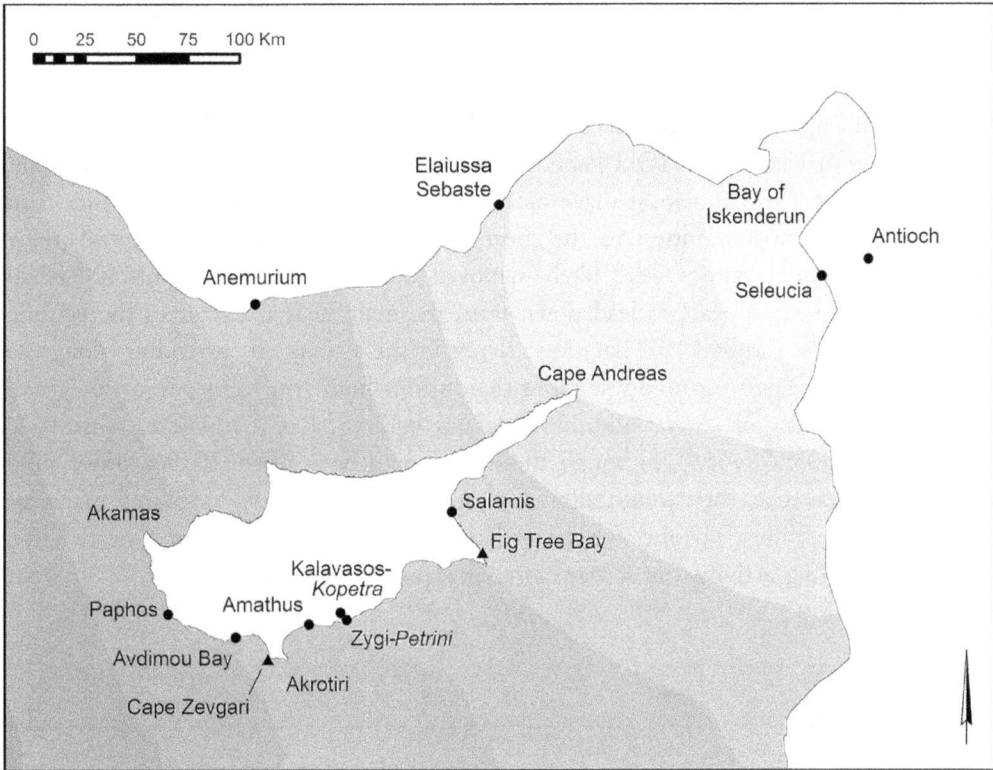

FIGURE 11.8 Approximate sailing times, represented as 1-day contours, from the mainland to Cyprus, based on an origin at Seleucia.

anywhere along the island to this coast could have been completed easily within a span of less than a week or slightly more. Realistically, journey times were probably even shorter; unlike sailors headed off on long trips, a small-time mariner traversing these distances probably had more freedom to wait out an unhelpful wind or ominous sky. The records of consumption and cargos suggest a distinctly local and regional scale of activity for the merchants and other mariners who frequented these coastal landing sites, quite distinct from the grander contours of Mediterranean connectivity.

How widespread was this busy maritime landscape phenomenon? If one goal of the present evaluation of evidence for coastal activity is the diversification of the maritime landscape and appreciation of the range of community interactions with the sea, then we should not imply that it was universal or consistent across space and time. Even in an area as richly studied as Cyprus, with large-scale terrestrial survey as well as sustained maritime and underwater investigations, it is exceedingly rare that the complementary detailed evidence is available to ascertain individual coastal landing site hinterlands, let alone their contrasting material culture imprints, as at *Kopetra*. Yet even in the fragmentary record, some evidence hints that the examples discussed here are not unique

(Figure 11.9). One intriguing case study comes from the island's administrative center under Rome, Paphos, together with its eastward sprawl of towns, villages, and farmsteads identified by David Rupp through the Canadian Palaipaphos Survey Project (Rupp 1997; Sørensen and Rupp 1993). More recent work offshore directly south of the millennium-old sanctuary site of Palaipaphos (Old Paphos), approximately 17 km to the east of Paphos, brought to light a thriving local maritime stop with no real infrastructure. More than 120 simple stone anchors attest to the sheer intensity of maritime activity, and many more anchors and ceramics were likely removed in recent decades (Howitt-Marshall 2012). A short spur appears to lead down from the main coastal circuit to the landing site (Bekker-Nielsen 2004:119). For those living in the settlements extending along the island's southwest coast, no one was more than a four-hour trip from one of these two sites. The possibility of several additional coastal landing sites in this area was raised by Leonard (2005:577–584), although these remain to be verified. If they prove valid and contemporaneous, they would allow for an even more intensely localized maritime landscape where almost no one was more than two or three hours from a nearby site, whether for fishing activity, quick transport, or export/import by sea.

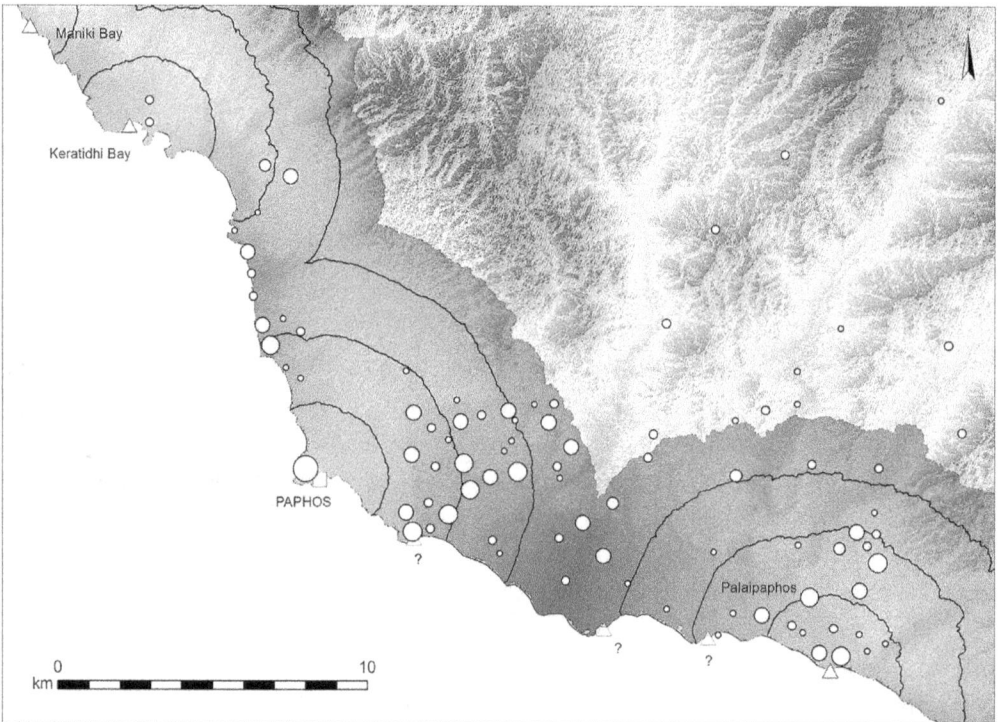

FIGURE 11.9 Approximate travel times, represented as 1-hour contours, from known coastal maritime sites around Paphos. The three potential maritime sites identified by Leonard (2005) are shown east of Paphos but have not been included in the analysis. Data for the settlements is based on Rupp 1997 and Sørensen and Rupp 1993, while maritime sites are based on Howitt-Marshall 2003 and 2012, and Leonard 2005.

Given the nature of preservation, the present archaeological exploration of coastal sites draws heavily on the movement of pottery, particularly durable transport amphoras, with the result that trade and exchange feature more prominently in the discussion than fishing, for which the material record is even more ephemeral. Yet this should not lead us to conclude that the economic—or the social—impact of fishing within such communities was insignificant. Perhaps the most obvious testimony to the utilization of this marine resource in general across the Mediterranean was the presence of fish processing installations, which represent in certain contexts an important economic investment with no doubt significant social ramifications (Wilson 2006). Epigraphic records attest to routine taxes on fish brought into harbor for sale in several urban contexts (e.g., Ephesus, Kaunos: Marzano 2013:243–245), but little evidence is available for the importance of fishing in the local maritime landscape and economy outside the larger cities. On Cyprus, the inclusion of various fishing implements in a domestic dump context at the small late antique site of Ayios Kononas, near the anchorage of Kioni, suggests that this simple inlet sufficed in antiquity as it does today for local fishing (Papacostas 2001:120). John Lund's (2002) attribution of a popular form of western Cypriot frying pan—accounting for 12 percent of the ceramic finds of survey in this same Akamas region—to the preparation of small fish meals would seem to indicate a prominent role for fishing in the local economy. Basic rock-cut and occasionally more elaborate fishponds are known from the island, and although the simple versions are difficult to date confidently, most were likely operational in the Roman era (Marzano 2013:206 and 226–227; Nicolaou 1976). The small size of fishing boats and often the seasonality of this occupation meant that useful landing sites could arise seemingly anywhere along the coast. Traditional small-scale fishermen in Morocco today utilize more than 90 landing sites in only 512 km of Mediterranean coastline (on average only 5.69 km between sites), and Italy boasts some 800 along its 8,000 km of coast.[9] Shared infrastructure and traditions may support the logical assumption that fishing was often carried out alongside maritime exchange, as implied by the Fiumicino 5 fishing vessel found together with merchant craft at Portus. Scholars have long linked the two fundamental maritime activities, raising the possibility that an expansion of fishing may have helped to give rise to prehistoric seaborne trade (Bintliff 1977:117–122; Powell 1996:54). The two practices are probably more deeply connected than the model outlined here, but little evidence is at hand to push the suggestion further.

TOWARD A MARITIME SOCIOECONOMIC LANDSCAPE FOR CYPRUS

Issuing a call for scholarly attention to the modern history of what he termed "unimportant ports," Gordon Jackson (2001:7) challenged that "we should forget about their comparative status and study them for what they did on their own terms and within the overall port system." From an economic and social standpoint, their contribution extended beyond outposts of the larger urban harbors; they variously functioned as market nodes, engaged in fishing as well as direct exchange overseas, and served myriad communities active on the water. Unimportant ports and the broader swath of Roman coastal landing sites merit similar attention and should take on new importance alongside recent emphasis on the large-scale harbor networks of the ancient Mediterranean. Fishing and exchange are just two of the economic activities that drew locals to their nearby coasts. Distinguishing confidently on the basis of archaeology between these and other seaside pursuits—like construction, layup, and breaking of ships—will be impossible without systematic coastal survey, and exploring the social and economic interdependence of these different activities is of paramount importance for understanding their role in local communities across the Mediterranean. Equally critical are defining and analyzing these various coastal landing sites in such a way that makes them explicit and testable against the material record both on- and offshore (Ilves 2009).

With its communities clustered along the narrow coastal plains and up river valleys at the Troodos foothills, south and southwest Cyprus offers a quintessential Mediterranean topography and an ideal case study through which to explore the patterning of seagoing activities among communities and the creation more generally of different facets of maritime consciousness. A closer look at the spatial relationships within and among coastal sites reveals a complex negotiation of power and centrality, in which access to the sea and the agency to exploit resources and to distribute agricultural surplus played a key role. These examples illustrate how a dense network of maritime facilities and ease of mobility on and around the island aided the development of extra-urban seafaring dynamics. Opportunistic coastal landing sites provided the crucial focal points for quick maritime access throughout the landscape as well as short sails to destinations elsewhere across the island and beyond to the opposite mainland. In this way, water formed a fundamental organizing principle behind the emergence of a distinctly regional socioeconomic community.

And yet, even as Cyprus increasingly exploited its maritime resources on a variety of scales, not all islanders cared about the sea. With the incorporation of Cyprus into the Roman state and expanding settlement and productivity in the countryside, new roads began to connect cities with their respective hinterlands in a secondary network tied into the broader coastal circuit completed largely during the Hellenistic period (Bekker-Nielsen 2004:230). The primary purpose for this transportation infrastructure was surely to integrate the cities into an efficient urban-oriented political unit. The concurrent development of outlying maritime sites and city-centered local road networks raises issues regarding potential shifts in economic power and productivity across the island, with urban areas taking steps to exert territorial control and to ensure their own supply from nearby towns, villages, and farmsteads. Meanwhile, some rural areas ensured their own autonomy by engaging more directly with separate maritime centers around the island and across the sea. Cities may have remained at the center of certain types of daily, year-round, and especially elite market exchange, but the increasing productivity of the countryside indicates new wealth and economic potential outside Cyprus's traditional urban areas. Here, Rupp's (1997) description of the environs east of Paphos as "suburban" might not wholly fit the economic or social situation, which might better be described not as peripheries but as small centers unto themselves. In these hinterlands, a rural elite certainly controlled substantial sectors of agricultural and other production as well as certain mechanisms of exchange (Rautman 2001:255). Their wealth and economic independence are reflected in their expenditures—including imported marble and the like—on public displays of civic pride situated very much within their own local communities (Papacostas 2001:115–121). The sea offered new opportunities to multiple people at multiple scales for agency and control over the movement of goods to, from, and across the sea. With the impetus of both terrestrial ants and amphibious frogs, the development of the maritime landscape and the accompanying exploitation of economic resources alongside and across the sea fundamentally changed the traditional rhythms of rural life in Roman and late antique Cyprus.

ACKNOWLEDGMENTS

Much of the initial intellectual stimulation for the present inquiry was provided by seven seasons of survey fieldwork off the coast of Cyprus (2003–2009), for which gratitude is owed to the Department of Antiquities as well as various sponsoring institutions whose financial and logistical support facilitated the work. The reactions from several test audiences in the past have been helpful for developing different components of this research, and special thanks are due to Elizabeth S. Greene for thoughts on the present text. The ideas here were much improved from their initial presentation thanks to lively discussion and exchange through the IEMA conference and community, and I am grateful to Emily Holt for the opportunity to participate.

NOTES

1. On Cyprus's most prominent inward turn for several millennia before and during the Early Bronze Age, see Broodbank 2013:342–343. To cite just one example, perhaps nowhere is this preconception as wrong as in diet. While fish is often highly prized, the Cypriot table today is dominated by meat, with per capita consumption of pork, chicken, beef, and mutton each eclipsing that of fish; pork consumption is nearly fivefold that of fish. See Stephanou 1996 and 2007.

2. A recent and notable exception is Ober (2015:61–70), who focuses on the ants of Plato's pond as successful examples of the communication and information exchange upon which participatory democracy is predicated.

3. I adapt the term "Med Wide Web" from Malkin's (2011:25) description of the "Greek Wide Web" of the Archaic Mediterranean.

4. In addition to intermittent earlier surveys for ports, anchorages, and other maritime sites (Giangrande et al. 1987), fieldwork during the 1990s and 2000s preliminarily documented large stretches of the Cypriot coastline, especially along its southwest, south, and southeast coasts: see Leonard 2005 in general, along with Howitt-Marshall 2003; Howitt-Marshall 2012; Leidwanger 2005; Leidwanger 2007; Leonard and Hohlfelder 1993.

5. This simple technology was probably sufficient to meet the needs of fishing vessels, but is also well attested in the context of merchant vessels traveling occasionally over longer distances, for example on the Dor D wreck in Israel: see Kingsley 2002:9–10.

6. Kaldeli's (2008:153–158, 238–241, and 500 tbl. 13 and fig. 23) quantification of transport amphoras from several urban contexts at Amathus show that products from around Cyprus comprise the greatest part of the assemblage at 63.3 percent; the southern Levant

and Egypt are well represented at 20.8 percent, while at 7.8 percent Aegean finds are not uncommon. Perhaps surprisingly, Cilicia and Syria/Lebanon account for just 3.0 percent of the imports, less than those farther-flung examples from the western Mediterranean at 5.2 percent.

7.   GIS analysis undertaken here was accomplished using ArcGIS 10.2.2. Estimates of time were derived through the Cost Distance tools using a table of values based on Tobler's Hiking Function (Gorenflo and Gale 1990; Tobler 1993).

8.   The GIS models utilized for these time calculations are based on average sailing times in different wind conditions (direction and strength) as outlined in Leidwanger 2013b.

9.   Figures are provided by Henri Farrugio in his 2013 report to the General Fisheries Commission for the Mediterranean ("Current situation of small-scale fisheries in the Mediterranean and Black Sea: strategies and methodologies for an effective analysis of the sector"), which draws on various United Nations Food and Agriculture Organization projects: http://www.ssfsymposium.org/Documents/FullVersion/BPI.pdf; accessed November 6, 2015.

REFERENCES CITED

Abulafia, D. 2005 Mediterraneans. In *Rethinking the Mediterranean*, edited by W.V. Harris, pp. 64–93. Oxford University Press, Oxford.

Arnaud, P. 2005 *Les routes de la navigation antique: itinéraires en Méditerranée*. Éditions Errance, Paris.

Bekker-Nielsen, T. 2004 *The Roads of Ancient Cyprus*. Museum Tusculanum, Copenhagen.

Beltrame, C. 2010 Fishing from Ships. Fishing Techniques in the Light of Nautical Archaeology. In *Ancient Nets and Fishing Gear. Proceedings of the International Workshop on "Nets and Fishing Gear in Classical Antiquity: A First Approach," Cádiz, November 15–17, 2007*, edited by T. Bekker-Nielsen and D. Bernal Casasola, pp. 229–241. Universidad de Cádiz and Aarhus University Press, Cádiz.

Bintliff, J. L. 1977 *Natural Environment and Human Settlement in Prehistoric Greece; Based on Original Fieldwork*. BAR-IS 28. British Archaeological Reports, Oxford.

Boetto, G. 2006 Roman Techniques for the Transport and Conservation of Fish: the Case of the Fiumicino 5 Wreck. In *Connected by the Sea. Proceedings of the Tenth International Symposium on Boat and Ship Archaeology, Roskilde, 2003*, edited by L. Blue, F. Hocker, and A. Englert, pp. 123–129. Oxbow, Oxford.

Boetto, G. 2010 Fishing Vessels in Antiquity: the Archaeological Evidence from Ostia. In *Ancient Nets and Fishing Gear. Proceedings of the International Workshop on "Nets and Fishing Gear in Classical Antiquity: A First Approach," Cádiz, November 15–17, 2007*, edited by T. Bekker-Nielsen and D. Bernal Casasola, pp. 243–255. Universidad de Cádiz and Aarhus University Press, Cádiz.

Brandon, C. J., R. L. Hohlfelder, M. D. Jackson, and J. P. Oleson. 2014 *Building for Eternity: The History and Technology of Roman Concrete Engineering in the Sea*. Oxbow, Oxford.

Braudel, F. 1972 *The Mediterranean and the Mediterranean World in the Age of Philip II*. Translated by S. Reynolds. Harper Colophon Books, New York. Original edition, 1949, Colin, Paris.

Broodbank, C. 2013 *The Making of the Middle Sea: A History of the Mediterranean from the Beginning to the Threshold of the Classical World*. Oxford University Press, Oxford.

Conolly, J., and M. Lake. 2006 *Geographic Information Systems in Archaeology*. Cambridge University Press, Cambridge.

Finley, M. I. 1977 The Ancient City: from Fustel de Coulanges to Max Weber and Beyond. *Comparative Studies in Society and History* 19(3):305–327.

Giangrande, C., G. Richards, D. Kennet, and J. Adams. 1987 Cyprus Underwater Survey, 1983–1984: A Preliminary Report. *Report of the Department of Antiquities Cyprus*:185–197.

Gorenflo, L. J., and N. Gale. 1990. Mapping Regional Settlement in Information Space. *Journal of Anthropological Archaeology* 9:240–274.

Heikell, R. 2006 *Turkish Waters & Cyprus Pilot*, 7th edition. Imray Laurie Norie & Wilson, St. Ives.

Horden, P., and N. Purcell. 2000 *The Corrupting Sea: a Study of Mediterranean History*. Blackwell, Oxford.

Howitt-Marshall, D. S. 2003 Cyprus Underwater Project 2002: a Preliminary Report. *Enalia* 7:28–37.

Howitt-Marshall, D. S. 2012 The Anchorage Site of Kouklia-*Achni*, Southwest Cyprus: Problems and Perspectives. In *Cyprus: An Island Culture. Society and Social Relations from the Bronze Age to the Venetian Period*, edited by A. Georgiou, pp. 104–121. Oxbow, Oxford.

Houston, G. W. 1988 Ports in Perspective: Some Comparative Materials on Roman Merchant Ships and Ports. *American Journal of Archaeology* 92(4):553–564.

Ilves, K. 2004 The Seaman's Perspective in Landscape Archaeology: Landing Sites on the Maritime Landscape. *Estonian Journal of Archaeology* 8(2):163–180.

Ilves, K. 2009 Discovering Harbours? Reflection on the State and Development of Landing Site Studies in the Baltic Sea Region. *Journal of Maritime Archaeology* 4:149–163.

Ilves, K. 2011 Is There an Archaeological Potential for a Sociology of Landing Sites? *Journal of Archaeology and Ancient History* 2:1–31.

Jackson, G. 2001 The Significance of Unimportant Ports. *International Journal of Maritime History* 13(2):1–17.

Kaldeli, A. 2008 *Roman Amphorae from Cyprus: Integrating Trade and Exchange in the Mediterranean*. PhD thesis, University College London.

Kantner, J. 2012 Realism, Reality, and Routes. Evaluating Cost-Surface and Cost-Path Algorithms. In *Least Cost Analysis of Social Landscapes: Archaeological Case Studies*, edited by D. A. White, and S. L. Surface-Evans, pp. 225–238. University of Utah Press, Salt Lake City.

Karmon, Y. 1985 Geographical Components in the Study of Ancient Mediterranean Ports. In *Harbour Archaeology. Proceedings of the First International Workshop on Ancient Mediterranean Harbours, Caesarea Maritima 24–28.6.83*, edited by A. Raban, pp. 1–6. BAR-IS 257. BAR, Oxford.

Keay, S., and L. Paroli (editors). 2011 *Portus and Its Hinterland: Recent Archaeological Research*. Archaeological Monographs of the British School at Rome 18. British School at Rome, London.

Kingsley, S. A. 2002 *A Sixth-Century AD Shipwreck off the Carmel Coast, Israel: Dor D and the Holy Land Wine Trade*. BAR-IS 1065. Archaeopress, Oxford.

Leidwanger, J. 2005 The Underwater Survey at Episkopi Bay: a Preliminary Report on the 2004 Field Season. *Report of the Department of Antiquities Cyprus*:269–277.

Leidwanger, J. 2007 Two Late Roman Wrecks from Southern Cyprus. *International Journal of Nautical Archaeology* 36(2):308–316.

Leidwanger, J. 2013a Between Local and Long-Distance: A Roman Shipwreck at Fig Tree Bay off SE Cyprus. *Journal of Roman Archaeology* 26:191–208.

Leidwanger, J. 2013b Modeling Distance with Time in Ancient Mediterranean Seafaring: A GIS Application for the Interpretation of Maritime Connectivity. *Journal of Archaeological Science* 40:3302–3308.

Leidwanger, J., C. Knappett, P. Arnaud, P. Arthur, E. Blake, C. Broodbank, T. Brughmans, T. Evans, S. Graham, E. S. Greene, B. Kowalzig, B. Mills, R. Rivers, T. Tartaron, and R. Van de Noort. 2014 A Manifesto for the Study of Mediterranean Maritime Networks. *Antiquity+* 342. http://journal.antiquity.ac.uk/projgall/leidwanger342.

Leonard, J. R. 1995a The Anchorage at Kioni. In *Ancient Akamas,* Vol. 1, *Settlement and Environment,* edited by J. Fejfer, pp. 133–170. Aarhus University Press, Aarhus.

Leonard, J. R. 1995b Evidence for Roman Ports, Harbours, and Anchorages in Cyprus. In *Cyprus and the Sea,* edited by V. Karageorghis, and D. Michaelides, pp. 227–246. University of Cyprus, Nicosia.

Leonard, J. R. 2005 *Roman Cyprus: Harbors, Hinterlands, and Hidden Powers.* PhD dissertation, State University of New York at Buffalo.

Leonard, J. R., and R. L. Hohlfelder 1993 Paphos Harbour, Past and Present: The 1991–1993 Underwater Survey. *Report of the Department of Antiquities Cyprus*:365–379.

Lund, J. 2002 Frying Pans and Other Cooking Wares from the Akamas (Western Cyprus). In *Céramiques hellénistiques et romaines, productions et diffusion en Méditerranée orientale (Chypre, Égypte et côte syro-palestinienne),* pp. 43–58. Maison de l'Orient et de la Méditerranée Jean Pouilloux, Lyon.

Malkin, I. 2011 *A Small Greek World: Networks in the Ancient Mediterranean.* Oxford University Press, Oxford.

Manning, S. W. 2002 *The Late Roman Church at Maroni* Petrera. A. G. Leventis Foundation, Nicosia.

Manning, S. W., S. J. Monks, D. A. Sewell, and S. Demesticha. 2000 Late Roman Type 1A Amphora Production at the Late Roman Site of Zygi-*Petrini,* Cyprus. *Report of the Department of Antiquities Cyprus*:233–257.

Manning, S. W., D. A. Sewell, and E. Herscher. 2002 Late Cypriot 1A Maritime Trade in Action: Underwater Survey at Maroni *Tsaroukkas* and the Contemporary East Mediterranean Trading System. *Annual of the British School at Athens* 97:97–162.

Marzano, A. 2007 *Roman Villas in Central Italy: a Social and Economic History.* Columbia Studies in the Classical Tradition 30. Brill, Leiden.

Marzano, A. 2013 *Harvesting the Sea: the Exploitation of Marine Resources in the Roman Mediterranean.* Oxford University Press, Oxford.

McCormick, M. 2001 *Origins of the European Economy.* Cambridge University Press, Cambridge.

Morris, I. 2003 Mediterraneanization. *Mediterranean Historical Review* 18(2):30–55.

Nicolaou, K. 1976 Ancient Fish-Tanks at Lapithos, Cyprus. *International Journal of Nautical Archaeology and Underwater Exploration* 5(2):133–141.

Ober, J. 2015 *The Rise and Fall of Classical Greece.* Princeton University Press, Princeton.

Papacostas, T. 2001 The Economy of Late Antique Cyprus. In *Economy and Exchange in the East Mediterranean during Late Antiquity,* edited by S. Kingsley, and M. Decker, pp. 107–128. Oxbow, Oxford.

Parker, A. J. 1992 *Ancient Shipwrecks of the Mediterranean and the Roman Provinces.* BAR-IS 580. Tempus Reparatum, Oxford.

Parker, A. J. 2008 Artifact Distributions and Wreck Locations: The Archaeology of Roman Commerce. In *The Maritime World of Ancient Rome,* edited by R. L. Hohlfelder, pp. 177–196. Memoirs of the American Academy in Rome Suppl. 6. University of Michigan Press, Ann Arbor.

Powell, J. 1996. *Fishing in the Prehistoric Aegean.* SIMA-PB 137. Åström, Jonsered.

Preiser-Kapeller, J., and F. Daim (editors). 2015 *Harbours and Maritime Networks as Complex Adaptive Systems*. Verlag des Römisch-Germanischen Zentralmuseums, Mainz.

Rautman, M. L. 2001 Rural Society and Economy in Late Roman Cyprus. In *Urban Centers and Rural Contexts in Late Antiquity*, edited by T. S. Burns, and J. W. Eadie, pp. 241–262. Michigan State University Press, Lansing.

Rautman, M. L. 2003 *A Cypriot Village of Late Antiquity: Kalavasos-Kopetra in the Vasilikos Valley*. Journal of Roman Archaeology Suppl. 52. Journal of Roman Archaeology, Portsmouth.

Rautman, M. L. 2013. Late Roman Amphorae and Trade in the Vasilikos Valley. In *Transport Amphorae and Trade of Cyprus: Proceedings of a Seminar at the Danish Institute at Athens, 23–24 April 2007*, edited by M. L. Lawall, and J. Lund, pp. 191–199. Aarhus University Press, Aarhus.

Rautman, M. L., H. Neff, B. Gomez, S. Vaughan, and M. D. Glascock. 1999 Amphoras and Roof-Tiles from Late Roman Cyprus: a Compositional Study of Calcareous Ceramics from Kalavasos-Kopetra. *Journal of Roman Archaeology* 12:377–391.

Rickman, G. E. 1985. Towards a Study of Roman Ports. In *Harbour Archaeology. Proceedings of the First International Workshop on Ancient Mediterranean Harbours, Caesarea Maritima 24–28.6.83*, edited by A. Raban, pp. 105–114. BAR-IS 257. BAR, Oxford.

Rickman, G. E. 1988 The Archaeology and History of Roman Ports. *International Journal of Nautical Archaeology and Underwater Exploration* 17(3):257–267.

Rogers, A. 2013 Social Archaeological Approaches in Port and Harbour Studies. *Journal of Maritime Archaeology* 8:181–196.

Rupp, D. W. 1997. "Metro" Nea Paphos: Suburban Sprawl in Southwestern Cyprus in the Hellenistic and Roman Periods. In *Urbanism in Antiquity: from Mesopotamia to Crete*, edited by W. E. Aufrecht, N. A. Mirau, and S. W. Gauley, pp. 236–262. Sheffield Academic Press, Sheffield.

Scheidel, W. 2013 Explaining the Maritime Freight Charges in Diocletian's Prices Edict." *Journal of Roman Archaeology* 26:464–468.

Scheidel, W. 2014 The Shape of the Roman World: Modelling Imperial Connectivity. *Journal of Roman Archaeology* 27:7–32.

Schörle, K. 2011 Constructing Port Hierarchies: Harbours of the Central Tyrrhenian Coast. In *Maritime Archaeology and Ancient Trade in the Mediterranean*, edited by D. Robinson and A. Wilson, pp. 93–106. Oxford Centre for Maritime Archaeology, Oxford.

Smith, C. A. 1974 Economics of Marketing Systems: Models from Economic Geography. *Annual Review of Anthropology* 3:167–201.

Smith, C. A. 1976 Regional Economic Systems: Linking Geographical Models and Socioeconomic Problems. In *Regional Analysis*, Vol. 1, edited by C. A. Smith, pp. 3–63. Academic Press, New York.

Sørensen, L. W., and D. W. Rupp (editors). 1993. *The Land of Paphian Aphrodite*, Vol. 2, *Artifact and Ecofactual Studies*. Paul Åströms Förlag, Göteborg.

Steffy, J. R. 1985 The Herculaneum Boat: Preliminary Notes on Hull Details. *American Journal of Archaeology* 89(3):519–521.

Stephanou, D. 1996 *On the Supply and Consumption of Fish in Cyprus*. Cahiers Options Méditerranéennes 17. CIHEAM, Zaragoza (ressources.ciheam.org/om/pdf/c17/96605672.pdf).

Stephanou, D. 2007 *Review of Aquaculture Development in Cyprus*. Mèze (ftp://ftp.fao.org/fi/document/aquaculture/ReviewAquacultureDevCyprus.pdf).

Swiny, H. W. 1982 Other Medieval Remains. In *An Archaeological Guide to the Ancient Kourion Area and the Akrotiri Peninsula*, edited by H. W. Swiny, pp. 160–161. Department of Antiquities, Nicosia.

Theodoulou, Th. 2012 Ναυτική δραστηριότητα και λιμενικά έργα στην Κλασική Κύπρο. *Enalia* 11:152–156.

Tobler, W. 1993 *Non-Isotropic Geographic Modeling*. Technical Report No. 93-1. National Center for Geographic Information and Analysis, Santa Barbara.

Todd, I. A. 2004 *Vasilikos Valley Project*, Vol. 9. *The Field Survey of the Vasilikos Valley*, Part 1. P. Åströms Förlag, Göteborg.

Todd, I. A. 2013 *Vasilikos Valley Project*, Vol. 12. *The Field Survey of the Vasilikos Valley*, Part 3. P. Åströms Förlag, Göteborg.

United Kingdom Hydrographic Office (UKHO). 2008 *Admiralty Sailing Directions. Mediterranean Pilot, Vol. V: Coasts of Libya, Egypt, Israel, Lebanon and Syria, South Coasts of Greek Islands from Kríti to Ródos and Turkey with the Island of Cyprus*, 10th edition. United Kingdom Hydrographic Office, London.

Wachsmann, S. 2000 *The Sea of Galilee Boat: A 2000-Year Old Discovery from the Sea of Legends*. Perseus, Cambridge.

Westerdahl, C. 1992 The Maritime Cultural Landscape. *International Journal of Nautical Archaeology* 21(1):5–14.

Westerdahl, C. 2011 The Maritime Cultural Landscape. In *The Oxford Handbook of Maritime Archaeology*, edited by A. Catsambis, B. Ford, and D. L. Hamilton, pp. 733–762. Oxford University Press, Oxford.

Wickham, C. 2005 *Framing the Early Middle Ages: Europe and the Mediterranean 400–800*. Oxford University Press, Oxford.

Wilson, A. 2006 Fishy Business: Roman Exploitation of Marine Resources. *Journal of Roman Archaeology* 19(2):525–537.

Wilson, A. 2011 Developments in Mediterranean Shipping and Maritime Trade from the Hellenistic Period to AD 1000. In *Maritime Archaeology and Ancient Trade in the Mediterranean*, edited by D. Robinson and A. Wilson, pp. 33–59. Oxford Centre for Maritime Archaeology, Oxford.

PART IV

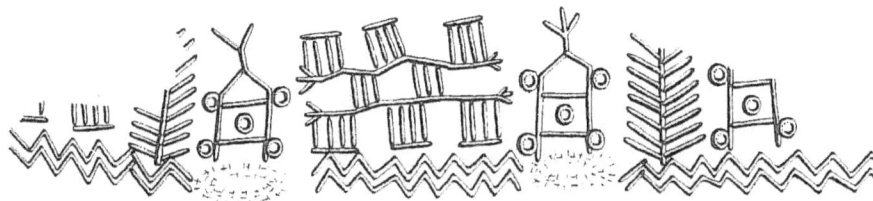

Water Archaeology: Pasts, Presents, Futures

CHAPTER TWELVE

Rivers as Material Infrastructure

A Legacy from the Past to the Future

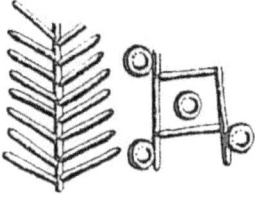

Matt Edgeworth

Abstract   *In 2010, a total of almost 26,000 sites on rivers and streams were identified as having potential for small-scale hydropower generation in England and Wales alone. This paper examines the historic character of many of the river features, structures, and layouts involved. It argues that a material infrastructure for the development of hydropower already exists in the form of heavily engineered watermill landscapes representing more than a thousand years of human-river interaction, at least from the Late Saxon period (ninth-eleventh centuries CE) to the present day. As a legacy from the past, this infrastructure of leats, weirs, and reservoirs could potentially be modified and reused for production of renewable energy in the present and the future.*

INTRODUCTION

The starting point for this paper is a map produced by the UK Environment Agency in 2010 (Figure 12.1 on page 244). It identifies sites on rivers with potential for small-scale hydropower generation. Astonishingly, the map pinpoints nearly 26,000 sites in England and Wales alone. The report does not give detail on what these sites consist of, where they come from, or how they got to be there. It simply classifies them in terms of the potential kilowatt power that might be generated at each site (Environment Agency 2010).

The report acknowledges that not all the sites identified on the map will be adapted and utilized for hydropower generation. Some are in unpopulated areas where maintenance would be difficult, or too far away from points of connection with the National Grid.

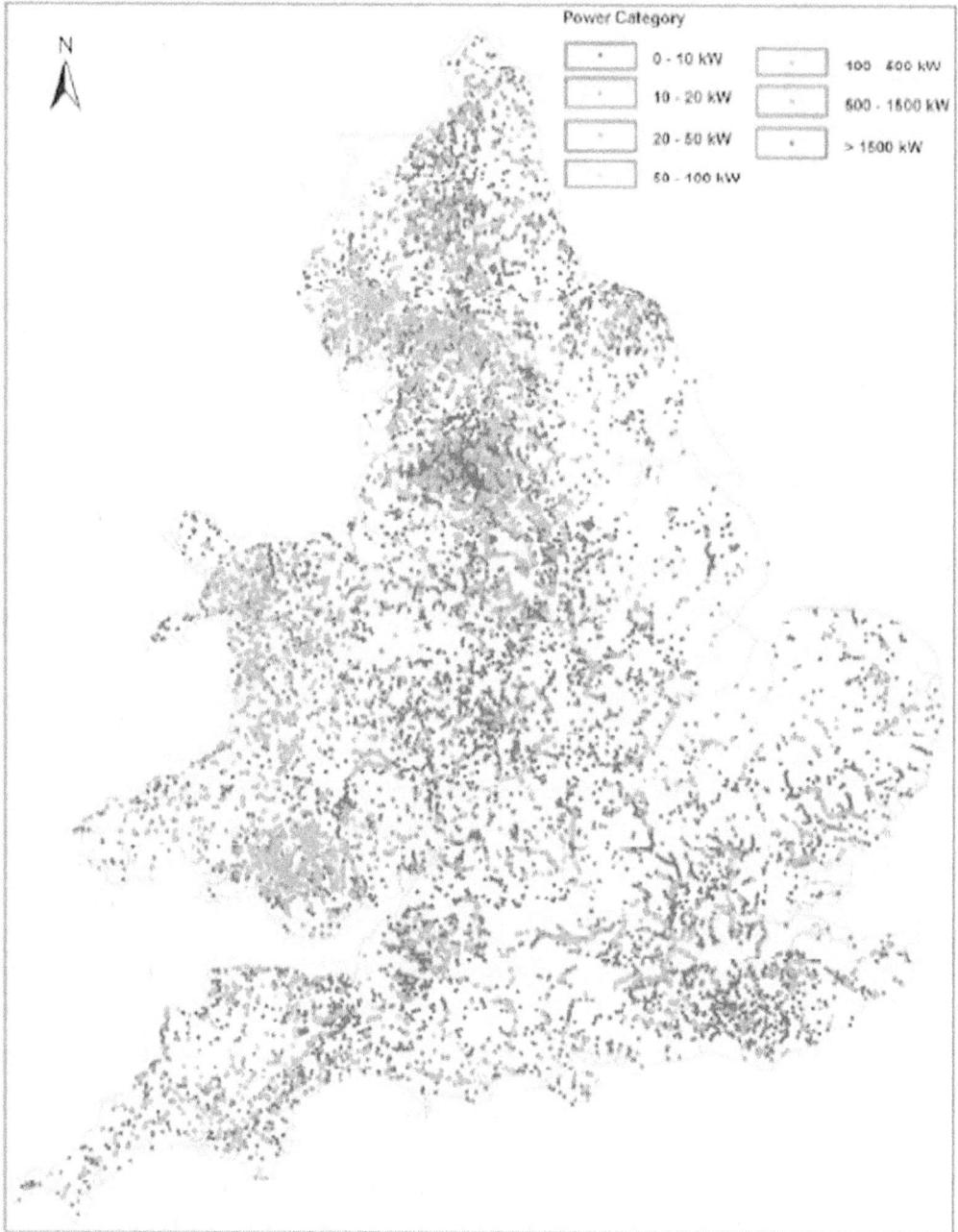

FIGURE 12.1 Map of sites in England and Wales with potential for small-scale hydro-power generation (Environment Agency 2010).

Even if all the identified sites were developed, small-scale hydropower can never match the scale of output from coal-fired or nuclear power stations. The theoretical maximum outage for all of the sites together is 1,178 MW, which is equivalent to just 1 percent of the UK's projected electricity demand in 2020 (Environment Agency 2010:19).

But that is beside the point. Renewable energy has important symbolic value to society that goes far beyond economic value, and in this context the small scale of operation can have advantages over more industrial processes of energy production. Development of "green" energy programs is crucial to the broader aim of achieving sustainable living, and to tackling problems associated with climate change, environmental pollution, and depletion of resources. Installation of small hydropower turbines can have the positive effect of re-connecting communities with the rivers and streams which run through local landscapes.

Even so, this paper takes a neutral stance toward energy policy and argues neither for nor against development of small-scale hydropower. Issues, as always, are complex and there are valid arguments on both sides, as in the debate about wind farms. The aim of the paper is to use the debate on hydropower as a kind of window through which to look in on aspects of the state of rivers in England, and to explore implications of the concept of rivers as material infrastructure.

What is truly extraordinary about the map, as this paper will show, is that the vision of the potential future development of rivers it presents is based upon a material infrastructure that is already there, in the form of older but often still functioning river structures and layouts. This temporal and cultural dimension to rivers—the fact that they have been shaped by past generations of human beings in ways that both enable and constrain what can be done in the future—will be crucial to the analysis presented here.

The first step is to look in detail at some of the individual sites indicated on the Environment Agency map, to establish what kind of sites they are and why they are deemed so suitable for development for hydropower generation.

Weirs and Associated River Structures

The Environment Agency map was generated mainly from mathematical data on river water levels, assembled by the use of LIDAR (Light Detection and Ranging) and other remote sensing techniques on rivers and floodplains throughout England and Wales. River "barriers" were identified wherever a sudden drop in water level of at least 1.5 m was indicated. For each barrier, data on height of the structure and amount of flow was used to calculate an estimate of the amount of power that could potentially be produced if a hydropower turbine were installed on that location.

What exactly is meant by the term *river barrier*? The report notes, "These sites are mostly weirs, but could be other man-made structures, or natural features such as a waterfall" (Environment Agency 2010:7). Beyond this basic information, no further enquiries were made about the historic character of many of the sites. Environmental sensitivity of sites was evaluated on the basis of likely impact of the structures on the movement of fish. Since few if any weirs are designated to be sites of historic interest, and none are protected as Scheduled Ancient Monuments (archaeological sites or buildings protected by law), the potential historic significance of the structures was not taken into account.

Let us therefore zoom in to focus on a particular group of "river barriers" or weirs, on the edge of one of the densest clusters on the map.

CASE STUDY 1: NEW MILLS, DERBYSHIRE

The following case study takes as its subject area a 500 m stretch of the River Goyt in the town of New Mills in Derbyshire.

In this short section of river there are five river barriers or weirs, neatly spaced about 100 m apart. Each weir is effectively a small dam, retaining and deepening the water on the upstream side, while allowing flow of water over the top and down a sloped apron or series of descending steps on the downstream side (Figure 12.2). These structures are mainly made from large blocks of quarried local stone, sometimes augmenting rocky formations in the river bed. The weir creates a "head" or "fall" of water, which is the vertical distance between the respective levels of water upstream and downstream of the weir. This artificially created drop in level is typically part of a more extensive river lay-out, where several weirs in succession effectively step the river into a series of descending levels in the direction of flow, as in this case (Figure 12.3).

As the place name New Mills suggests, the weirs on the river were associated with watermills. Before the introduction of steam turbines, in the eighteenth and early nine-teenth centuries, it was water that powered the development of the cotton industry. The weirs created the head or fall of water needed to turn the waterwheels, which in turn were connected through gearing to further machinery for industrial production and process-ing. All the mills had fallen out of use by the mid-twentieth century. Some of the mill buildings are still standing while others survive only as ruins or have been demolished.

The weirs were never intended to be standalone features, but rather were designed to be part of complexes of water features that functioned together. In most cases, water was directed into a leat or head-race, the inlet of which was placed at the higher water

FIGURE 12.2 Weir on the River Goyt, New Mills, Derbyshire.

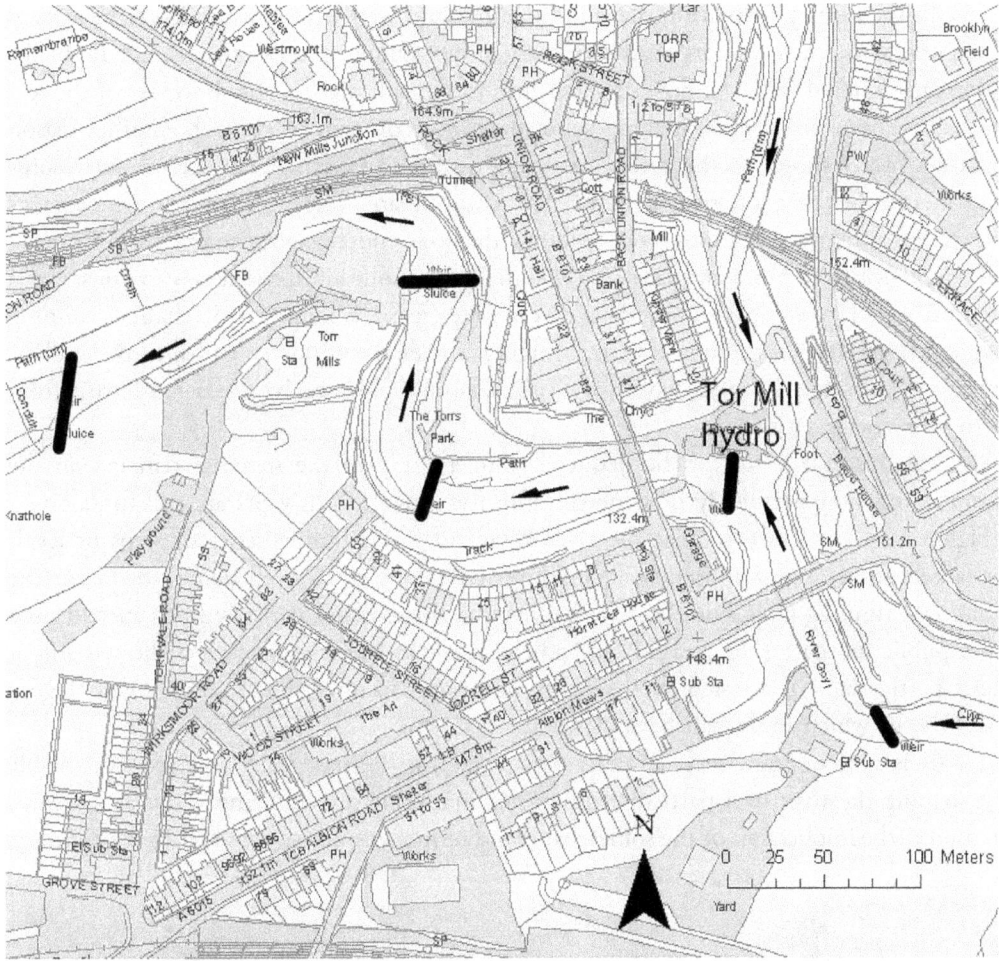

FIGURE 12.3 Map of New Mills, showing a stepped river layout with five weirs marked by bars. Direction of flow is indicated by arrows.

level *above* the weir. This brought the water to the mill, where the fall of water in the wheel-pit can be understood as a direct counterpart of the fall of water at the weir itself. Once the energy of the falling water had been used, a continuation of the leat or tail-race took water back to the river, with the outfall at the lower water level *below* the weir. The traces of several such leats can be discerned on the map shown in Figure 12.3.

The functioning of weirs and their associated leats was subject to the vagaries of river flow, and modifications to the system had to be made accordingly from time to time, leading to complex developmental histories. Disentangling these histories comes within the remit of an interpretive approach that I call "archaeology of flow"—a form of analysis that takes account not only of human agency in the past but also the agency of material currents flowing through the landscape, and the entanglement of these different kinds of forces (Edgeworth 2011a).

In the case of Torrs Mill, the mill buildings and weir were constructed right next to each other, with a very short head-race and tail-race taking water to the wheels. Problems were encountered with the flow of water into the leat, however. The shortness of the leat may have been one reason, making water flow more difficult to control. Another reason was that water supply to the wheel was being disrupted by flow from the tributary coming in to join the main river a short distance upstream, causing eddies and inconstant flows. An attempted solution was to build the weir much higher to increase the head of water—but the problem persisted. Eventually, the solution devised was to construct a second weir farther upstream and to divert water using a long leat or channel running alongside the river for about 100 m, bringing it over the tributary and into the mill by means of a bridge. In other words, the mill was now powered by water fed into it from two weir-and-leat systems.

All this and more can be deduced from a study of the material remains on the ground (or more accurately in some cases, in the water). Both weirs are still functioning (Figure 12.4A, 12.4B), so that the river layout of a descending series of steps or levels is largely intact and working. Mill buildings have long since been demolished. But the long leat running alongside the river survives, albeit dry and partially filled in and used as a public footpath (Figure 12.4C). And the fact that the system of water flow is still at least partly viable is attested by the recent addition of a small hydropower plant (Figure 12.4D), of which more will be said below.

It is evident from such remains that people in the past were involved not merely in shaping the river to a particular design, or managing and utilizing water as a passive resource (the implication of the somewhat bland term *water management*). On the contrary,

FIGURE 12.4 Systems of flow at Torrs Mill: (A) first weir, built higher than normal to increase head of water, (B) second weir 100 m upstream, (C) former leat from second weir to mill, now a footpath, (D) Torrs Hydro.

B

C

D

they were engaged in a kind of wrestle with a material force that, though it could be channeled and corralled up to a point, acted back in unpredictable ways, forcing original schemes to be adjusted and further measures to be taken to deal with it. The archaeologist of flow, like a kind of river detective, has to unravel the ways in which human projects and river currents have become materially woven together. Rivers are artifacts (Edgeworth 2011; Scarpino 1997) to be sure, but something more than that as well. It is not just about human agency. River forces and human forces intermingle—sometimes

FIGURE 12.5 Former mill building: (A) head-race with inflow upstream of weir, and (B) tail-race downstream of weir, River Goyt, New Mills, Derbyshire.

flowing together, sometimes pitched against each other. Instead of calling them artifacts, the term *human-river entanglements* would be more appropriate.

An example of how existing and still functioning structures such as weirs can be reused to serve contemporary and future needs is provided by the Torrs Hydro, built next to the weir on the site of the former mill in 2008. The first hydro plant in England to be owned and maintained by a local community, it uses a "reverse Archimedes screw" turbine to generate about 200,000 kilowatt hours of electricity over a typical year—the equivalent of the annual electricity consumption of around 50 typical British homes. It utilizes the same head of water as the old mill did before the construction of the second weir. This is an exemplar of exactly the kind of contemporary reuse of existing river structures that the Environment Agency has in mind when it speaks of the potential of the 25,000+ sites identified on rivers and shown on the map.

Although the generation of hydroelectric power at Torrs Hydro is a success, problems are still encountered with irregularities of water input caused by disruptive flows from the tributary. Should the problem ever become more serious, a viable course of action, already tried and tested in the past, might be the reopening of the leat from the second weir 100 m upstream, and the construction of a small bridge to carry it over the tributary to the hydropower plant.

Figure 12.5 depicts a large mill building that is still standing about 200 m downstream of Torrs Hydro, around a bend or two in the river, showing (A) where the water entered the mill through a metal sluice and short head-race, taking water from above the weir, and (B) where the water came back out again through a short tail-race below the weir.

Head-races and tail-races are short on the River Goyt because the watercourse here is fast and steep and it is relatively easy to create the necessary fall of water through construction of a weir alone. On slower rivers, races or leats tend to be much longer, as illustrated by a later example.

The Force of Local Community Action

A significant force in the movement toward small-scale hydropower generation, as in the example of Torrs Hydro above, comes from local community involvement. This is often more than just community groups being led by national policies and strategies of state bodies such as the Environment Agency: there are notable instances of local groups taking the lead and pioneering a way forward.

This is certainly the case with the *Power in the Landscape* project in the Upper Calder Valley, based at the Alternative Technology Centre (ATC) in Hebden Bridge, West Yorkshire. The River Calder runs about 60 miles to the north of the River Goyt in the middle of a dense cluster of river barriers shown on the Environment Agency map. Numerous tributary streams flow into the Calder down steeply wooded valleys, with the same steplike succession of weirs that was identified on the Goyt. Nearly all the weirs here too, as in New Mills, were associated with textile mills. And again, the weirs are linked with other structures and features, such as connected chains of leats and reservoirs running alongside and above the water—mostly either ruined, silted up, or overgrown. But many of the weirs are still intact and functioning. The project has (1) drawn attention to the existence of all these interconnected features through historical research and field survey, (2) shown the high potential for reuse for small-scale hydropower generation, and (3) provided support to communities and organizations to encourage the installation of hydropower turbines (refer to the Power in the Landscape website, listed in the references section).

This adds something very important to the Environment Agency map shown in Figure 12.1. What is missing from the map is the dimension of time, for the historical aspect of river barriers is almost completely neglected in the accompanying report. Yet the sites identified as having such potential for present and future are clearly inherited from the past. The stepping of watercourses into staircase-like series of descending levels, far from being a natural feature, is the product of human-river interaction over many hundreds of years, a part of historical process. Weirs are components of a material infrastructure that has been inherited as a legacy from the past, to be passed on to the future as a kind of river heritage.

The concept of river heritage may seem strange. *River* and *heritage* are words not often used together, and river features are rarely described as being of historic or archaeological value. Bringing the terms together may mean a rethinking of the definitions of both. For in seeing rivers as culturally and historically constituted rather than as natural entities, rivers challenge us to think of heritage and heritage conservation in new ways. Many historic river structures and layouts are best preserved precisely by keeping them in use, or by adapting them to present and future needs. Weirs need water running over them or they quickly dry out, develop cracks, and become ruins. Mill leats and other channels need water running through them or they rapidly silt up, clog with vegetation and become buried archaeological features.

An example of such reuse is provided by the hydropower turbine installed on a tributary of the River Calder at Gibson Mill on Hebden Water. Here the turbine has been placed not on the weir itself but in the former wheel pit of the mill, replacing an earlier turbine of 1925. It makes use of an elaborate water system that includes the weir on the river, the head-race taking water from above the weir, a large reservoir that stores the water, the former wheel pit in the mill itself, and the tail-race taking water back into the river below the weir. All these river features are preserved by the act of using them. Gibson Mill is now run by the National Trust and is its flagship sustainable building, using the hydropower turbine alongside solar panels to generate all its own electricity (refer to National Trust webpage on Gibson Mill).

OTHER EXAMPLES

It has not been possible in such a short paper to give examples of the full range of rivers that have been shaped or stepped extensively through the construction of weirs, mainly for the purpose of milling, although the map in Figure 12.1 gives a good indication of the number of river barriers that exist. The Upper Calder and the Goyt are both small but fast-running rivers in upland areas. But similar processes have been at work on larger and slower-running lowland rivers too, with variations in the form of weirs and especially on the length of leats (which tend to be longer in order to create the necessary fall of water).

While referring here mainly to rivers in England, very relevant examples could be drawn from other countries. An important paper about streams in Pennsylvania and Maryland, U.S.A., appeared in *Science* (Walter and Merritts 2008), drawing the attention of the scientific community to the impact of mill dams or weirs on the geomorphology of meandering rivers and their floodplains, previously thought to be natural. Here numerous seventeenth- and eighteenth-century mill dams had mostly fallen out of use and been partially buried, due to buildup of sediment behind them, with river barriers inserted across streams (and across the floodplains too) every kilometer or so. The paper shows how floodplains were transformed through changing patterns of sedimentation and erosion, leading to development of a distinctive type of meandering channel running through a deeply layered floodplain easy to mistake for a natural formation, but in which human as well as river agency has played a part. The paper by Walter and Merritts is highlighted here as a must-read for anyone researching the impact of mill weirs on wider landscapes. Many of its conclusions can be applied (with modification to allow for variations in river type and forms of technology) to understanding of historical transformations of rivers and floodplains in lowland areas of England and other parts of Europe.

All the examples looked at so far are from the Industrial Age. Would it be reasonable to assume, then, that this great transformation of rivers has occurred solely in the last few hundred years since the start of the Industrial Revolution? That would be an easy but mistaken assumption to draw. Suppose we had a database listing river barriers on English rivers a thousand years ago, from which we could generate a map roughly equivalent to that produced by the Environment Agency of river barriers today. How would the two maps compare?

Actually, such a database exists, at least for most parts of England. The Domesday Survey of 1086 recorded mills along with other information for taxation purposes. Although there were some animal-powered mills at that time, nearly all the mill sites recorded would have been watermills and most would have required a weir or dam to function properly. There are upward of 7,000 mill sites recorded in England alone. Allowing for those sites where two or more waterwheels on the same site were counted separately, it can be estimated that at least 6,000 water mills existed at that time. Most of these would have used weirs or dams on the river to provide the head of water to drive the waterwheels. In some cases a single weir might have served more than one mill, but it can be reasonably inferred from the Domesday records that several thousand weirs existed at the time, perhaps equivalent to about one-fifth of the number of river barriers shown on the Environment Agency map. That is a significant proportion, and even if the assumptions and inferences drawn are only half correct, there are indications that the artificial stepping of riverscapes was essentially already well under way by the Late Saxon period (ninth to eleventh centuries CE). There was undoubtedly considerable acceleration of the river stepping process in the industrial period, but this and other kinds of human-river interaction go back much farther in time than might be assumed (Blair 2007).

Material evidence also exists in the form of archaeological structures in abandoned river channels. A stone dam of eleventh-century date was recently excavated on a former course of the River Trent at Hemington in Derbyshire (Clay and Salisbury 1990). The line of a medieval weir has been identified, from an aerial photo on Google Earth, as an "underwater crop mark" or linear pattern of vegetation rooted in the disturbed riverbed (Edgeworth 2011:92). Such structures impacted in multiple ways on the geomorphology of rivers.

It must not be thought, however, that weirs of medieval and Saxon date are necessarily buried or submerged—or for that matter swept away, dismantled or ruined, though some certainly are. Many have been in continuous use, regularly repaired and sometimes rebuilt on the same site since Middle Saxon times (seventh-eighth centuries CE). The same is true of mill leats. Generally, the water management systems associated with mills show an extraordinary durability and longevity of use. A considerable number of those listed in the Domesday Survey remained in use until the advent of electricity in the early twentieth century. Some, such as Otterton Mill described below, are still functioning.

CASE STUDY 2: OTTERTON MILL, RIVER OTTER, DEVON

Otterton Mill on the River Otter comprises a whole watermill landscape rather than just the mill building itself. The mill is part of a much broader system of flow, which includes the weir, head-race, and tail-race (leat). In fact, a good way of defining the extent of a watermill landscape in space is to take it from the place where water is taken from the river to the place where it is directed back in again. At Otterton there is a fine example of the longer type of leat mentioned earlier, in this case measuring 400 m from inflow to outflow, as shown in Figure 12.6. These long leats were used, in conjunction with weirs, to create the required fall of water in low-lying areas where slope of land was slight. This was done by skilled manipulation of gravity-driven water flow—raising the height of the head-race above river level as it approached the water wheel, and lowering the height of the tail-race below river level immediately downstream of the mill.

Note the medieval priory south of the mill. This would have used water from the mill leat to service its fishponds, flush out its drains and sewage systems, and so on. In such ways the water management system extended far beyond the river itself, and was interbedded with other forms of social and economic life.

Otterton Mill was only one of a series of such mills, each with its own weir, on the river. Thus, the Otter was stepped into the same characteristic staircase-like formation discussed earlier. It was a pattern that could be added to in later periods, by increasing the number of levels within the already existing stepped layout. The great acceleration in the building of mills and their associated landscapes in the industrial period often took place on riverscapes that had already been stepped in preceding periods. Thus, on the stretch of the River Goyt at New Mills described in Case Study 1, for example, there was at least one mill—and therefore at least one weir and change in river level—in existence in the Late Saxon period.

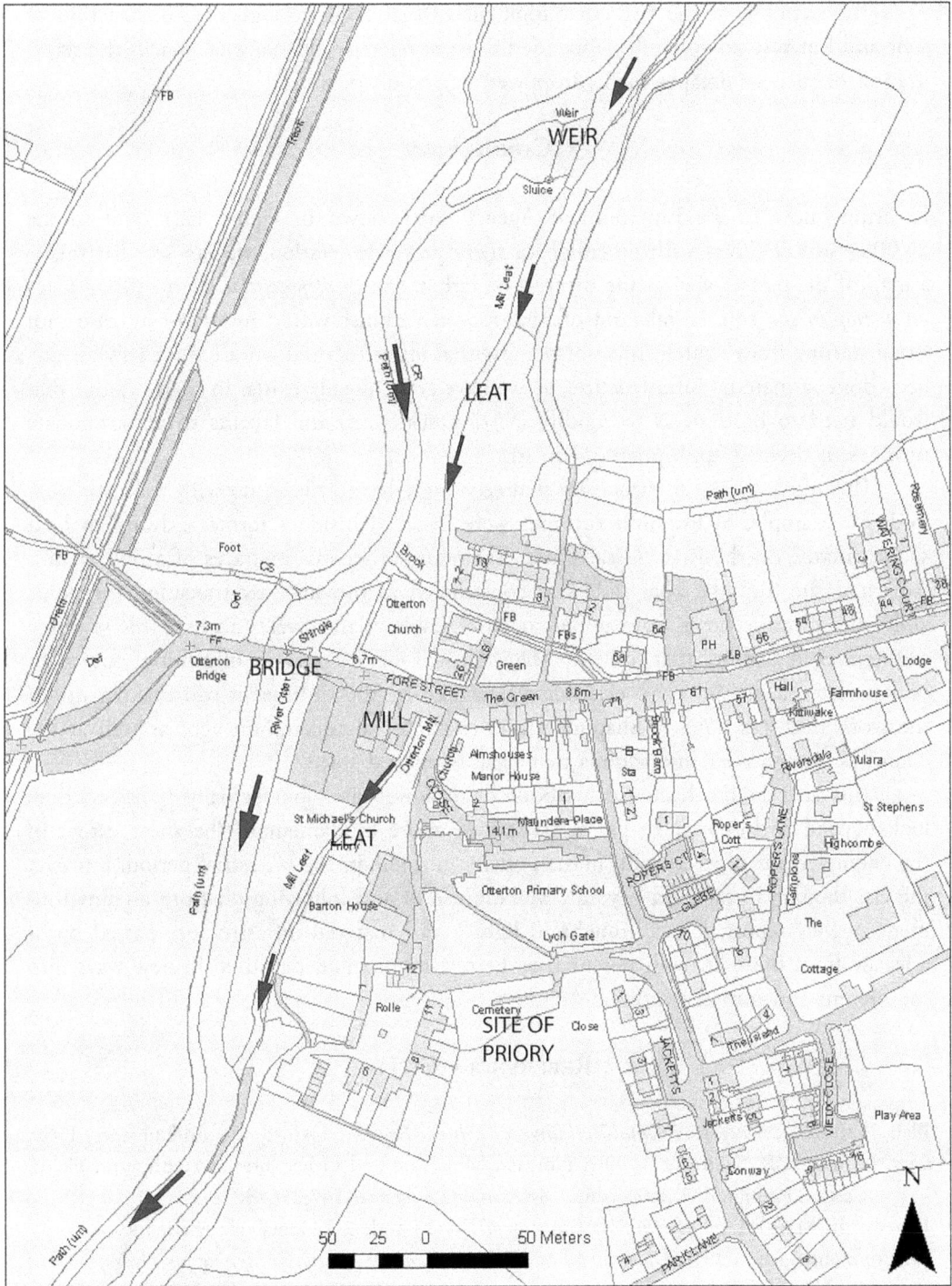

FIGURE 12.6 Watermill landscape on the River Otter, Otterton, Devon, listed in the Domesday Survey and dating to the Late Saxon period.

The stepping of the river that took place back then through the construction of weir-and-leat systems for mills, appended onto in later periods, is what makes the reutilization of such landscapes for hydropower generation possible.

CONCLUSION

Returning now to the Environment Agency map shown in Figure 12.1, and to the 25,000+ sites it shows with potential for hydropower generation, we can see that this is a map of the past as well as the future—or rather, a *map of potential for the future based on a map of the past*. Installation of hydropower turbines would in almost all cases not entail starting from scratch. Most of the essential infrastructural work has actually already been done: a material infrastructure, as we have seen, already exists. In many cases, what would need to be done is to modify existing structures and layouts to accommodate turbines, if deemed appropriate to do so.

This often applies to structures that seemingly have little to do with mills. In Bedford, for example, hydropower turbines were installed inside a former Edwardian boat slide structure on the River Great Ouse. There are no records or traces of a mill on this particular site. But the boat slide was constructed to provide easy transition for punts and other pleasure boats from upper to lower levels of the river, and it is this stepping of the river in Bedford that (initially accomplished for the purpose of milling) goes right back to late Saxon times. So electricity generated by the turbines is still making use of the work that was done in shaping the river almost a millennium ago, as well as the countless human-river interactions that have happened since.

This chapter has been partly about hydropower sites, but actually it has tried to look beyond hydropower to get at something more fundamental—the sheer extent of the entanglement of rivers with human affairs, not just in the industrial period, but over the last thousand years and beyond. Making use of and following on from an Environment Agency report, it has brought to light a vast material infrastructure passed on as a legacy from the past, with potential to be refashioned and reutilized in new ways into the present and into the future.

REFERENCES CITED

Blair, J. 2007 *Waterways and Canal-Building in Medieval England*. Oxford, Oxford University Press.

Clay, P., and C. R. Salisbury. 1990 A Norman Mill Dam and Other Sites at Hemington Fields, Castle Donington, Leicestershire. *Archaeological Journal* 147:276–307.

Edgeworth, M. 2011 *Fluid Pasts: Archaeology of Flow*. London, Bloomsbury Academic.

Environment Agency. 2010 *Opportunity and Environmental Sensitivity Mapping for Hydropower in England and Wales*. EA Report.

National Trust website, undated Gibson Mill. http://www.nationaltrust.org.uk/article-1356399403 913/; accessed April 20, 2016.

Power in the Landscape website, undated www.powerinthelandscape.co.uk/; accessed April 20, 2016.

Power from the Landscape website, undated http://www.powerfromthelandscape.co.uk/; accessed April 12, 2014.

Scarpino, P. V. 1997 Large Floodplain Rivers as Human Artifacts: A Historical Perspective on Ecological Integrity. Special Report for the US Geological Survey.

Walter, R., and D. Merritts. 2008 Natural Streams and the Legacy of Water-Powered Milling. *Science* 319(5861):299–304.

CHAPTER 13

Geologies of Belonging

The Political Ecology of Water in Central Anatolia

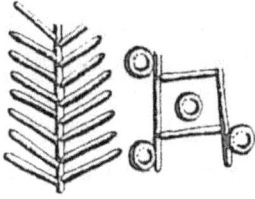

Ömür Harmanşah

Abstract *Human communities have been continuously drawn to bodies of water. Scientific discourse on water characterizes it primarily as a natural resource that is increasingly scarce and unevenly distributed globally. Contrary to this extractive discourse, one can argue that bodies of water are also landscapes of water, which are constituted by the animate ecologies of springs, mountains, lakes, and rivers, and participate in the political and geo-social configuration of the world. Archaeological field projects offer opportunities to engage with political ecologies of water. Firstly, the archaeological past offers the possibility of tracing the genealogies of water ecologies and understanding the powerful impact of water on regional histories of settlement. Secondly, archaeologists often work in contexts of development such as the construction of dams, power plants, irrigation programs, or other infrastructure projects. In the context of salvage projects, archaeologists are implicated in the conflicts over water ecologies among multiple stakeholders. This paper investigates the politics of water in the southwestern borderlands of the Hittite Empire of the central Anatolian plateau during the last centuries of the Late Bronze Age (roughly 1400–1175 BCE) in the regional context of the construction of two imperial Hittite water monuments: Yalburt Yaylası Mountain Spring Monument and the Köylütolu Yayla Earthen Dam.*

A lake is the landscape's most beautiful and expressive feature. It is the earth's eye; looking into which the beholder measures the depth of his own nature.

—Henry David Thoreau, *Walden*

Introduction

Human communities have been continuously drawn to bodies of water, and not just as a *natural resource* for basic sustenance for living. Scientific discourse on water has long characterized it primarily as a *natural* resource that is increasingly scarce globally and unevenly distributed among the world communities (e.g., Frérot 2011). This discourse has produced an understanding of water as a neutral mineral substance, whose cultural meanings, geographical diversity, and complex place-based associations are frequently ignored or undermined. Studied from the perspectives of economic value, commodification, pollution/sanitation, and supply, water is often reduced to an abstract and benign substance. Frérot (2011:11) writes in this vein that "water symbolizes the perfection and purity of a nature before creation, the ineffable trace of a world before the world." Such neoliberal capitalist imagination of water then puts water as a substance *before culture,* a "pristine shrine," and water's value "lives beyond the fluctuations and contingencies of human history" (Frérot 2011:11). Frérot then explicitly evacuates water from its local contexts of place and landscape, its special ecologies of flow, appearance, and disappearance, while he strips water from its historicity and cultural specificity. The material power, agency, and geo-social biography of waters that flow through specific landscapes and histories are reduced to a pristine nature, that is to say, a *natural resource* substance that can be extracted, commodified, and redistributed around the globe.

Yet flowing through wildly diverse geologies and landscapes, embroiled in complex ecological processes and histories, reaching to human communities in vastly different geological contexts, sources of water always have distinctive qualities from taste to smell, from temperature to bodily impact, including water's associations with particular memory places. At places of pilgrimage such as the Sanctuary of Our Lady of Lourdes in France, the Sufi Dergah of Husayn Tekri in India, the Zamzam Spring at the Ka'aba in Saudi Arabia, the sources of the Ganges River in India, the springs in the *agiasma* churches of the Byzantine Empire, or the sacred lakes of the Maya in Belize, water is believed to have healing or miraculous qualities.[1] Many local health pilgrims visit thermal and mineral springs for healing and their well-being every day around the world. Small towns and villages prior to the introduction of industrial infrastructure and centralized water distribution often had multiple sources of water, which are distinguished and qualified by their taste, level of coldness, or fittingness for making tea, and the like. Culturally speaking, then, water is not a neutral substance that can be abstracted to a certain chemical formula but it is a historical and sociopolitical agent that impacts the lives of communities and the shaping of landscapes through its vibrancy, fluidity, and its vital, irreducible materiality. This paper attempts to interrogate *this politics* of water both as a life-giving substance and an animated actor in ancient Anatolian landscapes.

The Political Ecologies of Water

The politics of water has been frequently evoked for the long history of the Middle East from antiquity to modern nation-states as a persistent, signature phenomenon in a geography that is historically dependent on water for agricultural production and transportation. This politics provoked many water-based historical models, such as the environmentally determinist, universalist hypotheses of "hydraulic civilizations" and the notorious orientalist-evolutionary perspectives on "oriental despotism," which had suggested that the relations of state power and social hierarchy were conditioned by the inevitable dependency of preindustrial (esp. Mesopotamian and Egyptian) agriculture on large-scale irrigation systems, which then led to despotism (Butzer 1976, 1996; Davies 2009; Harrower 2009; Wescoat 2000; Wittfogel 1957). This history has been somewhat related to the contemporary politics of the Tigris, the Euphrates, and the Nile between the nation-states who struggle for water rights (see, e.g., Dolatyar and Gray 2000). These debates on water politics and resource access, use/management, and ownership remain heavily anthropocentric as they tend to leave out bodies of water themselves as agents within political ecologies or render them powerless, inert, or subservient.

Beyond its conceptualization as mineral substance, water plays an even greater role in *bodies of water*, namely, lakes, ponds, marshes, streams and rivers, and prominent springs. These are *landscapes of water* that are dynamic, fluid, and act as habitats for distinct animal and plant communities (Campbell 2011; Edgeworth 2011), which then form what I would like to call in this article *"geologies of belonging."* This term articulates the human interaction with the mineral world as a constitutive force in the making of landscapes where the nature and culture binaries collapse. Landscapes of water are by no means static backdrops or dependable environments upon which cultural practice is inscribed. Neither are they stages on which the human-centered drama of history is performed, nor Cartesian spaces on which archaeological sites are distributed (Knapp and Ashmore 1999). Such imaginations of landscape as resourceful nature, romantic backdrop, or space of quantification have been strong in the post-Enlightenment landscape painting tradition in Europe and evocatively revived in the late capitalist economies of extraction.

Contrary to this extractive discourse, one can argue that bodies of water constitute animated ecologies of springs, mountains, lakes, and rivers, which participate in the political and geo-social configuration of the world. My interest in focusing on the archaeology of places in recent years has largely been, on the one hand, an attempt to understand bodies of water or landscapes of water as inalienable features that define locality and as powerful actors in the deep histories of geo-biological life and human settlement (Harmanşah 2015). On the other hand, it can be construed as a political reaction toward the widespread, globalist discourse of abstraction of water as natural resource, commonly used to legitimize the ruthless extraction of water and alienation of local communities of their rights to water (Harmanşah 2015:54–82). Archaeological field projects offer rich opportunities to engage with such political ecologies of water. First and foremost, the archaeological past offers the possibility of tracing the genealogies of water ecologies for those of us who are willing to engage with watery landscapes and their powerful impact on regional histories of settlement. Such histories may be traced through what we might call a critical geomorphology that traces the regimes of flow, appearance and disappearance of water in conjunction with evolving landscapes, alluvial burial of landscapes, human interventions such as irrigation projects, canal digging, or forest clearing, as well as the politics of and practices around water.[2] Secondly, archaeologists often work in contexts of neoliberal development such as the construction of dams, large-scale irrigation programs, or other infrastructure projects. In the context of salvage or rescue projects, archaeologists are then implicated in the conflicts over resources between sovereign states, multinational companies, local communities, and ecological activists in contexts of social movements for human rights and environmental justice (Wilson 1987; Shoup 2006).

An excellent example of a political conflict over water was narrated in the 2010 movie *Even the Rain*, by the Spanish director Icíar Bollaín (Cilento 2012). The political battle between discourses of water as natural resource and discourses of water as part and parcel of livelihood and local ecology emerges starkly in this film. This is the story of a Mexican film crew with a young idealist director, arriving at a Bolivian town to shoot a postcolonial movie, a historical drama about the Spanish colonization of Latin America and the violent resource extraction that accompanied it. As they shoot the movie, they find themselves entangled with a rising water crisis when the municipal government decides to privatize the drinking water. This is the well-known Cochabamba water wars of December 1999 and April 2000, a painful yet successful example of a social movement of ecological activism against water privatization (Albro 2005). In order to be able to finish their movie, the film crew faces a paradoxical position between helping the locals with their water activism and collaborating with the local government that is identified with violent state power. The completion of the movie depended on the locally hired indigenous actors. Finding themselves in precisely the colonial situation they were there to critique, the filmmakers are drowned in their complacency. The film brilliantly juxtaposes two episodes of political ecology for indigenous communities, in a multitemporal reenactment of colonial intervention into the indigenous landscape and resources.

Archaeologists, while doing fieldwork, often find themselves in similarly complex and paradoxical situations, especially when they are involved with salvage projects that aim to recover archaeological data and materials of cultural heritage from sites and landscapes that are under the threat of destruction in late capitalist contexts of development. Cornelia Kleinitz and Claudia Näser (2011), in the case of Merowe Dam Archaeological Salvage Project in Northern Sudan, tell us that local communities, namely the Manasir ethnic group, banned "archaeologists from their land as a political strategy against the developers, in order to improve the terms of compensation and resettlement" (Kaleinitz and Näser 2011:253). Kleinitz and Näser report the miserable failure of archaeological salvage projects in this instance, not only in their archaeological coverage but also in their care for local communities. Up to 78,000 people were forcibly resettled due to the construction of this controversial dam.

The flourishing field of political ecology aims at creating critical and democratic platforms for addressing questions of the environment without abandoning the subject matter to environmental scientists and policymakers but opening the field to social sciences and humanities in the academic world and putting them in direct contact with ecological activists, nongovernmental organizations, and local communities. Place-based struggles of local communities across the world in coming to terms with development projects and effects of globalization, and their claims to their rights to local resources such as water, land, clean air, ecological biodiversity, and cultural heritage are central in this manner (Escobar 2008; Latour 2004). Political ecology also urges archaeologists to reconnect with indigenous, descendant, and local communities who have direct interest and claim to the studied deep past, and therefore offers important potentials for archaeological projects' engagement with their landscapes of field practice (Atalay, Clauss, McGuire, and Welch 2014).

BRONZE AGE ANATOLIA: WATER AND BORDERLANDS

In the second half of this paper, I turn to Bronze Age Anatolia to discuss political ecologies of water in borderland landscapes of south central Turkey. During the last centuries of the Late Bronze Age (roughly 1400–1175 BCE) on the Anatolian peninsula, rulers and political elites of the Hittite Empire and other competing rulers at the edges of that empire seem to have transformed prominent springs into dynastic monuments (Ehringhaus 2005; Glatz 2009, 2011; Glatz and Plourde 2011; Harmanşah 2015). These sites where water appears, flows along, or disappears were marked with rock-cut inscriptions and pictorial imagery, and sometimes monumentalized by stone-lined reservoirs or ceremonial pools (Erbil and Mouton 2012; Ökse 2011). Found both in the context of urban centers as well as in the remote corners of the countryside, several of these monuments are located in the southern and western Hittite borderlands (Harmanşah 2017). In *Place, Memory, and Healing,* I argued that these monuments of the ruling elite were deliberately carved at sites that were already significant places of cultural practice, and that such sites were appropriated by sovereign elites who managed to link them to broader networks of state power and territorial discourses of imperialism while building their borderlands as a constellation of landscape monuments, where violent military discourse, dynastic narratives of kingship, and mythopoetical imagination of the world were negotiated (Harmanşah 2015:113).

At the site of Eflatûn Pınarı on the eastern shore of Beyşehir Lake, for example, a spectacular stone monument was built in the fourteenth or early thirteenth century BCE and featured a complex representation of mountain and spring deities clustering around presumably the enthroned Sun Goddess of the Earth and the Storm God, as a mimetic creation of a mountain spring in a lowland setting (Figure 13.1 on page 264). This is clearly indicated in the performative architectonics of the ashlar monument: in the way that fresh spring waters squirt out of the punctured bellies of anthropomorphized spring deities in the bottom of the monument (Harmanşah 2014). This kind of a mimetic architecture is also found in the Hittite capital as well, in the famous Südburg Sacred Pool Complex, which featured a stone-lined water reservoir in the eastern part of the city, built on perennial springs, and two stone chambers (Hawkins 1995). The wall surfaces of one of the stone-built chambers was inscribed in Luwian hieroglyphics featuring a commemorative inscription of the King Šuppiluliuma II, commemorating his military expeditions and foundation of new cities. A similar merging of state discourse

Figure 13.1 Eflatûn Pınarı. Hittite Sacred Pool, ashlar monument with carved reliefs (author's photograph).

of military violence with the monumentalization of a ritual place is known from Yalburt Yaylası Sacred Pool Monument near Ilgın (Figure 13.2) (Johnson and Harmanşah 2015; Temizer 1984). Yalburt Yaylası is a pastoral village and an abundant spring located on the southern slopes of Karadağ in the karst uplands directly north of the modern town of Ilgın (northwest of Konya in the Konya Province). The monument sits in the middle of an impressive (albeit eroded) landscape filled with deep sinkholes, karst depressions, and abundant springs. Here, at the fresh water spring in the midst of a parched upland landscape, the Hittite king Tudhaliya IV (1237–1209 BCE) commissioned a stone-lined reservoir in local limestone and adorned the interior surfaces of one course of ashlar blocks with a lengthy commemorative inscription in hieroglyphic Luwian (Hawkins 1995:68–70; Poetto 1993). The inscription recounts the king's military campaign to the southwest of the Anatolian peninsula.

These water monuments are very clearly intimately linked in their ideology, architectural form, and site-specific character, and in their distinct choice of framing or mimicking a geological feature through which water flows, while they demonstrate to us the entangled character of territorial politics, religious practice, and water management broadly within the empire. However, when considered in their local and regional scale, the political associations and the cultural biographies of all such monuments tell different stories. In the next section, I turn to the preliminary results of Yalburt Yaylası

FIGURE 13.2 Yalburt Yaylası Monument (Ankara Anatolian Civilizations Museum Archives).

Archaeological Landscape Research Project, a diachronic regional survey that I have been directing since 2010.

REGIONAL POLITICS OF WATER IN THE YALBURT SURVEY REGION

Hittite diplomatic texts, particularly the interpolity treaty documents from Boğazköy, describe the Hulaya River Land and Pedassa as the borderland between the Hittite Lower Land and the Kingdom of Tarhuntašša. Hulaya River land has been identified quite convincingly extending from the Beyşehir and Suğla Lake Basins into the Konya Plain along the Çarşamba River (Figure 13.3 on page 266) (Barjamovic 2010:371; Hawkins 1995:50; Yakar, Dinçol, Dinçol, and Taffet 2001). This identification has been further confirmed by the discovery of the rock monument of Kurunta, king of Tarhuntašša, at Hatip springs in the neighborhood of Hatip (Yakar 2014:501–502). Kurunta's terse yet scandalous inscription that announced him as a "Great King" (a title usually reserved for the kings at Hattuša) was carved on the living rock a few meters right above the gushing waters of Hatip spring. His inscription further testifies to the contested nature of this region as a borderland between Hatti and Tarhuntašša. Pedassa likewise is usually identified to be located north of Hulaya River Land, in the uplands that stretch from Sultan Mountains all the way to the Sakarya River Valley and separated from the Hulaya River

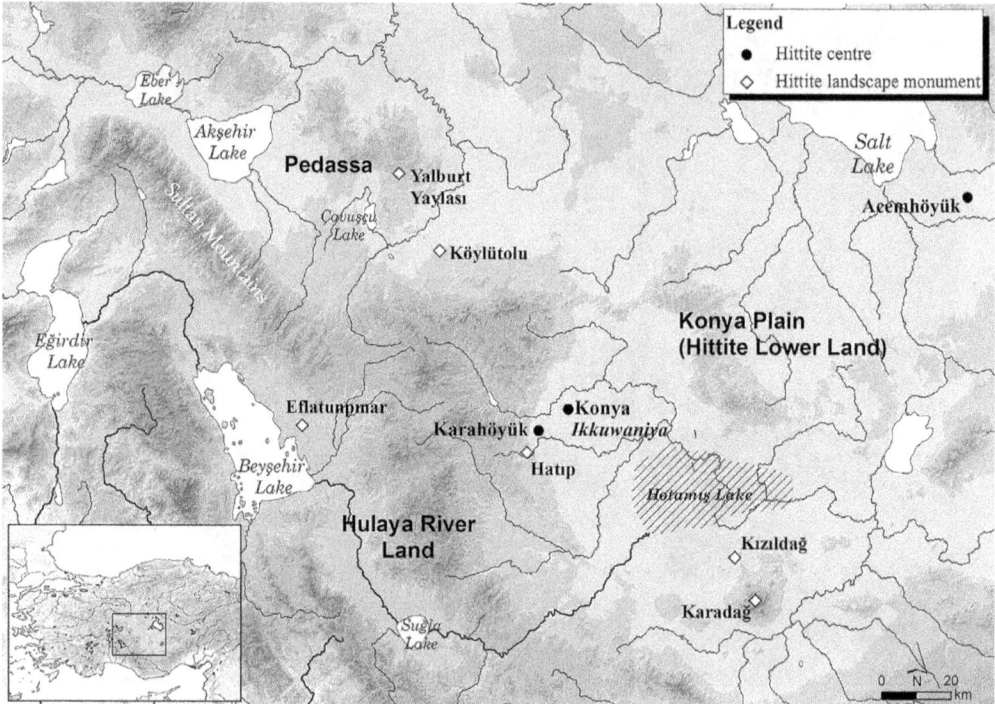

Figure 13.3 Map of Hulaya River Land and Pedassa during the Late Bronze Age (Base Map by Peri Johnson, using ESRI Topographic Data [Creative Commons]: World Shaded Relief).

Land by a mountain called Huwatnuwanda (Barjamovic 2010:371; Hawkins 1995:55). Tudhaliya IV's commemorative pool at Yalburt Yaylası and its environs then can possibly conceived as part of this borderland landscape.

Yalburt monument was discovered in the fall of 1970, when the General Directorate of Roads, Electricity, and Waterworks was excavating the spring to distribute its waters to nearby villages, and they came across a series of inscribed ashlar blocks (Temizer 1984; Temizer 1988). It was excavated and restored to its current state by Raci Temizer, then the director of Anatolian Civilizations Museum in Ankara, and his team between 1971 and 1975. None of the stratigraphic soundings the team placed on the nearby mound, the pool, or the medieval cemetery downhill from the monument produced any stratified remains of a Hittite settlement at the *yayla* site. Why exactly had Tudhaliya IV chosen this remote mountain spring in the uplands of Ilgın, and what kind of a water politics was he involved with when appropriating the local spring to commemorate his military victories in a sacred pool complex while managing its waters within a reservoir? What was the nature of the so-far undocumented episodes of colonial violence that took place in this local place?

These research questions are further complicated when one takes into consideration another nearby Hittite water monument: Köylütolu Yayla Earthen dam, located only about 21 km (as the crow flies) to the southeast of the Yalburt Monument. At the site, known as the Yazılıtaş Mevkii, about 4 km northwest of Köylütolu village, Polish art historian, philologist, and conservator Maryan Sokolowski came across a limestone basin, inscribed with a brief Luwian inscription. The inscription has three lines and is provisionally dated to the time of Tudḫaliya IV, although it does not name the Great King explicitly but a local governor, whose name is variously read as Sausga-Ru(wa)-ti or Sauskakuruntis, and who is attested in four seal impressions from Ḫattuša/Boğazköy (Masson 1980). The findspot of the inscription is right next to a massive arc-shaped earthen dam structure, today known among the local community of Köylütolu as "Büyük Büvet" (Emre 1993:8–9; Johnson and Harmanşah 2015:258–259) and first suggested by Hans Güterbock to be an earthen dam associated with the inscription (Güterbock 1946). The dam is a colossal landscape feature today. In plan it is formed by a gentle East-West arc at least 750 m long that creates a basin to its south. The embankment rises up to 20 m from the surrounding plain. The earthen structure is built up of several layers of imported soils while the dam was topped with a layer of rubble stone fill. The construction of the dam seems to have been an excessively labor-intensive activity, although coring by our geomorphologists in the reservoir showed no trace of sedimentation.

The two water monuments of Yalburt Yaylası and Köylutolu Yayla, both dating to the reign of the Hittite king Tudhaliya IV (r. 1237–1209 BCE) clearly belong to the same local landscape that is organized around the three hydrologically connected former lake basins of the Ilgın Plain, the Atlantı Plain, and the Çavuşçu Lake Basin (Figure 13.4 on page 268). The three basins are linked to each other also by the Bulasan River Valley, and the microregion is bracketed by the heavily eroded karst uplands of the Gavur Dağ-Karadağ Massif to the north and the verdant terraces of Boz Mountain to the south. Initiated in 2010 as a diachronic regional survey in Ilgın district of Konya, Yalburt Yaylası Archaeological Landscape Research Project has been investigating the history of settlement in this complex and varied landscape, while attempting to understand the historical circumstances and the cultural context of the making of the two water monuments. Yalburt Project combines both extensive and intensive archaeological survey, architectural documentation, material culture analysis, environmental research, and geomorphological prospection to understand the politics of water management, land use, and settlement in this contested borderlands region. The Ilgın and Atlantı plains have a long history of alluviation and have witnessed substantial irrigation projects, and are therefore largely buried with alluvial deposits up to 2–4 m, occurring in some places since the Hellenistic period. The burial of landscapes, the changing patterns of land use, water regimes, and the management of resources from antiquity to modernity are essential for a nuanced understanding of the historical ecology of the region.

The contemporaneous construction of the Yalburt Pool and the Köylütolu Dam at the time of Tudhaliya IV prompted us to suggest that the imperial intervention in this region by the Hittite state was done through the control and management of water resources. The monumentalization of springs and the creation of new water reservoirs clearly point to both symbolic and large-scale strategic gestures to reorient and intensify the agricultural landscape, modify the established patterns of land use, and introduce a new settlement program. Yalburt project surveyed the archaeological site of Boz Höyük at the southern edge of the Ilgın Plain in 2011 (Harmanşah and Johnson 2013:76–77) and this site is an example of a new urban foundation where the ceramic assemblage closely

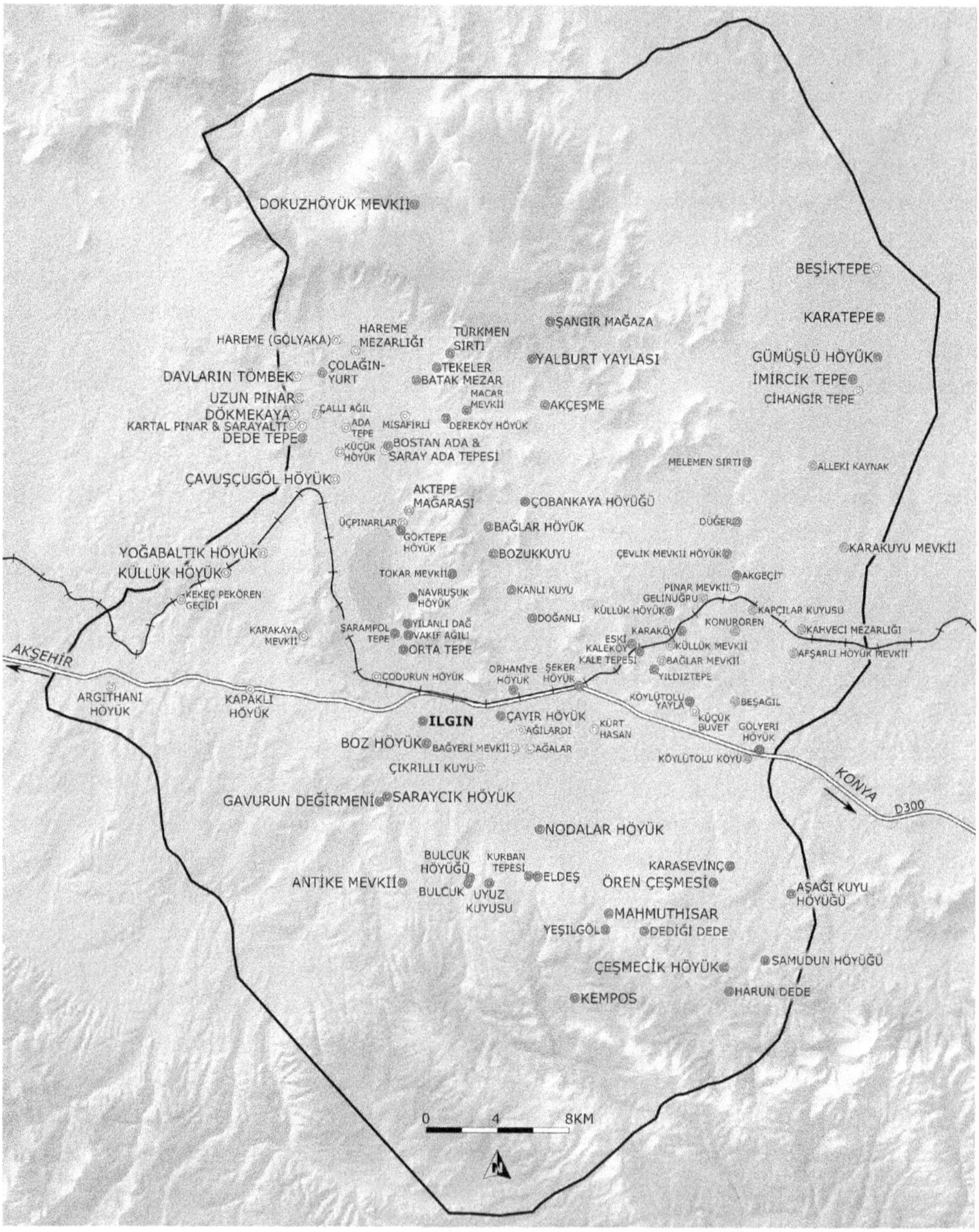

FIGURE 13.4 Map of Yalburt Yaylası Archaeological Landscape Project Survey area and survey units (2010–2015) (Map by Peri Johnson, © Yalburt Yaylası Archaeological Landscape Project).

connects with the production of the ceramic workshops of the Hittite capital cities to the northeast and elsewhere.[3] The settlement at Boz Höyük is a sizeable mound (at least 5 ha) built on the banks of one of the major tributaries of the Bulasan River, which flowed through the Ilgın Plain in antiquity. It is a short-lived, single-period site with an extensive assemblage of Hittite palatial wares of ceremonial consumption, and therefore presumably functioned as an administrative center for the agricultural production in the Ilgın Plain and its environs at the time of the late Hittite Empire.

Several seasons of work at the Yalburt Yaylası site itself revealed only a small amount of ceramic evidence for cultural activity at the site during the Late Bronze Age (ca. 1600–1175 BCE) and earlier, although the archaeological site around the monument, developed into a sizeable settlement with notable evidence for textile industry during the Late Iron Age (540–330 BCE), Hellenistic (330–30 BCE), and Roman Imperial periods (ca. 30 BCE–300 CE). The Hittite pool seems to have been continuously used, maintained, and at least once rebuilt during the early centuries of the Roman Empire. The settlement at Yalburt Yaylası grew exponentially during the Late Roman and Byzantine periods (300–1100 CE) into a massive village of houses with stone foundations. The dense clustering of the Hittite sites therefore had to be found elsewhere in the survey region. The survey results from the first five seasons of fieldwork now suggest that the two focal points of monumentalization during the Late Bronze Age were (1) the southwestern end of the Bulasan River valley where it is connected to the Ilgın Plain through a narrow isthmus—this is a landscape that is well connected to the Köylütolu Yayla Earthen Dam—and (2) the Dökmekaya ridge on the western edge of the Kuru Göl Basin, directly southwest of the Yalburt Monument, on a route that connected this monument to the major east-west running common road that connected the Konya Plain to the western Anatolia (Figure 13.5).

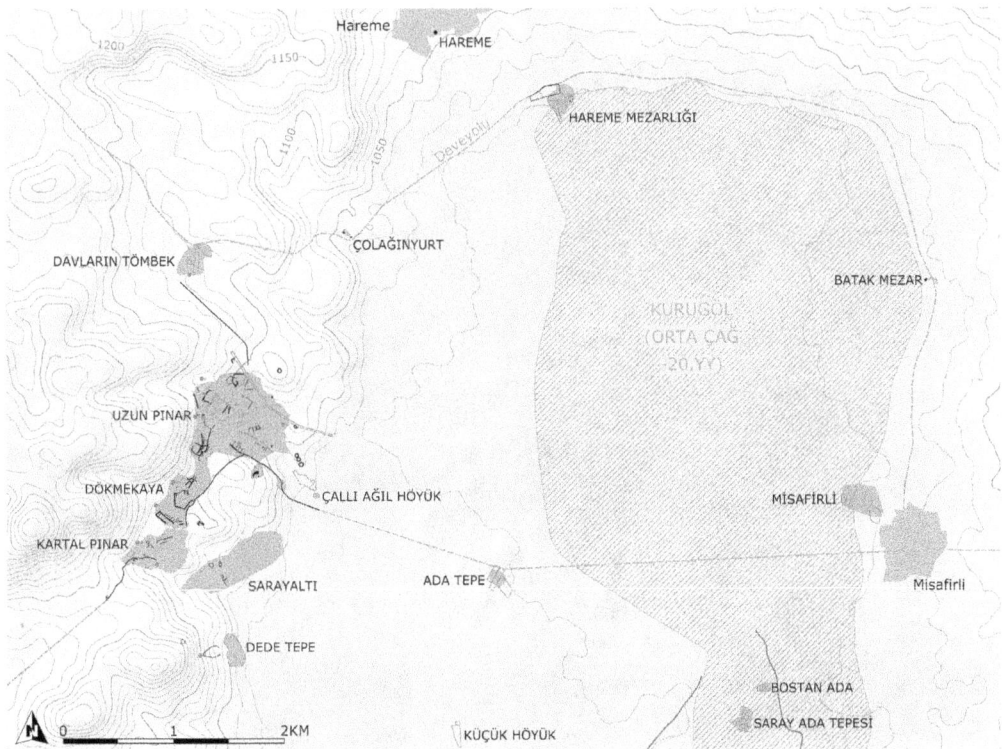

FIGURE 13.5 Map of Kuru Göl Basin (Map by Peri Johnson, © Yalburt Yaylası Archaeological Landscape Project).

The narrow isthmus on the southwestern end of the Bulasan River Valley is flanked by a massive limestone outcrop, sitting in between the three major villages in its vicinity: Karaköy, Kaleköy, and Zaferiye (Harmanşah and Johnson 2013:77–78; Harmanşah, Johnson, and Durusu-Tanrıöver 2014:16; Johnson and Harmanşah 2015:269–271). On the northeast foot of this massif where limestone comes into contact with the underlying schist, a major spring (*Kale Çeşmesi*) is located. The sweet waters and the abundant flow of the spring are famous in the whole region among the villages of Ilgın and Kadınhanı, and the spring is surrounded by orchards and fish farms. On the steep slopes immediately above this spring rises a well-preserved monumental fortress built of massive ashlar blocks of marl, overlooking the Bulasan River Valley and the isthmus (Figure 13.6). The fortress is known locally as Kale Tepesi. Prior to the work of Yalburt project in the 2010 season, the fortress and the extensive archaeological remains on the terraces surrounding the fortress had not been the subject of any major archaeological study.[4] The detailed study of the stone-cutting techniques at the fortress, the scatter of ceramics in and around the fortress, and our discovery of its quarries allowed us to propose that the fortress must have been built during the Late Bronze Age, but continued in use during the Hellenistic and Roman periods. The ashlar blocks do not present any evidence of the use of chisels or mortar, while the blocks are fitted to the adjacent blocks through gentle, cushion-like details of finely fitting joints, with close similarity to the ashlar bonding techniques that are observed at Yalburt Pool. The central rectangular space of the fortress is further

FIGURE 13.6 Kale Tepesi Fortress (Yalburt Yaylası Archaeological Landscape Project).

strengthened by additional towers especially visible on the southwestern edge as well as in the cascading series of towers on the steep slopes of the northeastern edge of the fortress.

According to Ben Marsh, the project's geomorphologist, the ashlar blocks that were used at the Hittite fortress were not quarried from the locally available limestone bed-rock of Kale Tepesi but must have been brought in from a quarry of marl that offered the better quality building blocks. Yalburt Project team's search for a marl quarry in the vicinity of Kale Tepesi site was fruitful, and the team identified and documented Yıldız-tepe marl quarry site about 1.2 km south-southeast of Kale Tepesi fortress, on the first ridge across a saddle. Our intensive survey at Yıldıztepe site, the only marl rock outcrop in the close vicinity of Kale Tepesi, identified several layers of ashlar blocks that have been quarried out (Johnson and Harmanşah 2015:270–271). The identification of the quarry as a predominantly Bronze Age quarry was based on a very dense assemblage of nonendemic green gabbro hammer fragments and chips that were distributed across the quarry site, most likely used as the quarrying tool at the site (Harmanşah and Johnson 2014:380). Because of the general absence of any evidence of the use of iron chisels and other tools, it can be suggested that this quarry must have provided the marl blocks of Kale Tepesi fortress at the time of its construction during the Hittite Empire. Yalburt team's fieldwalking survey in the lower slopes of Kale Tepesi, as well as other nearby mound sites revealed a rich collection of ceramics dated to the Hittite Empire period comparable to the fine and common wares of our Hittite ceramics-type site Boz Höyük, which was discussed above. It is then notable to point out that we consider Kale Tepesi Hittite fortress and the Yıldız Tepe quarry as a combined assemblage of Hittite urban-ization in the Bulasan River valley. Köylütolu Yayla Earthen Dam is located only about 3 km southeast of this ensemble to the East of the Ilgın Plain. Further intensive survey is needed in the environs of Köylütolu Yayla dam. However, it is possible to suggest that Tudhaliya IV's massive investment of labor in the construction of this dam must have been related to the construction of the fortress at Kale Tepesi and possibly had an objective for the boosting of agricultural production in the hinterland of this new urban center.

I turn finally to the Kuru Göl Basin, both to illustrate another zone of settlement intensity during the Hittite Empire Period and also to connect my discussion of water politics to contemporary political ecology. One of the important caravan routes that crossed the Yalburt project survey zone is called "Ulu Yol" (literally, the Great Road), and links the Atlantı Plain to the agricultural fields immediately below Yalburt Yaylası, while it continues west and crosses the Kuru Göl basin before it reaches to the major east--west highway (Konya-Afyon road), which replaced the ancient common road to the west. A coal-operated power plant and its supplying open pit lignite mine and limestone quarries are planned to completely occupy the Kuru Göl Basin. This urgent situation prompted the Yalburt Survey Project to concentrate its efforts during the recent seasons on the endangered archaeological landscape of Kuru Göl (Johnson and Harmanşah 2015:272–274). Kuru Göl is the marshy northern half of Çavuşçu Göl, until it was drained when the freshwater lake of Çavuşçu Göl was transformed into a controlled reservoir for a massive irrigation project by the State Waterworks Department in the 1960s and 1990s, in order to provide water for irrigated agriculture in Atlantı and Ilgın

Plains. Several streams that used to have their beds flowing through the Ilgın Plain were canalized to feed this new, dammed reservoir. This newly implemented industrial-scale irrigation program introduced an intricate network of distribution and diversion canals, overflow channels, and concrete-lined irrigation channels, and not only dramatically transformed the favored agricultural landscape in the Ilgın and Atlantı plains, but also further marginalized landscapes such as the Kuru Göl basin, which has now been completely drained of its groundwater. This marginalized and ruined landscape further legitimizes the prospect of the construction of the coal-operated power plant.

In the spirit of a salvage operation with the looming construction of the power plant, Yalburt Project team surveyed the archaeological landscape of the Kuru Göl basin. Travelers' accounts and previous archaeological and official reports had implicitly or explicitly suggested the absence of any archaeological heritage in the basin. Contrary to such historical conviction, the project team encountered a rich archaeological landscape of a series of mounded settlements in and around the lake basin as well as a series of fortress-like settlements on the Dökmekaya ridge overlooking the basin to its western edge. A series of active and fossil springs are attested on the limestone-schist hills of the Dökmekaya ridge. Associated with these springs and in the terraces that descend to the basin, Yalburt Project identified a dense clustering of settlements, including the Early Bronze Age mounds of Çallı Ağıl Höyük and Davların Tömbek Höyüğü, the low mound at Kartal Pınarı dating from the second millennium BCE, a looted pithos cemetery of the Hittite Empire period downslope from Uzun Pınar spring, the Hellenistic fortress at the highest point by Uzun Pınar spring, and the vast terraces of undated stone-built compounds spread over a vast area on the slopes of Dökmekaya and Uzun Pınar. This intensive settlement forms a rich archaeological landscape of approximately 80 ha across the well-watered Dökmekaya ridge and represents another focus of settlement during the second millennium BCE along with the earlier clusters discussed above. Hittite settlement in the Kuru Göl Basin is further supported by two important mound sites of Misafirli Höyük on the eastern edge of the basin and Hareme Mezarlığı on the northwestern edge.

Conclusions: Political Ecologies of Water, Ancient and Modern

The construction of the two major water monuments during the reign of the Hittite Great king Tudhaliya IV in the varied regional landscape of Ilgın points to an ambitious project of agricultural as well as sociosymbolic and political investment in the borderland region of Pedassa by the Hittite imperial administration. Ilgın's dramatic karst geology especially in the uplands of Gavur Dağ-Karadağ massif and the alluvial lowlands and river valleys offers an eventful geological landscape of water with its marshy lakes, multiple streams, abundant springs, sinkholes, caves, and swallow holes, where water continuously appears and disappears. Flows of water have been impacted by human communities over the ages (perhaps a bit more dramatically in the late twentieth century) through the introduction of irrigation systems, building of dams and reservoirs, or controlling water's use. It is important to highlight that water does not appear at any moment in history as a neutral, static, manageable substance but always appears to be a powerful actor in the negotiation of regional politics of settlement and landscape.

Also significant here is the entanglement among the political ecologies of different episodes within the genealogy of landscapes. Although some archaeologists may not feel responsible and may choose to engage only with the politics of place in the archaeological past, the contemporary politics of water is very much intimately linked to deep genealogies of water politics that is specific to places. In his monograph *Politics of Nature*, Bruno Latour (2004:9–52) argues that the commonly believed rift between scientific ecologies and political ecologies is not a real one. On the one side, we have the environmental sciences involving development studies, public health, sustainability studies, climate change initiatives, and archaeological salvage operations, where environment is consistently studied from a crisis-based perspective: problems and solutions for the environment. These scientifically addressed problems and their solutions are then delivered to the policymakers and local and indigenous communities around the world. On the other side of the debate we have political ecology and environmental humanities, with its challenges to neoliberal capitalism and activist resistance to development projects, critiques of colonialism and globalization, and cultural approaches to human landscapes. Latour suggests that the split between scientific research and politics of the environment is a problematic one: he argues we do not have the option of engaging with political ecology or not. This is done implicitly, surreptitiously, or explicitly in the sciences.

Watery landscapes are vibrant, eventful, and emergent places, where the flow of water is always negotiated. As seen successfully in Bollaín's movie *Even the Rain*, the juxtaposition of different episodes of such place-specific politics is revealing, and leads to creative evaluations of the past and contemporary situations. Archaeological inquiry over the cultural biography of landscapes may indeed become most fruitful if we are willing to address such cross-temporal entanglements and flows.

NOTES

1. On places and landscapes of holy water and healing, see, e.g., Strang 2004:83–102; Strang 2008; Gesler 2003; and Gesler and Kearns 2002. For an anthropological study of the Husayn Tekri Dargah, see Bellamy 2011. On history of the healing sanctuary at Lourdes, see Harris 2000. On Byzantine *agiasma* churches, see Talbot 2002. On the sacred lakes of Belize during the Mayan period, see Lucero and Kinkella 2014.

2. Excellent examples of such work of critical geomorphology can be seen in Marsh 1999, 2013; Beach, Luzzadder-Beach, Krause, Walling, Dunning, Flood, Guderjan, and Valdez 2015; Beach, Luzzadder-Beach, Krause, and Guderjan 2015.

3. See also Johnson and Harmanşah 2015. Second-millennium ceramic assemblages from the 2010–2012 seasons have recently been the subject of a PhD dissertation by Müge Durusu-Tanrıöver, entitled "Experiencing the Hittite Empire in its Borderlands" (Brown University, 2016). Durusu-Tanrıöver points out that the Middle Bronze Age local ceramics of Yalburt region align quite well with the ceramic assemblages of the Middle Bronze Age levels of Beycesultan mound, while during the Late Bronze Age Yalburt region

turns explicitly and increasingly toward the North Central Anatolian wares of the Halys bend.

4.   One exception is a brief mention of the fortress in Dinçol, Yakar Dinçol, and Taffet 2000, which evoked the possibility of dating the fortress to a pre-Hellenistic period. Hasan Bahar's survey team published a preliminary architectural survey of the fortress (Bahar, Karauğuz, and Koçak 1996 Plate CXXXIII).

REFERENCES CITED

Albro, R. 2005 Water Is Ours Carajo! Deep Citizenship in Bolivia's Water War. In *Social Movements: An Anthropological Reader*, edited by J. Nash, pp. 249–271. Blackwell, Malden, MA.

Atalay, S., L. Clauss, R. H. McGuire, and J. R. Welch (editors). 2014 *Transforming Archaeology: Activist Practices and Prospects*. Left Coast Press, Walnut Creek, CA.

Bahar, H., G. Karauğuz, and Ö. Koçak. 1996 *Eskiçağ Konya Araştırmaları I (Phyrgia Paroreus Bölgesi: Anıtlar, Yerleşmeler ve Küçük Buluntular)*. FS Yayınları, Istanbul.

Barjamovic, G. 2011 *A Historical Geography of Anatolia in the Old Assyrian Colony Period*. Museum Tusculanum Press, Copenhagen.

Beach, T., S. Luzzadder-Beach, S. Krause, S. Walling, N. Dunning, J. Flood, T. Guderjan, F. Valdez. 2015 Mayacene' Floodplain and Wetland Formation in the Rio Bravo Watershed of Northwestern Belize. *The Holocene* 25(10):1612–1626.

Beach, T., S. Luzzadder-Beach, T. Guderjan, and S. Krause. 2015 The Floating Gardens of Chan Cahal: Soils, Water, and Human Interactions. *Catena* 132:151–164.

Bear C., and J. Bull. 2011 Water Matters: Agency, Flows, and Frictions. *Environment and Planning A* 43(10):2261–2266.

Bellamy, C. 2011. *The Powerful Ephemeral. Everyday Healing in an Ambiguously Islamic Place*. The University of California Press, Berkeley.

Butzer, K. 1976. *Early Hydraulic Civilization in Egypt: A Study in Cultural Ecology*. University of Chicago Press, Chicago and London.

Butzer, K. 1996. Irrigation, Raised Fields and State Management: Wittfogel redux? *Antiquity* 70:200–204.

Campbell, S. 2011 Wet and Fluid. In *The Face of the Earth: Natural Landscapes, Science, and Culture*, edited by S. Campbell, pp. 120–181. University of California Press, Berkeley.

Cilento, F. 2012. Even the Rain: A Confluence of Cinematic and Historical Temporalities. *Arizona Journal of Hispanic Cultural Studies* 16:245–258.

Davies, M. I. J. 2009 Wittfogel's Dilemma: Heterarchy and Ethnographic Approaches to Irrigation Management in Eastern Africa and Mesopotamia. *World Archaeology* 41(1):16–35.

Dinçol, A., J. Yakar, B. Dinçol, and A. Taffet. 2000 The Borders of the Appanage Kingdom of Tarhuntassa—A Geographical and Archaeological Assessment. *Anatolica* 26:1–30.

Dolatyar, M., and T. Gray. 2000 *Water Politics in the Middle East: A Context for Conflict or Cooperation?* Palgrave Macmillan, New York.

Durusu-Tanrıöver, M. 2016. Experiencing the Hittite Empire in its Borderlands. Unpublished PhD Dissertation. Brown University, Providence, Rhode Island.

Edgeworth, M. 2011. *Fluid Pasts: Archaeology of Flow*. Bristol Classical Press Bloomsbury Academic, Bristol.

Ehringhaus, H. 2005 *Götter, Herrscher Inschriften: Die Felsreliefs der hethitischen Großreichzeit in der Türkei*. Verlag Philipp von Zabern, Mainz am Rhein.

Emre, K. 1993 The Hittite Dam of Karakuyu. In *Essays on Anatolian Archaeology*, edited by H.I.H. Prince Takahito Mikasa. Bulletin of the Middle Eastern Culture Center in Japan vol. 7, pp. 1–42. Harrassowitz Verlag, Wiesbaden.

Erbil, Y., and A. Mouton. 2012 Water in Ancient Anatolian Religions: An Archaeological and Philological Inquiry on the Hittite Evidence. *Journal of Near Eastern Studies* 71:53–74.

Escobar, A. 2008 *Territories of Difference: Place, Movements, Life, Redes*. Duke University Press, Durham.

Frérot, A. 2011 *Water: Towards a Culture of Responsibility*. University of New Hampshire Press, Durham.

Gesler, W. M. 2003 *Healing Places*. Rowman and Littlefield, Lanham, MD.

Gesler, W. M., and R. A. Kearns. 2002 *Culture, Place, and Health*. Routledge, Oxon and New York.

Glatz, C. 2009 Empire as Network: Spheres of Material Interaction in Late Bronze Age Anatolia. *Journal of Anthropological Archaeology* 28:127–141.

Glatz, C. 2011 The Hittite State and Empire from Archaeological Evidence. In *Oxford Handbook of Ancient Anatolia 10,000–323 BCE*, edited by S. R. Steadman and G. McMahon, pp. 877–899. Oxford University Press, Oxford.

Glatz, C., and A. M. Plourde. 2011 Landscape Monuments and Political Competition in Late Bronze Age Anatolia: An Investigation of Costly Signaling Theory. *Bulletin of the Schools of Oriental Research* 361:33–66.

Güterbock, H. G. 1946 *Ankara Bedesteninde bulunan Eti Müzesi Büyük Salonunun Kılavuzu = Guide to the Hittite Museum in the Bedesten at Ankara*. Translated by Nimet Özgüç. Milli Egitim Bakanlığı, Eski Eserler ve Müzeler Umum Müdürlüğü. Anıtları Koruma Kurulu. Seri I, Sayı X. Istanbul: Milli Egitim Basimevi.

Harmanşah, Ö. 2014 Event, Place, Performance: Rock Reliefs and Spring Monuments in Anatolia. In *Of Rocks and Water: Towards an Archaeology of Place*, edited by Ömür Harmanşah, pp. 139–167. Joukowsky Institute Publications 5. Oxbow Books, Oxford.

Harmanşah, Ö. 2015. *Place, Memory, and Healing: An Archaeology of Anatolian Rock Monuments*. Routledge, Oxon and New York.

Harmanşah, Ö. 2017 Borders are Rough-hewn: Monuments, Local Landscapes, and the Politics of Place in Hittite Anatolia. In *Bordered Places | Bounded Times. Cross-disciplinary perspectives on Turkey*, edited by E. Baysal and L. Karakatsanis. pp. 37–51. The British Institute at Ankara, London.

Harmanşah, Ö., and P. Johnson. 2013 Pınarlar, Mağaralar, ve Hitit Anadolu'sunda Kırsal Peyzaj: Yalburt Yaylası Arkeolojik Yüzey Araştırma Projesi (Ilgın, Konya), 2011 Sezonu Sonuçları. In *30. Araştırma Sonuçları Toplantısı*, edited by A. Özme, II. Cilt, pp. 73–84. T.C. Kültür ve Turizm Bakanlığı Kültür Varlıkları ve Müzeler Genel Müdürlüğü, Ankara.

Harmanşah, Ö., and P. Johnson. 2014 Yalburt'a Çıkan Bütün Yollar: Yalburt Yaylası Arkeolojik Yüzey Araştırması (Konya) 2012 Sezonu Çalışmaları. In *31. Araştırma Sonuçları Toplantısı*, edited by A. Özme, II. Cilt, pp. 377–394. T.C. Kültür ve Turizm Bakanlığı Kültür Varlıkları ve Müzeler Genel Müdürlüğü, Ankara.

Harmanşah, Ö., and P. Johnson. 2016 Hitit Ülkesi Sınırları'nda Peyzaj ve Yerleşim: Yalburt Yaylası ve Çevresi Arkeolojik Yüzey Araştırması Projesi Saha Çalışmaları 2014 Sezonu. In *33. Araştırma Sonuçları Toplantısı*, edited by C. Keskin, II. Cilt, pp. 235–250. T.C. Kültür ve Turizm Bakanlığı Kültür Varlıkları ve Müzeler Genel Müdürlüğü, Ankara.

Harmanşah, Ö., P. Johnson, and M. Durusu-Tanrıöver. 2014 A Hittite King at the Spring of Yalburt: Bronze Age, Cold Waters, and the Anatolian Landscape. *Actual Archaeology Magazine* 10 (Summer):10–16.

Harmanşah, Ö., P. Johnson, and M. Durusu-Tanrıöver. 2016 Kuru Göl Havzası'nda Yerleşim ve Çevre: Yalburt Yaylası ve Çevresi Arkeolojik Yüzey Araştırması 2013 Sezonu. In *33. Araştırma Sonuçları Toplantısı*, edited by C. Keskin, II Cilt, pp. 217–234. T.C. Kültür ve Turizm Bakanlığı Kültür Varlıkları ve Müzeler Genel Müdürlüğü, Ankara.

Harris, R. 2000. *Lourdes: Body and Spirit in the Secular Age.* Penguin, London.

Harrower, M. J. 2009 Is the Hydraulic Hypothesis Dead Yet? Irrigation and Social Change in Ancient Yemen. *World Archaeology* 41:58–72.

Hawkins, J. D. 1995 *The Hieroglyphic Inscription of the Sacred Pool Complex at Hattusa (SÜD-BURG).* Studien zu den Bogazköy-Texten Beiheft 3. Harrassowitz, Wiesbaden.

Johnson, P., and Ö. Harmanşah. 2015. Landscape, Politics, and Water in the Hittite Borderlands: Yalburt Yaylası Archaeological Landscape Research Project 2010–2014. In *The Archaeology of Anatolia: Recent Discoveries (2013–2014)*, edited by S. Steadman and G. McMahon, pp. 255–277. Cambridge Scholars Press, Cambridge.

Kleinitz, C., and C. Näser. 2011 The Loss of Innocence: Political and Ethical Dimensions of the Merowe Dam Archaeological Salvage Project at the Fourth Nile Cataract (Sudan). *Conservation and Management of Archaeological Sites* 13(2–3):253–280.

Knapp, A. B., and W. Ashmore. 1999 Archaeological Landscapes: Constructed, Conceptualized, Ideational. In *Archaeologies of Landscape: Contemporary Perspectives*, edited by W. Ashmore and A. Bernard Knapp, pp. 1–32. Blackwell, Oxford.

Latour, B. 2004 *The Politics of Nature: How to Bring the Sciences into Democracy.* Harvard University Press, Cambridge and London.

Lucero, L. J., and A. Kinkella. 2014 A Place for Pilgrimage: The Ancient Maya Sacred Landscape of Cara Blanca, Belize. In *Of Rocks and Water: Towards an Archaeology of Place*, edited by Ö. Harmanşah, pp. 13–39. Joukowsky Institute Publications 5. Oxbow Books, Oxford.

Marsh, B. 1999 Sakarya River History and the Alluvial Burial of Gordion. *Journal of Field Archaeology* 26(2):163–173.

Marsh, B. 2013 Reading Gordion Settlement History from Stream Sedimentation. In *The Archaeology of Phrygian Gordion, Royal City of Midas*, edited by C. B. Rose, pp. 39–46. Gordion Special Studies 7. University of Pennsylvania Museum, Philadelphia.

Masson, E. 1980 Les Inscriptions Louvites Hiéroglyphiques de Köylütolu et Beyköy. *Kadmos* 19:106–122.

Ökse, T. 2011 Open-Air Sanctuaries of the Hittites. In *Insights into Hittite History and Archaeology*, edited by H. Genz and D. P. Mielke, pp. 219–240. Peeters, Leuven.

Poetto, M. 1993 *L'iscrizione luvio-geroglifica di Yalburt : nuove acquisizioni relative alla geografia dell'Anatolia Sud-Occidentale.* Studia Mediterranea 8. G. Iuculano Editore, Pavia.

Shoup, D. 2006 Can Archaeology Build a Dam? Sites and Politics in Turkey's Southwest Anatolia Project. *Journal of Mediterranean Archaeology* 19(2):231–258.

Strang, V. 2004 *The Meaning of Water.* Berg, Oxford and New York.

Strang, V. 2008 The Social Construction of Water. In *Handbook of Landscape Archaeology*, edited by B. David and J. Thomas, pp. 123–130. Left Coast Press, Walnut Creek CA.

Talbot, A.-M. 2002. Pilgrimage to Healing Shrines: The Evidence of Miracle Accounts. *Dumbarton Oaks Papers* 56:153–173.

Temizer, R. 1984 Ilgın Yalburt Yaylası Hitit Anıtı. In *Konya*, edited by F. Halıcı, pp. 53–57. Güven Matbaası, Ankara.

Temizer, R. 1988 Introduction. In *İnandıktepe: an Important Cult Center in the Old Hittite Period*, edited by T. Özgüç, pp. xxiii–xxxii. Türk Tarih Kurumu Basımevi, Ankara.

Wescoat, J. L. Jr. 2000 Wittfogel East and West: Changing Perspectives On Water Development in South Asia and the US, 1670–2000. In *Cultural Encounters with the Environment: Enduring and Evolving Geographic Themes*, edited by A. B. Murphy and D. L. Johnson, pp. 109–132. Rowman and Littlefield, Lanham, MD.

Wilson, R. L. (editor). 1987 *Rescue Archaeology: Proceedings of the Second New World Conference on Rescue Archaeology*. Southern Methodist University Press, Dallas.

Wittfogel, K. A. 1957 *Oriental Despotism a Comparative Study of Total Power.* Yale University Press, New Haven.

Yakar, J. 2014 The Archaeology and Political Geography of the Lower Land in the Last Century of the Hittite Empire. In *Some Observations on Anatolian Cultures Compiled in Honor of Armağan Erkanal.* Edited by N. Çandarlı-Karaaslan, A. Aykurt, N. Kolankaya-Bostancı, and Y. H. Erbil, pp. 501–510. Hacettepe University Press, Ankara.

Yakar, J., A. M. Dinçol, B. Dinçol. and A. Taffet. 2001 The Territory of the Appanage Kingdom of Tarhuntassa—An Archaeological Appraisal. In *Akten des IV. Internationalen Würzburg 4–8 Oktober 1999 Kongresses für Hethitologie,* edited by G. Wilhelm, pp. 711–718. Studien zu den Bogazköy-Texten Band 45. Wiesbaden.

CHAPTER FOURTEEN

Some Perspectives on the Frequency of Significant, Historically Forcing Drought and Subsistence Crises in Anatolia and Region

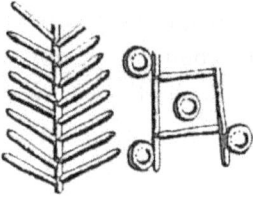

Sturt W. Manning

Abstract   *Challenges for, and the responses to, the agricultural basis of human societies—subsistence crises—are central themes when reviewing much of the history and prehistory of the Mediterranean. In particular, the major threat to human subsistence in this region is insufficient availability of water—ranging from minor to serious drought. Short-term (annual-scale) droughts are regular events in the Mediterranean and, over time, agricultural strategies evolved to cope with this recurrent threat. The potentially devastating circumstance is when there are two or more consecutive very dry (drought) years over a large geographical area, potentially defeating most defenses based on storage, diversification, or social networks/trade. A review of some precipitation proxies based on tree-ring records from Anatolia and the Levant from the second millennium CE indicate that such dangerous multiyear larger region very dry (drought) conditions are relatively rare, occurring only once every several centuries. But, when they occurred, such events could be transformative in premodern/mechanized circumstances and thus could be historically significant as drivers affecting historical trajectories.*

INTRODUCTION

In *Famine and Food Supply in the Graeco-Roman World: Responses to Risk and Crisis*, Garnsey (1988) argues the proposition that true famine is rare, but subsistence crises are frequent. He notes that "the boundary between famine and shortage is indistinct" and advocates analysis within a "continuum leading from mild shortage to disastrous famine" (1988:6). Garnsey reviewed recent meteorological and agricultural data and the ancient historical records in his groundbreaking study.

A quarter of a century later, today we have an increasing wealth of paleoclimate proxy reconstructions reaching back over several centuries to millennia to consider with reference to the Classical–East Mediterranean world (see, e.g., discussions and references in Clarke et al. 2015; Cook et al. 2015; Drake 2012; Finné et al. 2011; Haldon et al. 2014; Manning 2013; McCormick et al. 2012; Rosen 2007). If we consider paleoclimate records relating to precipitation, we nonetheless face similar challenges to Garnsey when attempting to integrate them into social history and a consideration of famine and subsistence crisis: What exact reconstruction represents what location on a continuum from mild shortage to disastrous famine? In this paper I explore some high-resolution precipitation proxy records from Anatolia and the Levant to gain perspective on what patterns emerge in terms of a likely subsistence crisis timescale and frequency when there are occurrences of two or more years of consecutive unusually drier conditions (I am not engaging in a detailed associated historical study—see for example Raphael 2013; White 2011). In particular, I focus on the issues of frequency of subsistence crisis episodes of a disastrous scale, both locally and regionally.

To anticipate the outcome, it will come as no surprise that I find Garnsey's proposition generally correct over the longer term: while instances of problematic low local precipitation (and so likely subsistence challenge) are frequent through time, widespread episodes of devastating precipitation shortfall over more than one year (and so likely famine or agricultural disaster) are relatively rare.

The bigger challenge is to define exactly what conditions (or thresholds) create crisis and disaster for humans and their societies in the premodern era. The essays in another influential book published in the late 1980s, *Bad Year Economics: Cultural Responses to Risk and Uncertainty* (Halstead and O'Shea 1989), nicely highlight that a number of complex practical and social mechanisms usually provide buffering against much of the expected variability at interannual scale in climate and local-regional context for human populations and their subsistence (see also Halstead 2014:191–251). In particular, "bad years" are expected and appropriate adaptive strategies are found in cases in all environments and periods. The usual exceptions occur when human-led political policy is unconcerned with the welfare of the population and negates such strategies, and, combined with climatic challenge, this can cause disaster as in the Ukraine under Stalin (e.g., Davies and Wheatcroft 2004) or China under Mao (e.g., Dikötter 2010) (while imperfect, I am thus accepting the general argument of Sen 2001 that famine does not usually occur under a functioning democracy).

In other "normal" situations, two patterns are evident in the case studies in the Halstead and O'Shea (1989) volume. First, larger geographic areas that are broadly homogenous in terms of environment (topography) and climate—placing any potential family, social, or political relations experiencing different circumstances a long way away—are potentially more at risk if general (e.g., climate) conditions become unfavorable (for the whole region). Second, episodes of clusters of growing seasons with inadequate rainfall over several years are likely to defeat any normal experiential "rule of thumb" storage and risk-buffering strategies (whether in terms of crops and sowing/cultivation options or social strategies: Halstead 2014)—and/or the practical or technological limits on storage in "traditional" circumstances until recent times—by human groups and especially farmers (whether individually or in any local area), and so create the conditions for subsistence crisis. The scale of possible buffering strategies varies, both by context (what is expected and how successfully given resources can be stored), and according to the social, economic, and political infrastructure available (major state–level society versus nonstate) and until recent times these rarely ran beyond a couple of years and rarely in reality to the seven-year model under Joseph in *Genesis* 41:47–48.

STORAGE AND THE TIMESCALE FOR SUBSISTENCE CRISIS

In their introduction to a collection of studies on (many aspects of) food in the ancient world, Wilkins and Nadeau (2015:10) observe that "ancient cultures seem to be a typical pre-industrial economy and social structure based on agriculture and pastoralism hugely dependent on the fairness of climatic conditions. A few years of bad harvests can mean social unrest and, even, the fall of great empires." Can we quantify a "few years"? Raphael (2013:56) observes of the Levant that "even well-organized regimes found it hard to cope with long periods (*more than two years*) of food shortage" (my italics), and, after a review of granaries and storage concludes (2013:66), that "the medieval Middle East was ill equipped to battle long-term droughts and famines"—with rulers usually able only to provide famine relief in their capital cities. In the larger states and empires we can observe that the main solution was an ability to import grain from other loci to meet various local shortages (e.g., Garnsey 1988; White 2011:31–34). However, the story at the bottom of the food chain is key: peasants and farms in the countryside. Problems here will migrate up the food chain, and so, despite perhaps the ability to buffer a capital (or other larger) city or military camp via transport logistics and from carefully monitored granary stores (e.g., Curtis 2015; Erdkamp 2015; Rickman 1971, 1980), problems in the countryside will affect the wider region or state or empire (as nicely illustrated and argued in White 2011, for the Ottoman world).

Reviewed in more detail, the approximate two-year threshold mentioned by Raphael keeps recurring as approximately the division between problem and serious problem. Ethnographic investigations in Greece indicate that individual traditional farmers aim to overproduce to achieve a surplus in average years so that even in a typical poor year they nonetheless have an adequate yield, and they also aspire to have an extra year of stored produce (e.g., grain) to cover one real failure year (Forbes 1989:93–94)—thus, household storage for up to two years is the aim for grain, etc., and four years for olive oil, since trees only produce every second year. Halstead (2014:162) similarly notes the aspiration of farmers to store enough grain for a second year "so they could ride one total crop failure," but says this was not always achieved. Sarpaki (1992:229; 2001:38 n.20) offers similar guidance, indicating storage of cereals and legume products typically for one or two years for the prehistoric Aegean (Akrotiri on Thera). Classical authors offer consonant information. Garnsey (1988:54–55) and Forbes and Foxhall (1995:76) cite Theophrastus (*Hist. plant.* 8.11) who says wheat seeds kept for just one year are best (for sowing a new crop), whereas those kept for two-three years are inferior and those kept longer infertile, while still edible—suggesting a usual one-to-two-year model. Garnsey (1988:55) observes testimony that "wheat kept less well than some other grains [e.g., millet] and dry legumes," but, as he concludes in general, the continuing "obsession" of all ancient agricultural writers "with the problems of keeping out moisture and pests" (Forbes and Foxhall 1995:76–77; Spurr 1986:79; White 1970:189) suggests real limits to the efficacy of long-term storage of grain despite various ancient and later authors claiming instances of very long-term storage (e.g., Pliny, *Nat. Hist.* 18.307—see also White 1970:196), such as (supposedly) 50 years for wheat or 100 years for millet. Sigaut (1988) discusses traditional storage techniques for grain and highlights especially the importance of sealed underground pits (1988:10–12), and other ethnohistoric and experimental evidence for underground pit storage of grain investigated by Currid and Navon (1989) further demonstrates the widespread use (and practicality) of the technique in the Mediterranean region (and beyond) (also Halstead 2014:158–160; Spurr 1986:79; White 1970:428). Currid and Navon (1989:67) cite the case from nineteenth-century France of grain being successfully stored in "hermetically sealed underground pits" for five years, but we must assume typically shorter utility in the premodern period in non-extreme-arid circumstances (moisture being a key threat to long-term storage). Halstead (2014) also documents typically one to two-year strategies, despite noting a few exceptions of informants successfully sowing after two or three or even, in two cases, four or six years of storage (2014:157) and of successful storage (underground pit) for two to three years (2014:159) or in a sealed container for up to five years (2014:160).

On the basis of these sorts of indications and discussions, and for the purposes of a heuristic starting point, I take a substantive threat to agricultural production—in this case considering drought as the main threat to subsistence farming in the Aegean–East Mediterranean region—of two or more consecutive years' duration to be potentially serious. This is not to dismiss substantial one-year droughts—a number of reconstructed one-year drought episodes correlate with historical records of drought, crop failure, food shortages, or famine (e.g., Griggs et al. 2014:2711; Köse et al. 2011:Table 6, 448)—however, likely historically significant episodes of food crisis will be those of ca. two or more years duration which have the potential to entirely undermine premodern farming and storage strategies—and especially, we may assume, in those areas that are more marginal in terms of access to water and precipitation, even in the best of times.

SOME PRECIPITATION PROXIES

Instrumental climate records for precipitation (or temperature, etc.) for the East Mediterranean rarely reach back beyond the start of the twentieth century CE (Luterbacher et al. 2012:Fig. 2.1). Thus, the only longer-term annual records of precipitation come from tree ring–based reconstructions (Luterbacher et al. 2012:98–103). Figures 14.1 and 14.2 compare spring precipitation reconstructions (in mm) published for the northern Aegean 1089–1989 CE from the analysis of *Quercus* sp. (Griggs et al. 2007) and from Southwest Anatolia 1339–1998 CE from the analysis of *Juniperus excelsa* (Touchan et al. 2003). The shaded areas show the 1 standard deviation (SD) (light gray) and 2SD (dark

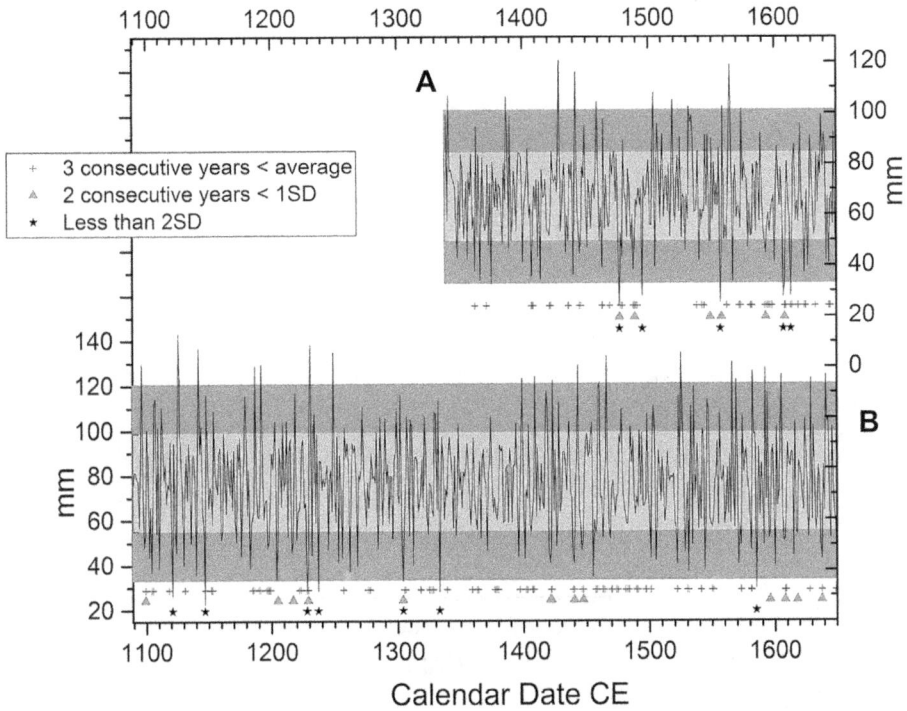

FIGURE 14.1 Tree ring–based spring (May–June) (note: not whole year total) precipitation reconstructions 1089/1339–1650 CE. (A) May–June precipitation (mm) in southwestern Turkey from *Juniperus excelsa* trees (in total 1339–1998 CE) from Touchan et al. (2003). (B) May–June reconstructed precipitation (mm) for NE Greece & NW Turkey from Griggs et al. (2007) employing *Quercus* sp. trees (in total 1089–1989 CE). The light gray area shows the region inside 1SD of the average; the dark gray area shows the region inside 2SD of the average. The + signs indicate years in each record when there have (to that point) been three consecutive years of below-average precipitation; the gray triangles indicate for each record when (to that point) there have been two consecutive years of precipitation more than 1SD below average; and the black stars indicate for each record single years when the precipitation is more than 2SD below the average. Datasets from: ftp://ftp.ncdc.noaa.gov/pub/data/paleo/treering/reconstructions/turkey/sw_turkey_precip.txt; and ftp://ftp.ncdc.noaa.gov/pub/data/paleo/treering/reconstructions/turkey/aegean-precip2007.txt.

gray) ranges around the average precipitation. Figure 14.3 on page 285 shows the same for a precipitation reconstruction for the southern Levant (south Jordan) from *Juniperus phoenicea* trees for 1600–1995 CE (Touchan et al. 1999).

Examination and comparison of Figures 14.1–3 show that while there are a number of reconstructed low-precipitation single years in all records, it is much less common to find periods of two or more consecutive such years and indeed rare to find instances where the reconstructed low-precipitation years are common among the different regions (of Anatolia or wider with the southern Levant). Indeed, not a single one of the >2SD below average reconstructed precipitation years is in common between the North Aegean

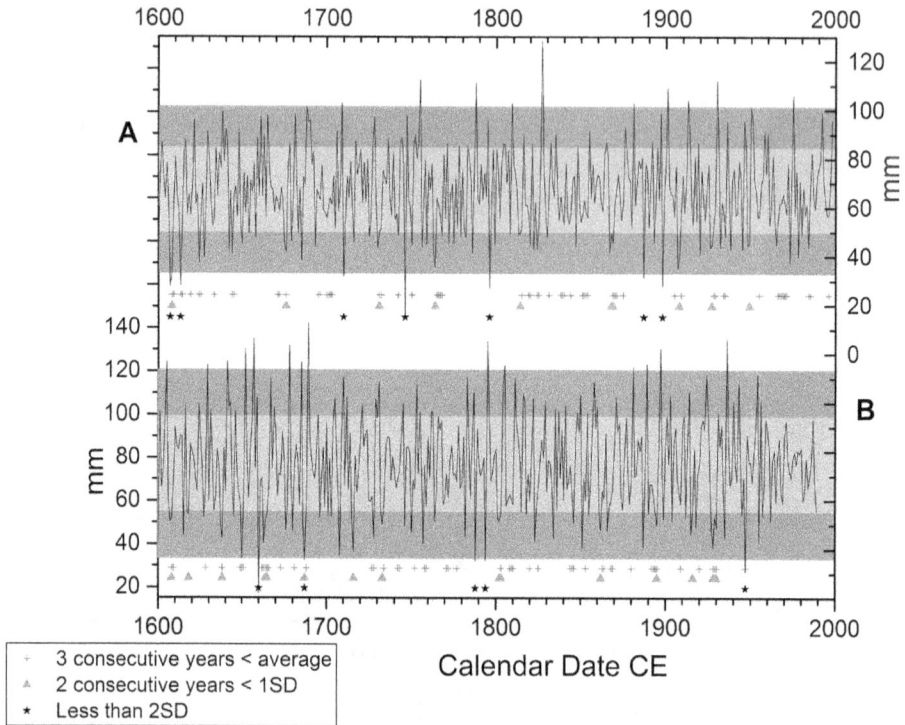

FIGURE 14.2 As Figure 14.1 but for the period 1600–1989/1998 CE.

and Southwest Anatolian records and only one North Aegean >2SD low year, 1788, corresponds to a similar >2SD low year in the southern Jordan record. Table 14.1 indicates the years when the drier reconstructed years for the two records in Figures 14.1 and 14.2, and/or another set of Anatolian reconstructions based on conifers from western Anatolia by Köse et al. (2011), coincide. Years in common for low reconstructed precipitation in the south Jordan juniper-based record—three such years only—and drought years (or groups of years) in a precipitation reconstruction from Cyprus (Griggs et al. 2014)—only nine of the 62 drought years observed in the Cypriot record are common with the Anatolian records—are also indicated in Table 14.1 on page 286.

The notable observation is that while one-year or even longer drought periods are relatively frequent in any of the local records or even wider reconstructions, instances where there are substantive episodes involving at least two consecutive years occurring in more than one (sub-) region and across more than one tree species and reconstruction methodology are in fact rare. In the period common to both the Griggs et al. (2007) and Touchan et al. (2003) records (1339 to 1989 CE) there are only two such episodes: 1607–1608 and 1927–1928—so, two episodes in 650 years.

The first doublet, 1607–1608, follows notably drier years in the Southwest Anatolia record: nine consecutive below-average years 1590–1598 (Figure 14.1) and is followed by another four consecutive such years: 1611–1614, including in 1613 a year more than 2SD below average.

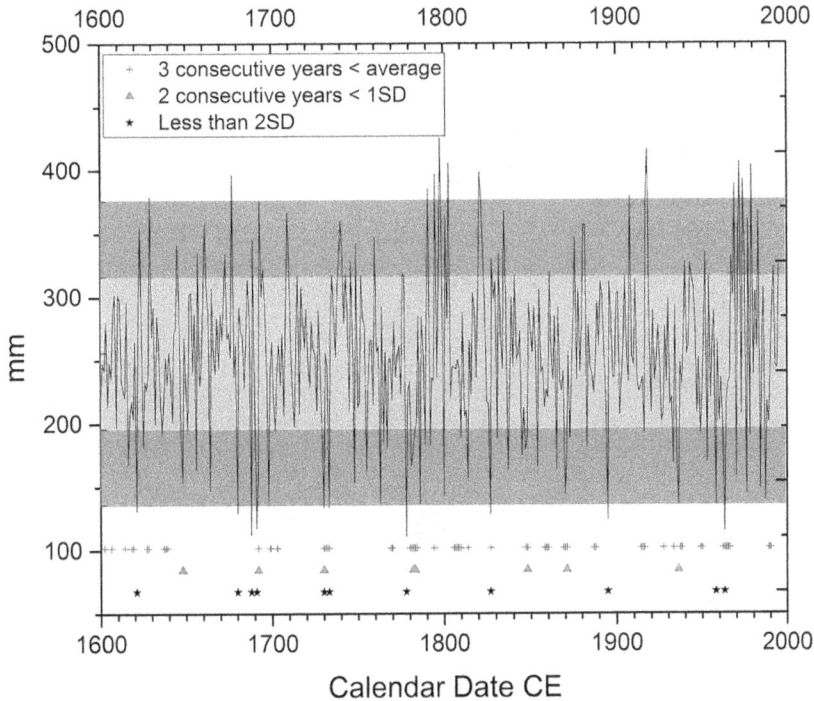

FIGURE 14.3 Tree ring–based October–May precipitation reconstruction (mm) for southern Jordan derived from a *Juniperus phoenicea* chronology from Touchan et al. 1999 (in total 1600–1995 CE). The + signs indicate years when there have (to that point) been three consecutive years of below average precipitation; the gray triangles indicate when (to that point) there have been two consecutive years of precipitation more than 1SD below average; and the black stars indicate single years when the precipitation is more than 2SD below the average. Dataset from: http://www1.ncdc. noaa.gov/pub/data/paleo/treering/reconstructions/asia/jordan/south-jordan-precip.txt.

Although this period is less dramatic in the North Aegean record, the years 1595–1596 are both more than 1SD below average and there are, as well, four consecutive below average years—1606–1609—with 1607 and 1608 both more than 1SD below average. This very dry period is evident also in the Isparta precipitation reconstruction based on *Pinus nigra* chronologies from Southwest Anatolia by Köse et al. (2011:444), which identifies 1607 as a very dry year and highlights the years 1607–1608 and 1610–1611 as dry. In Anatolia, there is rich historical testimony of drought and associated subsistence, social, economic, and political crises—the Celali Rebellion—in the 1590s to 1610 (White 2011:140–186) and these appear, as White argues, to be of a historically forcing scale. The years 1607–1608 are noted as among the worst of the worst of the Little Ice Age in Anatolia (White 2011:181–184), and this period is also conspicuous as unusually cold more widely in Europe and dry in the Mediterranean (Büntgen et al. 2011; White 2011:182). Here we do appear to have a period when climate creates an important part of the context of rebellion and political change within the Ottoman Empire.

TABLE 14.1
SPRING NORTH AEGEAN (GRIGGS ET AL. 2007) AND
SPRING SOUTHWEST ANATOLIA (TOUCHAN ET AL. 2003)
PRECIPITATION RECONSTRUCTIONS

Years CE	North Aegean (Griggs et al. 2007) Years precip. below average			SW Anatolia (Touchan et al. 2003) Years precip. below average			SW Antolia Köse et al.
	3 consec. (at least yr 2 of)	2x >1SD	>2SD	3 consec. (at least yr 2 of)	2x >1SD	>2SD	2011 2yrs(+)
1099	X	X					
1147	X		X		No		
1198	X	X			Data		No
1228	X		X		Until		Data
1229	X	X			1339		Until
1304	X	X	X				1459
1421	X	X					
1422	X	X					
1440	X	X					
1447	X	X					
1477				X	X	X	
1489				X	X		
1511							X
1512							X
1561							
1567							
1593				X	X		
1607				X		X	X
1608	X	X		X	X		X
1610							X
1611							X
1613				X		X	
1623							X
1624							X
1638	X	X					
1664	X	X					
1665	X	X					
1676				X	X		
1687	X	X	X				
1693							
1702							X
1703							X
1715							XX
1716							XX
1725							XX
1726							XX
1731				X	X		
1732				X	X		
1733*	X	X					
1763							X

| Years CE | North Aegean (Griggs et al. 2007) Years precip. below average | | | SW Anatolia (Touchan et al. 2003) Years precip. below average | | | SW Antolia Köse et al. |
	3 consec. (at least yr 2 of)	2x >1SD	>2SD	3 consec. (at least yr 2 of)	2x >1SD	>2SD	2011 2yrs(+)
1764				X	X		X
1789							XX
1790							XX
1793							XX
1794#							XX
1801							X
1802	X	X					X
1803	X	X					
1814				X	X		
1819##							XX
1820##							XX
1851#							XX
1852							XX
1862	X	X					
1867							XX
1868				X	X		XX
1869				X	X		
1870#							X
1871*							X
1878							X
1879#							X
1893							XX
1894							XX
1895*	X	X					
1908				X	X		
1927##				X	X		XX
1928##	X	X					XX
1929	X	X					
1930	X	X					
1947#	X		X				

Years in the spring North Aegean (Griggs et al. 2007) and spring Southwest Anatolia (Touchan et al. 2003) precipitation reconstructions shown in Figures 14.1 and 14.2 where two or more indicators of problematically drier conditions apply—either at least second year of three consecutive years of below average precipitation or the second of two years of precipitation more than 1SD below average or a year where the precipitation was more than 2SD below average. Years in italics and light gray shading are consecutive such drier years in just one of the records; years in larger bold and darker gray shading are common or in two or more records. The notably dry intervals of two or more years for any of the station reconstructions noted in the Köse et al. (2011: 443–444) study are also indicated—where two or more stations indicated in the same years these are marked as XX. For the period *after* 1600 CE (when the record starts), the three years marked with an * are those where either >2SD low precipitation or a combination of being at least in year 2 of a 3 consecutive year period of below average precipitation and two consecutive years of >1SD low precipitation occur in the southern Jordan record (Figure 14.3) and this is also a year flagged in one of the Anatolian records. For the period *after* 1756 CE (when the record starts) the years marked with # are also highlighted as single year drought years in the lower-elevation *Pinus brutia* dataset from Cyprus in Griggs et al. (2014) and the years marked ## are multi-year droughts.

The 1927–1928 drought, attested in other tree ring records from Anatolia (e.g., Akkemik et al. 2005; 2008), is well attested as a real and devastating drought in both natural and historical records (e.g., list of sources cited for 1927 and 1928 in Köse et al. 2011:Table 6), which impacted most of Anatolia (Köse et al. 2011:Fig. 4), and it is noted as largely stalling what had been rapid growth in the agricultural sector of the Turkish economy until then (Zürcher 2004:196).

Only three other years co-occur between one of the Griggs et al. (2007) or Touchan et al. (2003) records and the Köse et al. (2011) record: 1764, 1802, and 1868. Seventeen sixty-four is not notable in other records known to Köse et al. (2011:Table 6), while a two-year period, 1801–1802, is dry only in the Isparta station record of Köse et al. (2011:444), but 1868 (and a two-year period 1867–1868) is observed more widely (Köse et al. 2011:Table 6).

Discussion

The impact on agriculture, and the problems and suffering, caused by even a one-year dry episode should not be underestimated, and when such an event is severe (a real drought), as potentially indicated by reconstructed years around, or more than, 2SD from the average, these may still be of historical note. For example, the North Aegean record finds a rare concurrence of three consecutive below-average years, two consecutive years more than 1SD below average and a year more than 2SD below average in 1304, and, since this may be associated with the only year in the fourteenth century CE when there was drought recorded in both Syria and Egypt (Raphael 2013:95), and a sustained famine (1303–1309) recorded at Constantinople (Haldon et al. 2014:Appendix I), we might speculate that this was an East Mediterranean–wide episode (and, in all, really of greater than one-year total scale—with the "exception" sort of proving the rule).

However, overall, one-year dry episodes are relatively common in Anatolia and the East Mediterranean more widely. For example, 141 out of the the 900 years of the North Aegean record are more than 1SD below average precipitation (so just over one in about every six years), or 104 years in 659 years are more than 1SD below average in the Southwest Anatolia record (so, again, just over one in every six years) (Figures 14.1–2), and in the four western Anatolian areas studied by Köse et al. (2011:443–444) they found one in every 6.4 to seven years as 1SD or more below average. The Jordan record (Figure 14.3) offers a consonant picture: 59 years in the 395-year record are more than 1SD below average precipitation, or one in 6.7 years. Thus, dry years in which the wheat harvest will be threatened, or even hardier crops such as barley could be in difficulty, can be expected to occur relatively regularly in the overall Aegean-Anatolian and East Mediterranean region—and in particular in those areas classified (today) as semiarid—with the specific local frequency then depending on whether any given area has better/poorer rainfall than a regional average, or has access to water from sources other than direct local rainfall (e.g., river, irrigation system, etc.). The definitions of what exactly is semiarid or arid, and so "dry land farming," are imprecise (e.g., Steiner et al. 1988:81), but typically in areas with winter rainfall (such as the East Mediterranean) various approximations are made associating "semiarid" with annual rainfall in the range of, for instance, 200–500 mm (FAO 2004:chapter 2) or 300–600 mm (FAO 1987), with the label of "arid" applied to annual rainfall of respectively less than 200 mm or less than 300 mm. Dry land farming lies in the semiarid range, with Brouwer and Heibloem (1986:Table 3.1) giving an annual rainfall range of a generous 450–600 mm—although ethnographic observation indicates a real minimum annual rainfall threshold for "viable dry farming" in the East Mediterranean around 200–300 mm (Wilkinson 2004:13, 43 Fig. 3.3).

Noticeable rainfall deficit–linked agricultural problems in dry/drier land areas at least one in every six-seven years seems to be about as good as it gets for the East Mediterranean, and in reality the situation was probably worse in many marginal areas. For example, considering modern meteorological data and standard rules for approximate plant water thresholds or ethnographically observed crop presence/absences in dryland situations (ca. 300 mm per annum for wheat and ca. 200–250 mm for barley and generally ca. 200–300 mm as the limit for "viable dry farming": see, e.g., Wilkinson 2004:13, 43 Fig.3.3), Garnsey (1988:10) observes that in Attica the wheat crop would likely fail (or be challenged) one year in four, and barley one year in 20 (and Garnsey notes similar or even worse odds elsewhere, one in four and one in 10 years in Thessaly for wheat and barley respectively, and one in almost every two years for wheat and one in six-seven years for barley in the north Black Sea region [1988:11]). What is the scale of the challenge? Wilkinson (2004:Table 3.1) lists mean barley yields (kg per hectare) lumped together for a range of East Mediterranean climate/environment agricultural contexts versus annual rainfall, and we see that these decline rapidly as annual rainfall goes below 350 mm. Even rainfall in the 350–250 mm range produces yields of just 65 percent of those at 350+ mm, and this declines to 35 percent by 250–200 mm and 26 percent once under 200 mm. Such a dramatic scale of reductions/losses and meager harvest when a below-average situation occurs, which takes an area into the sub-350 mm, and especially sub-300 to 200 mm range of annual rainfall, could thus often be devastating. Large areas of central Anatolia, Syria, the southern Levant, and central Cyprus experience less than 500 mm average annual rainfall today, and significant parts of these areas only receive 400–200 mm (e.g., Black et al. 2011; Hijmans et al. 2005; Pashiardis et al. 2008; Unal et al. 2012; Wilkinson 2004:Fig. 2.1), and are, or are borderline, semiarid and thus are especially at risk in years with below-average and especially substantially below-average rainfall. Farmers in these areas anticipate these known risks and try to pursue strategies—overproduction in average years, storage, reserve seed, mixing crops, and so on (see Halstead 2014)—to overcome these expected challenges, along with water management strategies (and irrigation if possible). Manuring strategies are another variable. These can improve the use of available water for crops and are perhaps relevant in some archaeological cases from semiarid areas—although Styring et al. (2016) highlight that discriminating the relative role of manuring versus other constraints requires careful investigation.

However, if the past millennium is a reasonable guide (at least for the past few thousand years—and so we can adopt an approximate uniformitarian assumption), then once every three to four centuries an exceptional and sustained arid episode occurs that widely affects much of Anatolia and which might be anticipated to have had devastating and potentially historically forcing impacts. Figure 14.4 provides reconstructed temperature data for Central Europe and moisture availability in NW Anatolia as recorded by speleothem evidence at Sofular Cave over the past two millennia to gain a longer-time depth perspective. Three markedly drier episodes are evident (labeled 1–3), and perhaps four more minor periods (labeled i–iv) over the 2,000 years shown from the Sofular record. Episode 3 equates with the 1920s CE drought noted above, episode 2 begins around 1600 CE (and includes the 1607–1614 events noted above) and lasts to the mid-seventeenth century, and episode 1 lies in the fourth to mid-fifth century CE (this period falls within a general drought period in various Anatolian paleoclimate records as noted in Manning 2013:161). Thus, again there is a pattern of substantial arid events maybe only every three centuries or so, and of really major episodes more at a frequency of once in every 600–700 years (and plausibly linked to larger low-frequency climate processes, such as the Little Ice Age (ca. 1330–1840 CE), or the Medieval Climate Anomaly (ca. 1000–1330 CE), which amplified the high-frequency variations). While not entirely a clear coherent pattern, there is in addition something of an association between cooler conditions (and switches to substantially cooler conditions) in the Central European records (A and B in Figure 14.4) and the drier episodes in the Sofular Cave record—as, for example, around and after 1600 CE. It has been observed before that the Little Ice Age period generally appears to correspond with notably cool and drought-related climate stress to crisis in central Anatolia (White 2011)—in contrast with the Medieval Climate Anomaly (Roberts et al. 2012).

Overall, farmers themselves, and those investing or managing farming outputs, the elite, would have expected regular bad years (one-year variety), and thus planned (deliberately or subconsciously) to adapt and to employ strategies to overcome these expected problems: what we might term "known knowns" (adopting the terms made (in)famous in 2002 by Donald Rumsfeld, then United States Secretary of Defense: see endnote)—that is, some or all of the various options discussed by Halstead (2014) from early sowing, to use of crops not always aimed at human consumption, to managing any grazing and its timing, to use of irrigation if available, to use of alternative or stored resources, to prayer, etc. They would also have expected occasional worse circumstances—for example two bad years in a row. Garnsey (1988:17, Table 3) calculates this would see a failed wheat harvest two years running, maybe one in ca. 12–13 years at Athens or Larisa or a little more than one in every five years around Odessa, for example. Growing other crops, such as barley, which are much less drought susceptible, thus lowering the odds for two such consecutive failed harvests in the three cases just reviewed to around one in every 111, 333, or 42 years respectively, is just one of several strategies adopted in order to be prepared for, or to try to cope with, such challenges. These more occasional, but nonetheless anticipated, challenges might be termed, after Rumsfeld, as "known unknowns."

The real threats to humans and their societies are what Rumsfeld called the "unknown unknowns," in this case the irregular and very rare one-in-several-centuries (or longer) two-or-more-years severe droughts of the sort noted above as occurring just a very few times in the past 1,000–2,000 years—and especially if falling against a background of a generally drier period. These rare episodes were not anticipated and could overwhelm

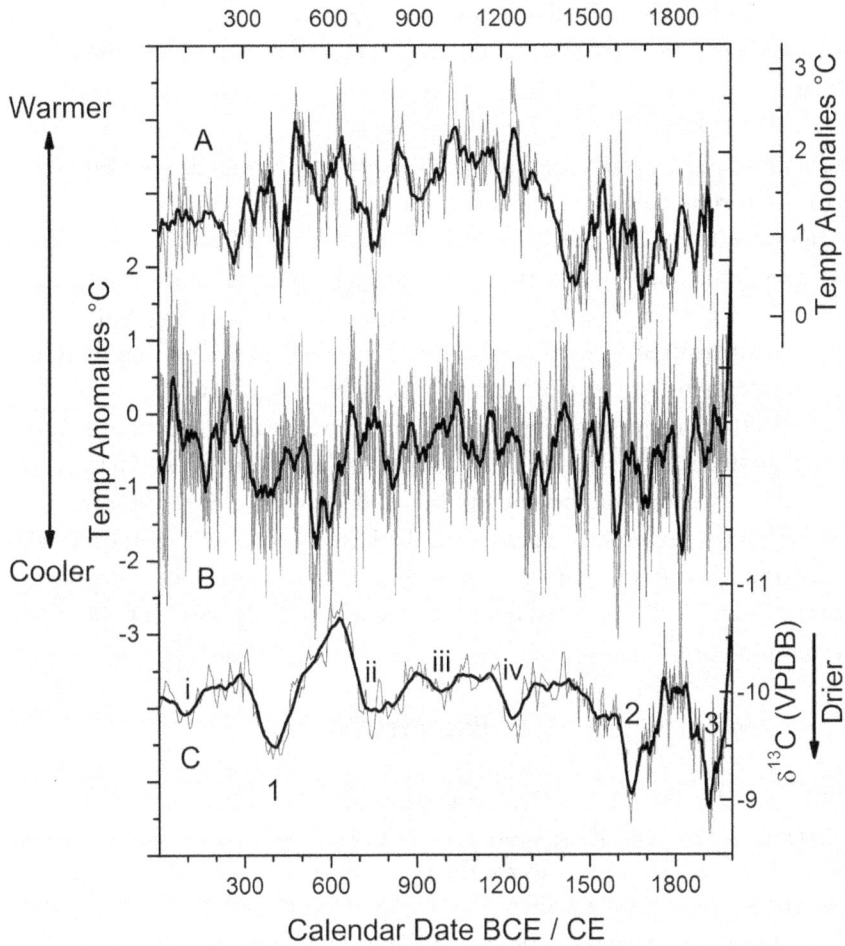

FIGURE 14.4 Comparison Central Europe temperature records with Sofular Cave speleothem (Northwest Anatolia) precipitation record. (A) Spannagel Cave, Austrian Alps, speleothem reconstructed temperature anomaly record from $\delta^{18}O$ measurements (Mangini et al. 2005)—gray shows the published data, black line shows a 10-year average; (B) Central Europe (Austrian Alps) temperature anomaly reconstruction from tree rings (Büntgen et al. 2011)—gray shows the annual data and the black line shows a 30-year smoothing; and C. $\delta^{13}C$ record from Sofular Cave (speleothem So-1) recording moisture availability (Fleitmann et al. 2009)—gray shows the published data and the black line is a 10 datapoint average. Datasets from: ftp://ftp.ncdc.noaa.gov/ pub/data/paleo/speleothem/europe/austria/spannagel2005.txt; ftp://ftp.ncdc.noaa.gov/ pub/data/paleo/treering/reconstructions/europe/buentgen2011europe.txt; and ftp://ftp. ncdc.noaa.gov/pub/data/paleo/speleothem/asia/turkey/sofular2009.txt.

and undermine all and any usual practices and adaptations. They might thus devastate (especially marginal) rural areas, creating instability and population unrest/movement and loss (in the very areas where premodern infrastructure was least able to be deployed to help—contrast large granaries in major centers or grain shipments to major ports/

cities—even if authorities wished to), and so promoting the circumstances that could lead to wider social, economic, and political problems for states and empires. The data available suggest that such severe and widespread precipitation reductions over two or more years, which could be historically significant, are very rare for Anatolia and the East Mediterranean, but might be important, and even potentially pivotal.

In earlier periods, such as the Bronze Age, when the main political centers seem to have specialized in large-scale cereal production (Halstead 2014:60), such rare, unexpected multiyear episodes could, even more directly, severely undermine the economic-political model and so force social change or even collapse. Although dating and resolution are so far often problematic (or even unsatisfactory) for several existing records (see citations and also critique in Knapp and Manning 2016), there is a general pattern of evidence indicating a shift to increasingly arid conditions around the close of the Late Bronze Age (during the thirteenth century BCE) (see also Neugebauer et al. 2015), and so this may be a time when one of the widespread, and only once in every several to many centuries, "unknown unknowns" occurred in the form of severe multiyear drought(s) that undermined the agricultural basis and rural territories of various of the palace societies of the Late Bronze Age East Mediterranean—and especially some of those already in marginal settings.

ENDNOTE

The initial Rumsfeld statement in a Defense Department briefing in early 2002 has been much quoted: "Reports that say something hasn't happened are always interesting to me because as we know, there are known knowns: there are things we know we know. We also know there are known unknowns: that is to say we know there are some things [we know] we do not know. But there are also unknown unknowns—the ones we don't know we don't know. And if one looks throughout the history of our country and other free countries, it is the latter category that tends to be the difficult one." Sources for, and discussion of, the quote include: Rumsfeld 2011; https://en.wikipedia.org/wiki/There_are_known_knowns. There are even academic articles highlighting that Rumsfeld was onto something—noting that the concept of the "unknown unknown" was not new, and can indeed be important in scientific research (Logan 2009).

REFERENCES CITED

Akkemik, Ü., N. Dagdeviren, and N. Aras. 2005 Preliminary Reconstruction (A.D. 1635–2000) of Spring Precipitation Using Oak Tree Rings in the Western Black Sea Region of Turkey. *International Journal of Biometeorology* 49:297–302.

Akkemik, Ü., R. D'Arrigo, P. Cherubini, N. Köse, and G. Jacoby. 2008 Tree-Ring Reconstructions of Precipitation and Streamflow for North-Western Turkey. *International Journal of Climatology* 28:173–183.

Black, E. 2011 The Influence of the North Atlantic Oscillation and European Circulation Regimes on the Daily to Interannual Variability of Winter Precipitation in Israel. *International Journal of Climatology* 32:1654–1664.

Brouwer, C., and M. Heibloem. 1986 *Irrigation Water Management*. Training Manual no. 3. FAO, Rome.

Büntgen, U., W. Tegel, K. Nicolussi,M. McCormick, D. Frank, V. Trouet, J. O. Kaplan, F. Herzig, K.-U. Heussner, H. Wanner, J. Luterbacher, and J. Esper. 2011 2500 Years of European Climate Variability and Human Susceptibility. *Science* 331:578–582.

Clarke, J., N. Brooks, E. B. Banning, M. Bar-Matthews, S. Campbell, L. Clare, M. Cremaschi, D. di Lernia, D., N. Drake, M. Gallinaro, S. Manning, K. Nicoll, G. Philip, S. Rosen, U.-D. Schoop. M. A. Tafuri, B. Weninger, and A. Zerboni. 2015 Climatic Changes and Social Transformations in the Near East and North Africa during the "Long" 4th Millennium BC: A Comparative Study of Environmental and Archaeological Evidence. *Quaternary Sciences Reviews* 136:96–121.

Cook, E. R. et al. (56 co-authors). 2015 Old World Megadroughts and Pluvials during the Common Era. *Science Advances* 1:e1500561.

Currid, J. D., and A. Navon. 1989 Iron Age Pits and the Lahav (Tell Halif) Grain Storage Project. *Bulletin of the American Schools of Oriental Research* 273:67–78.

Curtis, R. I. 2015 Storage and Transport. In *A Companion to Food in the Ancient World*, edited by J. Wilkins and R. Nadeau, pp. 173–182. Wiley Blackwell, Chichester.

Davies, R. W., and S. G. Wheatcroft. 2004 *The Years of Hunger: Soviet Agriculture, 1931–1933*. Palgrave Macmillan, New York.

Dikötter, F. 2010 *Mao's Great Famine: The History of China's Most Devastating Catastrophe, 1958–1962*. Walker, New York.

Drake, B. L. 2012 The Influence of Climatic Change on the Late Bronze Age Collapse and the Greek Dark Ages. *Journal of Archaeological Science* 39:1862–1870.

Erdkamp, P. 2015 Supplying Cities. In *A Companion to Food in the Ancient World*, edited by J. Wilkins and R. Nadeau, pp. 183–192. Wiley Blackwell, Chichester.

Food and Agriculture Organization (FAO). 1987 *Improving Productivity in Dryland Areas*. Committee on Agriculture (Ninth Session). COAG/87/7. FAO, Rome.

Food and Agriculture Organization (FAO). 2004 *Carbon Sequestration in Dryland Soils*. World Soils Resources Reports 102. FAO, Rome. http://www.fao.org/docrep/007/y5738e/y5738e00.htm#Contents.

Finné, M., K. Holmgren, H. S. Sundqvist, E. Weiberg, and M. Lindblom. 2011 Climate in the Eastern Mediterranean and Adjacent Regions, During the Past 6000 Years—A Review. *Journal of Archaeological Science* 38:3153–3173.

Fleitmann, D., H. Cheng, S. Badertscher, R. L. Edwards, M. Mudelsee, O. M. Göktürk, A. Fankhauser, R. Pickering, C. C. Raible, A. Matter, J. Kramers, and O. Tüysüz. 2009 Timing and Climatic Impact of Greenland Interstadials Recorded in Stalagmites from Northern Turkey. *Geophysical Research Letters* 36:L19707.

Forbes, H. 1989 Of Grandfathers and Grand Theories: The Hierarchized Ordering of Responses to Hazard in a Greek Rural Community. In *Bad Year Economics: Cultural Responses to Risk and Uncertainty*, edited by P. Halstead and J. O'Shea, pp. 87–97. Cambridge University Press, Cambridge.

Forbes, H., and L. Foxhall. 1995 Ethnoarchaeology and Storage in the Ancient Mediterranean. In *Food in Antiquity*, edited by J. Wilkins, D. Harvey, and M. Dobson, pp. 69–86. University of Exeter Press, Exeter.

Garnsey, P. 1988 *Famine and Food Supply in the Graeco-Roman World: Responses to Risk and Crisis*. Cambridge University Press, Cambridge.

Griggs, C. B., A. DeGaetano, P. I. Kuniholm, and M. W. Newton. 2007 A Regional High-Frequency Reconstruction of May–June Precipitation in the North Aegean from Oak Tree Rings, A.D. 1089–1989. *International Journal of Climatology* 27:1075–1089.

Griggs, C., C. Pearson, S. W. Manning, and B. Lorentzen. 2014 A 250-Year Annual Precipitation Reconstruction and Drought Assessment for Cyprus from *Pinus brutia* Ten. Tree-Rings. *International Journal of Climatology* 34:2702–2714.

Haldon, J., M. Cassis, O. Doonan, W. Eastwood, H. Elton, D. Fleitmann, A. Izdebski, S. Ladstätter, M. McCormick, S. Manning, J. Newhard, K. Nichol, N. Roberts, I. Telelis, and E. Xoplaki. 2014 Byzantine Anatolia: A "Laboratory" for the Study of Climate Impacts and Socio-Environmental Relations in the Past. *Journal of Interdisciplinary History* 45:113–161.

Halstead, P. 2014 *Two Oxen Ahead: Pre-Mechanized Farming in the Mediterranean.* Wiley Blackwell, Chichester.

Halstead, P., and J. O'Shea (editors). 1989 *Bad Year Economics: Cultural Responses to Risk and Uncertainty.* Cambridge University Press, Cambridge.

Hijmans, R. J., S. E. Cameron, J. L. Parra, P. G. Jones, and A. Jarvis. 2005 Very High Resolution Interpolated Climate Surfaces for Global Land Areas. *International Journal of Climatology* 25:1965–1978.

Knapp, A. B., and S. W. Manning. 2016 Crisis in Context: The End of the Late Bronze Age in the Eastern Mediterranean. *American Journal of Archaeology* 120:99–149.

Köse, N., Ü. Akkemik, H. N. Dalfsem, and M. S. Özeren. 2011 Tree-Ring Reconstructions of May–June Precipitation for Western Anatolia. *Quaternary Research* 75:438–450.

Logan, D. C. 2009 Known Knowns, Known Unknowns, Unknown Unknowns, and the Propagation of Scientific Enquiry. *Journal of Experimental Biology* 60:712–714.

Luterbacher, J., R. García-Herrera, S. Akcer-On, R. Allan, M. C. Alvarez-Castro, G. Benito, J. Booth, U. Büntgen, N. Cagatay, D. Colombaroli, B. Davis, J. Esper, T. Felis, D. Fleitmann, D. Frank, D. Gallego, E. Garcia-Bustamante, R. Glaser, J. F. González-Rouco, H. Goosse, T. Kiefer, M. G. Macklin, S. W. Manning, P. Montagna, L. Newman, M. J. Power, V. Rath, P. Ribera, D. Riemann, N. Roberts, S. Silenzi, W. Tinner, B. Valero-Garces, G. van der Schrier, C. Tzedakis, S. Vannière, S. Vogt, H. Wanner, J. P. Werner, G. Willett, M. H. Williams, E. Xoplaki, C. S. Zerefos, and E. Zorita. 2012 A Review of 2000 Years of Paleoclimatic Evidence in the Mediterranean. In *The Climate of the Mediterranean Region: From the Past to the Future,* edited by P. Lionello, pp. 87–185. Elsevier, Amsterdam.

McCormick, M., U. Büntgen, M. A. Cane, E. R. Cook, K. Harper, P. Huybers, T. Litt, S. W. Manning, P. A. Mayewski, A. F. M. More, K. Nicolussi, and W. Tegel. 2012 Climate Change during and after the Roman Empire: Reconstructing the Past from Scientific and Historical Evidence. *Journal of Interdisciplinary History* 43:169–220.

Mangini, A., C. Spötl, and P. Verdes. 2005 Reconstruction of Temperature in the Central Alps during the Past 2000 yr from a $\delta^{18}O$ Stalagmite Record. *Earth and Planetary Science Letters* 235:741–751.

Manning, S. W. 2013 The Roman World and Climate: Context, Relevance of Climate Change, and Some Issues. In *The Ancient Mediterranean Environment between Sciences and History,* edited by W. V. Harris, pp. 103–170. Brill, Leiden.

Neugebauer, I., A. Brauer, M. Schwab, P. Dulski, U. Frank, E. Hadzhiivanova, H. Kitagawa, T. Litt, V. Schiebel, N. Taha, and N. D. Waldmann. 2015 Evidence for Centennial Dry Periods at ~3300 and ~2800 Cal. Yr BP from Micro-Facies Analyses of the Dead Sea Sediments. *The Holocene* 25:1358–1371.

Pashiardis, S., and S. Michaelides. 2008 Implementation of the Standardized Precipitation Index (SPI) and the Reconnaissance Drought Index (RDI) for Regional Drought Assessment: A Case Study for Cyprus. *European Water* 23/24:57–65.

Raphael, S. K. 2013 *Climate and Political Climate: Environmental Disasters in the Medieval Levant.* Brill, Leiden.

Rickman, G. 1971 *Roman Granaries and Store Buildings.* Cambridge University Press, Cambridge.

Rickman, G. 1980 *The Corn Supply of Ancient Rome.* Clarendon Press, Oxford.

Roberts, N., A. Moreno, B. Valero-Garcés, J. P. Corella, M. Jones, S. Allcock, J. Woodbridge, M. Morellón, J. Luterbacher, E. Xoplaki, and M. Türkeş. 2012 Palaeolimnological Evidence for an East-West Climate See-Saw in the Mediterranean since AD 900. *Global and Planetary Change* 84–85:23–34.

Rosen, A. 2007 *Civilizing Climate: Social Responses to Climate Change in the Ancient Near East.* Alta Mira Press, Lanham, MD.

Rumsfeld, D. 2011 *Known and Unknown: A Memoir.* Sentinel, New York.

Sarpaki, A. 1992 A Palaeoethnobotanical Study of the West House, Akrotiri, Thera. *Annual of the British School at Athens* 87:219–230.

Sarpaki, A. 2001. Processed Cereals and Pulses from the Late Bronze Age Site of Akrotiri, Thera: Preparations prior to Consumption, a Preliminary Approach to Their Study. *Annual of the British School at Athens* 96:27–41.

Sen, A. 2001 *Development as Freedom.* Oxford University Press, Oxford.

Sigaut, F. 1988 A Method for Identifying Grain Storage Techniques and Its Application for European Agricultural History. *Tools and Tillage* 6:3–32.

Spurr, M. S. 1986 *Arable Cultivation in Roman Italy c.200 B.C.–c. A.D. 100.* Society for the Promotion of Roman Studies, London.

Steiner, J. L., J. C. Day, R. I. Papendick, R. E. Meyer, and A. R. Bertrand. 1988. Improving and Sustaining Productivity in Dryland Regions of Developing Countries. In *Advances in Soil Science, volume 8*, edited by B. A. Stewart, pp. 79–122. Springer, Berlin.

Styring, A. K., M. Ater, Y. Hmimsa, R. Fraser, H. Miller, R. Neef, J. A. Pearson, and A. Bogaard. 2016 Disentangling the Effect of Farming Practice from Aridity on Crop Stable Isotope Values: A Present-Day Model from Morocco and Its Application to Early Farming Sites in the Eastern Mediterranean. *The Anthropocene Review* 3:1–21.

Touchan, R., D. Meko, and M. K. Hughes. 1999 A 396-Year Reconstruction of Precipitation in Southern Jordan. *Journal of the American Water Resources Association* 35:49–59.

Touchan, R., G. M. Garfin, D. M. Meko, G. Funkhouser, N. Erkan, M. K. Hughes, and B. S. Wallin. 2003 Preliminary Reconstructions of Spring Precipitation in Southwestern Turkey from Tree-Ring Width. *International Journal of Climatology* 23:157–171.

Unal, Y. S., A. Deniz, H. Toros, and S. Incecik. 2012 Temporal and Spatial Patterns of Precipitation Variability for Annual, Wet, and Dry Seasons in Turkey. *International Journal of Climatology* 32:392–405.

White, K. D. 1970 *Roman Farming.* Thames and Hudson, London.

White, S. 2011 *The Climate of Rebellion in the Early Modern Ottoman Empire.* Cambridge University Press, New York.

Wilkins, J., and R. Nadeau. 2015 Introduction. In *A Companion to Food in the Ancient World*, edited by J. Wilkins and R. Nadeau, pp. 1–16. Wiley Blackwell, Chichester.

Wilkinson, T. J. 2004 *On the Margin of the Euphrates. Settlement and Land Use at Tell es-Sweyhat and in the Upper Lake Assad Area, Syria.* Oriental Institute, Chicago.

Zürcher, E. J. 2004 *Turkey: A Modern History.* New edition. I. B. Tauris, London.

CHAPTER FIFTEEN

A Framework for Facing the Past

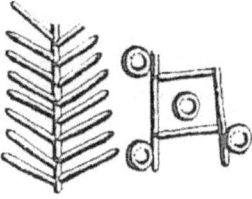

Vernon L. Scarborough

Abstract *Can archaeology meaningfully contribute to the dialogue of current affairs? Is the discipline in a position to pose theory, method, or technique in addressing our changing environmental and social conditions through time in a manner relevant to the present and future? This presentation will attempt to examine the role of anthropological archaeology as a school of thought capable of significant intercourse with other established sciences and social sciences, as well as archaeology's need to engage today's policymakers. As a focus, what water systems are and what they do to an environment, both in terms of societal actions and reactions, will underscore the examples incorporated in assessing our past evolving landscapes and their engineered effects.*

CAUSE TO EFFECT

For all sentient beings, the tenets of cause and effect drive survival. The logic of science has frequently assumed that deduction and hypothesis testing is their arena, and the rest of humanity is beholden and dependent on its rational development. Since Darwin and the evolving intricacies of that complex theory and its many extensions, science has built and codified a body of knowledge that has promoted stepwise discovery and innovation resulting in technologies and population growth unlike ever before. The quelling or amelioration of the effects of disease, the influence of pollution abatement controls, and the spectacular investments in eco-service exploitation—the latter permitting carbon-fuel abundance—have allowed an unprecedented spike in our biological success as a species. However, seven million of us now are threatening the very utility of technologies that have thrust us into this growth curve.

This trajectory has been a search for causal agents in our mission to explain the events or processes that initiate change and result in adaptation. We chose selectively—sometimes randomly—in identifying the variables or event packages that manifest themselves as causal links. The temporal arrow is past to present by way of explanation, with problem solving the temporal logic for explaining/understanding an effect—it is a conscious act and an irrepressible condition of the human mind. Effects are our tangible attempts at solving problems and always with degrees of unintended consequence. Frequently it is these unintended consequences that redouble our efforts to arrive at new solutions to problems that were either ill-defined or nonexistent in the past. We assume our "facts" identify causal agents, and this understanding becomes fixed—at least for a while or during the immediate problem-solving period. Societal institutions (Beddoe et al. 2008) have developed in concert with facts, conclusions, and worldviews predicated on the outcomes of these guiding logics, ultimately leading to a certain path dependency (Hegmon et al. 2008).

An interest here is to evaluate another approach to problem solving, one that slows the decision-making process, recognizes the intrinsic properties of the human mind, and attempts to identify points of discussion that society and its institutions may wish to cultivate for their well-being and longevity. By focusing on the extended future another kind of sister logic is apparent, outcomes we cannot know. Our ability to plan predictably is limited by the weight we give to variable sets as identified by past outcomes and poorly understood unintended consequences. Futures have the license of moving effects forward and designing outcomes that enhance well-being. Effects are given definition and fixity in this logic and this is the role of induction, a process less fettered by logical deductive thinking and well practiced in the humanities. What kind of world do we propose for our future and how can we now "unfix" causal agents to arrive at a well-plotted and discussed future, a fiction with predictive merit?

Societal overshoot of our natural resources as well as social upheaval between groups in part precipitated by the overreach of these resources is repeatedly argued to end in significant calamity for earth systems (Rockström et al. 2009; Steffen et al. 2015). Because predicting social or institutional collapse is counterproductive for a future, how can we take the immediate causal agents learned from the past and co-opt or appropriate them for a redirected positive end and outcome of our future? Archaeologists have a developed storyline for the longue durée; and though it is continually refined and enhanced for accuracy, our approach to the past has always been historical projection—and frequently with major gaps in identifying causal forces the farther we descend in time. In meaningful ways, however, archaeology is well positioned to discuss our futures because of our experience with treating lengthy periods of time and the many missing causal values that must be inferred to assess ancient (pre)histories. Our ways of piecing together convincing storylines that frequently ring true for even the most positivist in the greater scientific community permit anthropological archaeology the interpretative skill set to structure a logic to address the unknowable constraints of our futures. Our scientific logic provides credibility to our interpretations of the past and for the future in ways that no other disciplinary thought can identify as clearly. And our interface with the humanities provides the intellectual depth necessary for addressing what society requires for an acceptable and sustainable future.

Projections of a resilient and sustainable future for humanity require a remediation of past exploitative societal behaviors and institutions. Archaeology is again in a position to evaluate a broad range of ancient societies in a systematic and controlled manner drawing on material culture and societal infrastructures. A principal goal for identifying future outcomes is an assessment of slow-to-change institutional inertias and ways to adjust or modify change. Societal institutions have causal event sequences or path-dependencies, but they can be redirected at any stage both positively and negatively. Rates of change can be rapid over the short term and result in less control over unintended outcomes, while lengthy durations of change or the extended periods of time associated with the longevity of society frequently define successful adaptations and degrees of sustainable lifeways (see van der Leeuw 2012, 2014).

WHAT IS THE FUTURE?

Because the past is often devoted to explanations of events or those processes that culminate in an outcome, the emphasis in science is on causal agents. We frequently know the outcome or effect—an incurable disease, an infrastructural collapse, a climatic change—that is, a problem to be addressed and associated attempts at solutions. However, our projected futures are significantly our mental creations or our collective projections of well-being; they are a set of hopeful anticipations of effect. We identify these goals, but what will bring them about is unknown except by way of past assessments and understandings of cause. In this logic, only the effect is fixed, with causes unclear. In our past, the causes are viewed as fixed once an effect has been explained; in the future, only the effect can be fixed. Although the past is now inevitable, the future can never be; but the future can be parameterized.

If at least some of our goals as a species are to manage disease, curb violence, lessen inequality, and promote intellectual and physical stimulation for society while simultaneously providing adequate and renewable ecosystem services to all components of the biophysical environment, we need to study and model cause as revealed by examples of its fixity in the past. Enough archaeological data and knowledge now exist to identify multiple causalities in arriving at the fixed effects for which we wish. And the suite of causes requires narrowing and weighting variables to most predictably allow well-being as derived from data integration and its interdependencies (challenging the scientific logic of independent variables) based on tenets of cooperation and mutual respect.

Of special import is a need to recycle/reuse accumulated waste by redefining it. When our technologies develop material devices and residues, complementary efforts are required in anticipation of the tool's use life and ultimate discard. Discarded waste needs energy investments to cycle it back into the ecosystem in a productive and consumptive manner. The longevity of our earth system is derived from this axiom, perhaps most demonstrable by Lovejoy's Gaia principles and how plants oxygenate and animals carbonate. Social behaviors and institutions require similar kinds of monitoring in sustaining interdependencies within the ecosystem, but also within and between societies themselves. Our institutions necessitate mutual trust and collaboration between groups with thresholds for accommodating free riders or not (Cronk and Leech 2013).

To evaluate the two outlooks, past as opposed to future, time frames are required. Using a temporal partitioning in which duration as well as rapidity of change are identified, decadal to centennial to millennial time are adapted by way of using a recent approach to evaluate (pre)history (Costanza et al. 2007) (Figure 15.1). This orientation provided an organizational structure for a set of deliberations and book chapters by a group of scholars attempting to assess our planetary futures in the context of past trajectories. The merit of the work rests primarily in the cause and effect conditioning of the past to the present, as described above. However, some thought derived from the emphasis on causal agents as identified in that volume requires projecting futures in a different logic. What do we wish in the next several decades; how might it differ from the next several centuries; should we give even a passing thought to millennial time? Clearly, decadal intervals tend to resist change when compared to centennial or millennial time frames, with the weight of a decadal effect or event only evaluated at a historical level through

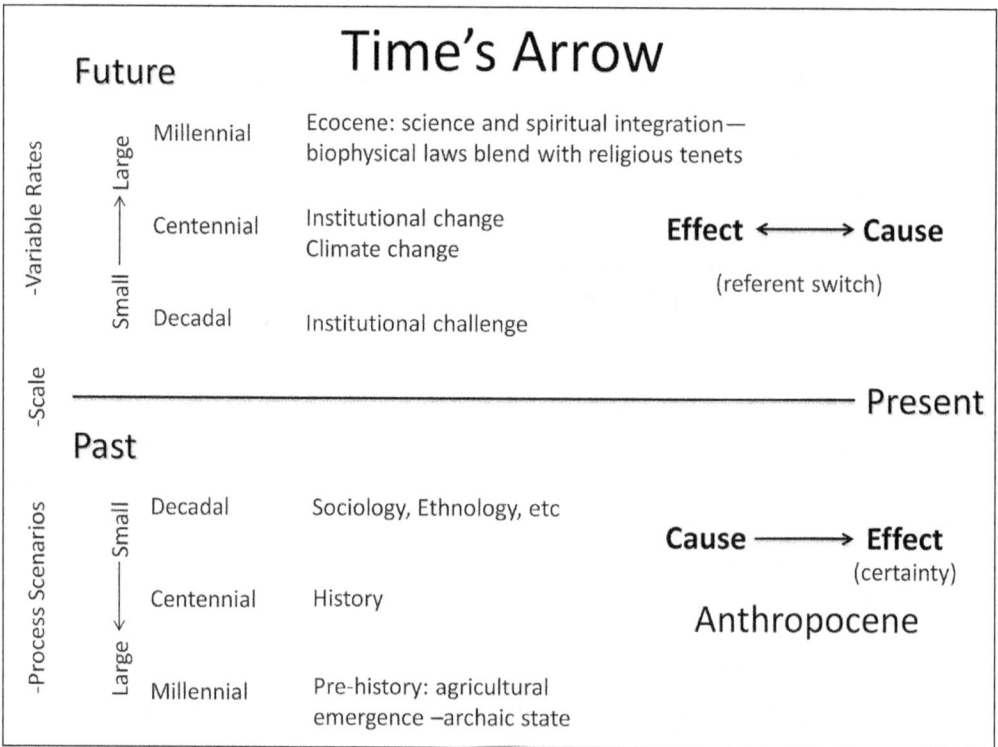

FIGURE 15.1 Graphic showing Past and Future Timeline.

longer periods of time. Social and environmental alterations over a few decades frequently cannot allow an assessment of the magnitude of those changes or the suite of variables and forces precipitating change. Over the longue durée, some decadal events may prove significant while others may be shown to have had little influence on (pre)history, though at the moment of decadal evaluation the latter may well have been viewed by society as pivotal. In this context, path dependency is subject to many concealed variables that may offset other internal change agents or even significant external forcings. Causal variables and their weighted influences are modified with decadal regularity making uncertainty and degrees of instability the only certainty for all socioenvironmental relationships. The fundamental questions associated with gradualism as opposed to punctuated evolutionary change, vulnerability versus resilience, and sustainability issues broadly are embedded.

WATER

Water for life is a biological given; a construction that is both inalienable and immutable on our green-blue planet. From a cultural perspective, water is foundational for our societal institutions; the rules and norms that direct and influence its access and allocation strongly affect all other raw and refined resources. Its scarcity or abundance to a region significantly dictates the kinds of social organizational adaptations we have made as a species. Our health and longevity depend on its availability; how it is delivered, who accesses it, and its quality and quantity identify levels of well-being. Ironically, those of us who are able to distance ourselves from a significant personal investment in water's immediate and fundamental access—because of highly developed technologies and infra-structures—are frequently the least aware of its quotidian impact. Like the air we breathe, we can assume that water is an inexhaustible resource needing little more attention than our immediate preoccupation with our own bodies.

However, water is an exhaustible resource with finite ends. Our scholarly assessments of both the past and the present demonstrate the lengths to which our ancestors have gone in establishing and maintaining water access in sustaining their societal identities and before degrading their environments. There is no doubt that we live in a world today of highly "progressive" interests—institutional arrangements—that promote economic growth dependent on technological advantage and advancing numbers of consumers. Past societies did not occupy as much geography or exploit it as intensively, a condition that frequently assumes that history cannot really affect our projections of our future; we are just so very different now than then. Nevertheless, there exist several benchmark societies that provide insights into a societal future of either more or less of it.

Because water is the most precious of all controllable resources—it is more basic than food, and next in line after air in life requirements—a review of its past and present role for a "sustainable society" merits discussion. My presentation will introduce aspects of water's influence and its implications for potentially less invasive approaches in its redeployment by way of addressing facets of our complex and frequently "wicked" institutional problem sets.

TWO PAST SOCIETIES WITH LESSONS

In an effort to evaluate aspects of these perspective, two past New World societies will be used as case studies; one is taken from the low-density urban occupation of the southern lowland Maya on the Yucatan Peninsula, and the other from ancestral Puebloan populations occupying Chaco Canyon of the U.S. Southwest. Although these two groups share a common ancestry with the colonization of North America by at least 12,000 years ago, they have had spatial and social separation for more than 3,000 years. During that period, and perhaps earlier, both populations adapted to highly dissimilar ecologies. The rainfall difference between the two regions represents both the wettest and the driest settings of North America, and their soilscapes differ profoundly, the former derived from a limestone seafloor and the latter from geologically recent volcanism as well as shallow inland sea deposition. How these two groups adapted to their landscapes and climatic conditions through time is used here as an introduction to archaeology's potential in addressing past and future time.

Of special import for evaluating the temporal trajectories of these two groups are the role and methods by which societies harvest or exploit resources and the energy cycles they employ. Water's availability and allocation are the landscape's underpinnings for both societies. Tainter's clever incorporation of an EROI (energy return on investment) approach (Tainter 2014; Tainter and Patzek 2012) meaningfully links developing technologies to newly identified ecosystem services through time (Costanza 1980). This orientation permits an assessment of the rate and process of change in assessing aspects of millennial time by way of a coupled human-nature dynamic that underscores both the past and the future.

THE ANCIENT MAYA

The Maya Lowlands are identified by a semitropical rainfall regime in which about 10 percent of the otherwise heavy seasonal precipitation curbs to drought-like conditions for four to five months. Nevertheless, at the type sites for this ancient Maya case study, both Tikal (northeastern Petén, Guatemala) and Cerros (northern Belize), rainfall averages around 1,500 mm/yr (Scarborough and Burnside 2010). Because the soils can be thin, especially in the northern reaches of the peninsula, the relatively rapid erosion of the limestone bedrock as a result of the tropical vegetation can allow for significant agricultural success (Dunning et al. 2012); when coupled with occasional enrichment of acidic volcanic ash from neighboring highland eruptions, the soils can be very productive (Tankersley et al. 2011). However, the pocked and jointed karst bedrock in association with the seasonally abundant precipitation percolating vertically downward prevents the development of major surface drainages resulting in limited access to riparian water sources; neither formal irrigation nor riverine navigation throughout peninsular Yucatan is significant (see Scarborough 2006).

The tendency to socially aggregate in dense populations is constrained in most tropical settings by degrees of rapid organic decomposition as well as fast-moving and quickly evolving species-specific disease vectors frequently dispersed through water. What has evolved in these settings is a magnificent abundance of biological diversity unlike that manifest in temperate or arid environments. However, in contrast to the vast wild fields of natural grains or the untamed herds of gregarious herbivores that led to Old World plant and animal domesticates, tropical environments are defined by very few members of the same species clustered together. Resource concentrations of naturally abundant food and related organic resources for supplying dense human populations are difficult to identify, establish, or maintain (Scarborough 2003; Scarborough and Burnside 2010). Once human population levels begin to ascend in these settings, decentralizing forces have resulted in a human settlement design emphasizing a low-density urbanism and a high-density "ruralism"—the latter indicative of the diversity richness of the environment more broadly.

Although occupation of the Maya area likely has a very deep history (Lohse 2010), the intensification associated with sustained generational sedentism probably occurred no earlier than 3,000 years ago (Pohl et al. 1996). By 400 BCE, and spanning a period of half a millennium, the Late Preclassic Maya (400 BCE–100 CE; Estrada-Belli 2011) had developed a broad-based landscape adaptation dependent on a passive natural system that used ̄stored ecosystem energy, energy that was "metabolized" by the early Maya to accommodate expanding human densities—early towns and low-density urbanism. Concentrating populations learned to tap the margins of huge wetlands that today make up about 40 percent of the Maya Lowlands (Dunning et al. 2002; cf. Kunen 2004) (Figure 15.2A). Many of their early communities were positioned in the low-lying reaches of

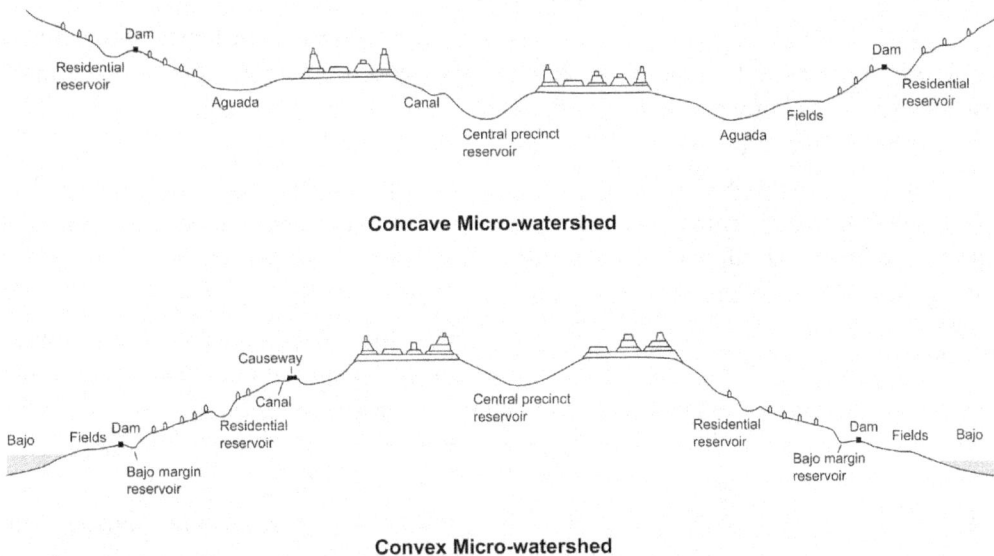

Concave Micro-watershed

Convex Micro-watershed

FIGURE 15.2 Southern Maya Lowland Water Management: (A) Concave Microwatershed and (B) Convex Microwatershed.

these *bajos* and drew from the elevated water table for wild and conserved plant varieties as well as landscape cropping designs emphasizing water storage and drainage infrastructures—drained fields (Scarborough 1991, 1994; 2003; cf. Scarborough et al. 2012). These environments were eventually compromised by accelerated erosion, human-induced sedimentation, and groundwater issues caused by the Late Preclassic occupants themselves and resulting in the fragmentation of community structures (see concave versus convex energy and landscape transitions at La Milpa [Dunning et al. 2002, 2003; Scarborough et al. 1995], Lake Salpeten [Anselmatti et al. 2007], and the site area of La Joyanca [Carozza et al. 2007]). These decadal changes were further compounded by evidence for a Late Preclassic drought (Dunning et al. 2014; Wahl et al. 2014). Population displacement and relocation, however, did not entail significant distances as the ridges and hillocks often flanking the low-lying depressions within the former geographical orbit of a Late Preclassic community became the new focus for occupation. In spite of elevated karst settings and their inability to retain significant quantities of water naturally, new ways of harvesting the seasonal resource were implemented.

By the advent of the Classic Maya (200–800 CE) and their literal rise to the challenge of seasonal drought by way of relocating to the summits of adjacent hillocks and ridge tops, the earlier passive, low-lying collection and manipulation of water and landscape resources had been compromised. The extensively raised and drained field systems that had been initiated during the Late Preclassic period were infilling with eroded soils derived from slash-and-burn activities along the upper slope margins of the great bajos and related depressions (Anselmatti et al. 2007). Unlike the Amazonian system of wetland reclamation occurring during a comparable period (Erickson 1993, 2006), extensive agricultural activities located on more rolling, elevated, and broken topography accelerated erosion and constricted the amount of bajo use. However, during the Early Classic period (200–500 CE), terracing of these slopes slowed the movement of previously lost soils (Dunning et al. 2002, 2003) in concert with active water storage management (Scarborough 2007; Scarborough et al. 1995). The relocation of several community centers to the newly engineered cut-and-fill landscapes of otherwise elevated, craggy karst hill surfaces ushered in a set of significant decadal changes (Figure 15.2B). The concave microwatersheds of the Late Preclassic were redefined by the Maya moving upward, claiming the tops of adjacent ridges, and creating convex microwatersheds. By paving these elevated surfaces—courtyards, plazas, pyramids, and acropolises—the heavy seasonal rainfall could be shed into locally elevated quarry depressions. City planning and the runoff from these elevated pavements directed significant catchments of water into sizable reservoirs modified from the deliberate placement of quarries for both the mining of construction fill to build the pyramids as well as the judicious positioning of tanks of potable water for gravity slope release and consumption. Most of the residential occupation at the larger centers was immediately below the most sizable reservoirs perched at elevated locations and within immediate proximity of a community's central precinct. Convex watershed systems required greater planning and active civic engagement than the previous Late Preclassic concave microwatersheds.

How can the socioenvironmental relationship between the homogenized linearity of millennial time compare to eventual but highly infrequent decadal punctuations? For the ancient Maya, Late Preclassic adaptations generated a societal trajectory of ecosystem harvesting that changed into exploitation as populations increased, natural resources were overused, and limited technologies developed—and likely over a relatively short period of time near the end of the Late Preclassic period. Nevertheless, the stored natural resources associated with an abundance of water flowing into the bajo wetlands, inclusive of the wild, conserved, and domesticated plants and animals then available, accommodated an initial and relatively long-lived florescence in society. If the Maya had attempted to maintain the same level of ecosystem use beyond their half-millennium of societal success, however, social collapse would have resulted.

Because of the proximity of the hills and ridges identifying the Maya Lowlands, some populations during the Late Preclassic did occupy elevated settings perhaps harvesting resources unique to those microenvironments. Valdez and I (Scarborough and Valdez 2009, 2014) have referred to this socioeconomic adaptation as that of "resource-specialized communities," a settlement and land-use model highly adaptive to the diverse and dispersed ecologies of the tropics. Regardless, during the Early Classic period, populations relocated from the concave microwatershed model to the convex microwatersheds of the adjacent high ground. The latter required a heavy investment in community planning and engineering, both sustained for nearly a millennium through continual construction and maintenance with limited additional built environment innovation. Because climate was cooperative, with precipitation presumed adequate for the manifested and envisioned infrastructure at the urban sites (see Kennett et al. 2012), costs for continuing the use of the ecosystem services were hidden. However, the artificiality of modifying the environment in such a significant manner, coupled with a growing population and its evolving and ever more demanding views of societal well-being, forced radical change around 800–1000 CE. Climate change also appears to have interceded (Gunn et al. 1995; Haug et al. 2003; Hodell et al. 2001; Kennett et al. 2012; Medina-Elizalde and Rohling 2012; Yaeger and Hodell 2008), forcing a severe fragmentation of what had been a Late Classic golden age.

ANCESTRAL PUEBLOANS

As a subset of the U.S. Southwest, ancestral Puebloans occupied its northern and eastern expanse. From their well-defined Pithouse period, or Basketmaker III times associated with long-term sedentism from 400–800 CE, groups in the San Juan Basin of northwestern New Mexico and adjacent portions of the present-day Four Corners region reveal degrees of social complexity (Lekson 2006; Vivian 1990), though much reduced from our starting point attributed above to the Late Preclassic Maya. Although Southwestern Native Americans never aspired to the kinds of complexities attributable to the archaic state, their lifeways in harnessing the limitations of arid lands ecosystem services provides a useful comparison by way of capturing a range of socioenvironmental adaptation through time.

The focus of this case study is Chaco Canyon, where precipitation is annually bimodal; snow and highly inclement temperatures followed by summer rains and a reversal in temperature readings—though also inclement. Total annual precipitation is about 200 mm or approaching a full order of magnitude less than in the southern Maya Lowlands.

Semiarid settings are identified by lower populations and patches of similar species types, significantly opposed to the biological characteristics noted for tropical climes (Brown 2014; Hawkins et al. 2003). Human population can concentrate and adhere to a specific setting based on the relative abundance of available resources; though without landscape enhancements those resources can be rapidly depleted. The kind and amount of stored resource energy by way of organics' availability and consumption is highly constrained in arid environments and this generally keeps populations small. However, during periods of relatively increased rainfall, food and water resources do multiply; though subsequent drought conditions—even if short-lived—can significantly interrupt a growth surge. In the case of human populations, this can result in highly disrupted path-dependency trajectories and institutional fragmentation. This condition may well force groups into collecting and foraging adaptations who were formerly agricultural sedentists, a pattern apparent through time and space among ancestral Puebloans (Wills 2003).

Throughout the Pithouse and Puebloan periods of Chaco Canyon (400–1200 CE), occupants operated at a (mid-) Preclassic level as defined by the ancient Maya and their use of the natural banking of the resource base in a nonexploitative manner. A set of complex environmental variables, principally water, soil, and topography, allowed an occupational period from 800–1200 CE to coalesce by way of employing a somewhat less passive harvesting strategy, in part induced by a complex climatic optimum (see Dean and Funkhouser 2002; Vivian et al. 2006a, b). A significant energy "release" occurred following a period of natural landscape "conservation" (after Holling and Gunderson 2002)—the latter a consequence of low population densities and minor harvesting of natural resources immediately prior to the Pithouse period and the millennia of natural environs building and storing energy forms before their human-induced release. Although the environments are/were extremely different, the ancient Maya of the Preclassic period tapped into the same relative resource abundance at the outset of permanent sedentism—though the amounts of precipitation in the latter allowed longer and more intensive resource harvesting than possible in the U.S. Southwest.

At Chaco Canyon, the ancestral Puebloans were highly vulnerable to settlement dissolution at any one time due to the scarcity of water—a decadal matter—but were able to assert a less passive state with incremental increases in the rainfall regime. Puebloans never attained the complexity of a Classic-period Maya associated with their clever "concave to convex" response induced by human degradation and a relative drought-like influence. Nevertheless, ancestral Puebloans did attain significant complexity during the "release" period from 800–1200 CE, though levels of complexity were reduced when a thirteenth-century drought descended; limited stores of energy capital as well as restricted technologies to further exploit the landscape prevented greater complexity. They simply could not institutionally "reorganize" rapidly enough to maintain their previous architectural and infrastructural order, and they were forced to abandon their Canyon home and its expansive regional networks (Lekson 2006; Vivian 1990).

Ancestral Puebloans are viewed as having had two phase cycles like the Maya, just not as sustained. Change was fast, as the span of Pueblo period exploitation—800–1200 CE—could not be extended given the external forcings of climate change. As was the case with the ancient Maya, many variables affected social change; but apparent broad climatic alterations at the regional level influenced centennial and millennial developments. With population success afforded by available soils and limited water sources during the Pithouse phase, another stage in social development was possible. Dean and Funkhouser (2002; Force et al. 2002; Vivian et al. 2006b; cf. Hall 2010; Love et al. 2011) translate dendroclimatological data into periods of channel cutting and channel filling, with early regional sediment aggradation spanning from 1–900 CE—an environmentally "conservative" (underexploited) period in Holling and Gunderson's terminology (2002; see Scarborough and Burnside 2010). From ca. 900–1000 CE, elevated temporal and spatial precipitation variability likely incited runoff erosion and sediment loss resulting in frequent stream and wash base–level alterations. However, the adoption of low-tech energy harvesting methods allowed the preservation and enhancement of soils and water sources (Vivian et al. 2006b), which otherwise were lost to overshooting the availability of organics in this fragile setting. These technical innovations on the landscape allowed the storage of energy inertias associated with water's diversion and containment. The advent of the tenth century, then, ushered in heightened temporal and spatial precipitation variability regionally, which likely accelerated erosional downcutting and challenged previous pithouse dwellers to further engage with their environment and initiate landscape engineering practices to control soil loss and compromised gradients (Vivian et al. 2006b).

Puebloan florescence was likely immediate, a decadal set of material modifications that were synergistically paired with new or significantly realigned social institutional developments. Degrees of environmental control were approached and demonstrably shown to positively affect the dynamically changing landscape by way of interfering with fluctuating base-level changes. Rapidly constructed check dams, floodwater recessional conservation methods, and short-segment canalization efforts were likely employed in expedient ways (see Vivian 1990). The continual and constant interplay with the many microenvironments in a canyon such as Chaco resulted in a set of suprafamily community interactions necessary to accommodate the influence of placing a suite of check dams at one margin of the drainage when their establishment and effectiveness would alter the flow and availability of sediments at another location farther down slope. The many rincons (incised mesa-top drainages) and associated runoff channels fueling the major wash arguably required societal coordination. And it was this cumulative investment in relatively ephemeral, small-scale agricultural production via less complex landscape alterations overseen by cooperative groups that changed societal order and organization. By instituting worldview changes, cultivating larger communities, accenting centralized resource concentrations, and coordinating agricultural practices and landscape maintenance the Puebloan world was established.

Recent work by Steve Plog concerning a ninth-century florescence at Chaco Canyon has revealed parrot dating to this period (Watson et al. 2015) and their significant travel investments from Central Mexico (Gilman et al. 2014), as well as reassessed room burials and associated furniture from Pueblo Bonito (Burials 13 and 14 identified with leadership identities in Room 33 containing rich elite status offerings [Plog and Heitman 2010]), possibly inclusive of Mesoamerican chocolate? (compare Crown and Hurst 2009; Neitzel 2007:139]. Lekson (1984; Lekson et al. 2006) makes the cogent case for the initial construction of the first four or five Great Houses occurring during the early tenth century, though followed by a period of consolidation or lack of building until the great spike in Great House architecture beginning about 1025 CE (Figure 15.3). Although several factors surely precipitated the architectural planning associated with the centralization of resources and the appearance of the first Great House in Chaco Canyon, investments made within the canyon to control base-level changes reflect an institutional change—"reorganization to exploitation" (Holling and Gunderson 2002). The efforts to rapidly adjust to a period of variable rainfall runoff, managed erosion controls and enhanced agricultural productivity led to developing administrative complexity.

Although the Pueblo period from 800–1200 CE represents the overall establishment and florescence of unprecedented development, not unlike the Maya Classic period, fragmentation was likely inevitable given Puebloan trajectories—a path dependency interrupted by increasing population demands from the built environment and the effects of climatic change. In some ways, the eleventh-century Chacoans effectively reinvented themselves by cloning their interests outside the canyon and linking a suite of outliers

FIGURE 15.3 The Great House of Pueblo Bonito (open access Wikipedia.org).

or system-wide Great Houses connected to and from the canyon, in part allowed by a century-long reduction of variable temporal and spatial precipitation and a period of channel filling or agradation associated with the now unincised Chaco Canyon Wash (Vivian et al. 2006a, b). This new social institutional strategy tapped unused resources elsewhere, harvesting thin natural energy sources outside the canyon and bringing them into a growing uber-canyon sustaining population. In an interestingly analogous manner to the earlier Pithouse to Puebloan transition, the Chacoan populations appear to have slowed their initial architectural investments in early canyon-focused Great Houses of the 900s, perhaps affected by an inability to further extract significant agricultural resources from their immediate canyon confines, only to fluoresce a century later. By extending their socioenvironmental networks up and away from the canyon's low-lying centrality, they were effectively moving from a "concave" or canyon-floor built environment focus to a "convex" or mesa-top roadway system and set of Great House outliers. These latter sites were positioned to best extract resources from a much broader range of territorial limits, even though their individual catchment areas were considerably less productive than that within the canyon itself. Cumulatively, over a relatively short period, these later Great Houses exploited resources in enough abundance to raise the level of regional connectivity and social complexity in accommodating a centrality within the canyon itself—the Chaco Phenomena of the eleventh and twelfth centuries (Lekson 2006; Vivian 1990). This socioeconomic and sociopolitical approach likely worked for a couple of hundred years, but the natural relative abundances and the socially engineered landscapes attributable to the canyon could not be mimicked at the local levels elsewhere; though the ideology of first founders and pilgrimages into the canyon were cleverly developed. In the end, not unlike the Maya (Scarborough 2003), the ideology proved too expensive for the environment (cf. Sofaer et al. 1979). And with an ensuing decadal or even centennial drought condition, the society abandoned the canyon. As with the famous Maya collapse of the tenth century, warfare and violent competition for diminishing resources resulted in social fragmentation as populations moved farther toward the Four Corners area and Mesa Verde of the thirteenth century (Vivian 1990).

DISCUSSION

Although scalar differences separate these two case studies, they do capture a broad array of environmental and societal responses to change: "the wet and the dry." A key difference between semiarid and semitropical settings is the harvesting and eventual exploitation of resources leading to degrees of centralization. Dispersed settlement designs in the tropics slow centripetal aggregations and result in low-density urbanism. The tendency not to build modular housing units that can be rapidly extended by adding additional walls prevents the kind of apartment-like living arrangements found in more arid settings (Flannery 1972, 2002). This adaptation complements the necessity to maintain a comfortable distance from a neighbor or extended kin due to disease vectors and related concerns over rapid organic decay rates. Although grand structures of stone identify the great centers of the ancient Maya, most sustaining population households were constructed of wood, reed, and thatch with stone foundations and plaster floors, building mediums that do not readily accommodate additional and subsequent wall or roof attachments.

In more arid settings, the cross-cultural tendency is to build with clay—frequently with sun-dried adobe. The great tells of the Near East are testament to the modular building efforts of several great cities and their concentration of refined resources from a relatively sparsely populated hinterland, unlike the high-density "ruralism" notable in several tropical regimes (Scarborough and Lucero 2011). Families literally build on top of one another through time. The ability to materially centralize over generations is a hallmark of many semiarid settings, and Puebloan period Chaco Canyon is no exception. Although unable to amass most of the population into one or two Great Houses through time at Chaco Canyon, an early set of socioenvironmental adaptations promoted the establishment of tightly constructed room blocks adopting the modular construction methods of apartment living. If ancestral Puebloans of the canyon had had more time, more precipitation, and less social upheaval, they may have been in a position to further centralize their "neighborhoods" or Great Houses into a concentrated urban setting, not unlike the riparian-rich Near East. It is important to note that several archaic cities in semiarid settings are shown to manifest "low-density urbanism," but several others do reveal extremely high densities perhaps most apparent with tell formations. Because we find tell development only in these environments, and not in the tropics, it suggests the impactful role of socioenvironmental dynamism and the different rates and processes in which a society harvests or exploits its available resource base (Scarborough 2016).

Most societies did not rise to the equivalent challenge of a concave-to-convex micro-watershed transition during their "release" period of nature's millennial accumulation and storage of harvestable resources. Nevertheless, six to eight societies did rise to a set of socioenviromental challenges with the first global primary states. This was the ultimate problem-solving exercise in the history of the modern world and resulted in the transformation of technology and infrastructure into societal power and a suite of inequality relationships—they, in turn, forming complicated positive feedback relationships ever since (see Flannery and Marcus 2012). Surely this was the onset of our Anthropocene (Figure 15.1) (Smith and Zeder 2013).

Returning to our "Time's Arrow" assessment (Figure 15.1), the causal effects of the past are deeply embedded in how our species interacts with the environment. Our regional histories globally identify a variety of causal factors stimulating historical processes and events. At the millennial level, most change agents are homogenized or blended and the variables difficult to weigh as individual triggering influences, but the archaeological effects can be evaluated. Centennial change, as we approach the present, allows for more variable scrutiny as the preservation of past causal forces are increased and the effects of those actions made more visible. Decadal assessments are clearly more immediate and causal agents easier to isolate, though their long-term effects require contextualization with centennial and millennial time frames.

In the case of two dissimilar culture areas with significant differences in rainfall and biophysical setting, but sharing similar levels of technology, their pathways remain surprisingly alike. Because technologies were not nearly as developed or sophisticated in the New World, the Maya and ancestral Pueblo examples introduce temporal change in a less accelerated manner. These two societies provide a comparative span of how humans have behaved within their environment and among themselves as affected by the environment. They allow us to trap and assess a limited number of stressors that are more opaque in other civilizations, especially our most recent manifestations.

Since the Industrial Revolution, the West and the rest have built societal complexity on rapidly developing technologies designed to extract growing amounts of energy from singular sources: water mills to steam to oil and gas. Today, there is the suggestion that "renewable" energy sources—from nuclear to solar to wind to voltaic—will allow the kinds of social well-being to accommodate resources for a less violent world with more opportunity. The past sequence of resource harvesting to exploitation as shown by the two archaeological cases demonstrates a need to adjust to external forcings and unintended consequences.

Given time's arrow, we are at a tipping point. Today, society is well positioned to project a future based not only on the millennia of previously reported human experience, but we can now draw on recently developed approaches and methodologies to assess those experiences derived from our rich archaeological past. Too, our highly global interconnectivity as a species allows a holism in an evaluation of our nuanced needs and wants. We can, more than ever before, project a future, define the effects we wish, and work in a much more conscious manner to select causal agents to implement effects. We can be deliberate in knowing when we will overshoot energy sources and how we will enter into the next phase transition of time's arrow. We must be able to break the carbon pollution cycle and productively consume our waste to maintain our ecosystem services in a manner compatible with our shared worldview. By assessing the nuanced (pre)histories at our disposal, anthropological archaeology can assess the rate and process of change through and into time (Scarborough 2003, 2010).

ACKNOWLEDGMENTS

Thanks to Emily Holt for the invitation to contribute to this volume and participate in the forum that made this volume possible, and to Joe Tainter, who read an early version of this chapter and provided his predictably thoughtful assessment.

REFERENCES CITED

Beddoe, R., R. Costanza, J. Farley, E. Garza, J. Kent, I. Kubiszewskia, L. Martineza, T. McCowen, K. Murphy, N. Myerse, Z. Ogden, K. Stapleton, and J. Woodward. 2008 Overcoming Systemic Roadblocks to Sustainability: The Evolutionary Redesign of Worldviews, Institutions, and Technologies. *Proceedings of the National Academy of Sciences* 106(8):2483–2489.

Brown, J. H. 2014 Why Are There So Many Species in the Tropics? *Journal of Biogeography* 41:8–22.

Carozza, J.-M., D. Galop, J.-P. Metaile, and E. Lemonnier. 2007 Landuse and Soil Degradation in the Southern Maya Lowlands from Pre-Classic to Post-Classic Times: The Case of La Joyanca (Petén, Guatemala). *Geodinamica Acta* 20:195–207.

Costanza, R. 1980 Embodied Energy and Economic Valuation. *Science* 210(4475):1219–1224.

Costanza, R., L. Graumlich, and W. Steffen (editors). 2007 *Sustainability or Collapse? Integrated History and Future of People on Earth (IHOPE)*. Dahlem Workshop Report 96R. The MIT Press, Cambridge, MA.

Cronk, L., and B. L. Leech. 2013 *Meeting at Grand Central: Understanding the Social and Evolutionary Roots of Cooperation*. Princeton University Press, Princeton.

Crown, P. L., and W. J. Hurst. 2009 Evidence of Cacao Use in the Prehispanic American Southwest. *Proceedings of the National Academy of Science* 106(7):2110–2113.

Dean, J. S., and G. Funkhouser. 2002 Dendroclimatology and Fluvial Chronology in Chaco Canyon: Appendix A. In *Relation of "Bonito" Paleo-channels and Base-level Variations to Anasazi Occupation, Chaco Canyon, New Mexico*, edited by E. R. Force, R. G. Vivian, T. C. Windes, and J. S. Dean, pp. 39–41. *Arizona State Museum Archaeological Series 194*. Tucson.

Dunning N. P., T. P. Beach, S. Luzzadder-Beach. 2012 Kax and Kol: Collapse and Resilience in Lowland Maya Civilization. *Proceedings of the National Academy of Science* 109:3652–3657.

Dunning, N. P., S. Luzzadder-Beach, T. Beach, J. G. Jones, V. L. Scarborough, and T. P. Culbert. 2002 Arising from the Bajos: Anthropogenic Change in Wetlands and the Rise of Maya Civilization. *Annals of the Association of American Geographers* 92:267–283.

Dunning, N., J. G. Jones, T. Beach, and S. Luzzadder-Beach. 2003 Physiography, Habitats, and Landscapes of the Three Rivers Region. In *Heterarchy, Political Economy, and the Ancient Maya: The Three Rivers Region of the East-Central Yucatan Peninsula*, edited by V. L. Scarborough, F. Valdez, and N. Dunning, pp. 14–24. University of Arizona Press, Tucson.

Dunning, N., D. Wahl, T. Beach, J. Jones, S. Luzzadder-Beach, and C. McCormick. 2014 The End of the Beginning: Drought, Environmental Change, and the Preclassic to Classic Transition in the East-Central Yucatan Peninsula. In *The Great Maya Droughts in Cultural Context*, edited by G. Iannone, pp. 107–129. University of Colorado Press, Boulder.

Erickson, C. L. 1993 The Social Organization of Prehispanic Raised Field Agriculture in the Lake Titicaca Basin, In *Economic Aspects of Water Management in the Prehispanic New World*, edited by V. L. Scarborough and B. L. Isaac, pp. 369–426. *Research in Economic Anthropology, Supplement 7*. JAI Press, Greenwich, CT.

Erickson, C. L. 2006 The Domesticated Landscapes of the Bolivian Amazon. In *Time and Complexity in Historical Ecology*, edited by W. Balée and C. L. Erickson, pp. 236–278. Columbia University Press, New York.

Estrada-Belli, F. 2011 *The First Maya Civilization*. Routledge, New York.

Flannery, K. V. 1972 The Origins of the Village as a Settlement Type in Mesoamerica and the Near East: A Comparative Study. In *Man, Settlement and Urbanism*, edited by P. J. Ucko, R. Tringham, and G. W. Dimbleby, pp. 23–35. Duckworth, London.

Flannery, K. V. 2002 The Origins of the Village Revisited: From Nuclear to Extended Households. *American Antiquity* 67:417–434.

Flannery, K., and J. Marcus. 2012 *The Creation of Inequality: How Our Prehistoric Ancestors Set the Stage for Monarchy, Slavery, and Empire*. Harvard University Press, Cambridge.

Force, E. R., R. G. Vivian, T. C. Windes, and J. S. Dean. 2002 *Relation of "Bonito" Paleo-channels and Base-level Variations to Anasazi Occupation, Chaco Canyon, New Mexico*. Arizona State Museum Archaeological Series 194. Arizona State Museum, University of Arizona, Tucson.

Gilman, P. A., M. Thompson, and K. Wyckoff. 2014 Ritual Change and the Distant: Mesoamerican Iconography, Scarlet Macaws, and Great Kivas in the Mimbres Region of Southwestern New Mexico. *American Antiquity* 79(1):90–107.

Gunn, J. D., W. J. Folan, and H. R. Robichaux. 1995 A Landscape Analysis of the Candelaria Watershed In Mexico: Insights into Paleoclimates affecting Upland Horticulture in the Southern Yucatan Peninsular Semi-Karst. *Geoarchaeology* 10:3–42.

Hall, S. A. 2010 New Interpretations of Alluvial and Paleo-vegetation Records from Chaco Canyon, New Mexico. *New Mexico Geological Society Guidebook, 61ˢᵗ Field Conference, Four Corners Country*, pp. 231–246. New Mexico Geological Society, Socorro, New Mexico.

Haug, G. H., D. Gunther, L. C. Perterson, D. M. Sigman, K. A. Hughen, and B. Aeschlimann. 2003 Climate and the Collapse of Maya Civilization. *Science* 299:1731–1735.

Hawkins, B. A., R. Field, H. V. Cornell, D. J. Currie, J.Franc Ois Gue'gan, D. M. Kaufman, J. T. Kerr, G. G. Mittelbach, T. Oberdorff, E. M. O'Brien, E. E. Porter, and J. R. Turner. 2003 Energy, Water, and the Broad-Scale Geographic Patterns of Species Richness. *Ecology* 84(12):3105–3117.

Hegmon, M., M. Peeples, A. P. Kinzig, S. Kulow, C. Meegan, and M. C. Nelson. 2008 Social Transformation and its Human Costs in the Prehispanic U.S. Southwest. *American Anthropologist* 110(3):313–324.

Hodell, D. A., M. Brenner, J. H. Curtis, and T. Guilderson. 2001 Solar Forcing of Drought Frequency in the Maya Lowlands. *Science* 292:1367–1370.

Holling, C. S., and L. H. Gunderson. 2002 Resilience and Adaptive Cycles. In *Panarchy: Understanding Transformations in Human and Natural Systems*, edited by L. H. Gunderson and C. S. Holling, pp. 25–62. Island Press, Washington, DC.

Kennett, D. J., S. F. M. Breitenbach, V. V. Aquino, Y. Asmerom, J. Awe, J. U. L. Baldini, P. Bartlein, B. J. Culleton, C. Ebert, C. Jazwa, M. J. Macri, N. Marwan, V. Polyak, K. M. Prufer, H. E. Ridley, H. Sodemann, B. Winterhalder, and G. H. Haug. 2012 Development and Disintegration of Maya Political Systems in Response to Climate Change. *Science* 338:788–791.

Kunen, J. L. 2004 *Ancient Maya Life in the Far West Bajo: Social and Environmental Change in the Wetlands of Belize.* Anthropological Papers of the University of Arizona, no. 69. University of Arizona Press, Tucson.

Lekson, S. H. 1984 *Great Pueblo Architecture of Chaco Canyon, New Mexico. Publications in Archaeology 18-B.* Chaco Canyon Studies. National Park Service, Albuquerque.

Lekson, S. H. 2006 Architecture. In *The Archaeology of Chaco Canyon: An Eleventh-Century Pueblo Regional Center*, edited by S. H. Lekson, pp. 67–116. School of Advanced Research Press, Santa Fe.

Lekson, S. H. (editor). 2006 *The Archaeology of Chaco Canyon: An Eleventh-Century Pueblo Regional Center.* School of Advanced Research Press, Santa Fe.

Lohse, J. C. 2010 Archaic Origins of the Lowland Maya. *Latin American Antiquity* 21(3):312–352.

Love, D. W., M. L. Gillam, L. V. Benson, R. Friedman, P. L. Miller, and K. R. Vincent. 2011 Geomorphology, Hydrology, and Alluvial Stratigraphy in Lower Chaco Canyon Do not Support the Possible Existence of Prehistoric Sand-dammed Ephemeral Lakes. *New Mexico Geology* 33(4):107–123.

Medina-Elizalde, M., and E. J. Rohling. 2012 Collapse of Classic Maya Civilization Related to Modest Reduction in Precipitation. *Science* 335:956–959.

Neitzel, J. E. 2007 Architectural Studies of Pueblo Bonito. In *The Architecture of Chaco Canyon, New Mexico*, edited by S. H. Lekson, pp. 127–154. University of Utah Press, Salt Lake City.

Plog, S., and C. Heitman. 2010 Hierarchy and Social Inequality in the American Southwest, A.D. 800–1200. *Proceedings of the National Academy of Sciences* 107:19619–19626.

Pohl, M. D., K. D. Pope, J. G. Jones, J. S. Jacobs, D. R. Piperno, S. de Franco, D. L. Lentz, J. A. Gifford, M. E. Danford, and J. K. Josserand. 1996 Early Agriculture in the Maya Lowlands. *Latin American Antiquity* 7:355–372.

Rockström, J., W. Steffen, K. Noone, A. Persson, F. S. Chapin 3rd, E. F. Lambin, T. M. Lenton, M. Scheffer, C. Folke, H. J. Schellnhuber, B. Nykvist, C. A. de Wit, T. Hughes, S. van der Leeuw, H. Rodhe, S. Sörlin, P. K. Snyder, R. Costanza, U. Svedin, M. Falkenmark, L. Karlberg, R. W. Corell, V. J. Fabry, J. Hansen, B. Walker, D. Liverman, K. Richardson, P. Crutzen, and J. A. Foley. 2009 A Safe Operating Space for Humanity. *Nature* 461:472–475.

Scarborough, V. L. 1991 Water Management Adaptations in Non-Industrial Complex Societies: An Archaeological Perspective. In *Archaeological Method and Theory, Volume 3,* edited by M. B. Schiffer, pp. 101–154. University of Arizona Press, Tucson.

Scarborough, V. L. 1994 Maya Water Management. *Research and Exploration* 10(2):184–199.

Scarborough, V. L. 2003 *The Flow of Power: Ancient Water Systems and Landscapes.* School of American Research Press, Santa Fe.

Scarborough, V. L. 2006 An Overview of Mesoamerican Water Systems. In *Precolumbian Water Management: Ideology, Ritual and Power,* edited by L. J. Lucero and B. L. Fash, pp. 223–236. University of Arizona Press, Tucson.

Scarborough, V. L. 2007 Colonizing a Landscape: Water and Wetlands in Ancient Mesoamerica. In *The Political Economy of Ancient Mesoamerica: Transformations during the Formative and Classic Periods,* edited by V. L. Scarborough and J. Clark, pp. 163–174. University of New Mexico Press, Albuquerque.

Scarborough, V. L. 2010 The Archaeology of Sustainability: Mesoamerica. *Ancient Mesoamerica* 20(2):197–203.

Scarborough, V. L. 2016 Human Niches, Cycling, and Humidity. *Water History* 7:381–396.

Scarborough, V. L., M. Becher, J. Baker, G. Harris, and F. Valdez Jr. 1995 Water and Land at theAncient Maya Community of La Milpa, Belize. *Latin American Antiquity* 6(2):98–119.

Scarborough, V. L., and W. R. Burnside. 2010 Complexity and Sustainability: Perspectives from the Ancient Maya and the Modern Balinese. *American Antiquity* 75(2):327–363.

Scarborough, V. L., N. Dunning, K. Tankersley, C. Carr, E. Weaver, L. Grazioso, B. Lane, J. Jones, P. Buttles, F. Valdez, and D. Lentz. 2012 Water and Sustainable Land Use at the Ancient Tropical City of Tikal, Guatemala. *Proceedings of the National Academy of Sciences* 109:12408–12413.

Scarborough, V. L., and G. G. Gallopin. 1991 A Water Storage Adaptation in the Maya Lowlands. *Science* 251:658–662.

Scarborough, V. L., and L. Lucero. 2011 The Non-Hierarchical Development of Complexity in the Semitropics: Water and Cooperation. *Water History* 2(2):185–205.

Scarborough, V. L., and F. Valdez Jr. 2009 An Alternative Order: The Dualistic Economies of the Ancient Maya. *Latin American Antiquity* 20(1):207–227.

Scarborough, V. L., and F. Valdez Jr. 2014 The Alternative Economy: Resilience in the Face of Complexity from the Eastern Lowlands. In *The Resilience and Vulnerability of Ancient Landscapes: Transforming Maya Archaeology through IHOPE,* edited by A. F. Chase and V. L. Scarborough, pp. 124–141. *Archaeological Papers of the American Anthropological Association, no. 24.* Wiley, Hoboken, NJ.

Smith, B. D., and M. A. Zeder. 2013 The Onset of the Anthropocene. *Anthropocene* 4:8–13.

Sofaer, A., V. Zinser, and R. M. Sinclair. 1979 A Unique Solar Marking Construct. *Science* 206(4416):283–291.

Steffen, W., K. Richardson, J. Rockström, S. E. Cornell, I. Fetzer, E. M. Bennett, R. Biggs, S. R. Carpenter, W. de Vries, C. A. de Wit, C. Folke, D. Gerten, J. Heinke, G. M. Mace, L. M. Persson, V. Ramanathan, B. Reyers, and S. Sörlin. 2015 Planetary Boundaries: Guiding Human Development on a Changing Planet. *Science* 347(6223):npn.

Tainter, J. A. 2014 Collapse and Sustainability: Rome, the Maya, and the Modern World. In *The Resilience and Vulnerability of Ancient Landscapes: Transforming Maya Archaeology through IHOPE*, edited by A. F. Chase and V. L. Scarborough, pp. 201–214. *Archaeological Papers of the American Anthropological Association, no. 24.* Wiley, Hoboken, NJ.

Tainter, J. A., and T. W. Patzek. 2012 *Drilling Down: The Gulf Oil Debacle and our Energy Dilemma.* Copernicus Books, New York.

Tankersley, K. B., V. L. Scarborough, N. Dunning, W. Huff, B. Maynard, and T. L. Gerke. 2011 Evidence for Volcanic Ash Fall in the Maya Lowlands from a Reservoir at Tikal, Guatemala. *Journal of Archaeological Science* 38:2925–2938.

Van der Leeuw, S. E. 2012 Global Systems Dynamics and Policy: Lessons for the Distant Past. *Complexity Economics* 1:33–60.

Van der Leeuw, S. E. 2014 Transforming Lessons from the Past into Lessons for the Future. In *The Resilience and Vulnerability of Ancient Landscapes: Transforming Maya Archaeology through IHOPE*, edited by A. F. Chase and V. L. Scarborough, pp. 215–231. *Archaeological Papers of the American Anthropological Association, no. 24.* Wiley, Hoboken, NJ.

Vivian, R. G. 1990 *The Chacoan Prehistroy of the San Juan Basin.* Academic Press, New York.

Vivian, R. G., C. R. Van West, J. S. Dean, N. J. Akins, M. S. Toll, and T. C. Windes. 2006a Ecology and Economy. In *The Archaeology of Chaco Canyon*, edited by S. H. Lekson, pp. 45–65. School of Advanced Research Press, Santa Fe.

Vivian, R. G., C. R. Van West, J. S. Dean, N. J. Akins, M. S. Toll, and T. C. Windes. 2006b Chacoan Ecology and Economy: Appendix B. In *The Archaeology of Chaco Canyon*, edited by S. H. Lekson, pp. 429–457. School of Advanced Research Press, Santa Fe.

Wahl, D., R. Byrne, and L. Anderson. 2014 An 8700 Year Paleoclimate Reconstruction from the Southern Maya Lowlands. *Quaternary Science Reviews* 103:19–25.

Watson, A. S., S. Plog, B. J. Culleton, P. A. Gilman, S. A. LeBlanc, P. M Whiteley, S. Claramunt, and D. J. Kennett. 2015 AMS [14]C Dates Provide New Evidence for the Early Procurement of Macaws by the Prehispanic Pueblo Inhabitants of Chaco Canyon, New Mexico. *Proceedings of the National Academy of Sciences* 112:8238–8243.

Wills, W. H. 2003 Economic Competition and Agricultural Involution in the Precontact North American Southwest. In *A Catalyst for Ideas: Anthropological Archaeology and the Legacy of Douglas W. Schwarz*, edited by V. L. Scarborough, pp. 41–67. School of Advanced Research Press, Santa Fe.

Yaeger, J., and D. A. Hodell. 2008 The Collapse of Maya Civilization: Assessing the Interaction of Culture, Climate, and Environment. In *El Niño, Catastrophism, and Culture Change in Ancient America*, edited by D. H. Sandweiss and J. Quilter, pp. 187–242. Harvard University Press, Cambridge, MA.

Contributors

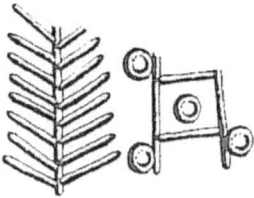

Knut Ivar Austvoll, Research Fellow, Department of Archaeology, Conservation and History, University of Oslo

Leigh-Ann Bedal, Associate Professor of Anthropology, Penn State Erie, The Behrend College

Matt Edgeworth, Honorary Research Fellow, Department of Archaeology and Ancient History, University of Leicester

Anette Sand-Eriksen, Graduate Student, Department of Archaeology, Conservation and History, University of Oslo

Jennifer L. Gaynor, School of Law, University at Buffalo

Emily Hammer, Assistant Professor, Department of Near Eastern Languages and Civilizations, University of Pennsylvania

Ömür Harmanşah, Associate Professor of Art History, University of Illinois at Chicago

Michael J. Harrower, Assistant Professor of Archaeology, Department of Near Eastern Studies, Johns Hopkins University

Emily Holt, Research Assistant Professor, Department of Anthropology, University at Buffalo

Eva Kaptijn, Postdoctoral Scholar, Quaternary Man and Environments Department, Royal Belgian Institute of Natural Sciences

Justin Leidwanger, Assistant Professor, Department of Classics & Archaeology Center, Stanford University

Kim Van Liefferinge, Postdoctoral Scholar, Department of Classics, Stanford University

Brenda Longfellow, Associate Professor, School of Art & Art History, The University of Iowa

Sturt W. Manning, Goldwin Smith Professor of Classical Archaeology, Department of Classics, Cornell University

Christopher T. Morehart, Associate Professor, School of Human Evolution and Social Change, Arizona State University

Christopher Prescott, Professor, The Norwegian Institute in Rome, University of Oslo

Vernon L. Scarborough, Distinguished Research Professor and Taft Professor, Department of Anthropology, The University of Cincinnati

Index

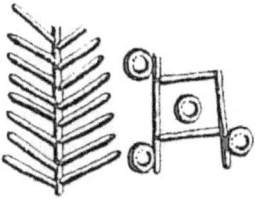

www.ingramcontent.com/pod-product-compliance
Lightning Source LLC
Chambersburg PA
CBHW080412270326
41929CB00018B/2998